Effective Implementation of Transformation Strategies

"An interesting and diverse assortment of articles addressing the connections between strategy and strategy implementation."
—Philip Bromiley, *Dean's Distinguished Professor in Strategic Management, UCI Paul Merage School of Business, United States*

"This is a must-read collection of papers from leading experts in strategy and change management, which bridges the worlds of academia and industry. The book is full of critical, cutting-edge and research-driven insights, enabling it to serve as a guide for leaders keen to formulate and implement strategies in dynamic business environments."
—Zhou Jiang, *Professor (MBA) at Graduate School of Business and Law, RMIT University, Australia*

"This book takes a comprehensive view of strategy and offers suggestions that should be of value to practitioners."
—Linda Duxbury, *Chancellor's Professor of Management, Sprott School of Business, Carleton University, Canada*

Angelina Zubac · Danielle Tucker ·
Ofer Zwikael · Kate Hughes ·
Shelley Kirkpatrick
Editors

Effective Implementation of Transformation Strategies

How to Navigate the Strategy and Change Interface Successfully

Editors
Angelina Zubac
University of Queensland
Brisbane, QLD, Australia

Danielle Tucker
University of Essex
Colchester, UK

Ofer Zwikael
Australian National University
Canberra, ACT, Australia

Kate Hughes
Technological University Dublin
Dublin, Ireland

Shelley Kirkpatrick
The MITRE Corporation
McLean, VA, USA

ISBN 978-981-19-2335-7   ISBN 978-981-19-2336-4 (eBook)
https://doi.org/10.1007/978-981-19-2336-4

© The Editor(s) (if applicable) and The Author(s), under exclusive license to Springer Nature Singapore Pte Ltd. 2022
This work is subject to copyright. All rights are solely and exclusively licensed by the Publisher, whether the whole or part of the material is concerned, specifically the rights of translation, reprinting, reuse of illustrations, recitation, broadcasting, reproduction on microfilms or in any other physical way, and transmission or information storage and retrieval, electronic adaptation, computer software, or by similar or dissimilar methodology now known or hereafter developed.
The use of general descriptive names, registered names, trademarks, service marks, etc. in this publication does not imply, even in the absence of a specific statement, that such names are exempt from the relevant protective laws and regulations and therefore free for general use.
The publisher, the authors, and the editors are safe to assume that the advice and information in this book are believed to be true and accurate at the date of publication. Neither the publisher nor the authors or the editors give a warranty, expressed or implied, with respect to the material contained herein or for any errors or omissions that may have been made. The publisher remains neutral with regard to jurisdictional claims in published maps and institutional affiliations.

Cover credit: © BHR GHN / 500px | GettyImages

This Palgrave Macmillan imprint is published by the registered company Springer Nature Singapore Pte Ltd.
The registered company address is: 152 Beach Road, #21-01/04 Gateway East, Singapore 189721, Singapore

CONTENTS

1   **Introduction: Navigating the Strategy and Change Interface Successfully**   1
Angelina Zubac, Danielle Tucker, Ofer Zwikael, Kate Hughes, and Shelley Kirkpatrick

Part I   The Strategy Process

2   **Introduction: The Strategy Process**   25
Angelina Zubac, Danielle Tucker, Ofer Zwikael, Kate Hughes, and Shelley Kirkpatrick

3   **A Social Context View of Strategic Cognition: Strategists Are Highly Emotional and Interactive Homo Sapiens!**   31
Steven R. Cofrancesco

4   **Implementing Strategy and Avenues of Access: A Practice Perspective**   65
Harry Sminia and Fredy Valdovinos Salinas

5   **Strategy Implementation and Organisational Change: A Complex Systems Perspective**   89
Czesław Mesjasz

Part II The Financial Strategy

6 Introduction: The Financial Strategy 131
Angelina Zubac, Danielle Tucker, Ofer Zwikael,
Kate Hughes, and Shelley Kirkpatrick

7 Implementing a Financial Strategy: Managing
Financial Capital, Investing in People, Balancing Risk
and Developing Critical Resources 139
Angelina Zubac

8 An Evolution: Turning Management Accounting
into a Strategic Function 177
Mark Pickering

Part III The Customer Value Creation Strategy

9 Introduction: The Customer Value Creation Strategy 205
Angelina Zubac, Danielle Tucker, Ofer Zwikael,
Kate Hughes, and Shelley Kirkpatrick

10 Business Models for Sustainability 213
Lenore K. Pennington

11 The Customer Value Concept: How Best to Define
and Create Customer Value? 261
Angelina Zubac

12 Strategic Processes and Mechanisms of Value Creation
and Value Capture: Some Insights from Business
Organisations in Poland 289
Wojciech Dyduch

Part IV The Resource Strategy

13 Introduction: The Resource Strategy 319
Angelina Zubac, Danielle Tucker, Ofer Zwikael,
Kate Hughes, and Shelley Kirkpatrick

14 Communicating and Shaping Strategic Change:
A CLASS Framework 327
Maris G. Martinsons

15 A Structured Approach to Project Management
as a Strategic Enabling Priority   355
Stephen Abrahams

16 Family Firms and Mergers and Acquisitions: The
Importance of Transfer of Trust   387
Danielle Tucker and Stella Lind

Part V Non-Market Strategies

17 Introduction: Non-market Strategies   409
Angelina Zubac, Danielle Tucker, Ofer Zwikael,
Kate Hughes, and Shelley Kirkpatrick

18 Towards a Strategic Change Management Framework
for the Nonprofit Sector: The Roll-Out of Australia's
National Disability Insurance Scheme (NDIS)   415
David Rosenbaum and Elizabeth More

19 When Everything Matters: Non-market Strategies,
Institutions and Stakeholders' Interests   451
Angelina Zubac

Index   479

LIST OF CONTRIBUTORS

Abrahams Stephen Swinburne University of Technology, Hawthorn, Australia

Cofrancesco Steven R. University of Advancing Technology, Tempe, AZ, USA

Dyduch Wojciech University of Economics in Katowice, Katowice, Poland

Hughes Kate Technological University Dublin, Dublin, Ireland

Kirkpatrick Shelley The MITRE Corporation, McLean, VA, USA

Lind Stella KPMG AG Wirtschaftsprüfungsgesellschaft, Frankfurt, Germany

Martinsons Maris G. Department of Management, City University of Hong Kong, Kowloon, Hong Kong, China

Mesjasz Czesław Management Process Department, Cracow University of Economics, Cracow, Poland

More Elizabeth Study Group, Sydney, NSW, Australia

Pennington Lenore K. University of Wollongong, Wollongong, NSW, Australia

Pickering Mark Swinburne University of Technology, Hawthorn, VIC, Australia

Rosenbaum David King's Own Institute, Sydney, NSW, Australia

Salinas Fredy Valdovinos QuodPraesens HR Consulting, Santiago de Chile, Chile

Sminia Harry University of Strathclyde Business School, Scotland, UK

Tucker Danielle University of Essex, Colchester, UK

Zubac Angelina University of Queensland, Brisbane, QLD, Australia

Zwikael Ofer Australian National University, Canberra, ACT, Australia

List of Figures

Fig. 1.1	The firm's strategic context: Two perspectives	6
Fig. 1.2	Examples of traditional vertical structures	9
Fig. 1.3	Example of structures at a large modern organisation	12
Fig. 1.4	An institutional approach to strategy and change	14
Fig. 1.5	Towards a strategically aligned organisation: Thinking, collaborating and acting strategically together	17
Fig. 2.1	Strategy and change at the contemporary organisation: implementing to learn and learning to implement within the institutional superstructure (*Source* Adapted from Zubac et al. [2021])	28
Fig. 3.1	The receipt of an affective interaction	45
Fig. 3.2	The giving of an affective interaction	50
Fig. 5.1	Coevolutionary interface—strategy and organisational change (*Source* own research)	102
Fig. 6.1	Implementing strategy and organisational change: a financial strategy focus	133
Fig. 6.2	Financial strategy: information flows and decision-making policies and processes	135
Fig. 7.1	The transformation of capital	143
Fig. 9.1	Implementing strategy and organisational change: a customer value creation strategy focus	207
Fig. 9.2	Strategic customer value creation	210
Fig. 9.3	Building a sustainable comprehensive customer value co-learning, co-creation and co-delivery system	211

Fig. 10.1	Sustainable value (*Source* Adapted from Evans et al. [2017: 600])	225
Fig. 11.1	Actioning customer value learning (*Source* Adapted from Woodruff [1997])	270
Fig. 11.2	Building customer value (dynamic) capabilities to transform the organisation into a customer value delivery powerhouse	277
Fig. 11.3	Learning about, and creating and delivering customer value within an institutionally complex ecosystem	280
Fig. 12.1	Strategic processes and mechanisms of value creation and capture influencing organisational performance	310
Fig. 12.2	The value creation and capture pillars	311
Fig. 13.1	Implementing strategy and organisational change: A resource strategy focus	321
Fig. 13.2	Building a strategically aligned organisation and positive culture	322
Fig. 13.3	Implementing/Continually refining a horizontally aligned and cooperation-based resourcing strategy	325
Fig. 14.1	The CLASS framework for an additive change	333
Fig. 14.2	The CLASS framework for a substitutive change	335
Fig. 14.3	The CLASS framework for interdependent strategic changes	349
Fig. 14.4	The CLASS framework for an integrated strategic change	350
Fig. 15.1	A Typically Siloed and Ad-Hoc Approach to Project Management (*Source* Author's own creation)	356
Fig. 15.2	Strategic Alignment and Enablement Pyramid (*Source* Author's own creation)	358
Fig. 15.3	Strategic goals roadmap against business themes (*Source* Author's own creation)	360
Fig. 15.4	Portfolio Management Decision Making Cycle (*Source* Author's own creation)	362
Fig. 15.5	Example Project Portfolio Matrix for determining project and Programme Priorities (*Source* Author's own creation)	363
Fig. 15.6	Strategic roadmap showing goals, key enabling programmes, projects and dependencies (*Source* Author's own creation)	365
Fig. 15.7	Portfolio, Programme, Project Resource Planning Challenge (*Source* Author's own creation)	367
Fig. 15.8	Effective portfolio, programme and project resource management (*Source* Author's own creation)	369

Fig. 15.9	Project-based resource management (not real figures) (*Source* Author's own creation)	370
Fig. 15.10	Functional resource management (not real figures) (*Source* Author's own creation)	371
Fig. 15.11	Example Organisational Project Governance Structure (*Source* Author's own creation)	373
Fig. 15.12	Example Project Life Cycle Phases and Activities (*Source* Author's own creation)	375
Fig. 15.13	Stakeholder Impact Assessment Checklist (*Source* Author's own creation)	376
Fig. 15.14	Project Approval and Reporting Flows by Project Size (*Source* Author's own creation)	377
Fig. 15.15	Example of indicators as measures of benefits that deliver strategic outcomes (*Source* Author's own creation)	379
Fig. 15.16	Example project life cycle adjusted for benefits realisation and sustainment activities (*Source* Author's own creation)	380
Fig. 15.17	Enabling Processes for Strategic Outcomes and Change Management (*Source* Adapted from the Model presented by Zubac et al., 2021: 487)	385
Fig. 16.1	A framework for family firm M&A trust transfer processes (*Source* Author's own creation)	393
Fig. 17.1	Implementing strategy and organisational change: a non-market strategies focus	411
Fig. 17.2	Integrating market and non-market strategies	413
Fig. 18.1	NDIS implementation framework—the high-level context	422
Fig. 18.2	A more accurate depiction of Lewin's 3-step model of change (Reproduced from Rosenbaum et al. (2018))	427
Fig. 18.3	NDIS implementation framework	427
Fig. 19.1	The firm's strategic context (*Source* Adapted from Zubac et al., 2007)	453
Fig. 19.2	Formulating and implementing integrated market and non-market strategies: The critical internal and external Knowledge flows and social interactions	471

List of Tables

Table 3.1	Cognitive styles: characteristics and outcomes	54
Table 4.1	Key terms and definitions	73
Table 4.2	Implementation practices	83
Table 5.1	Synthesis of philosophical interpretations of organisational change	98
Table 5.2	Perspectives of strategy implementation	112
Table 10.1	Stakeholder definitions	227
Table 10.2	Cultural values for SBMs	233
Table 11.1	Comparing accounting and software engineering firms	274
Table 12.1	Value creation and value capture: selected theoretical perspectives	296
Table 12.2	The questionnaire structure	301
Table 12.3	The influence of VCVC variables on firm performance	306
Table 14.1	CLASS Framework	332
Table 14.2	Summary of Propositions to Guide Strategic Change Based on the CLASS Framework	348
Table 16.1	Examples of specific actions for trust at family firms during the M&A/integration process	397

CHAPTER 1

Introduction: Navigating the Strategy and Change Interface Successfully

Angelina Zubac, Danielle Tucker, Ofer Zwikael, Kate Hughes, and Shelley Kirkpatrick

Book's Aims

There are no two ways about it, it is no easy task to significantly change how an organisation operates, much less transform it. There is always so much leaders need to think about and there are countless ways a programme of strategic change could be derailed. This partly explains why

---

A. Zubac (✉)
University of Queensland, Brisbane, QLD, Australia
e-mail: az@strategylink.com.au; a.zubac@business.uq.edu.au; angelina.zubac@aim.com.au

D. Tucker
University of Essex, Colchester, UK
e-mail: dtucker@essex.ac.uk

O. Zwikael
Australian National University, Canberra, ACT, Australia
e-mail: ofer.zwikael@anu.edu.au

© The Author(s), under exclusive license to Springer Nature Singapore Pte Ltd. 2022
A. Zubac et al. (eds.), *Effective Implementation of Transformation Strategies*, https://doi.org/10.1007/978-981-19-2336-4_1

it is regularly reported fewer than 30% of all strategies are fully implemented, if at all. Of course, not implementing a strategy or changing it mid-course may be a good thing if the management team is leading from the front and are continuously considering how the strategy could be improved or reimagined. Sometimes a strategy needs to be drastically tweaked or discarded entirely. Notwithstanding, it is more often the case that a strategy is badly or not implemented because the recursive practices required to effectively implement it or modify it over time are poorly understood or non-existent (Zubac et al., 2021), the organisation does not have a compelling vision for the future everyone can get behind (Kirkpatrick, 2016) and processes are not in place to ensure the organisation's strategic projects can realise their expected value (Zwikael & Smyrk, 2019).

Unfortunately, the management literature provides us with little definitive guidance about the best way to navigate the strategy process to create value and bring about meaningful organisational change regardless of the context. It is still replete with contradictions. For instance, even though MBA students are now taught there can be huge disparities between the planned strategy and what is actually realised, they are also taught the strategy process is essentially a mechanistic stepwise process, which may or may not involve everyone at the organisation. They are told the strategy process can only begin once the external and internal environments have been thoroughly analysed. The objective of this step is to understand the opportunities the organisation can viably pursue and to generate strategic options for the future. The options chosen from the final shortlist inform the strategic plan. Once the strategic plan is finalised, it is then possible to identify the programmes and budget allocations that are necessary to ensure the strategy can be successfully implemented. Further, top management accountabilities for each programme can then be confirmed

---

K. Hughes
Technological University Dublin, Dublin, Ireland
e-mail: kate.hughes@hughes-scm.com

S. Kirkpatrick
The MITRE Corporation, McLean, VA, USA
e-mail: skirkpatrick@mitre.org

to ensure the intended benefits are realised and organisational change happens.

Because most employees tend to resist change, MBA students are also taught that it is important to develop a change management plan as a cardinal last step in the strategy process. This plan defines the models of change and leadership that will be used to motivate everyone at the organisation to embrace the strategy and update their skills. However, it is not always clear why the organisation's people are being urged and/or incentivised to apply themselves differently because the people responsible for developing the change management plan are seldom the same as those who prepared the strategic plan. This vital connection is never established. As a result, it is not surprising that most leaders prefer to apply popular models of change instead of empirically validated models or are unable to learn valuable lessons from their implementation leadership experiences (Stouten et al., 2018).

With this in mind, differentiating itself from all other books on strategy implementation published to date, this book sheds light on the specialised (sub)processes and cognitions used by managers, singly or in combination, to navigate the strategy and change interface. Put another way, it demonstrates how the best managers make rationally derived strategies a reality in practical and sometimes very non-rational terms through the organisation's key processes and its people. The book applies the latest thinking from the resource-based literature, in particular the idea that high performing organisations have become adept at developing and utilising value creating dynamic capabilities to not only develop and implement a strategy but to make timely adjustments to it as is necessary. It builds on the idea that dynamic capabilities make it possible to sense opportunities and threats, seize profitable opportunities and mitigate threats, and reconfigure or transform the organisation as required. They are comprised of specialised (sub)processes and cognitions brought together, sometimes as platforms, to achieve these ends. The way dynamic capabilities are developed and utilised at different organisations will differ because no two organisations ever evolve in the same way (Teece, 2007).

This book also assumes that, unless managers understand the organisation's institutional context and accept that organisations are essentially all about their people, they will struggle or be unable to navigate the strategy and change interface successfully to bring about lasting change. Thus, it represents a break with past thinking about how to successfully enact change in organisations. Towards the end of the last millennium, it was widely accepted that organisations could be changed effectively if principles from industrial organisation (IO) economics and the resource-based view were judiciously applied. This is because these theories can be used by managers to understand the competitive environment, including how best to position the organisation within its industry and lever its unique portfolio of assets and capabilities. However, neither of these theories consider how an organisation can do well by emulating the behaviour of other organisations. This includes achieving success as a result of complying with the same laws, regulations and rules of the formal institutional environment, and the cultural and ethical norms and practices of the informal institutional environment of which their contemporaries are also subject. One more theory was required for this to happen. An institution-based view is such a theory because it acknowledges the social context within which strategic decisions are made. Decision-making is not limited to finding ways to outsmart the competition (Peng, et al., 2009). An institution-based view makes it clear that organisations can also thrive by becoming appreciably similar to competitors and other notable organisations.

Therefore, the book provides insight into how an organisation's leadership can effect strategic change by building a dynamic capability base designed to comprehensively address the institutional environment. Crucially, it develops a number of versatile frameworks leaders can utilise while leading a complex programme of strategic change to bring out the best in others.

The Corporate Strategy: The Market and Non-Market Domains

Accordingly, the corporate strategy in this book is conceived as being an amalgam of four fundamental strategies: the organisation's financial, customer value creation, resource strategies and its non-market strategies. This reflects the idea that organisations must constructively participate in the capital, product and service, and the resource markets, and the non-market environment of relevance to them if they are to succeed. This must be done while observing these institutions' parameters as is appropriate (Zubac et al., 2012). Hence, for-profit organisations need to use the market system (capital, product and services, and resource markets) while observing the rules of competition and pursuing their profit agendas. Not-for-profit organisations need to use the market system to achieve their stakeholders' social goals and their revenue neutral agendas. Comparable principles apply to the non-market institutions with the potential to impact the organisation. Regardless of their profit-seeking status, all organisations need to address the demands placed upon them by the non-market environment to gain legitimacy. However, the methods used to gain legitimacy by for-profit and not-for-profit organisations are likely to differ because they are driven by different value systems.

All organisations need to comply with the expectations of collectives of institutions. This is because all institutions are socially derived. They exist to serve society in some meaningful way. Many institutions are promoted through the auspices of an organisation too. When the organisation is not a for-profit or not-for-profit organisation as is commonly understood and has a legitimising objective, in all probability it was established to ensure compliance, for example, it was established to ensure compliance with the rules for safely driving a car, transacting commercially or manufacturing fit-for-purpose products. Markets, regulators, standards developers, enforcement agencies, the judiciary and governments are all institutions, as are the laws and conventions or behavioural norms that they exist to define, oversee or uphold. By the same token, for-profit and not-for-profit organisations are institutions. All of these institutions matter in different ways (North, 1994).

These ideas underpin the whole book. They are depicted diagrammatically at the top of (Fig. 1.1) in the area labelled "a". As shown, the corporate strategy informs the organisation's financial, customer value creation, resource and non-market strategies. However, as the double-headed arrows suggest, the organisation's people are always learning and finding new ways to improve upon the strategy or change it, as well as solve problems as they arise; therefore, it is inevitable the corporate strategy will be informed by the four lower-level strategies.

The opportunities inherent in the market and non-market systems are determined through the processes associated with the appropriate lower-level strategy. Accordingly, the financial strategy reflects the capital markets of relevance to the organisation. The customer value strategy reflects the product and service markets of relevance to it. The same can be said of the resource strategy—it reflects the resource markets of most relevance to the organisation. The non-market strategy reflects the specific non-market institutions that could impact the organisation. As the double-headed arrows connecting the strategies also suggest, each of

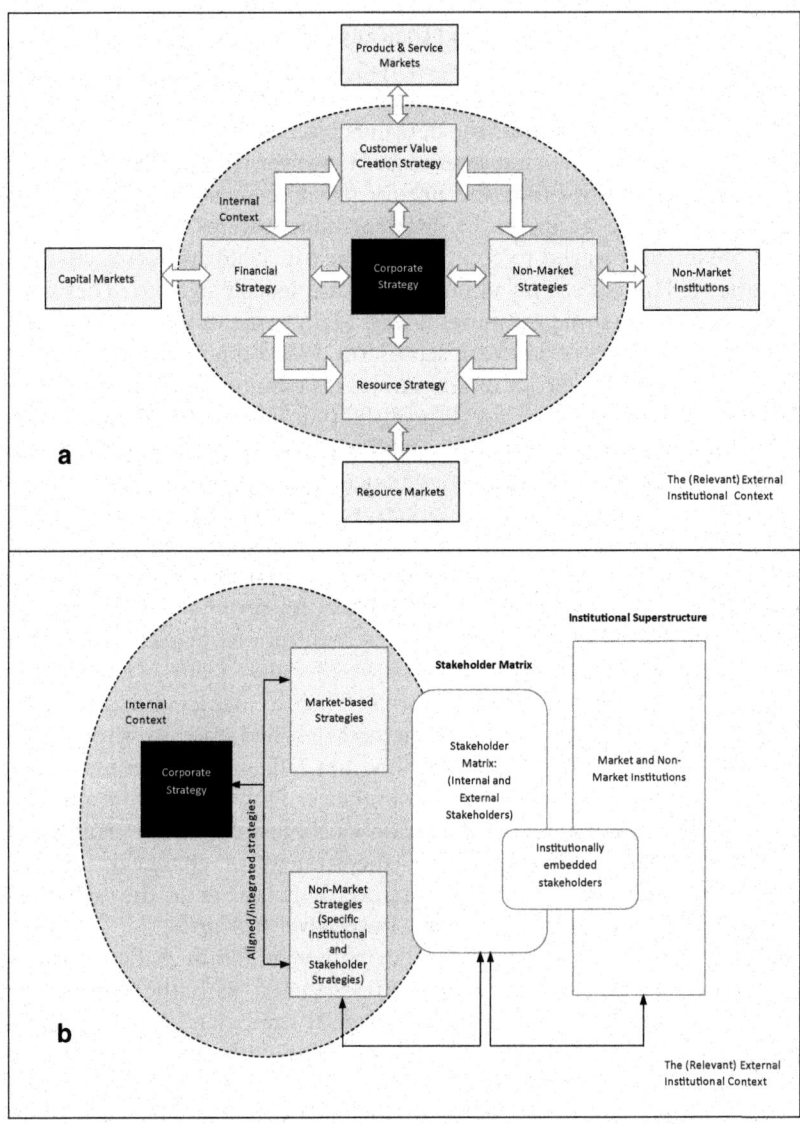

Fig. 1.1 The firm's strategic context: Two perspectives

these strategies are best developed, implemented and/or revised with an appreciation of how they complement or could impact each other.

The section labelled "a" similarly establishes the fact that all organisations evolve their own institutions and, consequently, their own unique internal context. Ideally, the strategies encourage the organisation's people to cultivate (sub)processes and cognitions, including mindsets that allow them to play a positive role at the organisation and contribute to its cultural development. Of course, it is conceivable that sometimes the (sub)processes and cognitions that are evolved are not particularly constructive. This is consistent with what we already know about institutions. Some organisations are very dysfunctional due to their inefficient processes or problematic cultures. In summary, the external institutional environment influences the evolution of the organisation's internal context, and organisations will influence the development of society's institutions over time. The extent to which this can occur depends on their intertwined histories, including the way in which certain institutions accumulated power.

The potential usefulness of this approach is further clarified diagrammatically in (Fig. 1.1) in the section labelled "b". In this perspective, the organisation's market strategies are grouped together because they have the same underlying drivers. These are distinct from the organisation's non-market strategies. Market strategies address the market environment while non-market strategies address the non-market environment, that is, market strategies focus on achieving the organisation's economic objectives while non-market strategies focus on achieving its non-economic objectives, including the organisation's ethical and cultural objectives. Just as was the case in "a", the corporate strategy informs the development of the organisation's market and non-market strategies. Each of the lower-level strategies informs the corporate strategy. When the market and non-market strategies are approached in an integrated manner, they are more likely to complement and support each other (Baron, 1995).

What is most significant about this second perspective is that it highlights how important it is to consider the interests and needs of stakeholders. This includes at all stages of the strategy process. This is indicated by the inclusion of the "stakeholder matrix". The stakeholder matrix makes it clear that while some stakeholders may be internal stakeholders, a large number of important stakeholders are likely to be external to the organisation. Both kinds of stakeholders may have some sort of association with, be embedded within, or be socially defined by an external institution, which may or may not be fronted by an organisation. No matter the type of organisation, organisations are more likely to achieve so much more through their strategy than they otherwise would have done if their stakeholders' needs are considered. Stakeholders help organisational leaders understand if the organisation is demonstrating the "right" set of values. This is important because when an organisation disappoints some stakeholders the organisation's reputation could suffer inordinately (Freeman et al., 2021). For example, we probably can all recount an instance where one extremely well-written and widely read published letter to a newspaper editor had a profound impact.

Of course, some stakeholders may end up having a larger say in how the organisation operates while others have very little. It is important to assess the potential of all stakeholders to impact the organisation regardless lest something of strategic importance ends up being missed. Organisations are stakeholder dependent for this reason. This second perspective also reinforces the fact that gone are the days when the sole objective of a strategy was to maximise the welfare of shareholders. Instead, the welfare of all stakeholders must be internalised by the organisation if it is to find its place in the world and be governed with foresight (Tirole, 2001).

THE STRATEGICALLY ALIGNED ORGANISATION

The two preceding frameworks provide insight into the organisational forms the contemporary organisation ought to aspire to evolve. In the past, it was taken as a given that young or growing organisations should build the same vertical, divisional structures as large multi-business industrial organisations of the last century. It was argued that these behemoths had achieved scale and scope efficiencies because the divisional structure enabled effective decentralised decision-making (Chandler, 2001). Of course, while growing and resource constrained, it was important to adopt organisational forms of a more intermediate nature, such as the functional form. What was important, no matter the structure that was ultimately adopted, was a structure that allowed decisions to be made by those most qualified to make them, no matter where that person sat within the organisation's hierarchy (Miles & Snow, 1984; Miller & Kirkpatrick, 2021).

These principles are illustrated diagrammatically in (Fig. 1.2). The section labelled "a" is an example of a functional structure. Functional

1 INTRODUCTION: NAVIGATING THE STRATEGY AND CHANGE ... 9

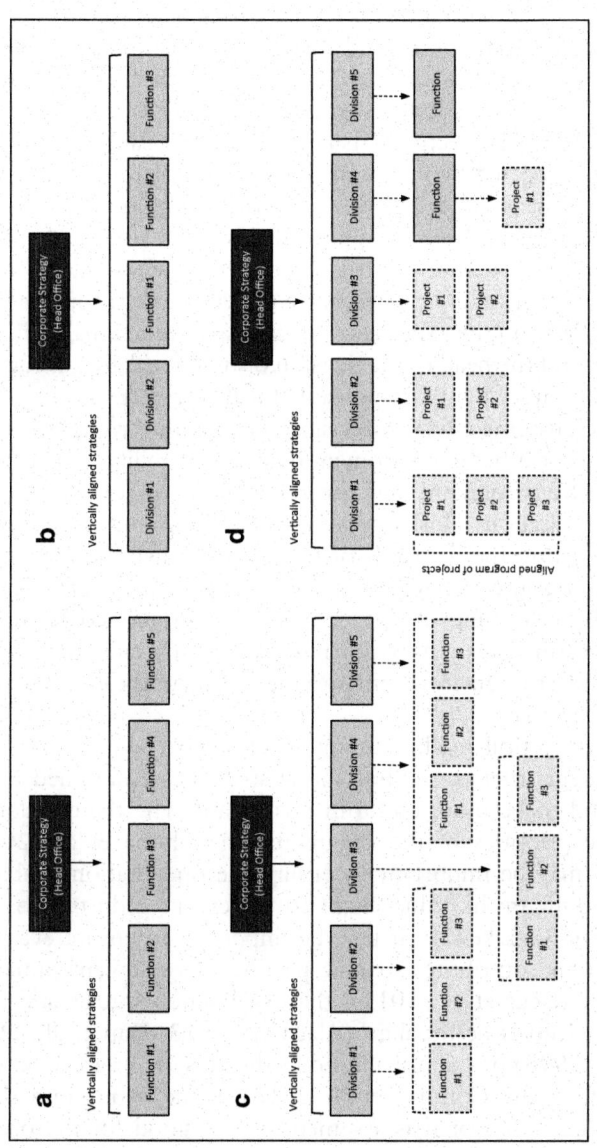

Fig. 1.2 Examples of traditional vertical structures

structures are normally adopted when an owner or single manager needs assistance from people with functional expertise. The section labelled "b" is an example of a divisional and functional structure. Such vertical structures are adopted when it is important to have decision input from managers with market or product expertise, as well as managers with functional expertise. The section labelled "c" is an example of a divisional structure supported by functions. Divisional structures of this type are adopted when head office requires divisional support, and the divisions require specialist functional support. The section labelled "d" is an example of a matrix structure. Matrix structures are adopted to ensure divisional or functional strategic projects are undertaken by project professionals who can draw on the expertise of divisional or functional staff. The project manager and the head of the division or functional area instigating the project are normally jointly responsible for the project.

In addition to ensuring effective decision-making, the "right" structure or organisational form became synonymous with the ability to achieve fit with the external environment and the related concept of the strategically aligned organisation. This is because high performing organisations were good at meeting the demands of the external environment, strategically using the resources they had at hand. When an organisation was sustainably high performing, it was because its managers could quickly adapt its structure and use organisational resources differently to meet the demands of the external environment and, thus, achieve the organisation's strategic objectives (Sarta, 2021).

Although both vertical and horizontal structures can be used to achieve a particular strategic theme, the horizontal structures established at the organisation tend to be more useful in this regard. The theme adopted depends on the priorities of the organisation (Kathuria et al., 2007). For instance, it may be important to ensure the organisation is able to consistently reconfigure its value chain to achieve its industry position goals (Porter, 1985). Likewise, it may be important to ensure everyone at the organisation contributes to new product development initiatives in the same way (Acur et al., 2012), the organisation's goals and individual employees' goals better align (Alagaraja, 2013; Han et al., 2019; Wright & Snell, 1998) or the organisation's digital systems are able to be used more strategically (Coltman et al., 2015). If the wrong underlying strategic driver is chosen or it is assumed what is good for the organisation today will be good for it tomorrow, then the organisation could struggle. Inconsistencies between the organisation and the greater institutional environment may emerge that become extremely problematic. They may be very difficult to bridge without completely transforming the organisation.

To avoid inconsistencies emerging, it is important to consider the cross-disciplinary and wide-ranging strategic implications of the organisation's unique institutional context. This is illustrated diagrammatically in (Fig. 1.3). As opposed to (Fig. 1.2), it is taken as a given that just as much effort should be placed on building suitable horizontal structures as is placed on building vertical structures. As illustrated in (Fig. 1.3), this is because market and non-market environments cannot be thoroughly addressed without establishing an appropriate set of knowledge sharing, learning, decision-making and collaborative action-oriented structures based on what was learned about the institutional environment. The ability to respond to the institutional environment may also be contingent on the ability to source resources from across the organisation and effectively use them. If the corporate strategy informs how the three market and non-market strategies are developed, implemented and/or revised over time, and the four lower-level strategies inform the corporate strategy, a diversity of people with expert knowledge and experience of all kinds will need to be involved in every single strategic decision made at the organisation. This needs to be enabled as much as is practicably possible through the formal structures. This includes by establishing platforms, self-forming teams and/or focused microdivisional structures (Zubac et al., 2021).

The Strategy and Change Interface

However, despite knowing more than we have known ever before about the strategy and change interface, it is still difficult to understand how organisations can approach strategic change problems consistently. Resource-based theory has come close to providing a solution. It is still the dominant theory for explaining why some organisations are able to outperform other organisations within their industry for sustained periods of time. Indeed, it deservedly pushed IO economic explanations for high performance from the top spot of explanations because it explains how the possession of a superior resource base could improve an organisation's competitiveness within its industry (Helfat et al., 2007). However, as previously discussed, an institution-based view has the potential to

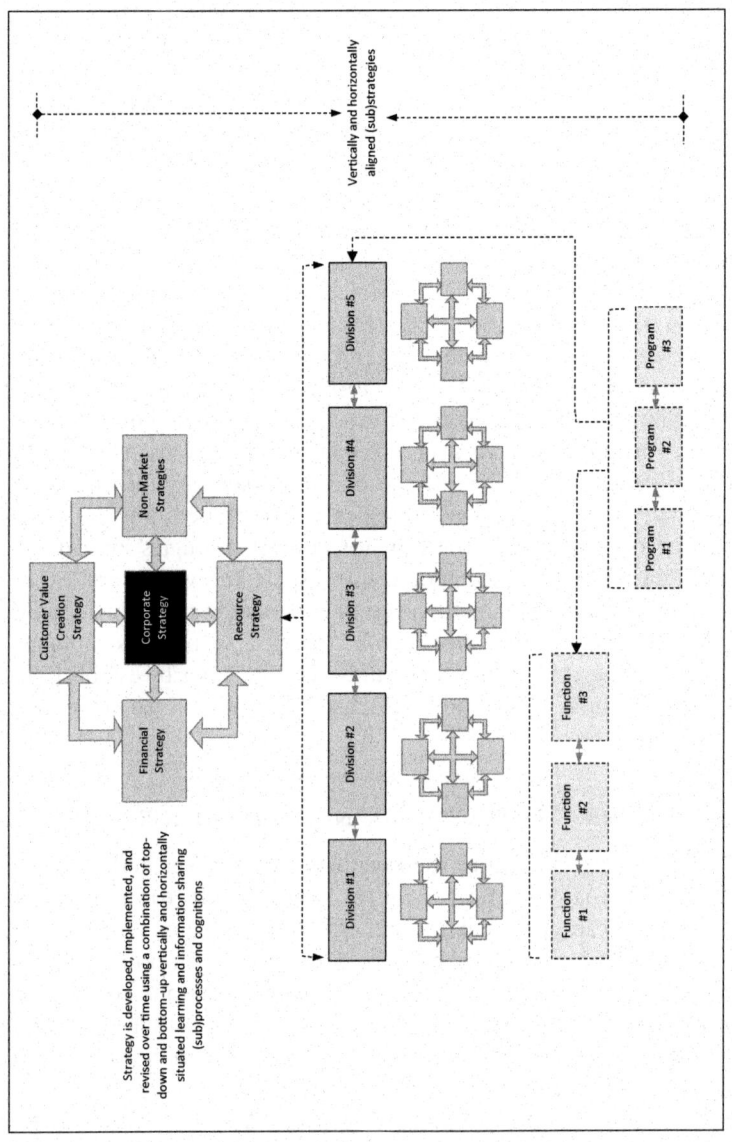

Fig. 1.3 Example of structures at a large modern organisation

provide even more insight into the sources of competitive advantage and high performance more generally because it also explains the benefits of becoming similar to other organisations.

Interestingly, there are situations when an institution-based view also explains a differential advantage. For instance, when an organisation is at the forefront of changing an institution with broad social implications, it may become known as the organisation that took the lead. Some organisations have been the first or only organisation to propose a change to a law or standard, to comment on a proposed change in government policy or to suggest and garner support for the establishment of a new industry body. Indeed, there are many potential reputational and knowledge-based advantages that an organisation can gain by taking the lead to transform an institution (Greenwood & Suddaby, 2006). Analogously, some organisations will imitate the competitive actions and business models of successful organisations during periods of uncertainty to avoid being left behind. There are many potential ways to benefit from being known as an industry leader or being the first to introduce a new type of business model to the market (DiMaggio & Powell, 1983). Thus, in addition to providing insights about the benefits of sameness, an institution-based view explains institution-based forms of differentiation. This is something that IO economics and resource-based explanations of differential performance have not explained.

Without a doubt, leaders face many challenges when navigating the strategy and change interface. In addition to determining the extent to which an organisation should differentiate itself from other organisations while simultaneously pursuing social legitimacy, leaders also need to understand the many different actions their organisations can take given the diversity of markets and non-market institutions that confront the organisation on any given day. The problem is only so much can be achieved at any one time too. Also, what works well one day may not work well another day. It may take years for an organisation to come even close to achieving its stated strategic objectives, if at all. Even if is able to achieve good things through its strategies, there is another challenge to overcome. Organisations cannot grow and perform sustainably over time unless they can develop the dynamic capabilities that they need to enable their people to sense, seize and reconfigure or transform the organisation as is necessary. Dynamic capabilities are the means by which organisations are able to meet the demands of a changing external environment. However, they need to be able to change too.

These ideas are illustrated diagrammatically in (Fig. 1.4). Just as before, it can be observed that corporate strategy informs the four lower-level strategies. The four lower-level strategies inform the corporate strategy. All of these strategies are important for addressing the capital, product and service, resource markets and non-market institutions of most relevance to the organisation. These can variously promote or constrain the organisation's growth. Most importantly, (Fig. 1.4) makes it clear organisations cannot effectively develop, implement and revise their strategies over time allowing for the institutional context unless it possesses sensing, seizing and reconfiguring/transforming dynamic capabilities. These need to be particularly attuned when the institutional environment is especially

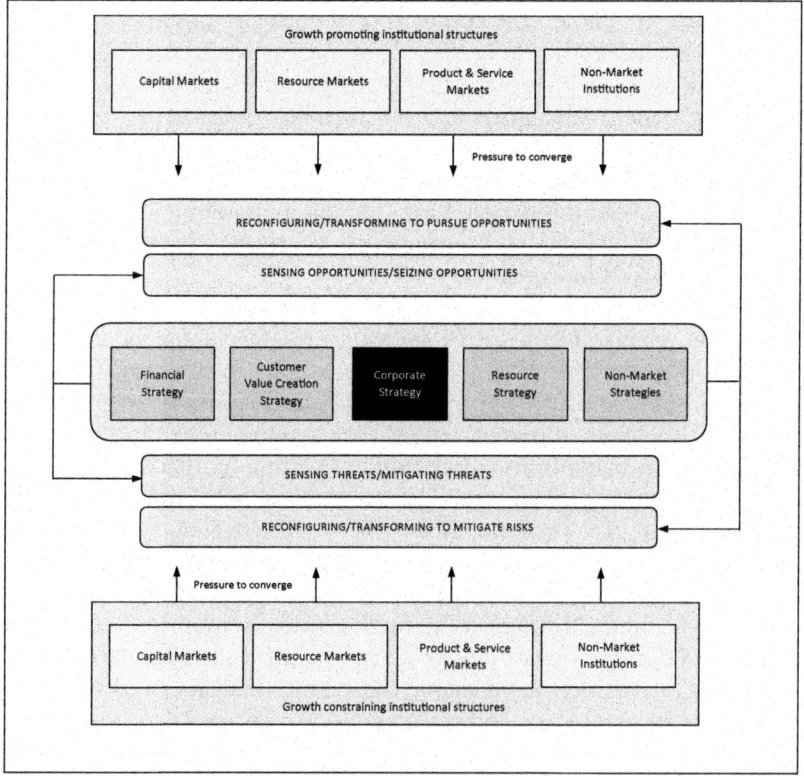

Fig. 1.4 An institutional approach to strategy and change

complex and diverse. As the double-headed arrows suggest, the dynamic capabilities organisations develop by utilising many (sub)processes and cognitions are always changing too because new ways to sense, seize and reconfigure/transform are always necessary to find to stay relevant.

Logically, since dynamic capabilities allow organisations to keep pace with change emanating from the external environment, organisations that find it difficult to address change in the external environment are less likely to possess dynamic capabilities. The capabilities they develop will be of a more ad hoc nature. This is not to say that the people leading such organisations should just give up. When an organisation becomes good at sensing, seizing and reconfiguring through the process of implementing the strategy, as bad as it might be, its people can change the strategy. The organisation can then pursue the opportunities that would have otherwise been overlooked (Lee & Puranam, 2016).

THINKING, COLLABORATING AND ACTING STRATEGICALLY TOGETHER

In summary, there are many good reasons why leaders should not take a rigid stepwise approach when developing and implementing its strategies. Although it can be helpful to run strategy workshops or go away to a strategy retreat to get to know each while setting the organisation's direction, this is only a small part of what strategy is all about. Ultimately, the strategy process works best when everyone, in every part of the organisation, understands that the concept of "the current strategy" is just that, a concept. It is simply a means by which everyone can learn about the organisation's longer-term strategic objectives and identify the projects that should be undertaken in future to achieve them. The strategy process also works best when everyone understands the strategy is not set in stone and that it will change over time as it becomes clearer how the organisation can more effectively address the external environment with the resources it has on hand.

As to the latter, it will be important to establish the ways in which the organisation's people can change the strategy, including improve upon how fit with the external environment is achieved over time. The dynamic capabilities, particularly the specific (sub)processes and cognitive methods that are key for enabling these changes, must be apparent and accessible. Everyone at the organisation should be aware of how they can use these tools for adapting the organisation and the extent to which they are authorised to use them to initiate change given the organisation's decision-making and operational structures. The organisation's people cannot contribute to the strategic development of the organisation over time otherwise. Likewise, how internal stakeholders think, feel and institutionalise knowledge and interact with each other, as well as interact with external stakeholders must be understood. Certainly, this is something that the astute leader needs to understand will be part of the mix.

These ideas are considered by the chapter contributors of this book in a variety of ways, reflecting a range of theoretical and disciplinary traditions. Consequently, the book has been divided into five sections. The first considers the nature of the strategy process. The second, third and fourth consider how the financial, product and service, and resource markets of most relevance to the organisation could impact it. The fifth and final section considers the non-market environment and how organisations could address it. The chapters demonstrate the relationship between the corporate strategy and the four fundamental strategies. Importantly, they demonstrate the many recursive practices and enabling structural, learning and cognitive mechanisms that should be in place and then effectively utilised to implement a strategy as a process of learning, as suggested diagrammatically in (Fig. 1.5). Each strategy is essentially a reflection of the other. The following is an overview of the sections and the chapters contained within them.

The Strategy Process

The three chapters in the first section of this book consider the nature of the strategy process in some detail from different disciplinary view-points. Chapter 1 by Steven Cofrancesco, *A social context view of strategic cognition: Strategists are highly emotional and interactive Homo sapiens*, argues that it is a mistake to assume strategy can be formulated and implemented linearly and rationally. The strategy process evokes strong emotions. These can be advantageously harnessed. Chapter 2 by Harry Sminia and Freddy Valdovinos Salinas, *Implementing strategy and avenues of access: A practice perspective*, argues that strategy is best conceived as a continuous implementation process. This is because the structures, incentives, cultural and people goals, and controls put in place to position the organisation in future can never be pursued with certainty. Concomitantly, Chapter 3 by Czeslaw Mesjasz, *Strategy implementation and organisational change:*

1 INTRODUCTION: NAVIGATING THE STRATEGY AND CHANGE ...   17

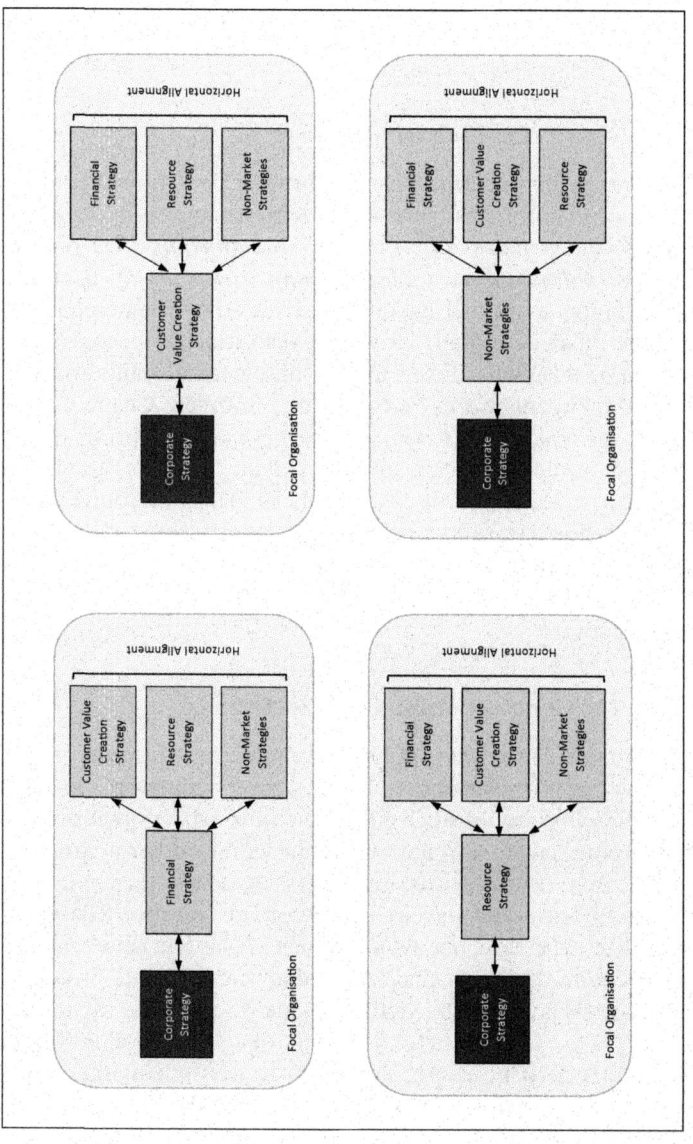

Fig. 1.5 Towards a strategically aligned organisation: Thinking, collaborating and acting strategically together

A complex systems perspective, considers how systems logic can be used to understand the strategy and change interface. Mesjasz considers how change can be instituted using well-established structuring, continually changing processes.

The Financial Strategy

The two chapters in this section considers how organisations approach the capital acquisition and management problem. Chapter 4 by Angelina Zubac, *Implementing a financial strategy: Managing financial capital, investing in people, balancing risk and developing critical resources*, argues that financial strategies are primarily concerned with the management and transformation of financial capital. However, very strategic choices need to be made about how capital can be used to utilise people's skills, manage risks and lever the organisation's non-human resources. Chapter 5 by Mark Pickering, *An evolution: Turning management accounting into a strategic function*, argues financial strategies define how organisations operationalise their strategic priorities using their financial resources over time. Particular attention is paid to how management accounting eventually evolved into strategic management accounting. Both chapters clarify how financial strategies empower organisational stakeholders to make better strategic decisions.

The Customer Value Creation Strategy

The three chapters in this section consider how organisations approach customer value creation. Chapter 6 by Lenore Pennington, *Business models for sustainability*, argues since customers now expect organisations to demonstrate a concern for the climate and the world's other megaproblems, it has become necessary to find ways to adapt their business models with this in mind and develop a concordant culture. Chapter 7 by Angelina Zubac, *The customer value concept: How best to define and create customer value*, explains that performance-enhancing customer value related decisions are more likely to be made if the "right" definition of customer value is used. A powerful definition of customer value should allow the organisation to be responsive to customers' changing needs, including in partnership with others. Chapter 8 by Wojciech Dyduch, *Strategic mechanisms of value creation and value capture: Some insights from business organisations in Poland*, explains his findings from an empirical study. He found that organisations operating in emerging market economies struggle to achieve a balance between value creation and value appropriation. The problem is that it can be difficult to consciously invest in the organisation's own processes when the environment is uncertain.

The Resource Strategy

The three chapters in this section highlight the criticality of the resource strategy. Without it, the rest of organisation's financial, customer value creation and non-market strategies cannot be implemented. They also make it clear that the process by which an organisation organises (coordinates) has strategic value in itself. Chapter 9 by Maris Martinsons, *Communicating and shaping strategic change: A CLASS framework*, considers the different kinds of leaders that are required to implement different strategic change objectives. It identifies the five contingent change-leadership related elements that must be managed to achieve a successful change outcome. Chapter 10 by Stephen Abrahams, *A structured approach to project management as a strategic enabling priority*, explains the ways in which an organisation can benefit by adopting a structured approach to project management, including by becoming more adaptable. Chapter 11 by Danielle Tucker and Stella Lind, *Family firms and mergers and acquisitions: The importance of transfer of trust*, discusses the criticality of the trust transfer process when it is necessary to integrate two family businesses post-merger/acquisition. When trust relationships are established, it is easier for everyone to learn from each other with integrity.

Non-Market Strategies

The two chapters in this section consider how the non-market environment must be addressed by different kinds of organisations. Chapter 12 by David Rosenbaum and Elizabeth More, *Towards a Strategic Management Framework for the Nonprofit Sector: The Roll-out of Australia's National Disability Insurance Scheme (NDIS)*, explains the findings of a study of the roll-out of the NDIS programme in Australia. It was found that disability service organisations with effective leaders, a supportive culture, processes for communicating and engaging with others could more readily adapt to a demand-driven services model from a service-driven model. Chapter 13 by Angelina Zubac, *When Everything Matters: Non-Market Strategies, Institutions and Stakeholders' Interests*, is a review of the extant institutions and stakeholder literatures. Using inductive methods, it found stakeholders play an important institutionalising role when strategising and implementing integrated market and non-market strategies.

Conclusion

At the start, the observation was made that, more often than not, strategies are badly or not implemented at all because of an inability to understand the recursive practices that must be in place to achieve strategic success over time, it is unclear why everyone should back the organisation's vision for the future, and processes are not in place to ensure the organisation's strategic projects achieve what was intended. The chapters in this book describe how these problems are being overcome at some organisations or could be at others with a little imagination. A number of frameworks are also developed that can be used by leaders to make better sense out of the challenges a complex programme of change might represent. The chapter's multidisciplinary insights confirm the importance of building dynamic capabilities to sense and seize opportunities, and to build supportive operational and strategic change structures. They also confirm how crucial it is to appreciate an organisation's own institutional context. More to the point, it is essential to encourage the right mindsets to get the best out of people. It is not possible to achieve great things through an organisation otherwise. In an increasing complex and hypercompetitive world, full of ambiguity and paradox, it is clear organisations need to be adaptable and strategic in many ways.

References

Acur, N., Kandemir, D., & Boer, H. (2012). Strategic alignment and new product development: Drivers and performance effects. *Journal of Product Innovation Management, 29*(2), 304–318.

Alagaraja, M. (2013). Mobilizing organizational alignment through strategic human resource development. *Human Resource Development International, 16*(1), 74–93.

Baron, D. P. (1995). Integrated strategy: Market and non-market components. *California Management Review, 37*(2), 47–65.

Chandler, A. D. (2001, March–April). The enduring logic of industrial success. *Harvard Business Review*, 130–140.

Coltman, T., Tallon, P., Sharma, R., & Queiroz, M. (2015). Strategic IT alignment: Twenty-five years on. *Journal of Information Technology, 30*(2), 91–100.

DiMaggio, P. J., & Powell, W. W. (1983). The iron cage revisited: Institutional isomorphism and collective rationality in organizational fields. *American Sociological Review, 48*, 147–160.

Freeman, R. E., Dmytriyev, S. D., & Phillips, R. A. (2021). Stakeholder theory and the resource-based view of the firm. *Journal of Management, 47*(7), 1757–1770.

Greenwood, R., & Suddaby, R. (2006). Institutional entrepreneurship in mature fields: The big five accounting firms. *Academy of Management Journal, 49*(1), 27–48.

Han, J. H., Kang, S., Oh, I.-S., Kehoe, R. R., & Lepak, D. P. (2019). The Goldilocks effect of strategic human resource management? Optimizing the benefits of a high-performance work system through the dual alignment of vertical and horizontal fit. *Academy of Management Journal, 62*(5), 1388–2142.

Helfat, C. E., Finkelstein, S., Mitchell, W., Peteraf, M., Singh, H., Teece, D., & Winter, S. G. (2007). *Dynamic Capabilities: Understanding Strategic Change in Organizations*. Blackwell.

Jacobides, M. G., Cennamo, C., & Gawer, A. (2018). Towards a theory of ecosystems. *Strategic Management Journal, 39*(8), 2255–2276.

Kathuria, R., Joshi, M. P., & Porth, S. J. (2007). Organizational alignment and performance: Past, present and future. *Management Decision, 45*(3), 503–517.

Kirkpatrick, S. A. (2016). *Build a better vision statement: Extending esearch with practical advice*. Lexington Books.

Lee, E., & Puranam, P. (2016). The implementation imperative: Why one should implement even imperfect strategies perfectly. *Strategic Management Journal, 37*(8), 1529–1546.

Miles, R. E., & Snow, C. C. (1984). Fit, failure and the hall of fame. *California Management Review, 26*(3), 10–28.

Miller, S. C. and Kirkpatrick, S. A. 2021. *The government leader's field guide to organizational agility: How to navigate complex and turbulent times*. Oakland, CA: Berrett-Koehler.

North, D. C. (1994). Economic performance through time. *American Economic Review, 84*, 359–368.

Peng, M. W., Sun, S. L., Pinkham, B., & Chen, H. (2009). The institution-based view as a third leg for a strategy tripod. *Academy of Management Perspectives, 23*(3), 63–81.

Porter, M. E. (1985). *Competitive advantage: Creating and sustaining superior performance*. The Free Press.

Sarta, A., Durand, R., & Vergne, J.-P. (2021). Organizational Adaptation. *Journal of Management, 47*(1), 43–75.

Stouten, J., Rousseau, D. M., & De Cremer, D. (2018). Successful organizational change: Integrating the management practice and scholarly literatures. *Academy of Management Annals, 12*(2), 752–788.

Teece, D. J. (2007). Explicating dynamic capabilities: The nature and microfoundations of (sustainable) enterprise performance. *Strategic Management Journal, 28*(13), 1319–1350.

Tirole, J. (2001). Corporate governance. *Econometrics, 69*(1), 1–35.

Wright, P. W., & Snell, S. A. (1998). Toward a unifying framework for exploring fit and flexibility in strategic human resource management. *Academy of Management Review, 23*(4), 756–772.

Zubac, A., Dasborough, M., Hughes, K., Jiang, Z., Kirkpatrick, S., Martinsons, M. G., Tucker, D., & Zwikael, O. (2021). The strategy and change interface: Understanding "enabling" processes and cognitions. *Management Decision, 59*(3), 481–505.

Zubac, A., Hubbard, G., & Johnson, L. W. (2012). Extending resource-based logic: Applying the resource-investment concept to the firm from a payments perspective. *Journal of Management, 38*(6), 1867–1891.

Zwikael, O., & Smyrk, J. R. (2019). *Project Management: A Benefit Realisation Approach*. Springer Nature.

PART I

The Strategy Process

CHAPTER 2

Introduction: The Strategy Process

Angelina Zubac, Danielle Tucker, Ofer Zwikael, Kate Hughes, and Shelley Kirkpatrick

The three chapters in this section demonstrate that, although it can be helpful at times to separate strategy formulation from the strategy implementation stage for pedagogical and communication purposes, when strategy is approached in this way, the wrong mindset ends up being adopted across the organisation. The process becomes the focus rather than the strategic outcomes the organisation needs to achieve. As a result,

A. Zubac (✉)
University of Queensland, Brisbane, QLD, Australia
e-mail: a.zubac@business.uq.edu.au; Angelina.zubac@aim.com.au; az@strategylink.com.au

D. Tucker
University of Essex, Colchester, UK
e-mail: dtucker@essex.ac.uk

O. Zwikael
Australian National University, Canberra, ACT, Australia
e-mail: ofer.zwikael@anu.edu.au

K. Hughes
Technological University Dublin, Dublin, Ireland

© The Author(s), under exclusive license to Springer Nature Singapore Pte Ltd. 2022
A. Zubac et al. (eds.), *Effective Implementation of Transformation Strategies*, https://doi.org/10.1007/978-981-19-2336-4_2

the organisation falls short of its potential to draw on its people's drive, passion and talents to pursue opportunities and solve the organisation's problems.

That being the case, Chapter 3 by Steven Cofrancesco, *A social context view of strategic cognition: Strategists are highly emotional and interactive Homo sapiens*, argues that it is a mistake to assume that strategy can be formulated and implemented rationally and, as a consequence, very successfully. This is because humans have evolved to respond to opportunities and threats as an affective response, that is, using verbal, bodily and other physiological signals for interpreting the social context. The nonconscious signals that are picked up and then interpreted during the process of formulating and implementing a strategy, including as a process of continual refinement, cannot be ignored. However, this does not mean that strategies cannot be formulated and implemented decisively or without integrity and commitment. If the strategist can work with others to harness the organisation's people's passion, creativity, knowledge, skills and ability to learn from the past and pre-empt the future, the strategy process can be successfully navigated, enabling the organisation to achieve its strategic objectives. For that reason, it is highly recommended that strategies are formulated and implemented with an understanding of who exactly will be contributing to it, if the strategy evokes strong emotions easily spread to others that can be productively levered, and how it might be possible to manage people's propensity to respond both rationally and nonconsciously to varying degrees as the social context dictates.

Analogously, Chapter 4 by Harry Sminia and Freddy Valdovinos Salinas, *Implementing strategy and avenues of access: A practice perspective*, argues that despite the appeal of approaching strategy in design terms, that is, as a series of steps that if properly enacted should lead to the organisation changing to be more strategic, strategy is best conceived as a continuous implementation process. The reality is that the structures, incentives, cultural and people goals, controls put in place, etc., that are pursued as part of the strategy to better position the organisation in the

---

e-mail: kate.hughes@hughes-scm.com

S. Kirkpatrick
The MITRE Corporation, McLean, VA, USA
e-mail: skirkpatrick@mitre.org

future can never be pursued with certainty. Everything in the organisation is so connected; when one practice is changed at an organisation, others will change. The strategy as originally intended may not be possible to achieve. Managers' behaviours during the implementation process can be interpreted by others in ways not intended too, leading to a shift in how it is subsequently approached. Organisations that are able to become "strategically aligned" may do so circumstantially rather than as a strategy being realised as intended.

Chapter 5 by Czeslaw Mesjasz, *Strategy implementation and organisational change: A complex systems perspective*, considers how systems logic can be used to better understand the strategy implementation process in non-sequential terms. In the past, the strategy process was described as involving two sets of processes—strategy formulation and strategy implementation. However, it became apparent that managers did not move from the strategic analysis to the decision stage and then to the implementation stage in a clear-cut manner. Strategic change, including the changes normally instituted by applying principles from the discipline of organisational change occurs non-sequentially. It also involves the interplay of many variables. After reviewing the systems related literature, explaining their relevance for solving different systems and complexity problems, it is concluded that the literature on coevolutionary complexity provides the most promising framework for studying the interface between strategy implementation and strategic change.

Taken together, these three chapters make it very clear that though it is important to set a direction for the organisation for practical reasons, the strategy process is all about learning. This includes learning about how people can be inspired to learn, and how the organisation's many systems and structures can be adapted to ensure that this learning can occur. Building on the themes underpinning this book, Fig. 2.1 demonstrates what is involved. The corporate strategy is continually refined by the market and non-market strategies of the organisation, and vice versa. This enables the organisation to invest in and develop the resources it needs for the future, including build dynamic capabilities. Dynamic capabilities are important to build as they allow the organisation to adapt itself on an ongoing basis by harnessing its people's creativity and commitment.

Importantly, Fig. 2.1 highlights the reasons why different organisations will build different capability bases and a corresponding ability to be suitably adaptable. Many recursive activities may need to be undertaken over time that are unique to the organisation. To make these activities

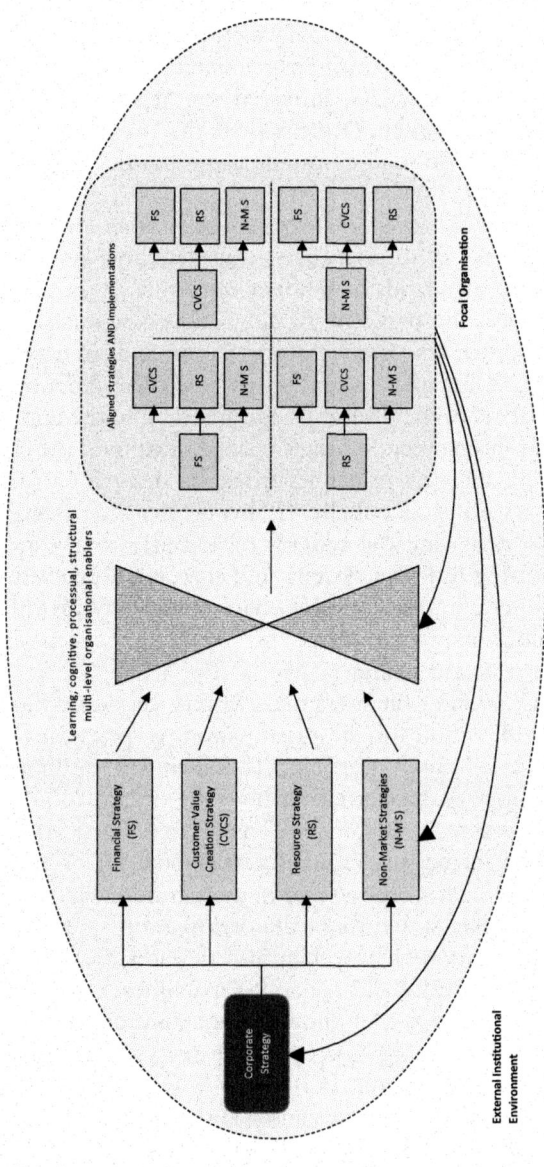

Fig. 2.1 Strategy and change at the contemporary organisation: implementing to learn and learning to implement within the institutional superstructure (*Source* Adapted from Zubac et al. [2021])

possible, a range of multi-level learning, cognitive, processual and structural enablers (or internal systems) will be necessary to establish allowing for the fact that all organisations are open systems. These may be realised as platforms or carefully crafted routines designed to help decision-makers overcome their cognitive shortcomings while implementing a strategy or when making necessary adjustments to it.

Reference

Zubac, A., Dasborough, M., Hughes, K., Jiang, Z., Kirkpatrick, S., Martinsons, M. G., Tucker, D. & Zwikael, O. (2021). The strategy and change interface: Understanding "enabling" processes and cognitions. *Management Decision*, *59*(3), 481–505.

CHAPTER 3

A Social Context View of Strategic Cognition: Strategists Are Highly Emotional and Interactive Homo Sapiens!

Steven R. Cofrancesco

INTRODUCTION

Cognition refers to thinking, i.e. how one processes information or one's form of thought, and strategic cognition therefore simply refers to how one processes information or thinks about strategic issues. The strategic cognition literature views strategy as over emphasising rational forms of cognition and methods (Ashton-James & Ashkanasy, 2008; Calabretta et al., 2017; Healey & Hodgkinson, 2015; Hodgkinson & Sadler-Smith, 2018; Powell, 2014; Robinson et al., 2017; Sibony et al., 2017), including strategy tools themselves (Hodgkinson & Healey, 2011; Kaplan, 2009; Moisander & Stenfors, 2009; Wright et al., 2013). This has resulted in one-dimensional research that does not account for the

---

S. R. Cofrancesco (✉)
University of Advancing Technology, Tempe, AZ, USA
e-mail: scofrancesco@uat.edu

whole of the phenomenon, which is problematic because it is misinforming both researchers and practitioners in their work (Ashton-James & Ashkanasy, 2008; Calabretta et al., 2017; Healey & Hodgkinson, 2015; Hodgkinson & Sadler-Smith, 2018; Powell, 2014; Robinson et al., 2017; Sibony et al., 2017). In turn, those misconceptions have resulted in a cognitive style that is emotionally and physically detached across strategists, their team members and even their work. This is problematic for strategy, perhaps explaining why it is described as a tumultuous rollercoaster (Bartunek et al., 2011; Sanchez-Burks & Huy, 2009), that does not facilitate the development of something new, unique and valuable for customers.

The social context view of strategy emphasises the concept of emergent strategy as opposed to rationally planned strategy (these two views are described in detail below). Therefore, viewing strategy as occurring within a social, emergent context suggests that emotional contagion and its related psychological impact on the strategists and others who contribute is significantly more sensitive, ubiquitous and influential on cognitive styles than previously portrayed. In fact, emotional human interaction emerges as a unifying concept throughout the whole of organisational change efforts. The experience of emotion is referred to as *affect*, and therefore the term *affect* is mostly used throughout the entirety of this paper. I think it is beneficial for practitioners and even educators to use the terms presented in this paper because it will change the way you think about doing the work of strategy with other human beings. Please give it a shot! Keep in mind that Organisations ARE our communities, and therefore strategic level decision-making directly impacts communities themselves, but also entire societies. This is the significance of this work.

The social context view also portrays strategy as an iterative and interactive activity performed by humans whose affect is present throughout the whole of their bodies, i.e. throughout their interconnected neurology and biology, and therefore throughout their interactions with each other. I think it's fascinating that the literature overwhelmingly suggests our cognition is dominated and controlled by our historical Homo sapien cognition from millions of years of living in the forest! This older form of cognition is commonly known as our subconscious or below-the-radar thinking, which the literature often refers to as *nonconscious* cognition. This work provides a fully contextualised, social view of strategy team interactions, which comprises those who contribute and their interactions, strategy work itself including its tools, and the physical environment within which it occurs. Addressing the full social context provides strategy practitioners with an accurate description of the whole of strategy, as current models and theories do not accurately explain how or with whom strategists interact (Balogun et al., 2003; Gary et al., 2012; Gavetti & Rivkin, 2007; Hodgkinson & Healey, 2008; Powell et al., 2011; Salas et al., 2010).

This article thematically synthesises theoretical concepts and thoughts from approximately 60 top journals and authors on the topic of strategic cognition. It begins by first extrapolating the misinformation realised from our focus on cold cognition, prescribing how it *should* be conceived based on the social context. The current state of strategic cognition follows. It begins by presenting our two cognitive processing systems: one that is older, affective, intuitive and nonconscious in nature, and one that is newer, rational, affect-free (without emotion) and conscious in nature. Then, a critical section on emotional contagion is presented, explaining how emotion is transmitted from one person to another and its potential for psychologically harming strategists, their team and even the organisation itself. Emotional contagion and psychological harm inspired development of a mechanism that deeply explains how strategists *receive* affect from the social context, *determine* an affective response, and in turn *give* affect back to the context. I *italicise* those three terms throughout this paper to clearly identify when referring to those specific affective steps of an interaction. The mechanism explains how emotion (affect) overwhelmingly drives our assessments of others and situations, i.e. our assessments are NOT driven by calm, rational cognition! The paper is rounded out by a section on cognitive regulation, which the literature presents as having the potential to produce supportive and kind environments instead of domineering and wicked environments. Each of those two environments leads to variations in cognitive styles and related outcomes. The paper concludes with a discussion of the implications for practising managers and even educators. Attention is also paid to questions that require further research and consideration by those three parties.

Misconceptions Due to Rational and Detached Thinking

Unfortunately, the one-dimensional, cold focus of strategy research has permeated the entirety of strategy producing damaging misconceptions. For example, the one-dimensional literature suggests formulation and implementation are considered mutually exclusive phases, where strategists are only top managers such as the CEO and the top management team (TMT) who do their work in calm, rational, linear manners without emotional debates or conflict (Ashton-James & Ashkanasy, 2008; Bartunek et al., 2011; Calabretta et al., 2017; Reitzig & Sorenson, 2013). In alignment with the rational view of strategy, the work is performed only in formal meetings in boardrooms or at getaway resorts, sometimes occurs in a single event (Healey, Hodgkinson, et al., 2015), never sporadically or informally, and those responsible for implementation are minimally involved even though their work is equally strategic, iterative and developmental in nature (Ashton-James & Ashkanasy, 2008; Huy, 2011; Jarzabkowski, 2008; Reitzig & Sorenson, 2013). Additionally, strategists' work is supported by data driven tools and analyses that suggest, without human input or critique, optimal courses of action in dogmatic fashions. Strategies are normally *disseminated* in a procedural manner to middle and project managers for implementation, not *communicated* to them, who efficiently and procedurally implement strategies through scientifically based, emotionless project management tools (Huy, 2011). This does not portray the work of strategy as developmental, passionate and creative, but rather as linear, procedural and emotionally and interactively neutral.

The apparent abdication of the social and emotional nature of the activity has become so ingrained that strategy now has an overarching philosophical view of the work and even the people as scientifically detached from each other. Only science, data, procedures and the almighty tools are valued. In other words, emergence and the social context are overwhelmingly underemphasised and undervalued (Balogun et al., 2003; Felin et al., 2015; Gary et al., 2012; Gavetti & Rivkin, 2007; Jarzabkowski, 2008). These misconceptions are highly problematic.

Correcting the Misconceptions: Strategy's Social Context

The strategic cognition literature overwhelmingly suggests the presence of an all-encompassing social context that comprises (1) strategists and their team members from both inside and outside the organisation, (2) strategy work and its tools and (3) even the physical environment (synthesised from: Akinci & Sadler-Smith, 2012; Ashton-James & Ashkanasy, 2008; Bakir & Todorovic, 2010; Barsade, 2002; Elbanna & Fadol, 2016; Healey & Hodgkinson, 2015; Powell, 2014; Pratt & Crosina, 2016; Salas et al., 2010; Walsh, 1995). Those three components of the social context, which are described in detail below, are interconnected via highly iterative and affective interactions among human beings, who are highly affective throughout their neurological and biological systems (Akinci & Sadler-Smith, 2012; Ashton-James & Ashkanasy, 2008; Barsade, 2002; Healey & Hodgkinson, 2015; Lieberman et al., 2002; Lieberman et al., 2004; Sibony et al., 2017). In other words, affect is not simply a feeling experienced in our heads, but rather permeates the entirety of our human body through its neurological and biological systems. The literature often combines those two terms into one: *neurobiological*, which I use throughout this paper.

Also, the social context tacitly comprises the concept of emergence (Felin et al., 2015), which suggests, for example, that strategizing occurs during both formal and planned meetings, and also during informal and emergent meetings such as around water coolers and in parking lots (synthesised from: Andersen & Nielsen, 2009; Andrews et al., 2009; Balbastre-Benavent & Canet-Giner, 2011; Elbanna, 2006; Jarratt & Stiles, 2010; Kjærgaard, 2009; Poister et al., 2013; Reitzig & Sorenson, 2013; Sminia, 2009). Strategists are loosely defined as those responsible for strategy work or the chief decision makers, which are normally the CEOs, department heads and possibly even supervisors. Interestingly, such behind-the-scenes, informal interactions described above might be even more important than the formal interactions (Bartunek et al., 2011). Therefore, the interactions of strategy work occur between many more strategists and contributors than normally portrayed, suggesting many more are contributing to both formulation and implementation activities than normally portrayed. The upcoming sections make it clear that almost an entire organisation could be considered strategy team members. For example, Lee Iacocca is touted and exalted for saving Chrysler with his now famous K-car strategy, but did he develop this strategy completely by himself? Considering the organisation was on the brink of failure, would he not have passionately and intensely discussed the problematic situation with his TMT, other CEOs, customers, line workers, governmental leaders, as well as interacted with the process and its tools? Stated another way, those who contribute are normally not recognised as strategy team members, and they might not even know that they have contributed!

The aforementioned social context clearly suggests the inclusion of nearly all organisational members into the concept of strategy (Bartunek et al., 2011), from both inside and outside an organisation, such as those who run workshops, write reports (Whittington et al., 2006), leaders from the competition, industry analysts, distributors (Reger & Huff, 1993), the corporate board, journalists and politicians (Bromiley & Rau, 2016), and include lower-level managers and even non-managerial staff (Balogun et al., 2003) because they are content experts (Balogun et al., 2003; Reger & Huff, 1993). Therefore, all who contribute to strategic organisational change efforts, whether formulation or implementation, shall heretofore be referred to as *strategy team members*, or just *team* or *members*. Additionally, there is significant cognitive confluence among formulation and implementation. For example, those involved in formulating ideas for new product strategies would simultaneously, in their heads, consider whether they have the skills and knowledge to actually make (implement) those products. Also, those involved in implementing new product strategies, whether planning and organising for the implementing or actually making the product, would simultaneously consider in their heads whether the new structures and systems recommended are adequate or even necessary for the implementation, which are formulation issues. In other words, formulation and implementation are intrinsically and tacitly linked and inseparable, not mutually exclusive phases (Bartunek, et al., 2011; Whittington et al., 2006).

Therefore, strategy work is NOT wholly or even mostly scientific and procedural with clearly delineated goals, but rather it is mostly ambiguous and complex with moving targets for goals that require passionate intensity and intuitive creativity (Dane & Pratt, 2007; Jarzabkowski, 2008; Salas et al., 2010; Sanchez-Burks & Huy, 2009; Tversky & Kahneman, 1981). Strategy work is developmental, iterative and based on interactions between and among people and activities, i.e. it is not linear, procedural and emotionally detached (Eggers & Kaplan, 2013; Marcel et al.,

2011; Whittington et al., 2006). In fact, it has significantly more intensity and passion than operational level decision-making (Ashton-James & Ashkanasy, 2008). Implementation also requires a certain amount of passionate intensity, iterations and creativity to be performed successfully (Bartunek et al., 2011; Dane & Pratt, 2009; Jarzabkowski, 2008; Pratt & Crosina, 2016), which is considered necessary for developing new, unique and valuable strategic alternatives (Barsade & Gibson, 2007; Calabretta et al., 2017; Dane & Pratt, 2009; Hodgkinson et al., 2009; Lieberman & Eisenberger, 2009).

In summary, the social context of strategy comprises the people, their work and their physical environment as *cognitive* sources of interaction. Therefore, the three are not mutually exclusive, but rather they are one. Even though we conduct research and write about these topics in a separatist methodological manner, because it facilitates our understanding of their complexities, the methods we use to research complex topics should not be used to "do" or perform strategy. Therefore, even though much information is presented in a slightly scientific and detached manner, I conclude with a more impassioned and practice-based discussion of what the information means for the practising manager.

I now address significant components of our human cognition identified by the literature, providing a more nuanced mechanism of interactions between and among strategists and their team members not normally emphasised in the literature. Such a nuanced view helps us to more deeply understand why the one-dimensional view is inappropriate, and understanding why often helps us to actually achieve perform activities (strategy) in a more optimal manner. Those sections conclude with a couple thoughts on how strategists can consciously regulate or control their emotions in order to enhance supportive and kind cognitive functioning in strategy work.

COGNITIVE SYSTEMS OF INFORMATION PROCESSING

This section begins by introducing human information processing systems, then describes their conflicting purposes and characteristics, which is followed by a fascinating mechanism describing how strategists *receive* and *give* affective interactions (Barsade & Gibson, 2007). This section is finalised by summarising the cognitive styles and outcomes that result from those affective interactions. In other words, this section describes and explains everything about strategic cognition that is excluded or misconceived from its current one-dimensional view. Once again, this is a significant because practising strategists, and even educators, are being misled and misinformed in their work. The following sections, therefore, address what those practising strategists, and educators, need to know in order to formulate and implement unique and valuable products!

The Two Systems

There is widespread agreement that human cognition comprises two overarching systems that operate iteratively and in unison: a newer system developed only tens of thousands of years ago that is overwhelmingly absent emotion (affect-free) and rational in nature, and an older system developed over many millions of years that is overwhelmingly affective and intuitive in nature (synthesised from: Akinci & Sadler-Smith, 2012; Epstein, 2010; Healey & Hodgkinson, 2015; Healey, Vuori, et al., 2015; Hodgkinson et al., 2008; Lieberman et al., 2002; Pratt & Crosina, 2016; Sadler-Smith, 2004). The older system provides this meaning by focusing on instantaneously recognisng risks to one's survival and reacting accordingly, e.g. by killing before being killed. The newer system provides this meaning by focusing on planning and organising in order to achieve goals, e.g. by working with other individuals or tribes to track and kill larger and stronger prey. However, this should NOT be interpreted to mean that the newer system is entirely superior to the old system. I believe this is one of the reasons (misconceptions) for the one-dimensional focus on the newer, affect-free and rational cognitive system. Let us now explore these two systems in greater depth to understand why focusing on rational cognition is detrimental…

The two cognitive systems have been described in numerous ways. For example, the newer, rational system has been called: reflective, cold, slow, analytical, effortful, controlled, intentional, cerebral and impersonal (synthesised from: Ashton-James & Ashkanasy, 2008; Carton & Lucas, 2018; Dane & Pratt, 2009; Healey & Hodgkinson, 2015, 2017; Healey, Vuori, et al., 2015; Powell, 2014; Pratt & Crosina, 2016; Salas et al., 2010). It is further described as logical reasoning responsible for planning and hypothetical cognition (Akinci & Sadler-Smith, 2012; Epstein, 2010). Conversely, the older, affective and intuitive system has been called: reflexive, hot, fast, spontaneous, nonconscious, heuristic, automatic, uncontrolled and effortless (synthesised from: Akinci & Sadler-Smith, 2012; Dane & Pratt, 2007; Epstein, 2010; Healey, Vuori, et al., 2015; Hodgkinson & Healey, 2008; Hodgkinson et al., 2008; Salas et al., 2010). It is further described as highly visceral and creative (Barsade & Gibson, 2007; Dane & Pratt, 2009; Hodgkinson et al., 2008, 2009), responsible for idea generation and divergent thinking suited for problems that lack concretely defined goals (Ashton-James & Ashkanasy, 2008; Epstein, 2010; Hodgkinson et al., 2008, 2009). Such goals include the making of new products because the formulators cannot know exactly when their new product strategy is "good". The same is true for implementers, albeit to a lesser degree, who cannot know precisely when their new manufacturing process or sales training programme is precisely what the strategists have prescribed. In other words, they cannot know whether they have implemented the new strategy with fidelity (as intended). The nonconscious is also considered to be a neurobiological system because of its highly intense and iterative connections between affect, intuition and the interconnected neurology and biology of the human body, as previously described (Ashton-James & Ashkanasy, 2008; Lieberman et al., 2002, 2004; Sibony et al., 2017). Notice that the two cognitive systems are nearly the antithesis of each other! This is significant to the practitioner's understanding of strategic cognition.

Based on these descriptions, I heretofore refer to the newer system as the *rational* system and refer to the older system as the *nonconscious* system. These two terms seem to capture the essence of their characteristics.

Conflicting Purposes and Characteristics

The overarching purpose of the newer, rational system is to make meaning (Carton & Lucas, 2018), which is the consciousness considered unique to human beings (Lieberman et al., 2002) providing us with the potential for greatly enhanced cognitive function, but also with confusion, stress, depression and even hopelessness associated with unanswerable questions such as: What is the meaning of life?! (Calabretta et al., 2017; Hodgkinson et al., 2009; Salas et al., 2010). Hence, the dog's life seems attractive (Lieberman et al., 2002). The rational system achieves this by evaluating life as fed to it by the older system, which is often inaccurate (Calabretta et al., 2017; Lieberman et al., 2002). It also seeks to take control of the nonconscious system and protect its identity and status by speaking and behaving in a socially and organisationally appropriate manner (Sibony et al., 2017). To be clear, this is the rational system's overarching purpose, but that does not mean it is always successful in its endeavours!

In contrast to the newer system's purpose of making meaning, the older nonconscious system has the overarching purpose of assessing risk and threats in order to enhance survival, as employed throughout our Homo sapien history (Akinci & Sadler-Smith, 2012). This system is based on our life's experiences (Akinci & Sadler-Smith, 2012; Ashton-James & Ashkanasy, 2008; Barsade & Gibson, 2007; Bartunek et al., 2011; Carton & Lucas, 2018; Eggers & Kaplan, 2013; Epstein, 2010; Gavetti et al., 2005; Lieberman et al., 2002; Marcel et al., 2011; Miller & Ireland, 2005; Salas et al., 2010), as well as millions of years of preprogrammed experiences, which is why it is referred to as ancient biological wisdom (Hodgkinson et al., 2008). It makes meaning by correlating analogies between past experiences and present situations (Carton & Lucas, 2018; Gary et al., 2012). For example, the strategists at Kodak probably never had the experience of their product (or perhaps any other product) becoming obsolete due to new technologies that completely changed the industry landscape. Therefore, their rational cognition made wonderfully positive statements about themselves, perhaps referring to their dominance in the market for so many years, and the greatness of their product. They simply did not have any similar analogies on which to base their thinking! Additionally, however, present situations eventually become past experiences, meaning that the experiential base changes over time and can even be intentionally modified (Akinci & Sadler-Smith, 2012), albeit with significant, passionate effort. You can be sure that those Kodak strategists now have the experiential base to make better decisions in those situations!

Because the two cognitive systems have completely different purposes, they are often in conflict with each other (Calabretta et al., 2017; Epstein, 2010; Gavetti & Rivkin, 2007; Healey, Vuori, et al., 2015; Hodgkinson et al., 2008; Pratt & Crosina, 2016). Making matters worse, the nonconscious is normally in charge of the rational (Ashton-James & Ashkanasy, 2008; Hodgkinson et al., 2009; Lieberman et al., 2002; Marcel et al., 2011), even if we do not realise it (Epstein, 2010)! The conflict is so intense that it has the potential to result in significant stress and confusion, and therefore produce destructive and damaging behaviour! This is highly problematic for the already ambiguous and stressful nature of strategy work. In order to cope with life's issues and overload (stress), the nonconscious seeks to maximise pleasure, minimise pain and avoid stable states—it is essentially consumed by hedonism (Epstein, 2010; Tversky & Kahneman, 1981), which distracts it from those issues and overload. Unfortunately, said distraction can represent damaging thinking and behaviour such as superstitions, phobias and even aggression towards others (Epstein, 2010; Lieberman et al., 2002). In other words, the nonconscious thinks and behaves according to what *feels* best and safest, which includes quickly choosing action over sitting still, and even electing to engage in negative thoughts and behaviours if there are no better options. In other words, negative feelings are better than no feelings! This is perhaps due to the system's evolutionary history, when inactive or complacent states might result in complacency and expose one to surprises, thereby risking injury or even death. As such, the nonconscious system uses affect (e.g. fear) to appraise a situation and guide its attention, cognitive style and decision-making (Ashton-James & Ashkanasy, 2008; Healey & Hodgkinson, 2015; Huy, 2012). Conversely, as stated previously, the rational system puts its stamp on the nonconscious' hedonism by (attempting to) speak and behave in accordance with social and organisational norms. All the above has very significant implications for interactions between and among strategists and their strategy team members because it appears to represent an untenable cognitive conundrum. How is one to navigate through this treacherous territory? As the following section demonstrates, such interactions often result in negative emotions that are both contagious (transmitted to others much like the common cold) and psychologically harmful to others. This is especially concerning considering the emergent nature of strategy work that includes many more strategists and members throughout almost the entirety of an organisation.

Contagion, Psychological Harm, and Emergence

Emotional contagion occurs constantly, automatically and without our awareness (Barsade & Gibson, 2007) through our nervous system (Akinci & Sadler-Smith, 2012; Healey & Hodgkinson, 2015). It results in bodily presentations such as facial musculature, postures and body language, and physiological presentations such as perspiration, tears and pounding hearts that are perceived and understood by others (Barsade & Gibson, 2007; Ashton-James & Ashkanasy, 2008; Lieberman & Eisenberger, 2009). In addition, the nonconscious has the tendency to copy or repeat others' bodily and physiological expressions with synchronised bodily movements such as facial expressions, postures, movements and vocalisations, known as mimicking, which results in experiencing the same emotion (Barsade, 2002; Barsade & Gibson, 2007; Healey & Hodgkinson, 2015). Contagion can be transferred from line and staff members to managers and other leaders, not only from leaders to line workers (Cropanzano et al., 2017; Reitzig & Sorenson, 2013). In other words, the affect of all verbal and visual signals from the entirety of the social context is received and comprehended by all strategists and members due to our highly sensitive perceptions of those signals! Human's nonconscious has developed and refined those abilities over our historical evolution. I think it is fascinating that emotional contagion is rather mechanical in nature, i.e. it is not magically transmitted through brain waves or ESP! Problematically, however, negative affect is more contagious than positive affect, and therefore the risk of psychological pain and damage is greater than the potential for psychological pleasure and enhancement (Barsade, 2002). This is why I suggest emotional contagion is an oversensitive, dangerous and omnipresent force in strategy work!

The concept of contagion is essentially absent from the rational view of strategy, perhaps receiving honourable mentions, and yet the cognition literature overwhelmingly suggests it is ubiquitous throughout the social context (synthesised from: Barsade, 2002; Barsade & Gibson, 2007; Bartunek et al., 2011; Healey & Hodgkinson, 2015, 2017; Huy, 2011; Jarzabkowski, 2008; Powell et al., 2011). This information has both detrimental and beneficial implications. In other words, humans understand emotion by seeing it in the form of bodily and physiological representations, not by hearing it, unless the vocalisations are impassioned or otherwise artistic in nature (Ashton-James & Ashkanasy, 2008; Barsade, 2002; Cropanzano et al., 2017; Epstein, 2010; Lieberman & Eisenberger, 2009; Lieberman et al., 2002). This is highly representative of strategy's social context and its structure of emergence where interactions are numerous and the stakes are high, i.e. passionate and intense. In other words, it is the optimal format for spreading each other's feelings, for better or worse. It is detrimental if feelings are negative, but can be beneficial if feelings are positive! Although some are less likely to be influenced by contagion and mimicry (Tasselli et al., 2015), it appears the average person is highly and significantly susceptible, and therefore emotions will most likely be received with fidelity by others. This means it is nearly impossible to hide or fake one's true feelings, especially if they are negative—Homo sapiens are masters at deciphering them! As an example, a master's student in one of my classes, who was a department head at a large hospital, said that his CEO does not like him at all. I asked how he knows this, and after pausing in reflection, he said: actually, I've never met him formally, but I just get that *feeling*. In other words, his nonconscious read the affect as portrayed to him by his CEO, either through direct a visual contact or perhaps even by interacting with a third party. This is the power, and danger, of emotional contagion!

Affect is normally described in an overarching manner as having either positive valence which simply means good or positive feelings, or negative valence which simply means bad or negative feelings. However, there can be varying magnitudes of those positive and negative feelings (valences), much like points on a continuum. In other words, severe psychological pain is located on one end of the continuum, which is experienced much like physical pain equal to a broken leg (Lieberman & Eisenberger, 2009), and psychological pleasure is located on the other end, assumedly experienced much like a euphoric physical experience. Further complicating the issue, psychological pain is in the eyes and ears of the beholder, i.e. the magnitude of the pain someone experiences is based in part on their individual perceptions. As you might expect, perceptions are real and the pain can actually be debilitating, just like physical injuries. I believe we're just beginning to understand the significance of our emotional health. Such emotional pain is probably based on our time in the forest, when experiencing pain was a signal that we were in need of social connection, food, water or shelter (Lieberman & Eisenberger, 2009). Therefore, considering the affectively sensitive social context, it seems an impossibility for strategists and teams to navigate their way through the complex and ambiguous process without realising psychological harm capable of debilitating the entire organisational change activity. Emotions are therefore suggested to be virally contagious in strategy work, placing affective interactions at centre stage of entire strategic change efforts! Incidentally, psychological pleasure is also in the eyes and ears of the beholder, suggesting there is hope within this cognitive conundrum. Yet another key thought for the strategist to put in his/her back pocket for future reference.

Positive Conflict

Not all conflict and negative affect is to be avoided, as it can actually translate into psychological pleasure. In other words, some mild negative affect can activate the nonconscious system and actually enhance emotional contagion (Lieberman et al., 2002), because people pay more attention to negativity (Barsade, 2002), which can also lead to more concentrated, detailed and analytic processing (synthesised from: Ashton-James & Ashkanasy, 2008; Barsade & Gibson, 2007; Cropanzano et al., 2017; Healey, Vuori, et al., 2015; To et al., 2015). This is especially the case if survival is at stake, whether of one's job or department, the strategy or the organisation itself, eventually resulting in psychological pleasure. When emerging unscathed from such conflict with new knowledge, experience, capabilities and confidence, we can experience psychological pleasure much like euphoria, with gratitude for the great relationships and interactions that occurred along the way. Once again, negative affect should not be avoided. Additionally, the entirety of strategy change efforts cannot be smooth socio-psychological sailing! Therefore, positive conflict possibly represents an arena for letting the conflict of our cognitive systems play out, at least if everyone is pursuing the organisation as the focus of that conflict.

I now introduce a mechanism of how affective interactions occur, beginning with *receiving* an affective interaction, followed by *determining* an affective response, and concluding with *giving* an affective interaction. The nature of our cognition and associated contagion suggests the interactions between and among strategists and their team members are highly complex and ubiquitously influential beyond our current portrayal, i.e. they are nothing less than the epicentre of strategy!

Receiving an Affective Interaction

Strategists and members receive visual and audible information simultaneously from all three components of strategy's social context. Interestingly, as can be seen in Fig. 3.1, the nonconscious receives most of its information from imagery through the eyes, which is in the form of bodily and physiological presentations, as previously described, but also from the physical environment's sights (synthesised from: Ashton-James & Ashkanasy, 2008; Kaplan, 2009; Moisander & Stenfors, 2009; Powell et al., 2011; Pratt & Crosina, 2016; Robinson et al., 2017; Stigliani & Ravasi, 2012) such as structures, busy office settings, computers, the

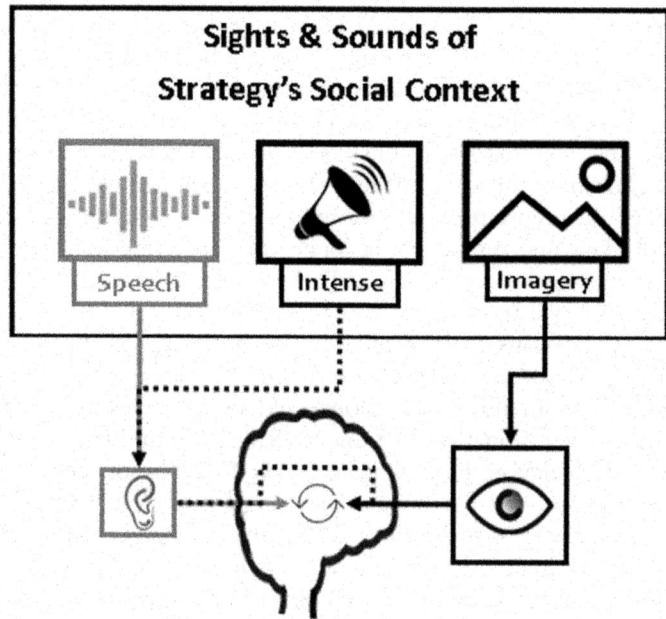

Fig. 3.1 The receipt of an affective interaction

humming of manufacturing equipment, palm trees at strategy getaways, and the work such as complex spreadsheets and colourful graphs on shinny screens. In addition to imagery, the nonconscious system can receive speech that is intense and passionate, which is represented by the dotted line (Barsade, 2002; Carton & Lucas, 2018; Cropanzano et al., 2017; Epstein, 2010; Lieberman et al., 2002; Miller & Ireland, 2005; Sadler-Smith, 2004). In short, signals that are affect-laden will be received by the nonconscious system for processing.

The rational system, conversely, is home to content-based verbal communication, which tacitly excludes nonconscious cognition and affect (Lieberman et al., 2002). The scientific and detached speech of strategy work, as currently emphasised, is received through the ears, containing only content, and essentially passes directly to the rational system for processing (Carton & Lucas, 2018; Epstein, 2010; Healey, Vuori, et al., 2015; Hodgkinson et al., 2008). Therefore, the receipt of an interaction comprises simultaneous verbal and visual signals from the entire social context, which is also the beginning of the emotional contagion process. Notice in Fig. 3.1 that the eye is considerably larger than the ear, and further that speech and the ear are grey, whereas imagery and the eye are black. This represents the human's overwhelming emphasis on information acquisition through imagery. However, notice also that highly impassioned or intense sounds, although physically entering through the ears, enter the same region of the brain for processing as imagery! So the key component to comprehend is that affect-laden signals, whether visual or verbal, will be directed to the nonconscious for processing. This has great implications for the physical surroundings of strategy work. To be clear, however, visual and verbal signals are received into the whole of the brain, not into disconnected hemispheres, as incorrectly purported by the rational view (Akinci & Sadler-Smith, 2012; Calabretta et al., 2017; Healey & Hodgkinson, 2015; Hodgkinson et al., 2009). Specifically, the rational and nonconscious systems are each controlled by three different parts of the brain, i.e. six total (Lieberman et al., 2002), but those parts are cross-hemispherical, interconnected and interactive neural systems (Hodgkinson et al., 2008; Lieberman et al., 2002, 2004). This means the myriad verbal, bodily and physiological signals from the social context are processed via both cognitive systems, simultaneously and collaboratively (although not cooperatively!), to construct an affective response. Once again, the whole of our bodies, i.e. brain, biology, neurology, psychology and physiology, are actually one highly interconnected system! Stated differently, since we are affective creatures, there is no way to exclude affect from strategy work. It simply is not possible. Attempting to do so seems to result in only suppressing it, which appears to exacerbate the conflict between the two systems, resulting in even more damaging cognition and behaviour!

Determining an Affective Response

Once a member receives an interaction, the nonconscious system almost instantaneously produces an affect in response, achieved by determining the interaction's: (1) emotional valence as either positive or negative in nature, and (2) the magnitude of that valence. I now describe each of those two steps.

Step one: First, the system determines whether the valence of the received interaction is positive affect and therefore representative of psychological pleasure, or negative affect and therefore representative of psychological pain (Barsade, 2002; Epstein, 2010; Neumann, 2017). It is believed this determination is based in the concept of moral intuition, where one decides whether a given situation *feels* right or wrong (Dane & Pratt, 2009). Over millions of years of evolution, Homo sapiens have developed the ability to assess imagery at near instantaneous speeds, with the purpose of assessing threats in order to enhance chances of survival. It is essential for recognising threatening facial musculature when happening upon a stranger in the forest (Hodgkinson et al., 2008), as it may preserve life. Extending that thought, that skill may also be useful for recognising threatening bodily and physiological presentations in the boardroom or on the shop floor, as it may preserve organisational life or ensure career success.

However, those near instantaneous assessments can be dysfunctional. In other words, we judge others based on the same method of visual assessment as when we lived in the forest, which excludes the context and reasons for people's behaviour, probably because what we see what our eyes is so salient visible (Lieberman et al., 2002). For example, humans usually ascribe negative affective assessments to someone who is belligerently yelling and screaming at another. However, even though yelling and screaming in response to the discovery of embezzlement is appropriate and moral, we normally do not include that reason in our instantaneous assessment of others. Therefore, because the possible outcomes from those inaccurate assessments in organisations are not life threatening as in the forest, humans have time to better understand the context of one's affective behaviour, which permits more accurate affective judgements of others (Bartunek et al., 2011; Epstein, 2010; Neumann, 2017; Tasselli et al., 2015). This would lead to reduced psychological pain, because inaccurate affective assessments can depersonalise individuals (Pratt & Crosina, 2016), and enhanced psychological pleasure, for both those directly involved as well as observers. Therefore, such dysfunctional assessments are perhaps far more significant than previously thought due to strategy's social context and emergence, resulting in highly facilitated contagion spreading such negative affect and even psychological harm ubiquitously throughout entire strategy teams.

In short, humans sincerely believe imagery and especially their associated *feelings*, anchoring to and defending them with visceral intensity if necessary, almost as if defending themselves against physical harm or death in the forest! Such inaccurate assessments of an interaction's valence (i.e. mistakenly assessing someone as negative instead of positive) could produce a downward spiralling culture of psychological harm within the entirety of the strategy context (Barsade, 2002; Cropanzano et al., 2017). That concludes how we determine the valence of an interaction.

Step two: Once the appropriate affective experience has been determined, the system seeks to determine the *magnitude* of that valence (Barsade, 2002; Epstein, 2010; Neumann, 2017). Once again, keep in mind the concept of a continuum from psychological harm to psychological pleasure, as previously described. For example, affective experiences such as elation, happiness, contentment and even serenity might be roughly considered euphoric psychological pleasure, whereas lethargy, depression, sadness, upset, stress and nervousness might be roughly considered severe psychological harm (Barsade & Gibson, 2007). If the nonconscious feels insulted with upset and stress, representative of psychological pain, it seeks a response appropriate for survival under these conditions, which might be to attack the offender with verbal lashings, vengeful back stabbings or even the development of alliances that carry out underhanded activities, whether through formal channels or underground channels. Sometimes the proper response is to flee and hide! Although such cognition and behaviour are appropriate for survival in the forest, it is not normally appropriate for survival (success) in the strategic organisational change environment. The rational system, conversely, seeks to take control of the nonconscious by determining whether, and to what degree, its affect should be expressed or suppressed—such a determination is based on the appropriateness of said affect for organisational and social expectations, which is achieved via carefully tweaked tactical speech (Lieberman et al., 2002).

Therefore, the combined influence of the sights and sounds from the social context, including contagion and mimicry and the battle between the two systems' purposes, results in a verbal rationalisation that has the ultimate effect of portraying oneself (or one's team or department) in a positive light (Epstein, 2010). However, the nonconscious is normally the victor in the battle between the two systems, whether we know it or not. This normally results in negative psychological affect and psychological harm, despite any spoken words of a positive nature, which is currently the norm in strategy work and is contagious for the team and beyond. Stated another way, members can unconsciously and unintentionally cause others psychological harm, as if in the forest seeking to protect oneself against physical harm or death. Humans behave this way because, much like ignoring painful situations is less painful than facing them (the ostrich effect) (Healey & Hodgkinson, 2017), insulting or attacking someone who is different feels better than facing one's own issues! We might also behave this way because, much like in the forest, we simply cannot take the risk of possible injury or death, and therefore its safer to attack or run away in order to enhance the certainty of preserving ourselves.

Giving an Affective Interaction

Now that an affective response has been determined, it will be *given* to others. Together, the rational and nonconscious cognitive systems produce neurobiological activity, i.e. both neurological and biological activity that produces signals that represent the *giving* of an affective response to others. Specifically, those signals are presented to others verbal, bodily and physiological, as previously described (see Fig. 3.2). As you might guess, speech is provided by the rational system, and bodily and physiological signals as well as passionate or intense vocalisations are provided by the nonconscious system. That briefly summarises the *giving* of an affective interaction. Of course, that *giving* is then *received* by strategy team members through their ears directly into their rational processing system, and through their eyes directly into their nonconscious processing system. This is part of the contagion/mimicking mechanism previously discussed, where affect is actually transmitted to, and received by, others. Once again, the verbal signals *given* to others seek to take care of one's status by making statements that make one look as good as possible, i.e. by telling people what they view as favourable, while the bodily, physiological and passionate vocalisation signals represent the actual affect experienced. This part of the mechanism describes how conflicts between the verbal and bodily/physiological signals are often *given* and therefore *received* as well. For example, a strategist's words can thank a member for great ideas and contributions, but the facial expression and body language might say the ideas will not even be considered! Even if the *recipient* does not consciously recognise the conflicting messages, their cognitive systems will most certainly recognise them.

The nonconscious system is essentially accurate in its interpretations of others' bodily and physiological presentations, i.e. when it *receives* them, because it has millions of years of evolutionary experience doing so. In other words, the nonconscious signals are most likely received

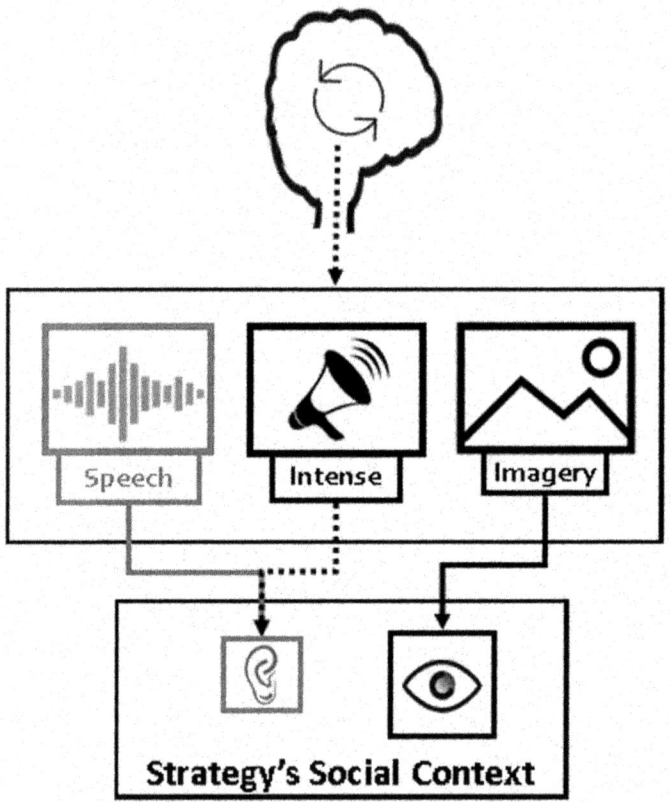

Fig. 3.2 The giving of an affective interaction

and understood as experienced and presented (*given*) by others, regardless of whether that nonconscious signal conflicts with verbal statements. Stated differently, due to the almighty nonconscious system, the receiver comprehends the affect experienced by the giver because it is in the ideal, highly iterative and interactive social format to be comprehended, as previously explained. Fascinatingly, however, there is usually no awareness of the nonconscious' power to decipher the very subtle nonconscious signals or its perceptions of those signals because it is… nonconscious (Akinci & Sadler-Smith, 2012; Epstein, 2010; Gary et al., 2012; Healey & Hodgkinson, 2015; Pratt & Crosina, 2016; Sibony et al.,

2017; Sinclair et al., 2010)! Therefore, the receivers are probably not fully aware that they comprehend both the verbal and bodily signals, focusing mostly on the verbal and yet *feeling* the conflictory bodily and physiological signals. Hence, the confusion and stress, which can actually be experienced by both *giver* and *receiver*, and by those who observe the interactions. This often leads to destructive cognition and behaviour such as conflicts and aggression towards others, especially those who have different appearances, opinions, group affiliations and personal values. Stated differently, we attack others as a method of avoiding the pains associated with the conscious (rational) evaluations of ourselves (Epstein, 2010; Lieberman et al., 2002).

Because the nonconscious system is not visible to us, especially its all-encompassing neurological and biological connections throughout the entire human organism, overcoming these destructive behaviours and the biases they cause is beyond the average person's abilities (Epstein, 2010; Powell et al., 2011; Pratt & Crosina, 2016). In fact, some actually prefer destructive behaviours and actually derive psychological pleasure from them because it is their historical pattern of existence and interactions (Powell et al., 2011; Sibony et al., 2017). In short, we simply cannot see our own cognition and behaviour as experienced by others (Pratt & Crosina, 2016), instead believing our self-perceptions represent our true selves (Lieberman et al., 2002). There appears to be no stopping it! Iterations of this nature probably permeate an entire strategy team, which might comprise the majority of an organisation, as affect becomes entrained over myriad iterations that produce an overarching affect representative of those interactions (Bartunek et al., 2011; Cropanzano, et al., 2017). Although the situation appears glim, there is hope for improving our thinking and behaviour. By regulating ourselves and our emotions, we can create kind environments that facilitate more valuable and successful strategic change initiatives.

Cognitive Regulation and Kind Environments

Thus far, strategic cognition has been portrayed as located in a battle between our two systems that can result in damaging forms of cognition and behaviours. However, there is overwhelming agreement in the research that self-regulation of our thoughts, feelings and behaviour is necessary (Barsade & Gibson, 2007; Healey & Hodgkinson, 2017; Salas et al., 2010; Sinclair et al., 2010; Tasselli et al., 2015), because left without oversight, the nonconscious will continue its clandestine control of the rational system in pursuit of hedonic pleasure and unstable states. Further, the rational system will continue to provide socially and organisationally acceptable niceties to protect its identity and status. Worse, emphasising the rational and suppressing the nonconscious, which is the current state of strategy, most likely exacerbates the tension and conflict between them, in turn exacerbating the already damaging cognition and behaviour. Not good. Neither of these pursuits is beneficial to the highly iterative and affective interactions required of strategy work that requires passionate creativity in order to develop and implement something truly unique and valuable.

Regulation suggests attaining control over both cognitive systems by learning about emotions, in general, but also by becoming familiar with one's and others' specific emotions and taking control of both (Barsade & Gibson, 2007; Huy, 2011; Pratt & Crosina, 2016; Salas et al., 2010; Sinclair et al., 2010). Of course, this should be performed with strategy team members in a transparent manner (Healey & Hodgkinson, 2015; Pratt & Crosina, 2016). However, incorporated into regulation is the concept of faking one's affective responses. Doing so is considered morally appropriate if the purpose of faking is considered sincere and genuine towards the good of the people and the organisation itself (Barsade & Gibson, 2007). In short, it appears some have the ability to regulate their cognitive systems, and perhaps even switch back and forth between them (Calabretta et al., 2017; Dane & Pratt, 2007; Hodgkinson & Healey, 2008; Hodgkinson et al., 2008). However, controlling and faking one's emotions is rife with challenges when considering the discussion thus far, as well as the fact that some have a natural attraction to either the rational or nonconscious style (Calabretta et al., 2017; Carton & Lucas, 2018; Hodgkinson et al., 2009; Sadler-Smith, 2004; Salas et al., 2010). One wonders whether it can actually be accomplished.

Emotional regulation appears to produce kind learning environments where discourse and feedback are encouraged that, as well as accepting multiple truths, has the effect of enhancing cognitive frames (Dane & Pratt, 2007; Epstein, 2010). This is aligned with positive affect and therefore psychological pleasure. Wicked learning environments, to the contrary, are those almost absent feedback, which actually suppress intuition and facilitate damaging cognition and behaviour (Epstein, 2010;

Hodgkinson et al., 2009). This is aligned with negative affect and psychological harm. Emotional regulation also suggests a more harmonious relationship between individuals' two cognitive systems, which is suggestive of optimal reasoning and judgement, and decision-making as well, implying that strategic change efforts will be more likely to produce unique and valuable products that can be implemented with fidelity.

In other words, some might have the ability to truly empathise with others, thereby stimulating their own neural networks and influencing their bodily and physiological presentations (Healey & Hodgkinson, 2015). This might be the most hopeful scenario for achieving serenity between the two systems and producing passionate creativity necessary for development work, because the source of nonconscious processing is its experiences, which can be modified. However, I suspect this challenging endeavour is simply not plausible for the average strategist or team member to overcome. One would have to sufficiently control their neurobiological system and associated bodily movements and presentations in order to fool the recipient's nonconscious system. In other words, one must control the entirety of their nonconscious organism—not an insignificant undertaking! Although certainly within the realm of possibility, it would most likely require very significant training, passion and socio-emotional skills.

Cognitive Styles

The two processing systems are actually said to represent cognitive styles—those cognitive styles control people's perceptions, memory, reasoning and judgement, and how they solve problems (Hodgkinson & Healey, 2008; Hodgkinson et al., 2008; Sadler-Smith, 2004). Of course, myriad iterations of *receiving* and *giving* affective interactions occurring over time will solidify an affective state or characteristic of an individual or the team. Therefore, the actual cognitive style embodied by any member or team as a whole depends on the stream of affective interactions between and among strategy team members, the strategy work and the physical environment at any particular moment. Restated: the nature of affect experienced determines the cognitive style. Both cognitive styles and their specific characteristics are described in Table 3.1, including the outcomes from each individual style.

Rational cognition is overwhelmingly, although not completely, associated with interactions that produce negative affect and psychological pain,

Table 3.1 Cognitive styles: characteristics and outcomes

	Rational style	Nonconscious style
Characteristics	Rational analysis, logical decision-making, convergent thinking, absent affect and therefore low intensity, commitment, and gratitude[a], and expert intuition[b]	Moral and creative intuition, judgemental decision-making, divergent thinking, affect laden and therefore high intensity, commitment and gratitude[e]
Outcomes	Wicked learning environments, separation of people, reduced/degraded interactions, pursuit of selfish myopic goals, ambiguity of strategy work, conflicting affect, and degraded sensing, ideation (creativity), commitment, and monitoring[c], with a little positive intensity[d]	Kind learning[f], close relationships, increased/enhanced interactions, pursuit of strategy, comprehension of work/strategy, shared affects, and sensing, ideation (creativity), commitment, and monitoring[g], with a little complacency and stereotyped/biased thinking[h]

[a]Synthesised from: Akinci and Sadler-Smith (2012), Calabretta et al. (2017), Cropanzano et al. (2017), Dane and Pratt (2007), Dane and Pratt (2009), Healey and Hodgkinson (2017), Epstein (2010), Powell et al. (2011), Pratt and Crosina (2016), and Sadler-Smith (2004)
[b]Akinci and Sadler-Smith (2012), Dane and Pratt (2009), Hodgkinson et al. (2008), Miller and Ireland (2005), and Salas et al. (2010)
[c]Synthesised from: Ashton-James and Ashkanasy (2008), Barsade (2002), Bartunek et al. (2011), Epstein (2010), Calabretta et al. (2017), Gavetti et al. (2005), Healey and Hodgkinson (2015), Healey, Vuori, et al. (2015), Hodgkinson et al. (2009), Narayanan et al. (2011), Pratt and Crosina (2016), Sinclair et al. (2010), and Whittington et al. (2006)
[d]Ashton-James and Ashkanasy (2008), Barsade and Gibson (2007), and Neumann (2017)
[e]Synthesised from: Akinci and Sadler-Smith (2012), Barsade and Gibson (2007), Cropanzano et al. (2017), Dane and Pratt (2009), Epstein (2010), Hodgkinson et al. (2008), Hodgkinson et al. (2009), Gary et al. (2012), Powell et al. (2011), and To et al. (2015)
[f]Dane and Pratt (2007)
[g]Synthesised from: Ashton-James and Ashkanasy (2008), Barsade (2002), Barsade and Gibson (2007), Bartunek et al. (2011), Carton and Lucas (2018), Cropanzano et al. (2017), Epstein (2010), Gary et al. (2012), Gavetti et al. (2015), Healey and Hodgkinson (2017), Healey, Hodgkinson, et al. (2015), Healey, Vuori, et al. (2015)), Huy (2011), Lieberman and Eisenberger (2009), Sadler-Smith (2004), and Sinclair et al. (2010)
[h]Synthesised from: Ashton-James and Ashkanasy (2008) and Epstein (2010)

whereas the nonconscious cognition is overwhelmingly, although not completely, associated with interactions that produce positive affect and psychological pleasure (Barsade, 2002; Dane & Pratt, 2009; Healey & Hodgkinson, 2017; Lieberman & Eisenberger, 2009; Neumann, 2017). More specifically, rational processing is suggestive of behavioural and relational separation between and among members. It values science, data and methods, not thoughts and feelings, and also damages relationships, degrades commitment, facilitates pursuit of one's own myopic goals, and yet has potential for unitedness and exceptional problem solving if occurring within the concept of positive conflict. This exacerbates an already-challenging strategy process and tools, possibly enacting a downward spiral that, if permitted to continue, becomes more tumultuous in nature with each iteration of interactions (Barsade, 2002; Cropanzano et al., 2017). The nonconscious processing style, conversely, is suggestive of more enhanced behaviours and relationships. It values emotion, enhances relationships through affective interactions, inspires working with unitedness and togetherness towards the common good of the strategy and organisation, and yet has the potential for complacency and mediocrity. These descriptions have very significant implications, because relationships between strategists and members have been almost absent from strategy work, and yet are considered critical to success in strategy work, both in formulation and implementation (Ashton-James & Ashkanasy, 2008; Bromiley & Rau, 2016; Cropanzano et al., 2017; Huy, 2012; Jarzabkowski, 2008; Salas et al., 2010). Notice that, however, despite the negatives associated with the rational processing style, it is not entirely detrimental for strategy work, nor is the nonconscious processing style entirely beneficial for strategy work. This thought is now explained in detail, as it is critical for the practising manager to understand that each style is necessary for certain types of strategy work.

The rational cognitive style is appropriate for work involving more routine procedures that are not developmental or creative, for which there are clear goals, whereas the nonconscious style is best suited for complex environments or those requiring significant developmental and creative activities, for which there are ambiguous goals (Dane & Pratt, 2007; To et al., 2015). The rational cognitive style is ideally suited for work rooted in planning and organising (Akinci & Sadler-Smith, 2012; Calabretta et al., 2017; Epstein, 2010; Dane & Pratt, 2007; Neumann, 2017; Sadler-Smith, 2004), and therefore such cognition is absolutely necessary for strategy work. This point should not be overlooked. For example, the gathering of information and recording it in an electronic database, whether for scanning for formulation or for development of a new operations system for implementation, is relatively unambiguous and procedural in nature, with clear and specific goals. This is where we excel as compared to other animals. Imagine trying to gather and organise massive amounts of information intuitively, without any rationality, logic or tools! However, the same may be said for developmental work: imagine trying to develop a unique and valuable product or trying to implement a new product strategy with its myriad potential permutations, using only rational, unpassionate, noncreative cognition! Hence the current crisis in strategy, as it currently emphasises the rational style. The development work of strategy change efforts requires higher levels of psychological pleasure and its associated intensity/passion in order to achieve the affective and intuitive creativity necessary for developing something new, unique and valuable (Barsade & Gibson, 2007; Calabretta et al., 2017; Dane & Pratt, 2009; Hodgkinson et al., 2009; Lieberman & Eisenberger, 2009). Positive conflict is also a necessary ingredient.

In summary, since the two systems operate simultaneously and are neurobiologically interactive, it is critical to conceive of any member's or team's style as one unified, blended style of the two. It seems an impossibility that any human could be entirely one or the other, especially one that is completely absent affect—only Dr. Spock from the Star Trek television series comes to mind as such a creature. Incidentally, he often made ineffective decisions, especially those involving complex human emotions and ambiguous problems without well-defined goals! Although the optimal blending of rational and nonconscious cognition for strategy work cannot be stated with precision, a certain ratio is likely, much like the ratio of two ingredients in a cocktail. For example, I speculate that strategy's current cognitive style represents 75% rational and 25% nonconscious, which might simply be called *mostly rational*. However, this review suggests the optimal cognitive style is the inverse, i.e. mostly nonconscious with a touch of rationality, or simply *mostly nonconscious*.

CONCLUSION

The main take away from this review of strategic cognition is clearly that the highly contagious interactions of affective Homo sapiens, which have been almost absent from the literature, are simply the epicentre of strategy! It is the concept that unites the members and their work. Therefore, strategists must be acutely concerned with what enters members' eyes and ears from within strategy social context, as it has the power to really hurt them and others in the organisation, and therefore hurt the organisation itself. Conversely, it also has the power to get people committed, passionate, intense and creative, benefitting them with feelings of euphoric teamwork and camaraderie! Sometimes members give their hearts and souls to this work, so a simple and cold "thank you" will not suffice. Those who contribute to strategy want to have their thoughts and feelings about strategy considered with sincerity and genuineness. They do not mind disagreement, as they enjoy discussing the very high stakes of strategy work because it is part of their lives. The strategist must be appreciative and gracious with all members, otherwise, negative affect can be perceived which hurts people's hearts and souls, who normally respond by *giving* it back viscerally to others, or even the work, right between the eyes (in the spirit of survival in the forest)!

In short, strategic organisational change efforts need the intense passion and creativity of all their members' knowledge, skills and life experiences if they are to produce unique products and services of value to others. To be clear: I'm not recommending niceties for the sake of niceties. Causing others psychological harm literally shuts down their passion and creativity. This means strategists will not *receive* positive and beneficial affect from their members. Keep in mind that affect helps strategists determine whether ideas for strategy are valuable and implementable. For example, external members know whether products align with customer needs and desires, and insider members certainly know whether they have the skills, knowledge and camaraderie to produce, sell, deliver and service particular products! Strategist cannot receive what those numbers truly think and feel about products and implementation issues if their affect is either shut off or negative. Strategists must pay attention to what they think and feel about interactions with others, no matter how brief or insignificant. This is the power of affect and contagion within strategy work!

In short, strategists must value people, emotion, intuition and the interactions themselves! Science, data and the strategy process are simply methods and tools. The romance and prestige associated with detached scientific thinking, behaviour and language are over! It is producing mediocrity. The strategist must take control of emotions in interactions with the team by enhancing his/her acting skills. In other words, express real appreciation for contributions, with passionate and expressive words, facial expressions and body language. SHOW them you care about them and their contribution! This means overcoming your own inaccurate Homo sapien assessments of people and situations. Judge people for their ideas and commitment instead of their appearances or group affiliations. Use passionate and expressive adjectives to describe data, as opposed to detached terms such as "statistically significant" and "competitive advantage". Finally, slow down, you have time to decide and discuss, even in the high-speed world of strategic decision-making. Deciding fast and confidently aligns with detachment and superiority, producing poor judgement. You will not die (as you would in the forest) if you slow down and sincerely entertain other's thoughts and feelings. But it must be sincere and real. No exceptions. Everyone knows what you are *really* thinking and feeling, even if you don't know, and even if they don't know that they know!

Achieving all of this will be a challenge. Given the entirety of this review, I wonder whether it is possible... I wonder whether we can get past the past! It seems the most hopeful route is for strategists to undergo very significant training on (1) the true structure of strategy and all who contribute, (2) emotion and its related contagion and (3) our two types of cognition. Business education programmes could begin training the next generation of strategists and strategy team members on these topics. In summary, strategists and their team members must acknowledge and embrace the work of strategy as messy, tumultuous and even conflictory, but also as exhilarating and rewarding teamwork. Strategists are NOT calm rational managers, but rather highly affective, intuitive and interactive Homo sapiens!

Implications for Future Research

This review clearly suggests that what comes into our eyes and ears must be accounted for and understood more fully. For example, more attention could be paid to the effect of passionate or intense speech on Homo sapien cognition and interactions. Other related possibilities include other senses such as touch, smell and taste. For example, researchers might explore the effect of *receiving* and *giving* affect related to a hand on the shoulder or a handshake.

Researchers could seek to better understand how and to what degree the valence and magnitude of affective interactions, the wickedness or kindness present in development work and components of the physical environment trigger the nonconscious to protect itself from potential harm. This appears to represent an enormous opportunity.

Finally, who should be learning about and doing the work of cognitive regulation? The lead strategists, the TMT or all members? How should they be trained? Through pre-strategy trainings, or through our education system? Should training on Homo sapien cognition be included as part of this training, as implied by this study? Due to the depth and the nascent nature of the affective cognition movement, I sincerely hope others will formulate additional research directions based on this important topic for strategy, organisations and in fact for societies.

Acknowledgements I am grateful to the editors for their insightful feedback, which significantly enhanced the quality of this work. I am also grateful to my daughter Anna Cofrancesco and great friend Roger Wyatt for their unique observations, which provided greater depth and meaning in this work. Thank you to everyone!

References

Akinci, C., & Sadler-Smith, E. (2012). Intuition in management research: A historical review. *International Journal of Management Reviews, 14*(1), 104–122. https://doi.org/10.1111/j.1468-2370.2011.00313.x

Andersen, T. J., & Nielsen, B. B. (2009). Adaptive strategy making: The effects of emergent and intended strategy modes. *European Management Review, 6*, 94–106. https://doi.org/10.1057/emr.2009.7

Andrews, R., Boyne, G. A., Law, J., & Walker, R. M. (2009). Strategy formulation, strategy content and performance: An empirical analysis. *Public Management Review, 11*(1), 1–22. https://doi.org/10.1080/14719030802489989

Ashton-James, C. E., & Ashkanasy, N. M. (2008). Affective events theory: A strategic perspective. In W. J. Zerbe, C. E. Härtel, & N. M. Ashkanasy (Eds.), *Emotions, ethics and decision-making (research on emotion in organizations, volume 4)* (pp. 1–34). Emerald Group Publishing Limited. https://doi.org/10.1016/S1746-9791(08)04001-7

Bakir, A., & Todorovic, M. (2010). A hermeneutic reading into "what strategy is": Ambiguous means-end relationship. *The Qualitative Report, 15*(5), 1037–1057. https://doi.org/10.46743/2160-3715/2010.1329

Balbastre-Benavent, F. F., & Canet-Giner, M. T. (2011). The strategy formation process in the EFQM excellence model: A critical review and new perspectives. *Total Quality Management & Business Excellence, 22*(7), 727–742. https://doi.org/10.1080/14783363.2011.585773

Balogun, J., Sigismund Huff, A., & Johnson, P. (2003). Three responses to the methodological challenges of studying strategizing. *Journal of Management Studies, 40*(1), 197–224. https://doi.org/10.1111/1467-6486.t01-1-00009

Barsade, S. G. (2002). The ripple effect: Emotional contagion and its influence on group behavior. *Administrative Science Quarterly, 47*(4), 644–675. https://doi.org/10.2307/3094912

Barsade, S. G., & Gibson, D. E. (2007). Why does affect matter in organizations? *Academy of Management Perspectives, 21*(1), 36–59. https://doi.org/10.5465/amp.2007.24286163

Bartunek, J. M., Balogun, J., & Do, B. (2011). Considering planned change anew: Stretching large group interventions strategically, emotionally, and meaningfully. *Academy of Management Annals, 5*(1), 1–52. https://doi.org/10.5465/19416520.2011.567109

Bromiley, P., & Rau, D. (2016). Social, behavioral, and cognitive influences on upper echelons during strategy process: A literature review. *Journal of Management, 42*(1), 174–202. https://doi.org/10.1177/0149206315617240

Calabretta, G., Gemser, G., & Wijnberg, N. M. (2017). The interplay between intuition and rationality in strategic decision making: A paradox perspective. *Organization Studies, 38*(3–4), 365–401. https://doi.org/10.1177/0170840616655483

Carton, A. M., & Lucas, B. J. (2018). How can leaders overcome the blurry vision bias? Identifying an antidote to the paradox of vision communication. *Academy of Management Journal, 61*(6), 2106–2129. https://doi.org/10.5465/amj.2015.0375

Cropanzano, R., Dasborough, M. T., & Weiss, H. M. (2017). Affective events and the development of leader-member exchange. *Academy of Management Review, 42*(2), 233–258. https://doi.org/10.5465/amr.2014.0384

Dane, E., & Pratt, M. G. (2007). Exploring intuition and its role in managerial decision making. *Academy of Management Review, 32*(1), 33–54. https://doi.org/10.5465/amr.2007.23463682

Dane, E., & Pratt, M. G. (2009). Conceptualizing and measuring intuition: A review of recent trends. In G. P. Hodgkinson & J. K. Ford (Eds.), *International review of industrial and organizational psychology* (pp. 1–40). Wiley-Blackwell. https://doi.org/10.1002/9780470745267.ch1

Eggers, J. P., & Kaplan, S. (2013). Cognition and capabilities: A multi-level perspective. *Academy of Management Annals, 7*(1), 295–340. https://doi.org/10.5465/19416520.2013.769318

Elbanna, S. (2006). Strategic decision-making: Process. *International Journal of Management Reviews, 8*(1), 1–20. https://doi.org/10.1111/j.1468-2370.2006.00118.x

Elbanna, S., & Fadol, Y. (2016). The role of context in intuitive decision-making. *Journal of Management & Organization, 22*(5), 642–661. https://doi.org/10.1017/jmo.2015.63

Epstein, S. (2010). Demystifying intuition: What it is, what it does, and how it does it. *Psychological Inquiry, 21*(4), 295–312. https://doi.org/10.1080/1047840X.2010.523875

Felin, T., Foss, N. J., & Ployhart, R. E. (2015). The microfoundations movement in strategy and organization theory. *The Academy of Management Annals, 9*(1), 575–632. https://doi.org/10.1080/19416520.2015.1007651

Gary, M., Wood, R. E., & Pillinger, T. (2012). Enhancing mental models, analogical transfer, and performance in strategic decision making. *Strategic Management Journal, 33*(11), 1229–1246. https://doi.org/10.1002/smj.1979

Gavetti, G., Levinthal, D., & Rivkin, J. (2005). Strategy making in novel and complex worlds: The power of analogy. *Strategic Management Journal, 26*(8), 691–712. https://doi.org/10.1002/smj.475

Gavetti, G., & Rivkin, J. W. (2007). On the origin of strategy: Action and cognition over time. *Organization Science, 18*(3), 420–439. https://doi.org/10.1287/orsc.1070.0282

Healey, M. P., & Hodgkinson, G. P. (2015). Toward a theoretical framework for organizational neuroscience. In D. A. Waldman & P. A. Balthazard (Eds.), *Organizational neuroscience (monographs in leadership and management, volume 7)* (pp. 51–81). Emerald Group Publishing Limited. https://doi.org/10.1108/S1479-357120150000007002

Healey, M. P., & Hodgkinson, G. P. (2017). Making strategy hot. *California Management Review, 59*(3), 109–134. https://doi.org/10.1177/0008125617712258

Healey, M. P., Hodgkinson, G. P., Whittington, R., & Johnson, G. (2015). Off to plan or out to lunch? Relationships between design characteristics and outcomes of strategy workshops. *British Journal of Management, 26*(3), 507–528. https://doi.org/10.1111/1467-8551.12038

Healey, M. P., Vuori, T., & Hodgkinson, G. P. (2015). When teams agree while disagreeing: Reflexion and reflection in shared cognition. *Academy of Management Review, 40*(3), 399–422. https://doi.org/10.5465/amr.2013.0154

Hodgkinson, G. P., & Healey, M. P. (2008). Cognition in organizations. *Annual Review of Psychology, 59*. https://doi.org/10.1146/annurev.psych.59.103006.093612

Hodgkinson, G. P., & Healey, M. P. (2011). Psychological foundations of dynamic capabilities: Reflexion and reflection in strategic management. *Strategic Management Journal, 32*(13), 1500–1516. https://doi.org/10.1002/smj.964

Hodgkinson, G. P., Langan-Fox, J., & Sadler-Smith, E. (2008). Intuition: A fundamental bridging construct in the behavioural sciences. *British Journal of Psychology, 99*(1), 1–27. https://doi.org/10.1348/000712607X216666

Hodgkinson, G. P., Sadler-Smith, E., Burke, L. A., Claxton, G., & Sparrow, P. R. (2009). Intuition in organizations: Implications for strategic management. *Long Range Planning*, 42(3), 277–297. https://doi.org/10.1016/j.lrp.2009.05.003

Hodgkinson, G. P., & Sadler-Smith, E. (2018). The dynamics of intuition and analysis in managerial and organizational decision making. *Academy of Management Perspectives*, 32(4), 473–492. https://doi.org/10.5465/amp.2016.0140

Huy, Q. N. (2011). How middle managers' group-focus emotions and social identities influence strategy implementation. *Strategic Management Journal*, 32(13), 1387–1410. https://doi.org/10.1002/smj.961

Huy, Q. N. (2012). Emotions in strategic organization: Opportunities for impactful research. *Strategic Organization*, 10(3), 240–247. https://doi.org/10.1177/1476127012453107

Jarratt, D., & Stiles, D. (2010). How are methodologies and tools framing managers' strategizing practice in competitive strategy development? *British Journal of Management*, 21(1), 28–43. https://doi.org/10.1111/j.1467-8551.2009.00665.x

Jarzabkowski, P. (2008). Shaping strategy as a structuration process. *Academy of Management Journal*, 51(4), 621–650. https://doi.org/10.5465/amr.2008.33664922

Kaplan, S. (2009). Strategy and PowerPoint: An inquiry into the epistemic culture and machinery of strategy making. *Organization Science*, 22(2), 320–346. https://doi.org/10.1287/orsc.1100.0531

Kjærgaard, A. L. (2009). Organizational identity and strategy: An empirical study of organizational identity's influence on the strategy-making process. *International Studies of Management and Organizations*, 39(1), 50–69. https://doi.org/10.2753/IMO0020-8825390103

Lieberman, M. D., & Eisenberger, N. I. (2009). Pains and pleasures of social life. *Science*, 323(5916), 890–891. https://doi.org/10.1126/science.1170008

Lieberman, M. D., Gaunt, R., Gilbert, D. T., & Trope, Y. (2002). Reflexion and reflection: A social cognitive neuroscience approach to attributional inference. In M. P. Zanna (Ed.), *Advances in experimental social psychology* (Vol. 34, pp. 199–249). Academic Press. https://doi.org/10.1016/S0065-2601(02)80006-5

Lieberman, M. D., Jarcho, J. M., & Satpute, A. B. (2004). Attitudes and social cognition evidence-based and intuition-based self-knowledge: An FMRI study. *Journal of Personality and Social Psychology*, 87(4), 421–435. https://doi.org/10.1037/0022-3514.87.4.421

Marcel, J. J., Barr, P. S., & Duhaime, I. M. (2011). The influence of executive cognition on competitive dynamics. *Strategic Management Journal*, 32(2), 115–138. https://doi.org/10.1002/smj.870

Miller, C. C., & Ireland, R. D. (2005). Intuition in strategic decision making: Friend or foe in the fast-paced 21st century? *Academy of Management Perspectives, 19*(1), 19–30. https://doi.org/10.5465/ame.2005.15841948

Moisander, J., & Stenfors, S. (2009). Exploring the edges of theory-practice gap: Epistemic cultures in strategy-tool development and use. *Organization, 16*, 227. https://doi.org/10.1177/1350508408100476

Narayanan, V. K., Zane, L. J., & Kemmerer, B. (2011). The cognitive perspective in strategy: An integrative review. *Journal of Management, 37*(1), 305–351. https://doi.org/10.1177/0149206310383986

Neumann, F. (2017). Antecedents and effects of emotions in strategic decision-making: A literature review and conceptual model. *Management Review Quarterly, Springer, 67*(3), 175–200. https://doi.org/10.1007/s11301-017-0127-1

Poister, T. H., Edwards, L., Pasha, O. Q., & Edwards, J. (2013). Strategy formulation and performance. *Public Performance & Management Review, 36*(4), 585–615. https://doi.org/10.2753/PMR1530-9576360405

Powell, T. C. (2014). Strategic management and the person. *Strategic Organization, 12*(3), 200–207. https://doi.org/10.1177/1476127014544093

Powell, T. C., Lovallo, D., & Fox, C. R. (2011). Behavioral strategy. *Strategic Management Journal, 32*(13), 1369–1386. https://doi.org/10.1002/smj.968

Pratt, M. G., & Crosina, E. (2016). The nonconscious at work. *Annual Review of Organizational Psychology and Organizational Behavior, 3*, 321–347. https://doi.org/10.1146/annurev-orgpsych-041015-062517

Reger, R., & Huff, A. (1993). Strategic groups: A cognitive perspective. *Strategic Management Journal, 14*(2), 103–123. https://doi.org/10.1002/smj.4250140203

Reitzig, M., & Sorenson, O. (2013). Biases in the selection stage of bottom-up strategy formulation. *Strategic Management Journal, 34*(7), 782–799. https://doi.org/10.1002/smj.2047

Robinson, J., Sinclair, M., Tobias, J., & Choi, E. (2017). More dynamic than you think: Hidden aspects of decision-making. *Administrative Sciences, 7*(3), 23. https://doi.org/10.3390/admsci7030023

Sadler-Smith, E. (2004). Cognitive style and the management of small and medium-sized enterprises. *Organization Studies, 25*(2), 155–181. https://doi.org/10.1177/0170840604036914

Salas, E., Rosen, M. A., & DiazGranados, D. (2010). Expertise-based intuition and decision making in organizations. *Journal of Management, 36*(4), 941–973. https://doi.org/10.1177/0149206309350084

Sanchez-Burks, J., & Huy, Q. N. (2009). Emotional aperture and strategic change: The accurate recognition of collective emotions. *Organization Science, 20*(1), 22–34. https://doi.org/10.1287/orsc.1070.0347

Sibony, O., Lovallo, D., & Powell, T. C. (2017). Behavioral strategy and the strategic decision architecture of the firm. *California Management Review, 59*(3), 5–21. https://doi.org/10.1177/0008125617712256

Sinclair, M., Ashkanasy, N. M., & Chattopadhyay, P. (2010). Affective antecedents of intuitive decision making. *Journal of Management and Organization, 16*(3), 382–398. https://doi.org/10.5172/jmo.16.3.382

Sminia, H. (2009). Process research in strategy formation: Theory, methodology and relevance. *International Journal of Management Reviews, 11*(1), 97–125. https://doi.org/10.1111/j.1468-2370.2008.00253.x

Stigliani, I., & Ravasi, D. (2012). Organizing thoughts and connecting brains: Material practices and the transition from individual to group-level prospective sensemaking. *Academy of Management Journal, 55*(5), 1232–1259. https://doi.org/10.5465/amj.2010.0890

Tasselli, S., Kilduff, M., & Menges, J. I. (2015). The microfoundations of organizational social networks: A review and an agenda for future research. *Journal of Management, 41*(5), 1361–1387. https://doi.org/10.1177/0149206315573996

To, M. L., Fisher, C. D., & Ashkanasy, N. M. (2015). Unleashing angst: Negative mood, learning goal orientation, psychological empowerment and creative behaviour. *Human Relations, 68*(10), 1601–1622. https://doi.org/10.1177/0018726714562235

Tversky, A., & Kahneman, D. (1981). The framing of decisions and the psychology of choice. *Science, 211*(4481), 453–458. https://doi.org/10.1126/science.7455683

Walsh, J. P. (1995). Managerial and organizational cognition: Notes from a trip down memory lane. *Organization Science, 6*(3), 280–321. https://doi.org/10.1287/orsc.6.3.280

Whittington, R., Molloy, E., Mayer, M., & Smith, A. (2006). Practices of strategising/organising: Broadening strategy work and skills. *Long Range Planning, 39*(6), 615–629. https://doi.org/10.1016/j.lrp.2006.10.004

Wright, R. P., Paroutis, S. E., & Blettner, D. P. (2013). How useful are the strategic tools we teach in business schools? *Journal of Management Studies, 50*(1), 92–125. https://doi.org/10.1111/j.1467-6486.2012.01082.x

CHAPTER 4

Implementing Strategy and Avenues of Access: A Practice Perspective

Harry Sminia and Fredy Valdovinos Salinas

From its inception, strategic management has been conceptualised as strategic planning (Ansoff, 1965). This presupposes a chronology in that a plan needs to be formulated first, which is then subsequently implemented. Strategy implementation is thence understood as a process of execution, a putting into action of explicitly formulated intentions; often requiring deliberate and managed organisational change. Thinking of strategy implementation in this way has achieved a level of sophistication in that over the years various frameworks have been developed by which managers can execute a strategy (e.g. Ansoff & McDonnell, 1990; Hrebiniak & Joyce, 1984; Okumus, 2003; Thompson et al., 2019). These frameworks present strategy implementation as a matter of designing

---

H. Sminia (✉)
University of Strathclyde Business School, Scotland, UK
e-mail: harry.sminia@strath.ac.uk

F. V. Salinas
QuodPraesens HR Consulting, Santiago de Chile, Chile
e-mail: fredy.valdovinos@quodpraesens.com

© The Author(s), under exclusive license to Springer Nature Singapore Pte Ltd. 2022
A. Zubac et al. (eds.), *Effective Implementation of Transformation Strategies*, https://doi.org/10.1007/978-981-19-2336-4_4

an appropriate organisation structure, establishing an incentive scheme, changing the organisational culture and of monitoring and control. This way of thinking has been labelled as the structural control view (Weiser et al., 2020).

Paradoxically, over the years there also appeared much research looking for explanations why implementation continues to fail, which then reach the conclusion that the frameworks are still lacking, and more research needs to be done (e.g. Cândido & Santos, 2015; Kaplan & Norton, 2001; Kiechel III, 1982; Nutt, 1999). Distinguishing strategy formulation from strategy implementation led to problematizing the successful realisation of a strategy as having to bridge the implementation gap (Martin, 2010; Whipp, 2003). Successfully executing a strategic plan appears to be as elusive as it ever was (Bourgeois III & Brodwin, 1984).

Roughly, there are two possible reactions to these observations. One reaction is of resignation and an acknowledgement that a top-down strategic management approach in which managers direct and the organisation responds and realises a strategy is an IDÉE FIXE perpetuated by a management rhetoric that can only be delusional. The other reaction, which is more prevalent, builds on what has been labelled as the adaptive view to strategy implementation (Weiser et al., 2020), which recognises that organisation and management is a social process. The aim is to find a way of retaining the possibility of managers intervening in this process to have an effect on eventual outcomes, albeit only a limited one. Instead of a top-down command and control style, more emphasis is put on the people in the organisation with them having to be empowered to decide what is best in the situations that they encounter yet being kept in check by a mission or a vision rather than a plan (Kanter, 1983; Wilkinson, 1998). This has recently been popularised again under the label of agility: an organisational capability to strategically deal with a continuous need for change (e.g. McKinsey, 2015; PwC, 2021). On the basis of this second reaction, what is then required is a specification of how implementation activity can make a contribution. For this we need to liberate implementation from planning and develop an alternative understanding that recognises strategy implementation as an activity in its own right.

Interestingly, implementation as execution is not the only way to define it. Execution comes from the Latin term EXECUTIONEM and includes the prefix EX, meaning "out", and the root SEQUI meaning "to follow" (Partridge, 2006). The word "sequel" has the same root. Etymologically, execution means "to follow out of". It signifies the process as an ex-post exercise of carrying intentions into effect. Implementation can also be understood as generating a whole, a more holistic effort. As a word, it comes from the Latin term IMPLERE, and includes the prefix IM, which means "in", and the root PLERE, meaning "to fill" (Partridge, 2006). Implementation shares this root with the word "plenary". Etymologically, implementation means "to fill in". In this sense, it is not an ex-post activity following on from formulating intentions. Instead, it must be understood as a set of activities aimed at creating a whole, at actualization, or at generating something from nothing. In a way, understanding implementation as execution and as a subsequent stage in a process does not do justice to its etymological origin. The latter understanding of implementation seems to be more appropriate if we take management and organisation to be a social process.

Implementation understood as a generative social process chimes with a conceptualization of strategic management as strategy formation, of realising a pattern in a stream of actions (Mintzberg & Waters, 1985). In this view, intentions can make contributions, but these tend to be drowned out by all the little and larger problems that need to be dealt with constantly. The endless succession of (half-baked) solutions is seen as contributing more to the pattern that emerges over time than the execution of periodically produced plans. Accordingly, strategic management has been described as wayfinding rather than planning; as a continuous coping with newly emerging situations (Chia & Holt, 2009).

The process conceptualization underpinning wayfinding is also different from the process conceptualization underneath planning. Wayfinding is more akin to the "strong" process approach that sees organisational reality as essentially processual (Langley & Tsoukas, 2010; Tsoukas & Chia, 2003). From a "strong" point of view, an organisation as it changes and persists exists as an ongoing process with the management challenge being about directing this process towards favourable outcomes. Planning is based on the "weak" process approach that sees process as happening to an organisation. The management challenge according to the "weak" process point of view is about effectuating change when it is deemed necessary. Strategic management as "wayfinding" does away with problematizing strategic management as having to bridge the implementation gap. Instead, the problem is about how strategic management contributes to an ongoing and continuous process by which an organisation performs and changes.

The ambition for this chapter is to look at strategic management from a strong process point of view to specify how implementation activities can have an effect. Implementing strategy then refers to those activities that direct and channel the process that is continuously going on anyway into a desired pattern. We will do that by basing ourselves on Schatzki's (2002, 2019) Theory of Practice. This will allow us to propose an understanding of strategic management as a continuous implementation process that generates both persistence and change. Interestingly, strategy formulation then becomes part of the implementation effort as well, instead of it being seen as a separate activity preceding strategy implementation. We will start by introducing Schatzki's Theory of Practice to then specify how implementation practices can make a contribution to an organisation's strategic management. We finish this chapter by drawing out some implications for strategic management and strategic change.

THE IMPLEMENTATION PROBLEM ACCORDING TO THE THEORY OF PRACTICE

Looking through the lens of Schatzki's practice theory, an organisation and everything associated with it come into being through and as practices that interact with material circumstances, i.e. *"an organization [...] is a bundle of practices and material arrangements"* (Schatzki, 2006: 1863). Practices in the bundle perform the organisation, with the patterning in this process as practices change, persists and relate to each other and to the wider "practice plenum" (Schatzki, 2019), taken to be what strategic management is about.

Practices are *"open-ended, spatial–temporal sets of organized doings and sayings"* (Schatzki, 2019: 26). "Doings" are the performances of action, events, things that happen—in short: activity. A "saying" is a particular type of "doing", singled out to be able to distinguish between discursive and non-discursive doings; a distinction we will come back to when discussing strategy formulation as an implementation practice. Open-ended means two things. One, a practice only persists if it happens again yet, and two, a practice happening does not guarantee that it will happen again and persist. Whether a practice will happen depends on whether something has happened that prompts a reaction. It is important to understand that to Schatzki, a practice happening is a reaction to something that happened rather than an activity being determined by what has happened. Practices are spatial–temporal because practices happen in and over time at specific locations. As with the strong process approach, organisations as a bundle of practices and material arrangements are essentially processual, as organisations appear and perform because practices happen. The emphasis is on activity and everything follows on from that.

A practice as it is happening is structured by practical and general understandings, rules and teleoaffectivity (Schatzki, 2002, 2019). Practical understanding refers to knowledge of how to perform the particular activity that makes the practice what it is. Frying an egg requires you to put a frying pan on a hot stove, add some butter, let it melt and heat up, break an egg and add the contents to the pan but throw away the shell to then wait a couple of minutes to let it solidify, but take it out before it burns. This practical understanding is part of the structure of the frying an egg practice. General understanding refers to the overall atmosphere to which the practice is attuned and, in a way, indicates the overall purpose. For instance, the egg is being fried to be served as part of a breakfast in a hotel and therefore serves a purpose in running a hotel business. Rules are directives or instructions that have been formulated to indicate what actions should and should not be taking place. If the frying of this egg is part of cooking a breakfast in a hotel, there are food hygiene regulations that instruct how food preparation is to be done. Teleoaffectivity refers to the particular projects, tasks and ends inherent in the practice as to what needs to be performed there and then. If an egg is being fried as part of preparing breakfast in a hotel, the breakfast is the project within which getting the stove heated up, cracking the egg to get at its contents and not letting the egg burn as it is solidifying are all ends that need to be accomplished. There might be all kind of issues with a practice as it is being performed like not having the right equipment, lacking practical or general understanding, flouting the rules or failing to get specific tasks completed—and we will come back to that later—but these are the four aspects that structure a practice.

As a practice is happening, it interacts with "*assemblages of material objects*" (Schatzki, 2006: 1864). In the case of frying eggs as part of making and eating breakfasts in a hotel, these material arrangements include the kitchen with all its equipment, the food ingredients, the building, but also the chefs, the waiting staff and the guests as bodily entities. The material arrangements are involved in or causally support the happening of the practices that are in the organisation's bundle. These material arrangements relate to a practice by contributing some causal effect (an egg reacts to heat by solidifying), by helping to constitute (a pan contains the egg to be heated on a stove) and to prefigure a practice (the hotel kitchen with a hot stove, a chef, a pan and an egg put together allow for the egg to be fried and served as breakfast), or embodying direction and meaning (an egg sizzling in a pan in a hotel's kitchen at 7:03am indicates that a breakfast is being prepared for a guest) (Schatzki, 2019).

Practices are interrelated in that practices link up as they are playing out Schatzki (2002, 2005). Providing a breakfast in the morning is part of the practices bundle of many hotels as is the checking in and out of guests, cleaning and preparing rooms and taking reservations. Without guests making reservations and checking in, breakfasts would not need to be made. Whether and how well breakfasts are provided prompts guests to book a room in this hotel. The practices and material arrangements and the way they interrelate are specific but not necessarily unique to a particular organisation. Frying eggs as part of preparing breakfasts happens in many hotels, although the people involved, the kitchens and how these are equipped, or what kind of breakfasts are prepared and whether these include fried eggs or not varies. The hotel bundle will connect and overlap with other bundles as well, creating larger constellations of practices, with all these constellations put together referred to as the "practice plenum" (Schatzki, 2019). For receiving and taking reservations, hotels sign up to booking companies who maintain websites where prospective guests look for availability and prices, and through which reservations are made, notwithstanding that people can book directly with the hotel as well. Washing towels and bedlinen tends to be outsourced to specialist laundry firms as well as the hotel's housekeeping practices in combination taking care of cleaning and preparing guestrooms. All of this happens as part of wider society.

Practices happening and linking up as they do is what makes an organisation what it is and how it performs. The pattern that emerges is what Mintzberg and Waters (1985) refer to as the realised strategy. It means that strategy is being implemented as long as there is activity, whether specific implementation efforts are part of the process or not. When you hire somebody as a chef, put her to work in a hotel kitchen in the morning, you can expect that breakfasts will be prepared. Schatzki (2002, 2019) stresses that this patterning is not a simple replication of practices time and time again. There is fluctuation to deal with smaller or larger contingencies, as these interfere with what is going on (cf. Feldman & Pentland, 2003). The number of breakfasts being cooked will vary with the number of guests being present every morning. There could be a sudden issue with the daily egg order and one morning the chef finds there are not enough eggs to go round, or a member of kitchen staff phones in sick and tasks have to be re-arranged. Or there is so little demand for porridge that the kitchen stops preparing a batch in advance to only make a portion on demand, which affects the speed by which porridge will be served and might lead to an unhappy guest, a negative review on a booking website, blemishing, say, the 4-star reputation of the hotel. And, as was written above, there might be all kind of issues with the practices as these are being performed like not having the right equipment, lacking practical or general understanding, flouting the rules or having trouble accomplishing specific tasks. An organisation as a bundle of practices and material arrangements allows for incorporating the fluctuation that is happening all the time.

All of this then qualifies the problem of how strategy implementation is happening into three interrelated questions. As the realised strategy is a consequence of how practices are performed, one question concerns why people in organisations do what they do in the way that they do it? This is about practical intelligibility. The second question is about what lets people do what they do, as surely not every course for action imaginable will be equally feasible. This is about prefiguration. The answers to these two questions pave the way for answering the third question that is central to this chapter. It concerns strategy implementation itself, or implementation practices, and how we are to understand how management activity can make an organisation perform in a preferred and particular way? This is about avenues of access.

With regard to why people do what they do, the answer is simple. People do what makes sense for them to do (Schatzki, 2001, 2002). Such sense making requires "practical intelligibility". This is a matter of every individual's teleology (to what ends would somebody want to do something) and affectivity (how it matters to somebody). What makes sense for a chef employed by a hotel to fry an egg is because it earns her a living, but maybe also because she likes people to enjoy food. Practical intelligibility is specific to each individual and is only informed, not determined, by practice structures, or more specifically by practices' practical and general understandings, rules and teleoaffectivity.

The answer to the question what lets people do what they do is a matter of prefiguration. Prefiguration in turn is about causality, constitution and meaning, as these are posed by how the practices in the bundle interrelate and how these interact with the material arrangements

(Schatzki, 2019). Prefiguration is about the extent to which courses for action are feasible options. Causality refers to an action as being a reaction to something that has happened, i.e. another practice in the bundle. An egg can be fried because it solidifies when exposed to heat. A chef only fries an egg after being notified by a waiter that a guest would like a fried egg for breakfast. As was said earlier, activity is a reaction to what has happened; that what happened does not determine what will happen next. Constitution is about what needs to be in place; about the practices that have to have happened ahead of or what needs to happen in conjunction with, as well as about the material arrangements that have to interact with the actions as these are happening. You cannot fry an egg without an egg. These need to have been ordered and delivered. The stove and the pans have to be present, cleaned and made ready. A guest needs to have woken up and appeared in the restaurant expecting a cooked breakfast. Meaning defines the situation. Being in a hotel kitchen early in the morning employed as a chef tells a person that she is expected to fry an egg when an order comes in. Whether a course for action is feasible is a matter of degree rather than a yes or no situation (Schatzki, 2002).

Consequently, the extent of the feasibility of a practice is very specific to a particular situation and relative to the feasibility of connected practices at that time and place. A chef employed by a hotel and present in the hotel's kitchen receiving an order to fry an egg at 7.09 AM, with eggs being available, will fry an egg, unless the fire alarm has just gone off and the kitchen staff are about to evacuate. She might also not fry the egg when the order is received at 10.33 AM, as breakfast service ends at 10.30 AM and her shift has finished with union regulations telling her not to work beyond her contracted hours. However, prefiguration prompts rather than determines, and with everybody's specific practical intelligibility eventually telling each individual person whether to engage in a practice, "*human activity is fundamentally indeterminate*" (Schatzki, 2002: 232).

Indeterminate does not mean random. The bundle of interrelated practices and material arrangements, which is the organisation, is an orderly but fluent process by which the organisation performs. The practical intelligibility of the people involved in combination with the prefiguration that is present sees to that. The organisation is a process and a bundle of practices and material arrangements, which fluctuates, changes and persists. It is as part of this orderly but fluent process that we can explore how we

Table 4.1 Key terms and definitions

Key term	Definition
Avenue of access	A causal chain of possible events across a number of practices, which links an implementation practice with a targeted practice when these practices are enacted
Practical intelligibility	An individual's teleology and affectivity that tells this individual whether it makes sense to do something
Practice	Doings and sayings of people while being prompted by the practice's structure that consists of general understanding, practical understanding and rules
Practice bundle	The practices and material arrangements that perform the organisation
Practice plenum	A constellation of practice bundles by which social reality exists
Prefiguration	The extent to which courses of action are feasible as posed by the interrelationship of practices by way of causality, constitution and meaning, and by the material arrangements
Strategy implementation	The enacted practices in the practice bundle that is the organisation, by which a strategy is realised

are to understand how implementation practices can make an organisation perform in a preferred and particular way? (Table 4.1).

IMPLEMENTATION REQUIRING AVENUES OF ACCESS

To understand the possibility and efficacy of implementation practices, we need to go back to Schatzki's (2002, 2019) notions of practice structure, practical intelligibility and of prefiguration. We also need to take into account Schatzki's claim about the fundamentally indeterminate nature of human activity.

For organisations to operate and be organised, there needs to be some persistence with the bundle of practices. This persistence appears if a number of things come together. The way in which practices are structured—a practice's practical and general understandings, rules and teleoaffectivity—informs people how to act. Organisations in particular have "practice memory" by which practice structures persist as long as practices happen (Schatzki, 2006). This combines with people's practical intelligibility—each individual's teleology and affect—by which they decide whether to engage in a practice, while also taking into account how the situation they face is prefigured by relations between practices in terms of causality, constitution and meaning, and by the material arrangements. Although a practice is open-ended and practices are never perfectly replicated, a specific configuration of practice memory, prefiguration and people's individual practical intelligibility can produce a pattern that shows persistence over time and across space. This persistence can even have the effect of returning to form when dealing with some disturbance, as the configuration of practice memory, prefiguration and practical intelligibility can make the process conform to how things have been done previously. Or the process reconfigures itself and adapts to the new situation, as people improvise and adjust. If the chef finds out at the beginning of a morning shift that again that there are not enough eggs to go round, she might instruct the kitchen porter to get some petty cash and go to the supermarket to buy some eggs. This engages various practices of workflow planning, procurement, accounting and kitchen hierarchy, as well as the way practices connect, the material arrangements and the practical intelligibility of the people involved, all in aid of delivering a breakfast service expected from a 4-star hotel. The kitchen porter's supermarket run can become a persistent part of the hotel's practice bundle to compensate for the intermittent food deliveries.

If we take strategic management to be about generating a pattern in a stream of actions (Mintzberg & Waters, 1985), the practice bundle that is the organisation has the ability to take care of that all on its own, even when fluctuations and disturbances need to be dealt with. All is well if this activity is what is generating preferred outcomes. However, it is not uncommon that the practice bundle that is the organisation is creating problems and issues rather than solutions, and something needs to change. Such an intervention would require what Schatzki (2019) labelled as "governance": the "*intentional shaping, directing, or making a difference*"(93). Strategy implementation then is about intervening in the bundle of practices and material arrangements, i.e. in the ongoing process that is the organisation, in order to direct the process towards preferred outcomes. For this, Schatzki (2015) developed the notion of "avenue of access".

An avenue of access is a possible "action chain" involving a range of practices including those targeted for change and those that are connected and implicated (Schatzki, 2015). An action chain is one of the forms by which practices connect (Schatzki, 2002). With a practice described as "a nexus of actions" (71), an event is one of these actions. An action chain appears when events react to events, with practices connecting when these actions are from different practices. In effect, because of the reactions, an action chain is where causality appears. Schatzki (2002: 41) understands causality "*as the relation of bringing about*". As was mentioned earlier, essential to this understanding of causality is that it appears only if there is a reaction. There is not anything in what triggers the reaction, which makes it inevitable that something has to happen as a consequence. It is the other way around. That what happens as a consequence happens because there is a reaction to what happened. Whether this reaction happens is decided by or built into whoever or whatever reacts. An egg solidifies as a reaction to heat. An egg does that because of the chemistry of the egg. Heat has the opposite effect when ice reacts to it. A chef in a hotel reacts to a breakfast order of two eggs on toast by putting a pan on a hot stove, breaking two eggs, and by adding the contents with some butter to the pan, and by putting a slice of bread in a toaster.

Because of the indeterminate nature of human activity, the chef can react differently if she wants to. She can boil the eggs, do nothing or even walk out. Although being informed by how practices are structured and prefigured, it is her own practical intelligibility that tells her whether and how to react at that moment in time. Practical intelligibility understood in this way is part of the argument why human activity is indeterminate. Nevertheless, because practices in the organisation's bundle are connected to each other and also link with practices in the wider practice plenum, events through causality appear as action chains (Schatzki, 2002, 2019). On the one hand, the fundamental indeterminacy of human action can make such activity chains rather haphazard. On the other hand, the persistence of practices and the recurrent patterning in the (re-)actions that appear are a pre-requisite of the social phenomenon of the organisation to occur. The result is that somebody can book a room with a hotel on a booking website and have the confidence that on arrival a room will be available. If the box to include breakfast has been ticked, then the guest can also be confident that an egg will be fried in the morning.

The notion of "avenue of access" makes use of action chains as these are occurring. It allows us to explore the efficacy of what can be identified as dedicated implementation practices. The first thing to recognise is that implementation practices are interventions in the ongoing process that is the bundle of practices and material arrangements by which the organisation exists and performs. The indeterminate nature of human activity makes that there is no guarantee that an intervention involving an implementation practice will result in the effect that was desired. However, the ordered but fluent process by which an organisation performs and persists can also harbour the possibility of an action chain that poses as an "avenue of access" because it connects an implementation practice through a sequence of events with some targeted practices where a change is needed. If such an avenue appears, it would be very specific to a particular organisation at a certain time in a certain place, posing as what is commonly referred to as a window of opportunity.

For instance, if the hotel is part of a hospitality conglomerate and top management has made the strategic decision to become more efficient, the kitchen porter's supermarket run to stock up on missing food items because of the intermittent food deliveries would be an obvious target to save some costs. Buying food ingredients at supermarket prices on a regular basis quickly adds up and will eat into the hotel's thin margin quite easily. There is a whole action chain that probably starts with the centralised procurement department that manages the contract with a national food service company who supplies every hotel that is owned by this larger hospitality conglomerate. The action chain includes the food service company having to manage the logistics of sourcing eggs and other ingredients and getting it delivered in the required quantities at the right time to every hotel that is covered by the contract. The action chain also includes local hotel management who have to keep track of food ingredient usage and food waste while hotel occupancy varies daily in order to communicate with the food service company about what the kitchen needs on a day-to-day basis. And this action chain interacts with the material arrangements that are present and involves the practical intelligibility of all those participating. It is in this action chain that one or more practices need to be targeted, with an implementation practice having to link up through an avenue of access that includes this action chain but extends across various hierarchical and coordination practices by which procurement, logistical and kitchen practices can be accessed, all in order to stop the daily early morning supermarket run.

THE EFFICACY OF IMPLEMENTATION PRACTICES

There are a number of implementation practices that are common to the various strategy implementation frameworks that have been developed over the years (e.g. Ansoff & McDonnell, 1990; Hrebiniak & Joyce, 1984; Okumus, 2003; Thompson et al., 2019). One of these implementation practices is about re-designing/re-structuring the organisation in line with a newly formulated strategy. Business Process Re-engineering (BPR) as an implementation effort, for instance, centres on organisational re-design (Hammer & Champy, 1993). The activity that comes with this implementation practice boils down to telling people what job they are supposed to do and how they have to do it. People are told about this by way of job descriptions and organisation charts. In terms of Schatzki's (2002, 2019) practice theory, job descriptions mostly concern the rules part in the practice structure. A job description in effect is a set of rules, directives and instructions telling somebody what actions should and should not be taking place. Nonetheless, the general and practical understandings as well as the targeted practices' teleoaffectivity have to be reflected in the job descriptions and in the organisation chart for these to make any sense. Organisation charts sketch out who is responsible for certain practices and how these are to link up. The organisation chart also indicates what the material arrangements are because it informs the resourcing that allows for the people to do their jobs.

Furthermore, it is the practices that are being subjected to a re-design attempt, which have to respond to the "organisation design" practice for it to be effective. Whether this happens depends on what is going on with the targeted practice, the interactions with the material arrangements and with other practices to which the targeted practice connects, and with the people's practical intelligibility. The organisation chart as well as the job descriptions should take the prefiguration into account for the re-design to make it feasible. The people's practical intelligibility will be telling them whether to change. To prevent the hotel porter's daily supermarket run from ever happening again, the job description could be tightened up to exclude any procurement activity. But to make that work, something also needs to be done about the intermittent food deliveries. The general understanding that this is a 4-star hotel that has to deliver a 4-star breakfast experience tells all the people involved in this that you cannot afford to run out of eggs, no matter what job descriptions have been formulated for kitchen porters. And because she cares, chef will sent out the hotel porter to buy eggs if they have run out.

To address the intermittent food deliveries, one or more practices need to be targeted in the action chain that involves the hotel chain's procurement department, the food service company and local hotel management. They could consider replacing fresh eggs with egg powder to deal with the fluctuations in demand for breakfasts in the morning because hotel occupancy varies so much on a day-to-day basis. Egg powder can be stored over longer periods and it is therefore easier to stockpile in a hotel kitchen and have it continuously available. This would compensate for the intermittent food deliveries. An alternative would be to improve yield management and to vary room rates depending on occupancy to have roughly the same number of guests using the hotel every night and consequently even out the demand on the kitchen, especially if room rates would always include breakfast. With less variability with regard to how many breakfasts need to be prepared every morning, food orders and delivery would settle into fixed quantities, which would make procurement and logistics better manageable. Other options could be contemplated but when these are, their avenues of access would need to be part of the considerations. The two options here already demonstrate how the various practices that are targeted are connected through action chains. By looking into the detail and into the extent to which the action chains pose an avenue of access, the feasibility of each option can be assessed.

Additionally, the avenue of access also has to include the practices by which an option is to be put into effect, i.e. the actual intervention. Apart from the intervention practice itself—which is the "organisation design" practice here—there are further management and coordination practices by which the connections are to be made. The egg powder option requires communication with kitchen staff to prompt alterations to their cooking practices so that fresh eggs can be replaced with egg powder. To assess the effectiveness of this action chain, the reaction on the basis of the practical intelligibility of the kitchen staff, with them being informed by the cooking practices that they undertake and the material arrangements with which these practices interact, is paramount to assess whether egg powder is a viable alternative to fresh eggs, especially because replacing fresh eggs with egg powder changes the material arrangements. A similar consideration needs to be made with regard to the yield management option. It requires communication with hotel marketing and sales staff to prompt them to vary rates on the basis of occupancy levels. This intervention also links into the booking practices of would-be guests, expecting that price is a deciding factor in their practical intelligibility. Again, it is practical intelligibility in combination with practices' structures and the material arrangements, which inform them how the feasibility of the yield management option will play out. What this illustrates is that an avenue of access on which the efficacy of an implementation practice relies is very specific and local to the organisation in which strategy is to be implemented.

Similar arguments apply to implementation practices like "incentivisation", "monitoring and control", or to "culture" interventions. The assumption with the "incentivisation" practice is that activity that is in line with a formulated strategy is rewarded, mostly in financial terms. From Schatzki's practice theory perspective, it directly intervenes in the general understanding of the practices in the bundle, which are targeted, with an expectation that the purpose of each practice by and large is about making money by those who are involved in them. Furthermore, incentivization as an implementation practice can be criticised for making the affect in practical intelligibility rather one-dimensional by dismissing any other reason than money as to why it matters to people to engage in a practice. An avenue of access could be present if the general understanding of the practices is mostly about financial rewards. Incentivisation would struggle to generate a reaction that helps to realise a strategy if people's affect is about non-financial rewards. If incentivisation would be an implementation practice in the hotel that wants to replace fresh eggs with egg powder and kitchen staff care more about preparing good food than about getting top dollar, incentivisation would not generate much of a reaction. If it does, it could skew general understanding away from preparing outstanding food for a 4-star breakfast experience and towards a "what-is-in-it-for-me" culture.

A number of implementation frameworks include the practice of changing an organisation's culture by propagating a set of shared values and understandings that support the strategy. Shared values and interpretations also chime with notions like mission and vision, which have been assigned a role in keeping empowered employees in check in organisations that are designed as "agile". Such "culture intervention" practices, by limiting the notion of organisational culture to shared interpretations and values, target the general understanding of practices in the bundle by which the organisation exists. The incentivization practice in effect has been elaborated as a "culture intervention" practice just now in as far that it propagates a specific shared value about the importance of money.

Alternatively, the hospitality conglomerate can have been advised by PwC or McKinsey to become an "agile" organisation. In doing so, kitchen staff in every hotel have been empowered to run their kitchens as they see fit but within the confines of a mission statement and an overall vision. With efficiency becoming more important, these could be reformulated to now state that the hotel is 4-star but also should be run on a tight budget. The solution to have the kitchen porter do an early morning supermarket run to stock up on eggs is a manifestation of the chef having felt empowered enough to solve a local problem with regard to delivering breakfasts in line with the 4-star rating of the hotel. A re-stated vision and mission that now also emphasises frugality would prompt chef to re-think this solution. In effect, the reformulated mission and vision has implications for practical understanding and for teleoaffectivity because the understandings and values that are being put forward refer to a specific but different way in which practices are to be done.

The expectation is that such explicitly reformulated values and interpretations are to become part of the practice structure. Again, the efficacy of such an intervention is a matter of the reactions that happen, with these reactions just as easily being the opposite of what was intended and the propagated shared interpretations and values getting an ironic ring to them. This mostly depends on the practical intelligibility of the people who are targeted with a culture intervention, which on this occasion includes kitchen staff who have been empowered to marry frugality with a 4-star breakfast service. They might find a way that avoids egg powder and dispels the need for a daily supermarket run. They might not and ignore the newly formulated mission and vision. A "culture" intervention can and should be more sophisticated than simply forcing shared interpretations and values on a supposedly empowered workforce. Aiming for dialogue and enhanced mutual understanding by way of a process of, for instance, Organisation Development or Large Scale Intervention (French & Bell Jr, 1998) could work better but the same argument of having to rely on an avenue of access applies.

"Monitoring and control" is an interesting implementation practice in this respect. It is particular popular in the guise of the Balanced Scorecard (Kaplan & Norton, 2001). The idea is that a set of indicators can be developed by which progress with regard to whether an intended strategy is realised can be assessed, in the expectation that deviations of the trajectory leading to realising the strategy can be picked up and measures put in place to put everything back on track again. It is interesting from a practice theory point of view because it can be appreciated in two ways. One way is about the reactions that might occur as a consequence of putting a monitoring and control practice like the Balanced Scorecard in place. The other way concerns the expected effects of the scores and assessments that are generated, especially, as is often the case, when the strategy that was intended is not being realised.

The activity that takes place to establish indicators that are to be monitored, and maybe even the monitoring itself, on its own can invoke reactions. In a way, this would be a variant of the supposed Hawthorne effect (Roethlisberger & Dickson, 1939) with attention being paid to what people are doing having an effect on how they are doing things. If, for instance, hotel kitchen staff activity is being scrutinised for measurement opportunities, then what they show as being observable might be different to what they normally do because they are being scrutinised. They might hide the supermarket run because they know it has been prohibited but still do it to safeguard their food supply. Or the measurement might actually capture what it intends to capture. The reaction to the monitoring and what the score on the scorecard turns out to be, is a consequence of the conjunction of the practice structure that is being monitored, of how this practice is prefigured as it relates to other practices and interacts with the material arrangements, and the practical intelligibility of the people involved in the practice.

The control part of the practice assumes that any deviation of the trajectory towards realising the intended strategy, once exposed, will lead to a corrective measure. From a practice theory point of view, such a mechanism is not a matter of course. Similar to the reaction to the monitoring, any control effect is a matter of how the practices about which this information is gathered will react to any such deviation when it is being revealed. This information can be ignored; it can be acted upon in that something about these practices will change. However, this change does not automatically direct all activity towards realising the intended strategy. Whether that happens or not, again, is a matter of how practices are structured and prefigured, and of people's, practical intelligibility. As with the other implementation practices, "monitoring and control" practice efficacy depends on how it connects with other practices through an "avenue of access". Probably for this reason, Kaplan and Norton (2001) present the balanced scorecard among a suite of other implementation practices because for monitoring and control to have an effect, at least it needs to connect with the other implementation efforts, although the overall effect depends on the presence of avenues of access across the wider organisation.

The practice of strategy formulation tends not to be seen as an implementation practice but rather as a practice preceding implementation activity. Intriguingly, the argument can be made that similar to monitoring above, the practice just happening can invoke a reaction. Just talking about what the strategy could be or should be can be picked up in other practices. Kitchen staff who catch a rumour that hotel management is considering replacing fresh eggs with egg powder could create an uproar because they feel that it makes it impossible to provide a 4-star breakfast experience. The only eggs that can be prepared for breakfast with egg powder are scrambled eggs. It would preclude serving fried eggs, poached eggs, boiled eggs or the proverbial 4-star breakfast of Eggs Benedict. However, the dialogue that could ensue between kitchen staff and hotel management about kitchen practices could lead to kitchen staff learning about the hotel's thin margins and the need to be frugal with food ingredients, and to minimise food waste. Strategy formulation is more of a "saying" than a "doing" when it comes to appreciating it as a practice (cf. Schatzki, 2019). Because it can be linked to an avenue of access or action chain by which a pattern in a stream of actions is changed, strategy formulation can be understood as being an implementation practice as well. Top management who are aware of strategy formulation already invoking reactions and contributing to strategy as it is being realised could be using this practice as such.

In summary, utilising Schatzki's Theory of Practice, strategy implementation turns into a collection of implementation practices in which efficacy is a matter of the reactions it generates in other practices in and beyond the organisation's bundle. The intervention needs to target specific practices that by themselves are part of an action chain, with the desired effect heavily dependent on how the targeted practice through the action chain of which it is part generates the desired effect. Additionally, practices that are targeted for deliberate change have to be accessible through an action chain themselves. All of these action chains make up a specific and essentially localised infrastructure of change that only appears as practices—with their practice structures and being prefigured by interconnections and material arrangements—line up and combine with people's practical intelligibility so that the action chain triggered by the implementation practice invokes the desired reaction in the targeted practice. Avenues of access are highly contextual because these appear only if all the elements that are required line up and happen to be in place (Table 4.2).

Table 4.2 Implementation practices

Implementation practice	Intervention	Considerations
Job description	Specifies the rules in the practice structure of the practices that are part of a job	Job content needs to consider practical intelligibility of job holders as well as prefiguration of practices that are part of the job. Job content has to reflect teleoaffectivity and material arrangements of practices that are part of the job
Organisation design	Specifies how practices in the bundle connect, who should be involved and what material arrangements are required	Design needs to consider practical intelligibility of position holders as well as prefiguration of practices that are part of the design
Incentivisation	Emphasises financial rewards in the general understanding of the practices in the bundle	Struggles to be effective if people's practical intelligibility is mostly non-financial
Culture	Specifies the general understanding and the rules of the practices in the bundle	Has to chime with people's practical intelligibility
Monitoring and control	Signals what general understanding is expected	Has to chime with people's practical intelligibility and needs to take into account how practices are prefigured
Strategy formulation	Signals what general understanding is expected	Has to chime with people's practical intelligibility and needs to take into account how practices are prefigured

Conclusion and Some Practical Implications

We approached strategy implementation from a strong process perspective utilising Schatzki's (2002, 2019) Theory of Practice. In doing so, strategic management is being understood as a continuous implementation process in which implementation practices aim to direct an organisation onwards on a continuous journey by which a pattern in a stream of activity is realised (Mintzberg & Waters, 1985). In this way, even strategy formulation can be appreciated as an implementation practice. Bearing in mind the indeterminacy of human activity, the efficacy of implementation practices can be gauged by way of the presence of avenues of access that connect the implementation effort with targeted practices. Such avenues are highly contextual in that they are sensitive to time and place. We can also expect avenues of access to open up and close down as the process moves on.

Consequently, implementation practices that have been put forward like designing an appropriate organisation structure, establishing an incentive scheme, changing the organisational culture, empowering people or monitoring and control cannot be expected to have universal applicability. Whether these have an effect is place and time sensitive and depends on the reactions that are triggered. There is no intrinsic causal force associated with any implementation practice that makes that certain effects can always be anticipated. Any anticipation of effects has to take into account the whole practice bundle, the practice's persistence, the prefiguration and the practical intelligibility of the people involved.

As with every practice, implementation practices have a practice structure in that there is practice understanding, general understanding and teleoaffectivity, and there are rules. Implementation practices are also prefigured in that their feasibility depends on how they connect to other practices and how they connect to material arrangements. The highly contextual nature of avenues of access in effect refers to the prefiguration aspect of implementation practices and indicates the fragility of their efficacy.

Using Schatzki's theory of practice also highlights the importance of managers and their role in the process, especially when we consider the role of their practical intelligibility. The practical intelligibility of top managers, with them often put at the centre of an organisation's strategic management effort, can be seen as essential in disentangling the mutual implication of the organisation as a bundle of practices and strategy as a pattern of actions. What this chapter tells us is that strategic management requires managers to always be critical and self-reflective about what is going on and how they go about doing management (Sminia, 2022). Top managers' individual affect and teleology is pivotal for them to appreciate what is happening with the organisation and seeing a necessity to intervene in what is going on or not, as well as being able to see it through. However, affect in particular is only recently being recognised as being of consequence in management and organisation (Gherardi, 2019).

Within the practice structure, practical understanding is particularly apt from the perspective of this chapter because the argument that has been put forward here indicates that this practical understanding has to include an appreciation of Schatzki's practice theory and particularly the notion of avenue of access. Having an appreciation of how the efficacy of an implementation practice is a matter of avenues of access would be an essential element in the know-how of strategy implementation. This is not to say that strategic managers should become experts in Schatzki's Theory of Practice. However, it might supply a vocabulary and a frame of reference, or at least a basic sense for understanding what is going on. What is of particular importance for understanding what is going on is that the practical applicability of any strategy tool or theory is not inherent in the tool or the theory. There is no universal applicability. Instead, usefulness and efficacy are born out of the specifics of the situation in two ways. Firstly, whatever a manager does, its effect is a matter of the reactions that it generates, not a consequence of some inherent power in the tool or method that has been used. Secondly, a manager can and needs to consider any intervention in the ongoing process by which an organisation exists in relation to the appearance of an avenue of access that links the intervention with the effect that needs to be generated.

Furthermore, this take on strategic management as effectively being a continuous implementation process urges managers to show some humility, firstly, because an organisation will realise a strategy because the process will be happening anyway, despite or in spite of what a manager does or does not contribute. In a way, this practice approach to strategy tells managers that in many instances they could and should trust the process for sorting itself out. Secondly, if they choose to intervene, they should be aware that to successfully implement strategy, their activity must invoke a reaction of the actual practices and actions that configure the organisational doings. Simply formulating a desired strategic position, identifying a strategic capability, stating the required culture through visions and missions, designing an organisational structure or acquiring new tangible assets is not enough to safeguard an organisation's viability and success. Whether any of this has any impact is a consequence of the reactions it generates. Chances are that whatever happens next is a circumstantial alignment of many factors. Attributing it all to the brilliance of a strategist is just another instance of what has been labelled the "romance" of leadership; of wanting to understand achievement as a consequence of deliberate managerial activity (Meindl et al., 1985). Practical strategic managers should primarily be focused on the avenues of access that pose as affordances (Gibson, 1979) as these open up and close down, to have interventions ready to be activated if and when this is required.

References

Ansoff, H. I. (1965). *Corporate strategy*. McGraw Hill.
Ansoff, H. I., & McDonnell, E. (1990). *Implanting strategic management*. Prentice Hall.
Bourgeois, L. J., III., & Brodwin, D. R. (1984). Strategic implementation: Five approaches to an elusive phenomenon. *Strategic Management Journal, 5*, 241–264.
Cândido, C. J., & Santos, S. P. (2015). Strategy implementation, What is the failure rate? *Journal of Management & Organization, 21*(2), 237–262.
Chia, R. C. H., & Holt, R. (2009). *Strategy without design: The silent efficacy of indirect action*. Cambridge University Press.
Feldman, M. S., & Pentland, B. T. (2003). Reconceptualizing organizational routines as a source of flexibility and change. *Administrative Science Quarterly, 48*(1), 94–118.
French, W. L., & Bell, C. H., Jr. (1998). *Organization development: Behavioral science interventions for organizational improvement* (6th ed.). Prentice-Hall.
Gherardi, S. (2019). Theorizing affective ethnography for organization studies. *Organization, 26*(6), 741–760.
Gibson, J. J. (1979). *The ecological approach to visual perception*. Houghton-Mifflin.
Hammer, M., & Champy, J. A. (1993). *Reengineering the corporation: A manifesto for business revolution*. Harper Business Books.
Hrebiniak, L. G., & Joyce, W. (1984). *Implementing strategy*. Macmillan.
Kanter, R. M. (1983). *The change masters: Innovation & entrepreneurship in the American corporation*. Simon & Schuster.
Kaplan, R. S., & Norton, D. P. (2001). *The strategy-focused organization—How balanced scorecard companies thrive in the new business environment*. Harvard Business School Press.
Kiechel III, W. (1982). Corporate strategist under fire. *Fortune*: 34–39.
Langley, A., & Tsoukas, H. (2010). Introducing "Perspectives on process organization studies." In T. Hernes & S. Maitlis (Eds.), *Process, sensemaking, and organizing* (pp. 1–26). Oxford University Press.
Martin, R. (2010). The execution trap. *Harvard Business Review*(July-August): 1–6.
McKinsey. (2015). *The keys to organizational agility*.
Meindl, J. R., Ehrlich, S. B., & Dukerich, J. M. (1985). The romance of leadership. *Administrative Science Quarterly, 30*, 78–102.

Mintzberg, H., & Waters, J. A. (1985). Of strategies, deliberate and emergent. *Strategic Management Journal, 6*, 257–272.

Nutt, P. C. (1999). Surprising but true: Half the decisions in organizations fail. *Academy of Management Executive, 13*(4), 75–90.

Okumus, F. (2003). A framework to implement strategies in organizations. *Management Decision, 41*(9), 871–882.

Partridge, E. (2006). *Origins: A short etymological dictionary of modern English.* Routledge.

PwC. (2021). *How to make agility more than a buzzword: Empower your teams, deal with disruption and drive productivity.*

Roethlisberger, F. J., & Dickson, W. J. (1939). *Management and the worker.* Harvard University Press.

Schatzki, T. R. (2001). Practice-minded orders. In T. R. Schatzki, K. Knorr-Cetina, & E. von Savigny (Eds.), *The practice turn in contemporary theory* (pp. 42–55). Routledge.

Schatzki, T. R. (2002). *The site of the social: A philosophical exploration of the constitution of social life and change.* Pennsylvania State University Press.

Schatzki, T. R. (2005). The sites of organizations. *Organization Studies, 26*(3), 465–484.

Schatzki, T. R. (2006). On organizations as they happen. *Organization Studies, 27*(12), 1863–1873.

Schatzki, T. R. (2015). Practices, governance, and sustainability. In Y. Strengers & C. Maller (Eds.), *Social practices, intervention and sustainability: beyond behavior change* (pp. 15–30). Routledge.

Schatzki, T. R. (2019). *Social change in a material world.* Routledge.

Sminia, H. (2022). *The strategic manager: Understanding strategy in practice* (3rd ed.). Routledge.

Thompson, A., Peteraf, M. A., Gamble, J., & Strickland, A. J., III. (2019). *Crafting & Executing Strategy: Concepts and Cases* (22nd ed.). McGraw-Hill.

Tsoukas, H., & Chia, R. (2003). Everything flows and nothing abides. *Process Studies, 32*(2), 196–224.

Weiser, A.-K., Jarzabkowski, P. A., & Laamanen, T. (2020). Completing the adaptive turn: An integrative view of strategy implementation. *Academy of Management Annals, 14*(2), 969–1031.

Whipp, R. (2003). Managing strategic change. In D. Faulkner & A. Campbell (Eds.), *The Oxford handbook of strategy* (pp. 729–758). Oxford University Press.

Wilkinson, A. (1998). Empowerment: Theory and practice. *Personnel Review, 27*(1), 40–56.

CHAPTER 5

Strategy Implementation and Organisational Change: A Complex Systems Perspective

Czesław Mesjasz

INTRODUCTION

The relations between strategy and organisational change constitute one of greatest challenge of management theory and practice. It is especially important since the low level of success in strategy implementation has become almost a mantric observation in multiple publications in strategic management, for example (Busulwa et al., 2019; Okumus, 2003; Hrebiniak, 2006; Kaplan & Norton, 2008; *The Oxford Handbook...*, 2016). Therefore, it is not incidental, that similarly as in other

---

The Project has been financed by the Ministry of Science and Higher Education of Poland within "Regional Initiative of Excellence" Programme for 2019-2022. Project no.: 021/RID/2018/19.

C. Mesjasz (✉)
Management Process Department, Cracow University of Economics, Cracow, Poland
e-mail: mesjaszc@uek.krakow.pl

© The Author(s), under exclusive license to Springer Nature Singapore Pte Ltd. 2022
A. Zubac et al. (eds.), *Effective Implementation of Transformation Strategies*, https://doi.org/10.1007/978-981-19-2336-4_5

areas of management, it was expected that new domains of knowledge such as cybernetics, systems thinking developed in the 1950s and 1960s and broadly defined complexity studies originated in the 1970s, would provide instruments for a better understanding of the interrelationship between strategic management and organisational change.

It is mirrored in the literature referring to strategic management and organisational change published since the 1950s. As examples, the following works can be quoted—strategic management (Ansoff, 1965), change and cybernetics (Beer, 1957), strategic management, change and systems thinking (Emery & Trist, 1965). The publications in the 1960s and 1970 were not numerous. The applications of complexity-related research in theory of strategic management organisational change have become one of decisive factor of development of theory and practice of management since the 1980s (Allen et al., 2011; Boulton et al., 2015; Stacey, 1996, 2000; Stacey et al., 2000; Stacey & Mowles, 2016).

One of the most challenging problems in relations between strategic management and organisational change is strategy implementation. In the initial concepts of strategic management, the implementation was treated just as an easily identifiable stage of the decision-making process: strategic analysis—strategic decision—strategy implementation. Following the development of economics and management, such an idealised picture became too simple. However, even when the intricacy of relations between strategy and organisational change is borne in mind, the transfer of results of decisions concerning changes of organisation, or in a broader sense, interaction of those two processes still is a source of multiple questions and doubts.

There are two research problems of the studies of interrelations between strategy implementation and organisational changes. The first, a more precise identification of those interrelations, and the second, identification of the factors of determining effectiveness of those interactions. In the modern theory and practice of strategic management, the process of development of strategy built on learning, adaptation and coevolution with non-linearity as a determining factor of its dynamics creates an additional hurdle in studying these interrelationships.

In the literature, a superficial divide can be observed. Some sources use the term strategy implementation examples, while the other tilt towards the concept of strategy execution examples. A closer look shows that in most cases these terms are treated as synonymous (Hrebiniak, 2005, 2006).

In spite of this terminological and theoretical divide, there is a need to study the interrelationships between strategy implementation and organisational change. Bearing in mind the impact of the applications of broadly defined complexity-related ideas on management theory, including, strategic management, the following question is arising: What is the impact of complexity-related ideas on a better understanding of the interrelations between strategy implementation and organisational change? These interrelationships are described with the concept of interface (Zubac et al., 2021) and they are defined in a more detailed way in the remainder of the paper.

The main research question can be decomposed into the following partial questions:

1. What are the interpretations of strategy implementation under the circumstances in which both strategy development and organisational change are interpretated as cyclical adaptive processes?
2. How have the ideas from broadly defined complexity-related studies been helpful in gaining a better understanding of the interrelations between strategy implementation and organisational changes?
3. What are the main advantages and disadvantages of those applications?

The study presented in this chapter aims at giving preliminary answers to the above questions. In addition to the traditional arguments favouring applications of complexity-related ideas in management the argument about time perspective can be added. The status quo of applications of complexity-related ideas in management allows for a more cautious assessment than was possible, say, in the 1990s and in the beginning of the twenty-first century when fascination of chaos and complexity theories too often led to excessive and naïve expectations.

The study is prepared with full awareness of terminological problems occurring in theory of management. Obviously, it will be pointless to strive for unequivocal definitions and interpretations but in the era of dominance of constructivist approach in management, it is not possible to fall into an opposite trap of terminological carelessness and negligence. A range of fundamental terminological doubts must be clarified in advance. Firstly, due to a multitude of definitions and interpretations of the terms applied in the studies of strategy and organisational change, instead of using the term definition, the term interpretation is applied. Secondly, the research dealing with various interpretated notions of complexity is so broad and differentiated so for the sake of clarity two terms are used: complexity-related ideas and complexity studies. Most significant terminological nuances are explained in the further part of the chapter. Due to the terminological clarity, the term organisational change is used consistently throughout this chapter.

The final formal introductory remark concerns the literature. Strategic management and organisational change were discussed in almost uncountable sources of various rank and scope of impact. In this survey-like introductory study, a necessary selection of sources had to be made. Usually such a selection could lead to omission or redundant quotes but it is an unavoidable aspect of modern management research affected by information overabundance.

The main method of research was a classical literature survey. It was selected purposively with a full awareness of availability of various methods of text mining and meta-analysis. Such analyses of a large number of publications are helpful when topics are well-defined and widely applied. This chapter embodies a preliminary study in which counting the occurrences of words in titles, abstracts and texts would be too superficial and useless. It is not a systematic survey but just a collection of representative examples.

The structure of the chapter is as follows. In the first part, strategy and interpretations of organisational change are described. The second part embodies the proposal of a simplified typology of interpretations of complexity-related ideas. In the third part, examples of applications of complexity-related ideas in the studies of relations between strategy implementation and organisational change are surveyed and preliminarily assessed.

Strategy and Systemic Interpretations of Organisational Change

Systemic Interpretations of Organisational Change

Change constitutes an important attribute—if not an element when seen in a constructivist perspective, of every social system, including artificially created purposive organisation.[1] Change is an intuitive concept thus instead of presenting attempts to define it in a classical way, it is more useful to enumerate its characteristics. As a conceptual background, a broad systemic interpretation is applied. In this interpretation, organisation is always treated as a system. This comment may seem self-evident but it is added here as to prevent the misunderstanding in which a dichotomy between systemic and processual interpretations of organisation is exposed. In the ultimate case, in processual interpretation, the organisation can be also viewed as a system of processes.

In the broadest systemic sense, the change of organisation can be depicted with the following characteristics:

- the relation between observer-participant and organisation in defining organisation—objective, subjective and intersubjective,
- definitions of organisations,
- the borders of organisation,
- interactions between organisation and its environment (mutual influence),
- causes of changes of organisation—external and internal,
- the aims of change of organisation,
- the structural elements and subsystems of organisation and the patterns of their changes organisation structure, motivation system, IT system, manufacturing system,
- changes of characteristics of elements and subsystems, e.g. changing patterns of behaviour of employees, their qualifications, motivation,
- phases of processes of change at each level of organisational hierarchy (classical structures and networks),

---

[1] Without definitional and philosophical considerations and using simple intuitive interpretation, it is assumed that the term change treated as an event or process means cause of difference observed over time in a specific feature of an observed object. As an inspiration for this interpretation, a more precise definition of intuitive interpretation of organisational change can be found by Van de Ven and Poole (1995: 512).

- continuity/discontinuity of the processes of change at each level of organisational hierarchy (classical structures and networks),
- relations between the changes of elements and changes of the entire organisation,
- time horizon and scope of change—strategic, tactical, operational,
- scope of change—partial (selected elements and subsystems) and complete (whole system),
- scope of difference between the initial and the final state of characteristics describing organisation, its elements and subsystems,
- scope of controllability of organisational change—controlled, spontaneous (emerging) and mixed,
- psychological aspect of change—change of mental models, cognitive patterns, motivation of stakeholders of organisation,
- cultural change—change of individual cognitive patterns and change of collective cultural norms,
- change of physical infrastructure of organisation.

Looking from a systemic point of view, a large variety of interpretations of organisational change can be proposed. This phenomenon seems understandable because of two reasons. First, the economic development was accompanied by different patterns of organisation of manufacturing and management. Second, in order to understand better the changing patterns of business organisation, inspiration was sought for in technology (classical management) and collective phenomena in physics, chemistry and biology. This variety of interpretations of organisational change was perceived as something natural after the observation of Morgan (1986) that organisation can be depicted with various metaphors.

Staying on the ground of systemic understanding of organisation and taking into account the impact of complexity studies, the following typology of interpretations of organisational change can be proposed:

- planned change as an instrument of improvement of organisation,
- specific (functional?) interpretations,
- universal interpretations,
- interpretations deriving from cybernetics and classical systems thinking,
- interpretations deriving from complexity studies.

Planned Organisational Change

The ideas of planned change stemmed from the need to enhance performance of organisation and to accommodate it to the changing environment. They are usually labelled as linear, goal-oriented, including clearly separable stages, rational and based on the decisive role of managers and/or other influential actors within the organisation.

Usually as the first attempt to develop a process of change, Lewin's ideas of freezing and unfreezing are quoted (1947). The majority of linear concepts of organisational change were developed in the 1990s, e.g. "power tools for change" (Grundy, 1992), "Ten commandments" (Kanter et al., 1992), "Eight steps to transforming your organization" (Kotter, 1996). Later some of them were developed into more flexible approaches in which the growing complexity of organisation and complexity and uncertainty of the environment was considered, e.g. Kotter et al. (2021).

Specific Interpretations

One of most popular and influential typologies of organisational change was developed by Van de Ven and Poole (1995). The ideas presented in this paper were later refined and extended by Van de Ven and Sun (2011). They proposed four universal ideal-type processes of change treated also as developmental processes which are applicable in the studies of organisational change. The authors use the terms theory and model interchangeably: teleological theory (planned change), life-cycle theory (regulated change), dialectical theory (conflictive change) and evolutionary theory (competitive change).

The teleological theory—planned change, is derived from the assumption that the purpose is the final cause for guiding movement of any entity. It means that an entity having its final state is purposeful and adaptive. The process of change, or in a broader sense, development, includes the following phases: goal formulation, implementation, evaluation and modification of goals based on what was learned or intended by the entity which can be an individual or any collectivity. This adaptive process is not sequential due to the learning loops. In some cases, the path of achieving the goals may be different as it is expressed in the concept of equifinality developed in systems thinking (Bertalanffy, 1968: 131). The process of change can be perpetual since the goal is not viewed as the state of equilibrium.

The life-cycle theory (regulated change) is built on the metaphor of the living organism for which the change is imminent. The linear sequential and deterministic process embodies all stages from the initiation to the termination of existence of an entity. Each stage determines the following stage and there is no possibility for any kind of learning. This theory is relevant to organisations, products and projects.

The Hegelian assumption of colliding forces: thesis-antithesis-synthesis constitutes the point of departure of the dialectical theory (conflictive change). The organisational entity exists in a pluralistic world of colliding events, forces and contradictory values, both inside and outside of the organisation. In dialectical process theory, stability and change are explained by reference to the balance of power between opposing entities. Change is occurring when one of those values, forces and events gains sufficient power to undermine the status quo. Although the concept is rooted in the Hegelian triad, it is not assured that dialectical conflicts lead to creative syntheses.

The evolutionary theory (competitive change) refers to classical biological evolutionary theory but not in an isomorphic sense. The concept of evolution is focused on cumulative changes in structural forms of populations of organisational entities across communities, industries or society at large. Similarly, as in biology, the change embodies continuous cycles of variation, selection and retention. The main object of interest is organisations which change their structural properties (variation) and then they are selected by the mechanisms of market competition. As a result, they can find their environmental niches. Retention serves to counteract the self-reinforcing loop between variations and selection. In this theory, evolution explains change as a recurrent, cumulative and probabilistic progression of variation, selection and retention of organisational entities.

The presentation of the four theories is extended with the metatheories referring to different cycles of events, the concepts of generating mechanisms called "motors", different units of analysis and different patterns of change. The above theories are split into two broader types: first-order change and second-order change. According to the first-order change, processes of change are building on what has gone on before or change within an existing framework that produces variations on a theme. The processes that produce these variations are prescribed and predictable because they are patterned on the previous state. The life-cycle and the evolutionary theories belong to this type of prescribed change. The second-order change is in some sense constructive, meaning that there is a conscious break with the past situation basic assumptions or framework. The level of predictability is lower but the change is more genuine. The teleological and dialectic theory are assigned to the second-order (constructive/emergent) change.

Universal Interpretations
Organisational change can be perceived in a broader perspective that gives an additional point of departure for a deeper understanding of a great variety of ideas associated with the theory of organisational change. Two examples of such a broader approach have been selected in order to show the scope and intricacy of the universal theoretical concepts and of their relations.

As the first, the typology of philosophical foundations of organisational change developed by Graetz and Smith (2010) can be recalled. In this study, only the ideas drawn from their paper are referred to, not from the book published a year later (Graetz & Smith, 2011). After criticising the abovementioned, traditional, simple concepts, they argue that 10 broader interpretations exploring prescriptive functions of metaphors can be helpful in a deeper understanding of organisational change by identifying the relations between various theories of change. For the purpose of our study, this typology is modified. The philosophy of change associated with cybernetics, systems thinking and complexity studies constituting the main topic of our study is scrutinised in detail separately. Instead, a constructivist philosophy is introduced because the postmodernist philosophy of change included in the original typology of Graetz and Smith should be explained with higher precision. It must be added that this additional philosophy is introduced with a full awareness of discussions about differences between constructivism and constructionism (Table 5.1).

The number and differentiation of theoretical concepts of change lead to the question: What are the relations between those theories? Are they competing or complementary, or perhaps, they are indifferent to each other?

According to the authors of this typology, the multiple universal interpretations of organisational change show that in the studies of change several perspectives have to be applied (Graetz & Smith, 2010: 149–151). In consequence of applications of various interpretations of organisational change, two approaches are proposed—modularity and ambidexterity.

Table 5.1 Synthesis of philosophical interpretations of organisational change

Philosophical interpretations of organisational change	Characteristics
Biological	Collective evolution—population ecology, evolution of organisations, natural selection, strive for effectiveness, competition for scarce resources Individual experience of organisation—lifecycle, imminent and progressive change
Rational (strategic)	Process of change—rational and linear, natural and universal patterns of change Goal-oriented change, rational managers who are pivotal for change
Institutional	Change is a function of transforming industrial landscape (institutional environment) External stimuli for change leading to homogeneity of industry
Resource	Organisational change deriving from search for necessary resources Change begins from identification of necessary resources Possibility of acquisition of scarce resources and not the impact of environment determines organisational change
Contingency perspective	Explanation of organisational change from a behavioural perspective concerning managers who have to identify the best fit between internal conditions and the environment in order to achieve maximum efficacy Impossibility of a proper identification of all factors leads to increased uncertainty

(continued)

Modular organisation is defined as composed from elements performing different functions. In consequence, modularity allows for independent evolution of elements. Organisations can be also ambidextrous unifying hierarchical structure and networks.

In another typology, Dooley (1997) proposed three universal approaches to organisational change, which he treats as paradigms: systems theory-based, evolutionary and information processing. In the

Table 5.1 (continued)

Philosophical interpretations of organisational change	Characteristics
Psychological	Continuation of tradition of Kurt Lewin
Individual and personal experience are the main determinants of organisational change
Organisational change is determined by individual emotions, feeling and learned slowing down of pace
Dealing with organisational change was included in the concept of organisational development
Political	Organisations are political systems with power games, coalitions and conflicting interests
Conflict as a decisive factor driving organisational change
Change managers must skillfully deal with the internal power system in the organisation and with external factors
Results of organisational change are uncertain
Cultural	Organisational change is treated as changes of organisational culture—unconsciously determined patterns of behaviour
Collective experience, norms and behaviour as elements of prolonged organisational change
Cultural change can be natural and also imposed as an instrument for determining motivation of managers and employees
Postmodernist	Change is a function of reality constructed by actors associated with the organisation
Departure from modernist, industrial and post-industrial society
The language of description of organisation is decoupled from real experience
Increased role of knowledge as a determinant of power
Power perceived not as a potential source of rational imposition of change but as an instrument of oppression and unjust relations within and without the organisation
Absence of overarching theoretical approaches

(continued)

Table 5.1 (continued)

Philosophical interpretations of organisational change	Characteristics
Constructivist	Associated with post modernism but exposes the processes and patterns of creating social systems Concentrated on the ways/how individuals and collectivities create an organisational "reality" Change as a social construct and sensemaking Necessity to consider relations between subjectivity, intersubjectivity and objectivity

Source own research based on (Graetz & Smith, 2010)

approach based on systems theory and cybernetics, the organisation is treated as analogous to a living organism changing in a coevolutionary process with its environment in order to maintain its equilibrium. In the evolutionary, or population ecology-based approach, attention is given to creation, diffusion and adoption of technical and managerial innovation. In this approach, including also neo-Darwinian evolutionary model, innovations are treated as memes (cultural genes) and the dynamics of innovation diffusion are described as self-organising systems allowing to compete successfully with other organisations. Change understood as an effect of information processing and decision-making processes is dependent on the limitations of rationality (bounded rationality) and adaptation of the organisation to its environment is built upon second-order learning. These three approaches presented here in a simplified form have been used by Dooley to build the foundations for studying change of organisations with the concept of Complex Adaptive Systems (CAS). Similarly, as in the case of typology of Graetz and Smith (2010), Dooley's typology is treated as an example of context for implementation of the CAS as a theoretical instrument for studying the relations between strategy, strategy implementation and organisational change.

This collection of systemic interpretations of organisational change is obviously not complete but it provides a point of departure for a better understanding of applications of complexity-related ideas in the studies of relations between strategy implementation and organisational change.

Strategy and Organisational Change

The studies of relations between strategy and organisational change are based on the idea of strategy process proposed by Mintzberg and Lampel (1999) and Van de Ven (1992). The strategy process can be then treated as interacting in various forms with the process of organisational change.

Additional explanation is also needed for strategic change. According to Van de Ven (1992: 211), strategic change has been used to denote "key" organisational changes. It is treated as being purposive and goal-oriented. Strategic change has also been used to denote changes undertaken to align an organisation with its environment. It can be also treated in a processual framework. Analysis of relations between implementation of strategy of various levels and scope—strategic, tactical, operational demands for further research. The above explanation of strategic change is added to signal additional complexity of relations between strategy implementation and strategic change.

From a broader systemic vantage point, the relations between strategy and organisational change are determined by the following factors:

1. Type of strategy and the processes of its realisation.
2. Interpretations of organisational change.
3. Organisational change and strategic change.
4. The interface between the processes of development and implementation of strategy and organisational change.
5. Limited possibility of separation of the phase of strategy implementation from the entire strategic management process.
6. Patterns of interrelations between strategy implementation and organisational change.

In consequence, the research area determined by the above factors is very broad, including competing ideas, affected by the lack of clarity of definitions and interpretations, and, last but not least, full of various dualities, predominantly the paradoxes, e.g. the distinction between strategy implementation and strategy execution.

The interrelations between the strategic management process and organisational change process can be described with the metaphor of interface. Zubac et al. (2021) proposed two interpretations of interface. The Interface between strategy and organisational change (*ibidem*,

p. 484) and the interface between strategy implementation and organisational change (*ibidem*, p. 482). Although the original concept of interface concerns predominantly the latter relation, in a systemic study both concepts must be given a more detailed interpretation.

The coevolutionary interface (Fig. 5.1) embodies all potential interactions between strategy process and organisational change process. It concerns both processes and all of their types—from linear to adaptive and all their potential interactions. It must be underlined that only some of the interactions are bi-directional, coevolutionary and even recursive with feedback since in the most general sense those two processes are constantly interacting with each other.

In some cases, the strategy implementation is traditional, one directional—strategy influences and determines organisational change. Zubac et al., (2021: 482) reaffirms this property of the interface: "if strategy implementation is defined as strategic decision-making processes 'put into action through the development of programmes, budgets and procedures' (Wheelen & Hunger, 2008: 16), while organizational change is the application of behavioral science, specifically as the 'planned development and reinforcement of organizational strategies, structures and processes for improving an organization's effectiveness' (Waddell et al., 2011: 4)". Under such circumstances, for purely operational reasons, this more precisely defined interface can be treated as one-directional.

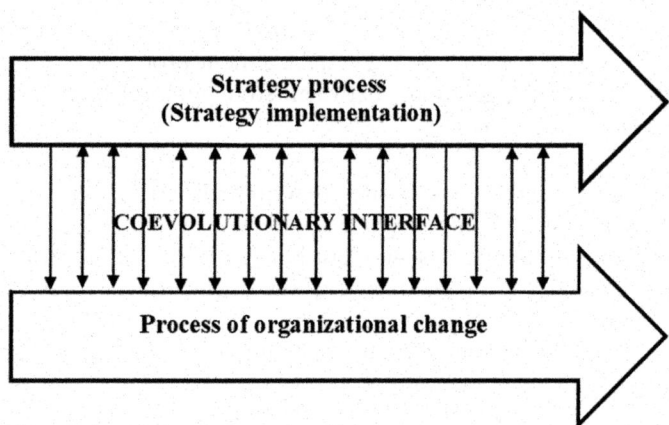

Fig. 5.1 Coevolutionary interface—strategy and organisational change (*Source* own research)

The above interpretations can be further specified and decomposed. They can be treated as a conceptual background for studying the role of complexity-related ideas in relations between strategy and organisational change. In this part, they are treated as the context for discussing the interrelationships between strategic management and organisational change, and relations between strategy implementation and organisational change.

COMPLEXITY AND ORGANISATION: A MULTITUDE OF APPROACHES

Since the 1960s management theory and practice have been developed under a strong influence of various areas of knowledge in which interpretations of complexity and complexity-related concepts were originated—cybernetics, systems thinking, broadly defined complexity studies. They have been used as mathematical models, analogies and metaphors. It is well-known that mathematical models can be used for description, explanation of causal relationships, prediction and in normative (prescriptive) approaches but it must be remembered that analogies and metaphors also can be applied for similar purposes.

First and foremost, we have to realise that there are not any commonly accepted definitions of complexity. There were multiple attempts to develop and to systematise definitions and interpretations of complexity-related terms, e.g. 45 interpretations of complexity by Lloyd (2001), attempts made in comprehensive synthetizing works (Bar-Yam, 1997; Castellani 2021). Similar efforts have been made in the management literature (Allen et al., 2011; Boulton et al., 2015; Brown & Eisenhardt, 1998; Jackson, 2019; Stacey, 1996; Stacey & Mowles, 2016; Stacey et al., 2000).

When discussing the role of complexity in management, we have to take a broader perspective including not only the impact of complexity science which has become popular since the 1970s but also the earlier ideas and the ideas developed in other areas. The typology proposed here in a simplified version refers to management but here it is tailored for the studies of relations between the strategic management process and organisational changes. The assumptions of the typology are as follows:

1. It is based on the experience of applications of complexity-related ideas in management which began with development of cybernetics and systems thinking.
2. It embodies not the definitions but various interpretations of the meaning of the term complexity.
3. The distinction between "hard" quantitative (computable) and "soft" qualitative aspects of complexity is considered but for the use in studying strategy implementation, the problems associated with computability and complexity are left for further considerations.
4. The role of observer in defining complexity as a set of characteristics of a system is taken into account.

Before presenting the typology, the following ideas are helpful in ordering the research area so they can be preliminarily defined: Complexity-related concepts which can be directly and indirectly associated with variously defined complexity. As examples, such terms as chaos, edge of chaos, emergence, feedback and self-organisation. All more or less specifically defined areas of knowledge, they are labelled as complexity-related studies. It is a significant simplification but it makes their application in management more relevant to reality.

The proposed typology includes the following interpretations of complexity.

1. Intuitive complexity.
2. Complexity is defined directly and indirectly in cybernetics, managerial cybernetics, system thinking and in associated areas, e. g. systems dynamics.
3. Complexity studies embodying quantitative and qualitative interpretations of complexity.

It is neither possible nor necessary to present here all the definitions. This typology is only a point of departure for presenting the main concepts and some representative patterns of their applications in management.

Intuitive Complexity

The following distinctive features allow to treat the interpretation of the notion complexity as intuitive (quantitative "hard" and qualitative "soft"):

- description of complexity with universal characteristics commonly treated as intuitive, e.g. number of elements, differentiation of elements and their states, number of interactions, hierarchy, etc. (structural complexity),
- dynamics of a collectivity described with simple intuitive quantitative and qualitative characteristics—speed of change of elements, of their interactions and of the whole collectivity, growth, decay, dissipation, uncertainty.

Complexity and Cybernetics

Cybernetics: first-order, objective, cybernetics without considering the role of the observer, and subjective, second-order cybernetics including the role of the observer and managerial cybernetics. The name cybernetics was coined by Wiener as to describe "the science of control and communication, in the animal and the machine" (Wiener, 1948). References to complexity can be found in such cybernetical concepts as feedback, information, communication, learning, non-linearity, self-organisation, self-reproducing machines. Another pioneer of cybernetics W. Ross Ashby (1957) understood complexity in general terms as a property of the brain, computing machines, human organisms, society and declared that his research aimed to develop methods for studying them as complex systems. Cybernetics was defined by Ashby as providing effective methods for the study, and control, of systems that are intrinsically extremely complex. He proposed a rank of complexity-related concepts as adaptation, Black Box, feedback, equilibrium, homeostasis, stability, regulation, self-organisation, the law of requisite variety and ultrastability.

The "soft" interpretations of complexity are deriving from the "second order cybernetics" in which the role of observer is taken into account (Foerster, 1982). In "soft" complexity, it is assumed that the object is not independent from the observer, what is reflected in the famous observation "complexity as beauty is in the eyes of the beholder".

Management Cybernetics

British scholar and practitioner, Stafford Beer, inspired by the ideas of cybernetics and neurology, developed a synthesis of the managerial cybernetics called the Viable System Model (VSM) which can be treated as an instrument of effective management of variety and complexity (Beer, 1972, 1979).

Systems Thinking

At the same time as cybernetics was being developed, the concept called systems thinking, systems theory or the systems approach was developed in the 1950s. Ludwig von Bertalanffy (1968) and Kenneth Boulding (1968) are regarded as founding fathers of systems thinking. They made attempts to develop General Systems Theory. The main idea of systems theory proposed by Bertalanffy is an open system such as a living organism interacting with its environment and exchanging information. Systems can be treated as organised complexity.

The concept of soft systems methodology, developed as an opposition to hard systems engineering (Checkland, 1999) applied in management theory and practice can be viewed as an extension of classical systems thinking. Soft systems methodology (SSM) is an approach for tackling problematical, complex messy situations of all kinds.

System Dynamics

System dynamics is an example of linking cybernetics and systems thinking with mathematical models including feedback and non-linearity as the characteristics of complexity. The core element of system dynamics is simulation models. The interpretation of complexity used in systems dynamics can be assigned to intuitive quantitative complexity, to quantitative complexity developed in systems thinking (feedback) and indirectly to complexity science (non-linear models). System dynamics have been applied in studying various social systems—company (business strategy), urban planning, world models (Forrester, 1975).

Complexity Studies

The term complexity studies, describing another group of interpretations of complexity-related ideas and concepts, is selected purposively as to make a distinction between the ideas called complexity science or complexity theory and other concepts not always directly associated with them. In this proposition complexity studies embody complexity science, the Stacey Matrix, Cynefin and the concepts of complexity of social systems of Niklas Luhmann.

Complexity Science

The impact of ideas relating to complexity which were developed in cybernetics and systems thinking had been significant but the real complexity revolution in science and in management theory and practice began with the development of a collection of mathematical models in the 1970s, including such concepts as deterministic chaos, non-equilibrium thermodynamics, synergetics developed by Hermann Haken, catastrophe theory, etc.

There are two terms used for describing this collection of mathematical models—complexity science and complexity theory without clearly delineated distinction. Bearing in mind the various opinions of authors using the terms complexity theory, e.g. (Jackson, 2019; Stacey, 2000;), complexity science (Richardson & Cilliers, 2001) or interchangeably (Stacey & Mowles, 2016), it is proposed to apply the term complexity science.

In consequence, complexity science embodies two areas. First, hard complexity science, including mathematical models of complexity and complexity-related ideas, and second, soft complexity including analogies and metaphors built with the terms in which those terms are treated as source domains. This interpretation of complexity science refers to the works of Nicolis and Prigogine (1989), Waldrop (1992), Kauffman (1993, 1995), Gell-Mann (1994), Holland (1995, 1998), Bar-Yam (1997) and was made popular by Gleick (1987/2011).

Complex systems are usually depicted by the following features: (1) Non-linearity of interactions among the elements, (2) Simple behaviour of elements contributing to intricacy of the system (3) Simple models describing and explaining the complex behaviour of systems.

Similarly, as in other cases, the typology of ideas belonging to complexity science is not unequivocal. Taking into account the surveyed general works on complexity, it may be assumed that the ideas viewed as the dominant interpretations in "hard" complexity science include the following, sometimes overlapping areas:

- chaos theory as the primary idea and associated with that concept complexity theory referring to non-linearity,
- the theory of dissipative structures developed in non-equilibrium thermodynamics,
- Complex Adaptive Systems (CAS)—mathematical models and soft (mixed) interpretations,
- the edge of chaos.

The vocabulary of complexity science includes a large variety of terms—intuitive, taken from other areas of complexity-related studies and specific indigenous terms, just quoting the most popular ones: adaptation, attractor, bifurcations, butterfly effect, catastrophe theory, chaos theory, coevolution, Complex Adaptive Systems, edge of chaos, emerging properties, far-from-equilibrium states, fractals, learning systems, non-linearity, open system, path dependence, scale-free networks, self-organisation, self-reflexivity, self-similarity, strange attractor, synergy, synergetics, turbulence.

The above list is an introduction to further studies in the multitude of works devoted to applications of complexity science in management theory and practice. They have become popular in the vocabulary of modern management theory and practice because they embody a strong appeal to intuition, sometimes even normative and emotional, not mentioning speculative, e.g. chaos, the edge of chaos, emergence, self-organisation, synergy, etc. They have to be treated with very high cautiousness and without fascination mirrored in such sentences—the environment is turbulent and chaotic, we are creative at the edge of chaos, the leader is a strange attractor, etc.

The multiple sources of these and similar approaches easily found in the management literature are purposively not quoted. Instead, the following reflections originated from the studies of complexity-related works in management theory and practice are presented.

1. They refer to organisations which in the ultimate resort are social constructs.

2. First and foremost, it must be remembered that those ideas are applied in management theory and practice as metaphors.
3. It should be then understood how those metaphors are created, what are their source domains and target domains.
4. It must be remembered that sometimes the names of the mathematical models used as the source domains were just incidental, e.g. the chaos theory (Li & Yorke, 1975; Lorenz, 1972, 1995), or the edge of chaos (Langton, 1992; Waldrop, 1992). The biggest error is to use them in management theory with an exact literal meaning.
5. They may have various interpretations and as the best example the Complex Adaptive Systems can be quoted. Their initial different mathematical interpretations Gell-Mann (1994) and Holland (1995) have turned into multiple quantitative, qualitative and mixed interpretations.

Before studying complexity of organisation of science a fundamental ontological question has to be answered. It concerns all social systems but here it is focused on organisation as defined in organisation and management theory. This question can be formulated as follows: What is an organisation? Is it a system understood as engineering or is it a pure social construct? It can be summarised with another question: Are organisations systems in the world or in the mind (Stacey & Mowles, 2016: 191)?

As to the first question, organisation is a complex adaptive system made of tangible and intangible components—human agents, physical and symbolic artefacts, which can be described and studied with mathematical models, verbal narratives and hybrid constructs. Does this pattern dominate the majority of applications of complexity-related ideas in management theory and practice? (McKelvey, 1997; Stacey, 1996).

An opposite understanding of organisation called complex Responsive Processes of Relating (later referred to as CRPR) has been presented in several works of Stacey and his co-workers (Stacey, 2000; Stacey et al., 2000). According to such interpretations, it is not the individuals who organise themselves but the pattern of their relationships in communicational and power terms. The process of communicating is an analogue of a complex adaptive system (Stacey, 2000: 148). These interpretations of complexity of organisation are mentioned here in order to show the depth of studies of strategy and change in the modern theory of management.

No unequivocal position is taken but it is only mentioned as to show the complexity of complexity-related discourse in organisation theory.

Stacey Matrix and Cynefin
These two concepts supported by well-known graphic illustrations have undoubtedly become one of most popular vehicles of transferring the complexity-related ideas to management theory and practice. They are presented here together as a part of complexity studies but it is necessary to underscore that the ideas of Ralph Stacey derive from mathematical models of complexity science while the Cynefin Framework is an indigenous idea from studying complexity of social systems developed by Dave Snowden.

The initial model, popularised as the "Stacey Matrix" embodying an attempt to distinguish degrees of simplicity, complication, complexity and chaos along two dimensions—proximity to certainty and proximity to agreement was for the first time published in Stacey (1996: 47). It is still used in the studies on the links between complexity-related ideas and various areas of management although the author had resigned from its application and explained the reasons for this decision (Stacey, 2012).

Cynefin, in Welsh equivalent to home, habitat, or as recently underscored, "Place of Your Multiple Belongings" (Snowden & Goh, 2021: 17) is another popular model of interpretations of complexity applied in management. It was developed by Snowden in the late 1990s and in the beginning of the twenty-first century (Kurtz & Snowden, 2003). The Cynefin Framework embraces five decision-making contexts (domains): known—simple (obvious), knowable—complicated, complex, chaos and disorder. Similarly, as was the Stacey Matrix, it has been widely applied in management with the use of a metaphorical sense of all these concepts. It is worthwhile to observe that the Cynefin Framework was constantly evolving in the subsequent versions of the works of its author and co-workers. The most recent version presented in Snowden and Goh (2021, p. 77) includes three domains, called also systems: Ordered, Complex and Chaotic. The domain described as Disorder is the state of not knowing which domain you are in. Since it is frequently confused with Chaos in this version it is labelled as A/C (Aporia/Confused).

Luhmann's Complexity of Social Systems
The concept of social system developed by Niklas Luhmann (2013) has gained a significant influence in management theory, especially in Europe.

The theory of social system is built on the idea of autopoiesis proposed by Maturana and Varela (1980) in theoretical biology. According to Luhmann, a social system can be treated as the system of meaningful communication. A complex system is one in which there are more possibilities than can be actualized. Complexity of operations means that the number of possible relations becomes too large with respect to the capacity of elements to establish relations. It means that complexity enforces selection. As an example, the survey of applications of Luhmann's ideas in organisation theory can be recalled (Seidl & Becker, 2006).

STRATEGY IMPLEMENTATION, ORGANISATIONAL CHANGE AND COMPLEXITY

Strategy Implementation: Comprehensive Approaches

It is not possible to elaborate a limited number of definitions, or in a broader sense, interpretations, of strategy implementation. It is usually treated as a process, which is distinguishable but at the same time interrelated with the process of strategy development (Hrebiniak, 2006). As to delineate the research area, several attempts were made to identify and to order these interpretations (Okumus, 2003; Reza & Hui, 2013; Yang et al., 2010). Okumus (2003: 875) proposed the following universal factors determining strategy implementation:

1. *Strategic content* including the development of strategy.
2. *Strategic context* is divided into external and internal context. The former including environmental uncertainty and the internal context including organisational structure, culture and leadership.
3. *Operational process* includes operational planning, resource allocation, people, communication and control.
4. *Outcome* including results of the implementation process.

Another attempt of ordering of interpretations of strategy implementation was made by Yang et al. (2010). They proposed three perspectives on the strategy implementation: process perspective, behavioural perspective and hybrid perspective. Coming out from their proposal, the following synthetic interpretations of relations between strategic management process, strategy implementation and organisational change are proposed (Table 5.2).

Table 5.2 Perspectives of strategy implementation

Perspective	Interpretation
Simple process perspective	Strategic management is a sequential process in which the stage of strategic decision is at the same time partly separated from the process of strategy implementation although they remain interdependent. Organisational change is treated as a result of this process
Behavioural perspective	Strategic process management, strategy implementation and organisational change are treated as actions resulting from the decision-making processes of managers (organisational units) involved in the process. Inherent limits of rationality (bounded rationality) and consequences of uncertainty are partly considered
Constructivist perspective	Strategy, organisation and their attributes are treated as social constructs developed in the processes of sensemaking. The processes of social construction of strategy and organisational change are perceived as parallel and interacting. Individual and organisational learning can be treated as an element of the process of social construction
Complex coevolutionary process perspective	Both processes—strategic management and organisational change are constantly mutually interacting, with processes of learning, feedback, iterations, recursion and reflexivity. Coevolution of various internal organisational units and coevolution of organisation with its environment are also considered. Strategy implementation is a part of this coevolutionary process. The constructivist (constructionist) perspective can be taken into account

Source own research based on (Hrebiniak, 2005, 2006; Lewin & Volberda, 1999; Okumus, 2003; Yang et al., 2010; Zubac et al., 2021)

The perspectives presented in Table 5.2 reflect the evolution of approaches to strategic management and interpretations of change in management. From a systemic point of view, the first perspective is somehow isolated from the remaining ones since it includes only one-directional interactions. The behavioural, the constructivist and the coevolutionary perspectives are interrelated. Seen from the same vantage point the last perspective, embodies the behavioural and constructivist perspectives. Treating the coevolutionary perspective as most universal gives ground for applications of all complexity-related ideas depicted earlier.

In the studies of strategy implementation, the distinction between strategy implementation and strategy execution constitutes another theoretical problem which cannot be reduced to a semantic puzzle. This distinction scrutinised by (Yang et al., 2010) is only signalled here and requires additional studies. Here only some examples are listed. In the literature on strategy implementations, two viewpoints can be distinguished.

In the first dominating one, strategy implementation is treated as synonymous, to strategy execution and no efforts are made to assign them different meaning. Hrebiniak (2006: 12) declares that: "Formulating strategy is difficult. Making strategy work – executing or implementing it throughout the organization – is even more difficult. Without effective implementation, no business strategy can succeed. Unfortunately, most managers know far more about developing strategy than they do about executing it". No distinction between strategy implementation and strategy execution was also made by Kaplan and Norton (2008) and Kotter et al. (2021). In the book with strategy execution in its title (Busulwa et al., 2019), those terms are also treated interchangeably but the explanation for such an interpretation is that it results from the iterative character of strategy implementation.

The following example of distinction between strategy implementation and strategy execution that has been invented in management consulting can be treated as a potential source of inspiration. Favaro (2015) treats the lack of distinction between strategy implementation and strategy execution as an important source of confusion influencing the practice of two-level strategic management—corporate strategy and business unit strategy. In this concept, implementing a strategy consists of all the decisions and activities required to turn the strategic choices at the corporate level and at the business level into reality. Strategy execution is defined as the decisions and activities which are undertaken in order to turn the implemented strategy into commercial success.

As it has been declared earlier, the terminological carefulness is decisive in sophisticated studies in those areas of management theory and practice where any complexity-based interpretative approaches are applied. The absence of distinctions between implementation meaning, a separate part of the strategic management process and strategy execution embodying the entire process, shows that by the majority of researchers this distinction is treated as purely semantic and negligible. It creates an important methodological hurdle in applying the complexity-related ideas in studying the relations between the strategic management process and strategy implementation. Taking this conclusion as an encouragement for the further, more profound research, in this chapter the term strategy implementation is used with full awareness of the above terminological subtleties and the need for further research.

Cybernetics and Systems Thinking

Focusing attention on the applications of complexity-related ideas originated in cybernetics and systems thinking in the studies of the relations between strategy implementation and organisational changes, the examples are drawn from the following areas are preliminarily depicted:

- cybernetics: feedback, requisite variety, disorganised and organised complexity,
- managerial cybernetics,
- systems thinking.

The ideas drawn from cybernetics and systems thinking have a significant impact on the concept of strategic management created by H. Igor Ansoff (1965, 1979), e.g. the idea of turbulence. In a comprehensive work on strategy implementation, broadly defined complexity echoing the ideas of organised and disorganised complexity of Weaver (1948), and the law of requisite variety are treated as an epistemological foundation of the study of the main issues of strategic management, including strategy implementation (Ansoff et al., 2019).

The Viable System Model (VSM), the key idea of managerial cybernetics developed by Beer (1957, 1979) as an instrument supporting strategy implementation in complex organisation, can be scrutinised from a double perspective. The first perspective concerns the time when it was originated. The VSM by definition was regarded as a comprehensive multi-level model of organisation whose aim was to improve its management in the complex environment. In the time of its development, the 1970s and 1980s, it was applied but without any specific emphasis put on strategy implementation. It was designated to deal both with strategy and its implementation.

The second perspective is connected with more recent proposals of applications of the VSM in strategy implementation. Two examples are representative for this perspective. In a conference paper (Espejo, 2000) shows a possibility to apply the general concept of the VSM and his original method, that in improving the process of implementation, new strategic and implementation processes are derived through the design of organisational structures which establish novel forms of co-operative relationships based on trust and self-organising autonomy. The main aim of the Espejo's concept is to develop a methodology of the strategic management process embodying process of strategy implementation, which in turn, is referring to complexity, to the law of requisite variety and to the learning process. This concept is only signalled here and can be treated as an example of applicability of ideas invented in cybernetics and in management cybernetics in the early period of their development in the 1950s. In order to achieve the balance implied by Ashby's law at a desirable level of performance, management must develop strategies, supported by others, for attenuating (reducing) the variety observed from the situation being managed, while "amplifying" its variety when transforming a decision into action. Such an approach is suggested in order to deal with hierarchical structure of organisation in the process of development and implementation of strategy.

In the second example, Espinosa et al. (2015) applied the VSM in order to facilitate the second learning so as to enable the company under scrutiny to redesign their structures, functions and roles in a way that would create a better context for strategy implementation. Without delving into other methodological details, e.g. the Soft Systems Methodology (SSM) Checkland, the VSM had proved its usefulness as a metalanguage, a hermeneutical tool allowing for a more profound engagement of managers and employees in the changes of their organisation.

Systems thinking was used as a conceptual foundation of a synthetic strategy implementation model by Reza and Hui (2013). After studying all the main models of strategy implementation, their main conclusion was that none of those models meets the standards of effectiveness of implementation. They have collected 40 determinants of the strategy execution process (they use implementation and execution as synonyms). Referring to the ideas of systems thinking (Bertalanffy, 1968; Boulding, 1968) they proposed a synthetic model of strategy implementation treated as system. The model embodies forty factors and their grouping are as follows: **montrol** (monitoring & learning, control and measurement/metrics/evaluation); **strategising** (strategy formulation, strategy, strategy planning and portfolio analysis); **structuring** (organisational structure, and operating structure), goal-setting (focus/direction, purpose/objective, goal breaks down, long-range goal, mid-range goal and operating objective); **alignment** (adjustment/adapt, and alignment), S4Ps (systems, processes, projects, procedures, programme and reward system); **human resource management (HRM)** (human resources, tasks, clarity of roles and performance); **capsources** (capability, capacity building, resource allocation and supportive budget); **cultentity** (culture, identity and commitment); **innocationship** (innovation, communication, strategic leadership and coordination), achieved objectives, and finally external environment. Classifying these forty factors based on their similarities or logical connectivity led to the creation of ten groups of factors and two individual elements, which constitute the synthetic system of implementation.

Without delving into a detailed description of the proposed system and expressing a sceptical approach as to whether describing any system with 40 characteristics is effective—possibility of clear delineation of those characteristics, without overlap, it must be concluded that this proposal constitutes an innovative example of ways of approaching strategy implementation and organisational change from a systemic point of view.

Complexity Studies

A comprehensive study of the role of complexity-related ideas in strategy implementation leads to the conclusion that publications on that topic are rather scarce, contrary to an impressive amount and thematic scope of works on complexity and change and complexity and strategic management, quoted in part 3. Two approaches can be distinguished in the use of complexity-related ideas in strategy implementation. The first, which can be called indirect, or universal, includes those ideas applied without detailed reference to the discourse on complexity, and the second, direct, where specific complexity-related ideas are directly referred to in the discourse.

In the first group undoubtedly the problem of relations between deliberate control and emergent strategy analysed by Mintzberg seems to be the most influential one. In his view managers always try to control, at least partly, the process of strategy formulation and implementation. On the other hand, strategy can be viewed as emerging via the interplay of stakeholders. In consequence Mintzberg (2007: 7) regards strategy formulation as deliberate and strategy implementation as both deliberate and emergent. He adds that it is difficult to imagine a total absence of intention as would be expected in purely emergent strategies. In a broader sense, it can be treated as the process of learning and sensemaking (Weick, 1995).

While treating emergence as a fundamental phenomenon in strategy formulation and implementation, a high level of cautiousness should be applied. Emergence together with self-organisation is likely the most frequently used and abused metaphors transferred from complexity studies to management. As an example of necessary cautiousness in applying the studies of strategy implementation and change, the subtleties of emergence are discussed in a more profound way. The conclusions from this discussion could be helpful both in more general considerations and in more specific examples of relations between strategy implementation and change.

A comprehensive critical approach to emergence in management based on a survey of interpretations of emergence in various domains of knowledge was prepared by Goldstein (2011). It is shown that emergence is a phenomenon which has several functional interpretations deriving from such areas as condensed matter physics, non-equilibrium thermodynamics (dissipative structures), non-linearity and chaos in dynamical systems, computational emergence, social emergence (social networks) and biological emergence. Additionally, Goldstein shows erroneous and simplified interpretations of emergence, for example, sudden emergence of complexity from simplicity, incorrect connection of emergence with self-organisation and incorrectness of the model of Langton which gave ground for the famous "edge of chaos" metaphor. The analysis of Goldstein leads to the conclusion that if it is assumed that the organisation is a complex system in engineering terms, then a better understanding of emergence could be helpful in developing its actions increasing adaptivity of organisation. If it is assumed, and this approach is more justifiable from a current perspective that emergence is usually treated as a metaphor, thus it is necessary to understand better for the source fields of this metaphor and to apply them in order to understand more profoundly the origins of strategy as a metaphorically understood phenomenon, and subsequently, to treat the emergence as a result of relations between strategy implementation and organisational change.

As a representative example of the second, detailed approach, a comprehensive study of Busulwa et al. (2019) in which strategy execution, synonymously understood as strategy implementation is studied with the use of a concept taken from complexity studies. They refer to a broad range of complexity-related ideas but as the fundamental ones they treat the definitions of complexity and related concepts taken from one of earlier versions of the Cynefin Framework (Snowden & Boone, 2007) are used as a conceptual framework for theoretical considerations, and the source of definitions of chaotic, complexity, complicated and obvious. It must be added that the Cynefin Framework is evolving and some ideas associated with complexity in management have been changed and added since those versions (Snowden & Goh, 2021).

The second main source of inspiration by complexity-related ideas in the studies of strategy execution is connected with the concept of simple rules from Sull and Eisenhardt (2012). Designed as an instrument for reducing complexity in management, simple rules were applied in the empirical studies, allowing the authors to identify the number of companies applying simple rules in executing their strategies. It is worthwhile to mention that in their book Busulwa et al. (2019) do not distinguish between strategy execution and strategy implementation; this is what makes the assessment of the role of complexity-related ideas in strategy implementation more difficult.

Direct reference to these specific complexity-related ideas was an inspiration to the identification of the ways/how complexity is affecting strategy implementation. First, complexity is the source of uncertainty affecting strategic management. Second, complexity influences whether deliberate strategy, emergent strategy or a mixture of both will be realised. Third, complexity influences the perceptions of employees and, as a result, their engagement levels (Busulwa et al., 2019, p. 11–13). It must be added, that these three patterns are associated not only with two ideas borrowed from complexity studies but can be treated as a commonly accepted framework.

The main conclusions of this study are general and relatively well-known: strategic leaders should recognise the types of complexity, and subsequently should be able to pursue a relevant strategy, to implement them in optimal way and be able to help to limit any negative impact of complexity on stakeholders among whom the role of employees is emphasised (Busulwa et al., 2019).

The applications of complexity-related ideas in studying the relations between strategy implementation and strategic change presented in the above examples show two patterns, which always should be taken into consideration. First, complexity studies are a source field of analogies and metaphors. Second, complexity-related mathematical models provide more profound insights into the functioning of organisations. However, when applying such models, the level of abstraction deriving from too strict boundary conditions could make them not relevant to the reality of organisation. Subsequently, when the complexity-related concepts are applied thus, a more profound analysis of their origins, advantages and limitations must be taken into account.

Coevolutionary Perspective

Seen in a systemic context, the coevolutionary approach is undoubtedly the most advanced and sophisticated interpretation of relations ("interface"), between strategy implementation and strategic change. In the most general sense, coevolution of any kind of systems with their environment and internal coevolution embodies all types of processes identified in complexity studies. The most important ones are adaptation, emergence, learning, mutual learning, selection, self-organisation, synergy.

In the concept proposed by Lewin and Volberda (1999), coevolution embodies variation, selection and retention. They treat the organisation as evolving internally and the external system and strategic management process is both influenced and influences the process of organisational change. Coevolution is viewed as the concept allowing to extend the dilemma selection vs. adaptation. Additionally, the coevolutionary approach is grounded in the state-of-the-art of knowledge concerning broadly defined complex systems (Holland, 1995, 1998; Kauffman, 1993, 1995; McKelvey, 1997, 1999).

The general research framework proposed by Lewin and Volberda (1999) includes ideas of McKelvey (1997) and later developed by McKelvey (1999) who directly used models taken from complexity science in studying coevolution in management and, in particular, in strategy implementation. The studies of coevolution developed by McKelvey, similarly as other works on complexity and management of this author, are built on abstract mathematical models of variously defined complexity. They are treated as applicable in management theory and practice. They are presented not in order to explain detailed characteristics of coevolutionary processes but to show primarily the potential usefulness of complexity-related models in studying the role of coevolution for a better understanding of relations between strategy implementation and organisational change.

In the studies of complexity of organisation, McKelvey (1997, 1999) treats organisations as socio-technical systems which derives from scientific realism (McKelvey, 1997). Without delving into the subtleties of philosophy of science and following earlier explanations of complexity, it may be stated that in this understanding the organisation can be described as a socio-technical system and can be studied with mathematical models drawn from various domains of complexity science. The term metaphor is used only twice in McKelvey (1997) and once in McKelvey (1999) and they do not refer to complexity. On the one hand, looking from the current perspective, such an approach may stir doubts concerning such strong boundary conditions in studying organisation, e.g. the possibility of operationalization of multiple characteristics of organisation. On the other, assuming that organisations can be modelled and simulated with models of various relevance to reality, such an approach seems to some extent relevant to theoretical and practical demands. This concept is treated as an inspiration for Lewin and Volberda in their narrative of coevolution inside and outside of the organisation which can be described with the following characteristics (Lewin & Volberda, 1999: 526–528).

1. Multilevelness/embeddedness constitutes the main universal idea of McKelvey applicable in studying strategy implementation and change (Lewin & Volberda, 1999; McKelvey, 1997, 1999). Coevolutionary effects exist at multiple levels and they are interacting with each other. McKelvey makes a distinction between coevolution within organisation (microcoevolution) and coevolution between the organisations and their niche (macrocoevolution). This distinction means that processes of variation, selection, and retention operate within the organisation and interact with similar processes operating at the population level. Macrocoevolutionary approach

refers to coevolutionary competitive context and microcoevolution concerns coevolution of intrafirm resources, dynamic capabilities. Under such circumstances it is necessary to consider multiple levels of coevolution. In consequence, microcoevolutionary order within organisations emerges in the context of macroevolutionary selectionist competitive pressure (McKelvey, 1997: 361).
2. Multidirectional causality meaning that the internal and external coevolution is the result of multitude of interactions with other units. In such a case, the identification of causal links are often difficult to identify.
3. Non-linearity meaning that changes in one unit may lead to unpredictable counterintuitive changes in other units through unexpected feedback connections.
4. Positive feedback and recursive mutual causality. Each organisation and its elements are mutually influenced internally and mutually interact with the environment.
5. Path and history dependence meaning that evolution of an organisation and of its elements is constrained by their past evolution.

In his subsequent paper, McKelvey (1999) applied the Kauffman's (1993) biological complexity models as to show how they could help in a better understanding of the processes of coevolution in organisation connected with strategy development and implementation.

The McKelvey's paper demands for a profound knowledge of mathematical models of complexity, therefore its content, is only initially signalled as to show the directions of research and the depth of potential analyses for strategy development and implementation. The main area of analysis is the multicoevolutionary complexity defined as follows (McKelvey, 1999: 294): "Multicoevolutionary complexity in firms is defined by moving natural selection processes inside firms and down to a 'parts' level of analysis". "Multicoevolutionary complexity concerns multilevel phenomena in organisation with the microagents at the lowest level".

The study of microevolutionary complexity was conducted at Porter's value chain level and was focused on microstate activities by agents (microagents). Intrafirm and interfirm multicoveolutionary complexity was modelled with the Kaufmann's concepts of fitness landscape, rugged landscape and the edge of chaos and non-equilibrium thermodynamics.

Additionally, the Kauffman model was used as an extension of network sociology as declared by the author (McKelvey, 1999: 314).

The main conclusions deriving from the relations between the coevolutionary approach and complexity-related ideas in studying strategy development and implementation are similar as in the previous example. Here they have some additional specificity. The coevolutionary character of strategy implementation and organisational change is self-evident. However, it is only the mathematical models of complexity and related ideas treated in a metaphorical sense which can be applied for refinement of description and analysis of coevolutionary processes in the organisation and between organisations. It was seen how profoundly the inspiration from the interpretations of mathematical models by McKelvey (1997) influenced more universal ideas of Lewin and Volberda (1999).

Conclusions

The aim of this chapter was to provide a preliminary assessment of how complexity-related ideas could be used to better understand the interrelationship between strategy implementation and organisational change. As a theoretical and research framework, the concept of such an interface proposed by Zubac et al. (2021) was used. It was assumed that this metaphorical interface can be used both as an introductory metaphorical framework and as a point of departure for more detailed studies.

This chapter is based on the fundamental assumption that, broadly defined, complexity studies embodying such domains as cybernetics, systems thinking and various areas of research called complexity science can play a significant role for understanding strategy implementation and change. A survey of the literature led to the following conclusions:

1. In the early period of development of cybernetics, systems theory and related ideas from the 1960s until the 1970s, applications of ideas borrowed from these domains in studying relations between strategy process, strategy implementation and organisational change were limited. Such a situation was partly caused by the dominance of simplified models of strategy implementation as a linear process to a large extent separable from strategy process.

2. In the subsequent developments, the ideas taken from broadly defined complexity science allowed much more advanced theoretical ideas, such as emergence, self-organisation, coevolution, edge of chaos, etc. which led to a better understanding of the relations between strategy process, strategy implementation (strategy execution) and organisational change. They were used both as analogies and metaphors and as mathematical models.
3. Experience stemming from applications of complexity-related ideas in strategic management shows that after an initial, sometimes superficial fascination, especially by such concepts as emergence and the edge of chaos, a more balanced perspective is emerging in which qualitative considerations are more cautious and mathematical models are more relevant to the reality of organisation.
4. This more cautious approach can help to conduct more profound, broader and practice-oriented studies of the relations between strategy process, strategy implementation and organisational change.

The results of the study suggest the following directions of research:

1. The concept of coevolutionary complexity seems to be the most promising framework of studying the interface between strategy implementation and strategic change. Its usefulness is enhanced by the possibility of applying both advanced mathematical models and more sophisticated complexity-related qualitative considerations.
2. Development of Industry 4.0 and changes in the business environment will be the other determinants for applying complexity-related ideas when studying the interface, between strategy implementation and organisational change.

References

Allen, P., Maguire, S., & McKelvey, B. (Eds.). (2011). *The Sage handbook of complexity and management*. Sage.
Ansoff, H. I. (1965). *Corporate strategy—An analytic approach to business policy for growth and expansion*. McGraw-Hill.
Ansoff, H. I. (1979). *Strategic management*. Wiley.

Ashby, W. R. (1957). *An introduction to cybernetics*. Chapman & Hall.
Ansoff, H. I., Kipley, D., Lewis, A. O., Helm-Stevens, R., & Ansoff, R. (2019). *Implanting strategic management*. Palgrave Macmillan.
Bar-Yam, Y. (1997). *Dynamics of complex systems*. Addison-Wesley.
Beer, S. (1957). *Cybernetics and management*. The English Universities Press Ltd.
Beer, S. (1972). *Brain of the firm*. Allen Lane, The Penguin Press.
Beer, S. (1979). *The heart of enterprise*. John Wiley & Sons.
Boulding, K. E. (1968). General systems theory: The skeleton of science. In W. Buckley (Ed.), *Modern systems research for the behavioral scientist* (pp. 3–10). Aldine.
Boulton, J. G., Allen, P. M., & Bow, C. (2015) *Embracing Complexity*. Oxford University Press.
Brown, S. L., & Eisenhardt, K. M. (1998). *Competing on the edge: Strategy as structured chaos*. Harvard Business School Press.
Busulwa, R., Tice, M., & Gurd, B. (2019). *Strategy execution and complexity*. Routledge, Kindle Edition.
Castellani, B., & Gerrits, L. (2021). 2021 map of complexiy sciences, Ar & science factory. https://www.art-sciencefactory.com/complexity-map_feb09.html
Checkland, P. (1999). *Systems thinking, systems practice. includes a 30-year retrospective*. John Wiley & Sons.
Cilliers, P. (1998). *Complexity and postmodernism: Understanding complex systems*. Routledge.
Dooley, K. J. (1997). A complex adaptive systems model of organization change. *Nonlinear Dynamics, Psychology, and Life Sciences, 1*(1), 69–97.
Emery, F. E., & Trist, E. L. (1965). The causal texture of organizational environments. *Human Relations, 18*(1), 21–32.
Espejo, R. (2000). *Giving requisite variety to strategic and implementation processes: Theory and practice*. Paper based on a talk given by the author at the London School of Economics in November, 1997. https://www.researchgate.net/publication/228772758_Giving_Requisite_Variety_to_Strategic_and_Implementation_Processes_Theory_and_Practice
Espinosa, A., Reficco, E., Martinez, A., & Guzman, D. (2015). A methodology for supporting strategy implementation based on the VSM: A case study in a Latin-American multi-national. *European Journal of Operational Research, 240*, 202–212.
Favaro, K. (2015). Defining strategy, implementation, and execution. *Harvard Business Review, 31*. https://hbr.org/2015/03/defining-strategy-implementation-and-execution
Forrester, J. W. (1975). *Collected papers of Jay W. Forrester* Pegasus Communications.

Gleick, J. (1987). *Chaos: Making of a new science.* Viking Press.
Gleick, J. (2011). *Chaos: Making a new science. enhanced edition,* Open Road. Integrated Media. Kindle Edition.
Goldstein, J. (2011). Emergence in complex systems. In P. Allen, S. Maguire & B. McKelvey (Eds.), *The SAGE handbook of complexity and management SAGE publications* (pp. 65–78). Kindle Edition.
Gell-Mann, M. (1994). *The quark and the jaguar: Adventures in the simple and the complex.* W.H. Freeman and Company.
Graetz, F., & Smith, A. C. T. (2010). Managing organizational change: A Philosophies of change approach. *Journal of Change Management, 10*(2), 135–154.
Graetz, F., & Smith, A. C. T. (2011). *Philosophies of organizational change.* Edward Elgar.
Grundy, T. (1992). *Implementing strategic change.* Kogan Page.
Holland, J. H. (1995). *Hidden order: How adaptation Builds complexity.* Addison-Wesley.
Holland, J. H. (1998). *Emergence: From chaos to order.* Addison-Wesley.
Hrebiniak, L. G. (2005). *Making strategy work: Leading effective execution and change.* Pearson Education.
Hrebiniak, L. G. (2006). Obstacles to effective strategy implementation. *Organizational Dynamics, 35*(1), 12–31. https://doi.org/10.1016/j.orgdyn.2005.12.001
Jackson, M. C. (2019). *Critical systems thinking and the management of complexity.* Kindle Edition.
Kanter, R. M., Stein, B. A., & Jick, T. D. (1992). *The challenge of organizational change.* The Free Press
Kaplan, R. S., & Norton, D. P. (2008). *The execution premium: Linking strategy to operations for competitive advantage.* Harvard Business School Publishing.
Kauffman, S. A. (1993). *The origins of order: Self-organization and selection in evolution.* Oxford University Press.
Kauffman, S. A. (1995). *At home in the universe. The search for laws of self-organization and complexity.* Oxford University Press.
Kotter, J. P. (1996). *Leading change.* Harvard Business School Press.
Kotter, J. P., Akhtar, V., & Gupta, G. (2021). *Change: How organizations achieve hard-to-imagine results in uncertain and volatile times.* Wiley.
Kurtz, C.F., & Snowden, D. J. (2003). The new dynamics of strategy: Sensemaking in a complex and complicated World. *IBM Systems Journal, 3*(42), 462–483.
Langton, C. G. (1992). Life at the Edge of Chaos, in Artificial Life II, *SFI Studies in the Sciences of Complexity,* 41–91.

Lewin, K. (1947). Frontiers in group dynamics: Concept, method and reality in social science; social equilibria and social change. *Human Relations, 1*(1), 5–41. https://doi.org/10.1177/001872674700100103

Lewin, A. Y., & Volberda, H. W. (1999). Prolegomena on coevolution: A framework for research on strategy and new organizational forms. *Organization Science, 10*(5), 519–534. https://doi.org/10.1287/orsc.10.5.519

Li, T. Y., & Yorke, J. A. (1975). Period three implies chaos. *The American Mathematical Monthly, 82*(10), 985–992.

Lloyd, S. (2001). Measures of complexity: A nonexhaustive list, *IEEE Control Systems Magazine, 21*(4), 7–8.

Lorenz, E. N. (1972/1995). Predictability: Does the flap of a butterfly's wings in Brazil set off a tornado in Texas? 139th Annual Meeting of the American Association for the Advancement of Science (29 Dec 1972). In E. N. Lorenz (Ed.), *Essence of chaos*. University of Washington Press, Appendix 1, 181–184.

Luhmann, N. (2013). *Introduction to systems theory*. Polity Press.

Maturana, H., & Varela, F. (1980). *Autopoiesis and cognition. The realisation of the living*. Boston Studies in the Philosophy of Science # 42. Riedel Publishing.

McKelvey, B. (1997). Quasi-natural organization science. *Organization Science, 8*(4), 352–380. https://doi.org/10.1287/orsc.8.4.351

McKelvey, B. (1999). Avoiding complexity catastrophe in coevolutionary pockets: Strategies for rugged landscapes. *Organization Science, 10*(3), 294–321. https://doi.org/10.1287/orsc.10.3.294

Mintzberg, H. (2007). *Tracking strategies: Towards a general theory*. Oxford University Press.

Mintzberg, H., & Lampel, J. (1999). Reflecting on the strategy process. *Sloan Management Review, 40*(3), 21–30.

Morgan, G. (1986). *Images of organization*. Sage.

Nicolis, G., & Prigogine, I. (1989). *Exploring complexity: An introduction*. W.H. Freeman.

Okumus, F. (2003). A framework to implement strategies in organizations. *Management Decision, 41*(9), 871–882. https://doi.org/10.1108/00251740310499555

Reza, A., & Hui, T. (2013). A synthetic strategy implementation model. *Series British Academy of Management Conference Proceedings 2013*, 10 September. https://www.bl.uk/collection-items/synthetic-strategy-implementation-model

Richardson, K., & Cilliers, P. (2001). Special editors' introduction: What is complexity science? *A View from Different Directions, Emergence, Complexity and Organization, 3*(1), 5–23.

Seidl, D., & Becker, K. H. (Eds.). (2006). *Niklas Luhmann and organization studies*. CBS Press.

Snowden, D., & Goh, Z. (2021). *Cynefin–Weaving sense-making into the fabric of our world*. Cognitive Edge Pte Ltd., Kindle Edition.

Snowden, D. J., & Boone, M. E. (2007). A leader's framework for decision making. *Harvard Business Review, 85*(11), 68–76.

Stacey, R. D. (1996). *Strategic management and organisational dynamics*. Pitman Publishing.

Stacey, R. D. (2000). *Strategic management and organizational dynamics. The challenge of complexity*. Pearson Education Limited.

Stacey, R. (2012). Comment on debate article: Coaching psychology coming of age: The challenges we face in the messy world of complexity. *International Coaching Psychology Review, 7*(1), 91–95.

Stacey, R. D., Griffin, D., & Shaw, P. (2000). *Complexity and management*. Routledge.

Stacey, R. D., & Mowles, Ch. (2016). *Strategic management and organisational dynamics: The challenge of complexity to ways of thinking about organisations*. Pearson Education Limited.

Sull, D., & Eisenhardt, K. (2012). Simple rules for a complex world. *Harvard Business Review, 90*(9), 68.

The Oxford Handbook of Strategy Implementation. (2016). Hitt, M. A., Jackson, S. E., Carmona, S., Bierman, L., Shalley C. E., & Wright, M. (Eds.). Oxford University Press.

Van de Ven, A. H. (1992). Suggestions for studying strategy process: A research note. *Strategic Management Journal, 13*(5), 169–188.

Van de Ven, A., & Poole, M. (1995). Explaining development and change in organizations. *The Academy of Management Review, 20*(3), 510–540.

Van de Ven, A. H., & Sun, K. (2011). Breakdowns in implementing models of organization change. *Academy of Management Perspectives, 25*(3), 58–74. https://doi.org/10.5465/AMP.2011.63886530

von Bertalanffy, L. (1968). *General systems theory*. Braziller.

von Foerster, H. (1982). *Observing systems: A collection of papers by Heinz von Foerster*. Intersystems Publications.

Waddell, D. M., Cummings, T. G., & Worley, C. G. (2011). *Organizational change: Development and transformation, Asia Pacific* (4th ed.). Cengage Learning.

Waldrop, M. M. (1992). *Complexity: The emerging science at the edge of order and chaos*. Simon & Schuster.

Weaver, W. (1948). Science and complexity. *American Scientist, 36*(4), 536–544.

Weick, K. E. (1995). *Sensemaking in organizations*. Sage.

Wheelen, T. L., & Hunger, J. D. (2008). *Strategic management and policy* (11th ed.). Prentice Hall.

Wiener, N. (1948). *Cybernetics: Or control and communication in the animal and the machine*. Hermann & Cie and MIT Press.

Yang, L., Guo-hui, S., & Eppler, M. J. (2010). Making strategy work: A literature review on the factors influencing strategy implementation. In P. Mazzola & F. W. Kellermanns (Eds.), *Handbook of research on strategy process* (pp. 165–183). Edward Elgar.

Zubac, A., Dasborough, M., Hughes, K., Jiang, Z., Kirkpatrick, S., Martinsons, M. G., Tucker, D., & Zwikael, O. (2021). The Strategy and change interface: Understanding "enabling" processes and cognitions. *Management Decision, 59*(3), 481–505.

PART II

The Financial Strategy

CHAPTER 6

Introduction: The Financial Strategy

Angelina Zubac, Danielle Tucker, Ofer Zwikael, Kate Hughes, and Shelley Kirkpatrick

A. Zubac (✉)
University of Queensland, Brisbane, QLD, Australia
e-mail: a.zubac@business.uq.edu.au; Angelina.zubac@aim.com.au; az@strategylink.com.au

D. Tucker
University of Essex, Colchester, Essex, UK
e-mail: dtucker@essex.ac.uk

O. Zwikael
Australian National University, Canberra, ACT, Australia
e-mail: ofer.zwikael@anu.edu.au

K. Hughes
Technological University Dublin, Dublin, Ireland
e-mail: kate.hughes@hughes-scm.com

S. Kirkpatrick
The MITRE Corporation, McLean, VA, USA
e-mail: skirkpatrick@mitre.org

© The Author(s), under exclusive license to Springer Nature Singapore Pte Ltd. 2022
A. Zubac et al. (eds.), *Effective Implementation of Transformation Strategies*, https://doi.org/10.1007/978-981-19-2336-4_6

Consistent with the notion that strategies are made up of an amalgam of strategies and, as a result, must be implemented with this in mind, the two chapters in this section explain the role of a financial strategy in markedly different ways. In a nutshell, Chapter 4 by Angelina Zubac argues that financial strategies are primarily concerned with the management and transformation of financial capital as an all-encompassing strategic function. Chapter 5 by Mark Pickering argues financial strategies define how organisations are required to operationalise their strategic priorities using its financial resources over time. Either way, both chapters clarify how the contemporary organisation can achieve high levels of strategic alignment by implementing an effective financial strategy.

Thus, as depicted in Fig. 6.1, both chapters explain how a financial strategy can enable an organisation, that is, help it achieve its various customer value creation and resource development objectives, as well as address its societal obligations. As one can see by examining Fig. 6.1, this means that both chapters explain how the financial strategy allows the organisation to deal with the pressures that emanate from the external environment. The idea that a potentially large number of (sub)processes and cognitions must be rationalised through a financial strategy is key here. Just as the external environment changes, the organisation must change how it coordinates its disparate parts. Therefore, managers need to continuously consider how best to utilise the organisation's financial resources to build capabilities in order to undertake necessary activities. When the capabilities that are built lead to high performance outcomes, it is because they enable the organisation's managers to sense and seize opportunities, as well as understand and mitigate threats, and judiciously reconfigure the organisation through its financial resources to set it up for the future.

The first chapter in this section by Angelina Zubac, *Implementing a financial strategy: Managing financial capital, investing in people, balancing risk and developing critical resources*, uses a firm theoretic framework to explain the two fundamental set of activities of which a financial strategy is concerned: (1) the management of financial capital, and (2) the transformation of financial capital into human, risk and resource capital. In regard to the management of financial capital, it is argued that even if an organisation starts very lean, in the long run, its scope will be limited unless it invests in growth or its own sustainability. To put it differently, to remain viable and stay in business, it will be necessary to fund its activities at some point by participating in the capital

6 INTRODUCTION: THE FINANCIAL STRATEGY

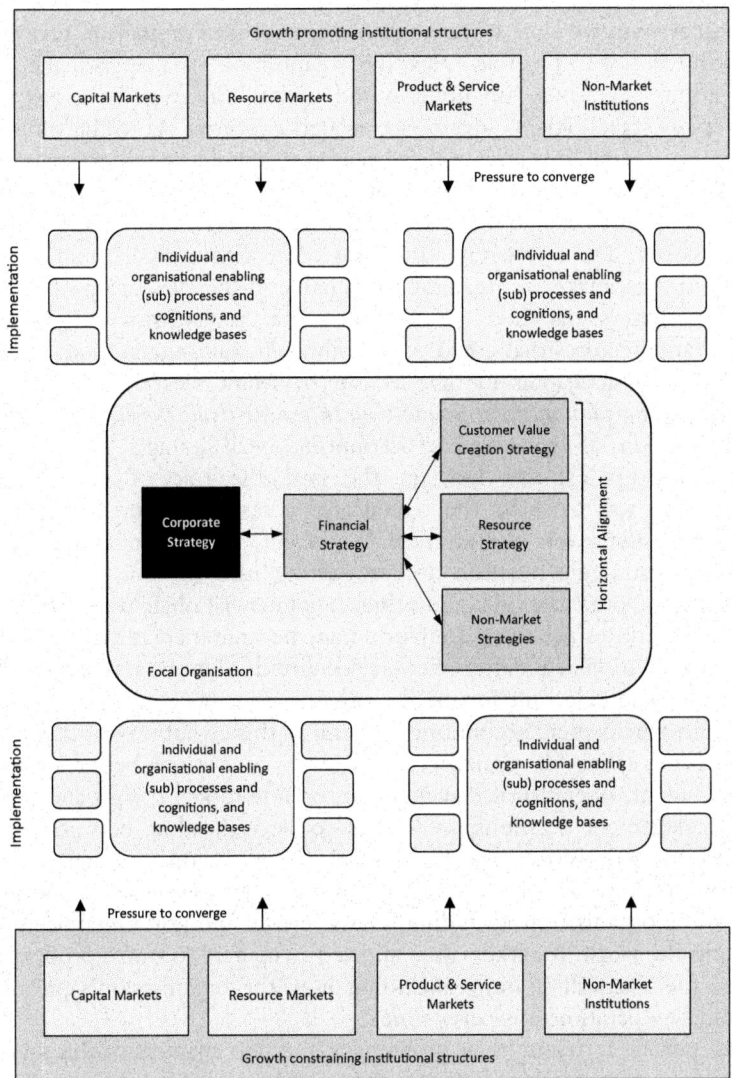

Fig. 6.1 Implementing strategy and organisational change: a financial strategy focus

market system, which is at the heart of the system of capitalism. Likewise, growth will not be possible unless the organisation's managers make debt and equity mix, and cash holding and capital allocation decisions that reflect key stakeholders' governance related concerns. As to the transformation of capital, it is argued that because stakeholders help to shape the organisation, it is necessary for the organisation to build stocks of human, risk and resource capital that also reflect what stakeholders want from the organisation. These different categories of applied capital, to all intents and purposes, make an organisation valuable in the eyes of stakeholders. The problem is that there are many potential human, risk and resource capital architectures that could potentially define an organisation.

The second chapter in this section by Mark Pickering, *An evolution: Turning management accounting into a strategic function*, describes the evolution of management accounting into strategic management accounting. It explains how in the past the role of management accounting was to assist the operational parts of the organisation to achieve greater levels of efficiency. As a result, it was not considered to be a very strategic function despite getting into the "nitty gritty" of ensuring the organisation could achieve its financial objectives. However, over time and as the market environment became increasingly competitive, an evolution as a matter of course occurred. Management accounting became a strategic function of the organisation, hence, it evolved into strategic management accounting. Central to this evolution was the desire to make it easier for managers at all levels to execute better strategic management, operational management, organisational design and financial management decisions, as well as connect the dots between all of these critical decision areas. Many tools and techniques of analysis and decision-making were subsequently fine-tuned or developed to be used across the organisation, including across vertical and horizontal decision-making domains. Together, they allowed managers to more proficiently frame the financial strategy, including how the organisation's priorities should be operationalised over time.

As indicated, despite their differences, the two chapters of this section complement each other. Their findings and arguments also overlap at times. As a result, the two chapters provide insight into how Fig. 6.1 can be further adapted to clarify the capabilities that allow an organisation to successfully articulate and implement its financial strategies. The two chapters' insights in toto are depicted in Fig. 6.2.

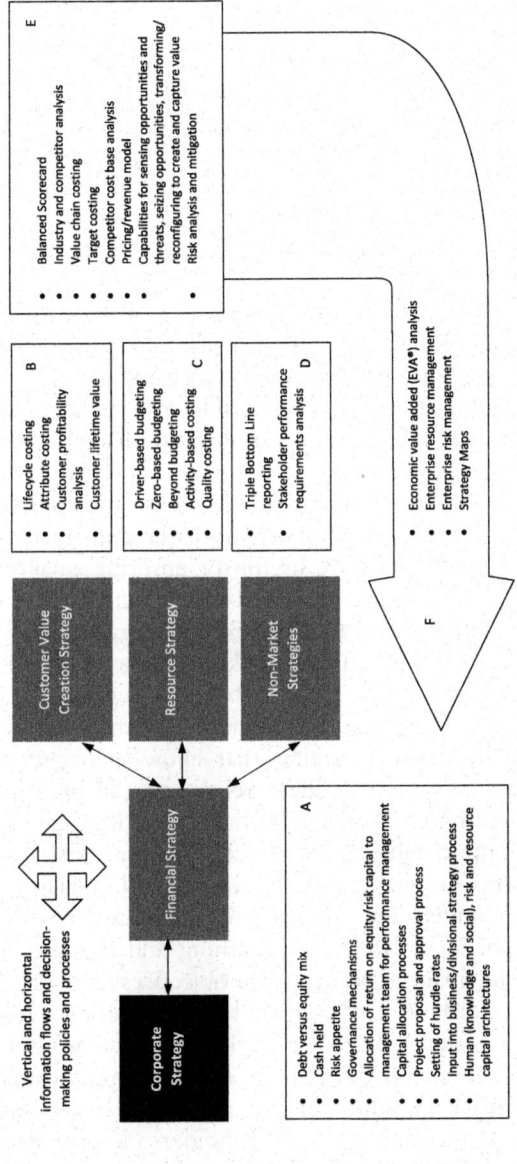

Fig. 6.2 Financial strategy: information flows and decision-making policies and processes

As the box labelled "A" in Fig. 6.2 shows by where it sits between the corporate strategy and financial strategy boxes, there are a number of capabilities, including tools and techniques of analysis and decision-making that enable the corporate (or overall) strategy and the financial strategy to align. For instance, once a decision has been made at the corporate level about what is a suitable risk appetite for the whole organisation to embrace, the financial strategy must be implemented with this in mind. Methods must be put in place to ensure the different parts of the organisation engage in activities or build capabilities in a manner that reflects the level of risk that has been deemed appropriate for the organisation to take.

The boxes, "B", "C" and "D" in Fig. 6.2 demonstrate the capabilities, that is, the tools and techniques of analysis and decision-making that can be used to support the organisation's customer value creation, resource and non-market strategies, respectively. For instance, managers implementing a customer value creation strategy are likely to find information about customer profitability over time very useful. Managers implementing a resource strategy that involves ensuring high levels of operational efficiency are likely to find activity-based and quality costing especially useful. These methods are useful for ensuring quality/fit-for-purpose products and services are produced cost effectively and without wastage. Managers implementing a non-market strategy are likely to find it is easier to communicate effectively with key stakeholders and comply with regulations if they get timely triple bottom line reports.

The boxes "E" and "D" in Fig. 6.2 demonstrate the tools and techniques of analysis and decision-making that allow managers to solve pricing and negotiation-related problems related to the marketplace or cooperating or competing inter-organisationally, as well as gain a "birds-eye view" of the opportunities and threats, and internal resourcing problems that confront an organisation. For instance, the Balanced Scorecard can be used to understand whether the organisation is effectively achieving its customer, operational, and learning and innovation objectives, in addition to its financial performance objectives. The organisation is more likely to perform in a coordinated manner along vertical and horizontal lines as a result. Likewise, the Balanced Scorecard can help managers gain even more clarity about the strategic initiatives that may need to be put in place in future to ensure the organisation remains relevant and able to satisfy its various stakeholders (Kaplan & Norton, 1996).

Although Fig. 6.2 is not exhaustive, it still demonstrates the two chapters' commonalities and overlaps. They both in essence argue that financials strategies are integral to organisational success, no matter how success is defined at an organisation or by its stakeholders or how the financial strategy is ultimately implemented.

Reference

Kaplan, R. S., & Norton, D. P. (1996). Linking the Balanced Scorecard to strategy. *California Management Review*, *39*(1), 53–79.

CHAPTER 7

Implementing a Financial Strategy: Managing Financial Capital, Investing in People, Balancing Risk and Developing Critical Resources

Angelina Zubac

Introduction

All organisations need capital in some form in order to exist and achieve their most important stakeholders' objectives. This is regardless of whether an organisation is small, medium or large in size, a not-for-profit organisation, a private or publicly listed entity, government run or a multinational. For instance, a street performer could sing in the street for an hour to earn some money after spending $2 on bus fare to get to their desired location; members of the same family could use family money,

---

A. Zubac (✉)
University of Queensland, Brisbane, QLD, Australia
e-mail: a.zubac@business.uq.edu.au; Angelina.zubac@aim.com.au;
az@strategylink.com.au

their individual time and effort to sell vegetables at a market stall; a charitable concern could take donations and use this money, as well as the time and effort of its volunteers to provide services to vulnerable people; a government organisation could be indirectly funded by taxpayers; and a large organisation could raise equity by listing on the stock market, take on some bank debt and earn revenue to ensure it can deliver a mix of products and services to target groups of consumers.

Likewise, it is rare for an organisation to form and become a going concern without at least one major stakeholder taking responsibility for its governance. However, in a modern economy, as an organisation grows in size, it is more likely that many people will have a vested interest in it and be keen to see it is governed effectively (Schumpeter, 1979[1943]; Stiglitz, 2012; Zambon & Zan, 2000; Zubac, 2018). Put another way, since capitalism is now the dominant economic system globally and has evolved to make possible multiple methods for investing capital into an organisation, organisations have evolved to be grown in a great number of ways to meet their key stakeholders' objectives, provided they follow the rules (Ingham, 2008; Stiglitz, 2001, 2010).

As a corollary, the more complex the organisation and its institutional context,[1] the more essential it is for the organisation to have a well-articulated financial strategy. Such a strategy should (ideally) spell out how the organisation will attract and gain access to capital, and how these inflows, once secured, should be structured and transformed or, said differently, it should spell out how the financial strategy, if effectively implemented, will benefit the organisation and achieve its most important stakeholders' objectives, such as those of its owners, employees, customers and regulators. Because organisations operate within a rules-based environment, its managers must proactively and strategically manage the financial capital at the organisation's disposal with stakeholders' needs in mind (Hodgson, 2006; Langlois, 1985; North, 1994). Financial capital must be proactively structured and regularly transformed, otherwise future inflows of capital investment cannot be assured (Lachman, 1978 [1956]; Lewin, 1999, 2005). However, there is so much to consider—much more than one might at first think is involved. It is no easy task

---

[1] Institutions are definable as the "systems of established and embedded social rules that structure social interactions". Markets are an example of a major institution (Hodgson, 2006: 17). It should be noted that many laypeople will use terms such as "society" or "the economy" instead of the term "institutional environment".

to transform capital. The more complex the organisation and the institutional context within which it operates, the more important it will be to have a thoughtfully crafted and implemented financial strategy.

In the next section, these ideas are elaborated upon through the use of a firm theoretic framework which was developed to explain these ideas (Zubac et al., 2012), albeit, for the purposes of this chapter, a modified and simpler version of it is used. The framework demonstrates the mechanisms that organisations use through their founders/owners and managers to access and build stocks of financial and applied capital. Thus, it demonstrates the two primary functions of which a financial strategy should be concerned: the management of financial capital and the building of applied capital through the transformation of financial capital. In the section that follows, the extant literature on the management of financial capital is discussed. This literature confirms the importance of articulating and implementing financial strategies that reflect the institutional context and stakeholders' requirements but that much remains to be learned about how to do this well. The next section reviews the relevant human, risk and resource literatures. The objective is to better understand how human, risk and resource capital can be built up, including the architectures that may be key. Special attention is paid to risk capital in this section because there is still very little about it in the management literatures compared to the corporate finance and banking literatures. The review demonstrates that though organisations will have much in common when they build stocks of human, risk and resource capital, there will also be differences. They will uniquely use stocks of human, risk and resource capital to create and appropriate value at the organisation. The chapter concludes with a discussion of the implications of its arguments for researchers and practice.

FINANCIAL CAPITAL AND ITS TRANSFORMATION

The modern capitalist system is defined by three "institutional clusters": (1) the monetary system, which is coordinated and regulated by governments, and serviced by financial organisations, such as banks, (2) the market exchange system, which is made up of many markets, such as products and labour markets, and (3) organisations which produce and distribute products and services (Ingham, 2008: 53). Thus, in most countries, almost invariably, business owners and/or the managers appointed to run the business are required to consider how to develop and grow their organisation by gaining access to capital and then transforming it (Ferguson, 2008; Hall & Soskice, 2001). Even if the organisation starts very lean and without a source of money to fund its activities, utilising the time and effort of its founders and other interested parties instead, such as what occurs at some microbusinesses, small family businesses or non-profit organisations, after a certain point, it will be very difficult to increase the organisation's scope and become a going concern unless financial capital is accessed and actively transformed.

Figure 7.1 illustrates what is involved. Although the original framework was designed to explicate the nature of the bilateral relationship managers have with capital owners and the investing stimulated by this relationship, that is, "(1) the combination of resources that the firm's managers acquired or developed and deployed to produce and deliver products and services and/or grow or contract the firm to be an increasingly market-sensitive and efficient institution, and (2) the capital that the firm's owners invested in the firm to allow its managers to implement strategies able to achieve owners' future payment demands" (Zubac et al., 2012: 1868), the modified framework explains, very simply, why it is important to satisfy an organisation's most important stakeholders within the given institutional context.

By explicating how managers gain access to capital on behalf of their organisations and those with capital can invest in an organisation for gain, Fig. 7.1 demonstrates the inherent circularity of the investment system and how this leads to organisations thriving. The framework in its entirety describes the potentially complex set of interactions and capital/value flows that lead to organisations gaining the ability to build their stocks. The accumulation of capital stocks stimulates more inflows of capital from external institutional sources[2] and then even more over time; this demonstrates how organisations and markets perpetuate each other, that is, unless enough organisations or markets or stakeholder groups or institutions or a combination of these become seriously dysfunctional or fail.

As an adjunct, Fig. 7.1 uses payments to elucidate the nature of the value drivers that underpin the capital system, and lead to organisations

---

[2] These can vary significantly in size, complexity and scope, for instance, from loans from one's parents to a complex loan facility from a consortium of banks. Similar principles apply to investing capital to acquire an equity stake.

7 IMPLEMENTING A FINANCIAL STRATEGY: MANAGING FINANCIAL ... 143

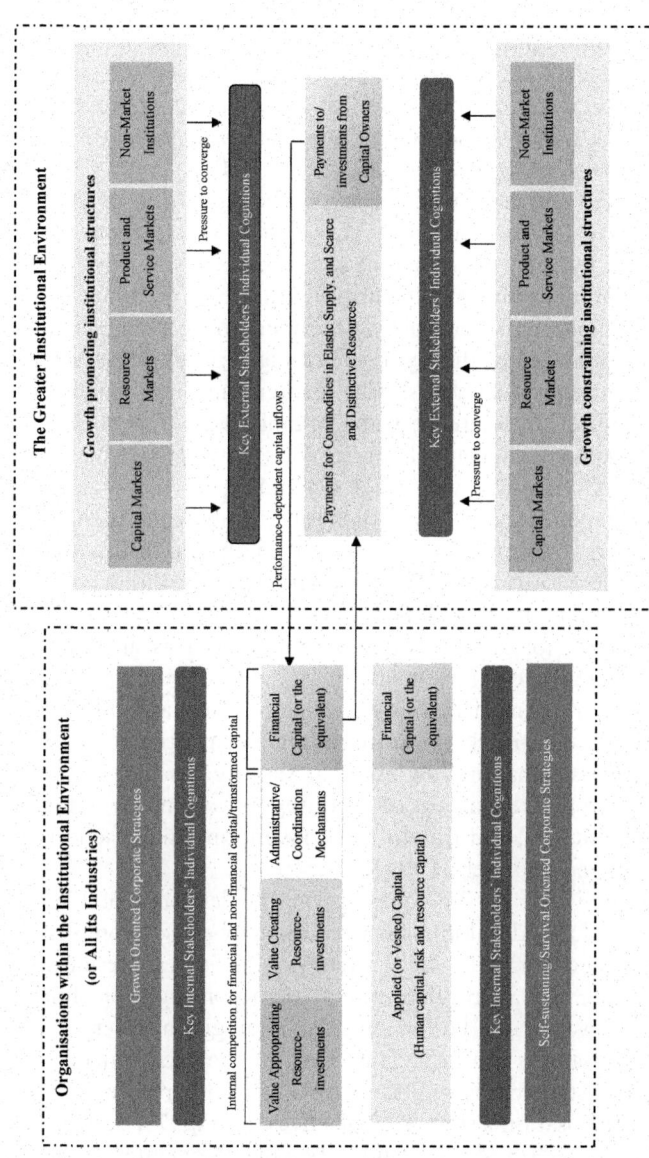

Fig. 7.1 The transformation of capital

forming and coordinating; this perspective is used as it is "appropriately reductionist" (explains the fundamental elements of a complex phenomenon). Prime among these value drivers is capital owners' need to have their payments expectations met or be given assurance they will be met. For a more technical discussion of the payment perspective and how it allows one to understand capital investment-accumulation process in purely value terms, please see the Zubac et al. (2012) paper.

Critically, as one can see by focusing on the right side of Fig. 7.1, which describes the institutional context, the flow of capital to organisations is enabled by the capital markets, resource markets, product and service markets, and non-market institutions that exist within the institutional environment. It is not solely dependent on capital markets as might be assumed. Similarly, the right side of Fig. 7.1 suggests that some capital, resource and product and service markets, and non-market institutions will be more important to some organisations than they are to others. This is because the capital investments (payments) they attract and the value this represents will differ depending on the organisation or institutional stance taken. Put another way, value depends on whose point-of-view is in question, for instance, from the point-of-view of a manager, an investor looking for an organisation to invest in, a consumer keen to identify organisations selling products they want at a good price or a person looking for a good organisation to join as an employee. Regardless, as suggested on the left side of Fig. 7.1, stakeholders external to the focal organisation moderate how capital, resource and product and service markets, and non-market institutions enable investments of capital, and then their transformation and usage at the organisation over time. This is because the greater institutional context is very much influenced by people's psychologies, and the norms, conventions and practices they give rise to over time (Samuels, 1995).

Likewise, as one can see by focusing on the left side of Fig. 7.1, it is highly desirable to develop a financial strategy which complements the organisation's corporate (overall) strategy. This is because individual organisations create and appropriate value and, accordingly, use financial capital (or its equivalent) to be (potentially) strategic in different ways. This means organisations can be defined by how they accumulate stocks of financial capital, structure it and transform it into other forms of capital to achieve the organisation's strategic objectives. As Fig. 7.1 suggests, for an organisation to be "strategic", it must be able to operate or compete and/or cooperate in the most pertinent capital, resource and product and service markets, as well as demonstrate an appropriate degree of compliance with a range of non-market institutions. Crucially, an organisation must be able to build stocks of human, risk and resource capital over time with a capacity for change (Zubac et al., 2012). Since the greater institutional environment is subject to change, organisations must be able to change too. This is why a financial strategy involves far more than the management of liquid assets through the budget cycle, and why concepts of value associated with different stakeholders are key.

To put this in yet another way, if an organisation is to become valuable, that is, represents value from many viewpoints, many analytical and activity-directed (sub)processes and useful cognitions must be developed by its managers to transform the financial capital others have invested into the organisation into transformed capital, that is, into valuable forms of human, risk and resource capital. Indeed, no matter the size of the organisation, an organisation will have more capacity to become a going concern if the most appropriate activity-directed (sub)processes and cognitions are developed and applied to define and implement the financial strategy. Of course, the larger the organisation and the more complex its institutional context, that is, the markets and non-market institutions in total that can affect it, the more complex the analytical and activity-directed (sub)processes and cognitions that will be required to come into play.

The extant organisation and management literatures have examined many such financial strategy related processes already. However, as will be discussed in more detail in the next sections, drawing on this literature, much remains to be learned and clarified.

What We Know About Financial Capital Management

The problem of how organisations gain access to financial capital in order to operate is essentially a theory of the firm problem (Zingales, 2000). However, no theory of the firm or, more generally, of organisation as of yet definitely explains why organisations exist and limits to their scope (Garrouste & Saussier, 2008; Williamson, 2010). However, since financial capital is managed within the given complex institutional environment, where there are many rules and interacting (complex) systems, the theories of corporate finance, corporate governance and organisational design point to what it is that organisations do that is of valuable to so many and why (Stiglitz, 2001).

The Theory of Corporate Finance

The theory of corporate finance is the study of the financing patterns used to advance an organisation's objectives allowing for its institutional context (Tirole, 2006). The models developed in this field are used by managers to make financing decisions (Bodie et al., 2005). However, the models break down when an organisation's unique circumstances are taken into account (Goldstein & Hackbarth, 2014). The most prominent of these are discussed in the next subsections.

Debt Versus Equity and Cash

The Modigliani and Miller (MM) theorem remains one of corporate finance's most important theories (Harris & Raviv, 1991). The theory states that without considering taxes, information advantages and various costs, it does not matter how an organisation is financed; firm value will remain unaffected regardless of the financing mode. The theory stimulated a prolific amount of research on the situations in which the MM theorem does not hold true (Tirole, 2006).[3] This research stream confirmed that in the real world the "size of the [organisational] pie" is impacted by different groups, such as managers and debt holders. For instance, managers' shareholdings and contract terms can impact organisations' future earnings (Hart, 1988, 2001). Likewise, Simerly and Li (2000) found that choice of capital structure is constrained by the level of environmental dynamism, with debt less preferred in intensely dynamic environments or when managers' orientation is short-term. The same applies to the degree of complexity confronting an organisation and its ability to access capital (Shleifer & Vishny, 1991), the intensity of entrepreneurs' control concerns (Kaplan & Stromberg, 2002) and when the projects at the organisation represent significantly different cashflows, risk, liquidation values and management incentives profiles over time (Rajan, 2012: 1174). Managers tend to be given a great deal of discretion in how their projects are to be implemented. As organisations mature, it will also be necessary to renegotiate the stake different stakeholders have in the organisation (Zingales, 2000).

---

[3] Financial contracting refers to the deals "made between financiers and those who need financing". Contracts can be the source of many forms of moral hazard (Tirole, 2006: 1079–1080).

In the past, the excess holding of cash was associated with a failure to pursue opportunities. However, organisations now hold more cash now than ever before. For instance, the average cash-to-assets ratio in the United States is more than double than it was during the period 1980 to 2006. Previously, cash was held for four reasons: to avoid the transaction costs incurred when converting noncash into liquidity, to better cope with unexpected external shocks, for tax reasons and because managers believed it was more important to pursue opportunities rather than pay dividends. However, the trend is now better explained by managers' greater willingness to explore and exploit opportunities, shorter payments terms, lower inventory levels, a reluctance to invest in major capital projects and greater R&D intensity. The research does not support the thesis that the increase in cash holdings is essentially an agency-related problem, although recently listed organisations, those that do not pay dividends or which operate in extremely volatile environments hold more cash (Bates et al., 2009). The cash trend is essentially a "lemons" problem related to the mismatch of knowledge held by managers and investors during high growth periods (Harris & Raviv, 2017: 162).

Internal Capital Markets and Capital Allocation
A disconnect also exists between the theories of internal capital markets and capital allocation and what occurs in practice. In theory, internal capital markets are assumed to be more efficient than external capital markets (Stein, 1997). However, in real life, so much depends upon the context. Also, internal capital markets have both an up- and down-side in practice. For instance, Dickler and Folta (2020) found that multi-business firms are generally more efficient than single-business firms because multi-business firms can more easily exit unprofitable businesses than single-business firms. They can also expand their revenue base far more nimbly. However, in line with the "dark side" of capital markets literature, when organisations are doing very well, powerful managers tend to obtain larger allocations of capital than their less well-connected counterparts, demonstrating that internal capital markets are not as impartial as is normally assumed. However, it may be possible to avoid this problem by establishing clear-cut rules about the allocation of windfall capital, regularly redeploying managers to other areas to allow them to learn about them, and periodically evaluating resource allocation patterns (Glaser et al., 2013: 1577).

Sengul et al.'s (2019) extensive review of the intra-firm capital allocation literature identified three general contexts (or pillars) for critically evaluating how inefficiencies occur in real life. The first involves understanding how managers identify, compare and choose between different and potentially advantaging strategic investments. This can be thought of as better understanding the horizontal dimension. The second involves understanding how investment occurs up and down hierarchical levels. This can be thought of as understanding the vertical dimension. The third involves understanding the influences and constraints emanating from the external environment. On the whole, the research confirms that corporate centres (Head Offices) allocate capital more efficiently than external markets because of their inherent informational and control advantages. They also possess capital allocation competences specifically designed over time to address the organisation's path dependencies (Burgelman, 1996; Christensen & Bower, 1996; Noda & Bower, 1996) and its managers' decision-making biases (Arrfelt et al., 2015; Cyert & March, 1963; Lovallo & Kahneman, 2003).

The research also revealed the problems inherent in using the capital asset pricing model (CAPM) at some organisations to determine project hurdle rates. The use of marketable assets and prices to determine a hurdle rate is problematic because resource-based theory states above average performance is not possible unless resources are combined uniquely. An organisation can only outperform the market during periods of disequilibrium, such as when an organisation has a first mover advantage. Thus, in most cases, it may not be practicable or strategic to separate the resources or use CAPM unless competitors are pursuing similar strategies:

> The fundamental premise of organizational economics is that the productivity of an asset owned by a firm is greater than the asset's productivity in the absence of the firm. The equilibrium pricing of a firm's assets therefore is truly meaningful only if those assets are evaluated as an inseparable unit. A market price attaches to the firm as a whole, but market pricing of the constituent parts of the firm is inherently misleading if the firm meets organizational-economic criteria for viability. (Robins, 1992: 530)

By the same token, it can be difficult, if not outright impossible, to calculate CAPM in some parts of the world (Bettis, 1983). Indeed, many organisations choose hurdle rates subjectively and many managers write business cases that "back into" the desired rate. In addition, some divisions may be given significantly different hurdle rates to that of other divisions. Even if this is not for political reasons, it may be interpreted to be political. These perceptions of bias problems could be avoided by applying a variation of portfolio logic, for instance, by imposing hurdle rates based on the level of volatility in the divisions' markets and its expected growth rate compared to the rest of the organisation. The problem is that such techniques are still rarely employed (Calandro et al., 2015: 72).

In summary, there is a corporate effect. Organisations with sophisticated capital allocation processes tend to be higher performing than those with unsophisticated or ad hoc capital allocation processes (Arrfelt et al., 2015). Regardless, internal markets are more rigid than external markets. It is only possible to lever financial capital's inherent fungibility so much. Ultimately, financial capital is more likely to be efficiently allocated if the strategy is sound and the timing of its implementation is well-judged. Managers' equity concerns, lack of balance in the business portfolio, the approval process being too bottom-up or top-down, and serious instability in the external (market) environment may also be constraining factors (Lovallo et al., 2020).

The Theory of Corporate Governance

In broad terms, "corporate governance deals with the ways in which suppliers of finance to corporations assure themselves of getting a return on their investment" (Shleifer & Vishny, 1997: 737). It can also be conceived of as the methods adopted at organisations for dealing with agency problems occurring at different levels. However, it is now customary to define it as "the design of institutions that induce or force management to internalise the welfare of stakeholders". Crucially, corporate governance is no longer synonymous with the maximisation of shareholder value (Tirole, 2001: 4). This may be one of the few positives to have come out of the many corporate scandals of the last decades (Barton, 2011; Langlois, 2003).[4]

---

[4] Corporate governance is different to the concept of governance in transaction cost economics, since governance in transaction cost economics refers to the decision to govern via the firm (organisation), markets or a hybrid of the two (Mahoney, 2005).

Corporate Governance: An Evolving and Increasingly Stakeholder-Oriented Field

Thus, corporate governance research has largely focused on understanding the governance capabilities and mechanisms that lead to an organisation outperforming its rivals and/or satisfying its stakeholders (Aguilera et al., 2007; Bies et al., 2007; Bonardi et al., 2005; Capron & Guillen, 2009; Hoetker, & Mellewigt, 2009; Kim & Prescott, 2005; Kim et al., 2009). In their extensive review of the corporate governance literature, Shleifer and Vishny (1997) found that most problems of governance were viewed from an agency lens. Managers were less likely to work in the best interests of shareholders because their contract was incomplete, they were insufficiently or incautiously incentivised, manager's decision-making methods were not scrutinised and they had unfair informational advantages. Of course, it is helpful if those investing in an organisation have some semblance or assurance of control:

> The principal reason that investors provide external financing to firms is that they receive control rights in exchange. External financing is a contract between the firm as a legal entity and the financiers, which gives the financiers certain rights vis a vis the assets of the firm. (Shleifer & Vishny, 1997: 750)

The agency problem is not just a trust problem. It is also an assurance of organisational value problem; indeed, the value an organisation represents and how a strategy might augment that value over time will mean different things to different stakeholders. Likewise, different corporate governance characteristics will mean different things to different stakeholders, for instance, the impact of certain stock-based incentives for managers, the proportion of block-holder or institutional ownership, past equity ownership holdings, and the number of shares sold prior to listing to venture capitalists and internal board members will be interpreted vastly differently in value terms by some (Sanders & Boivie, 2004).

So much depends on which governance characteristic is being put under the spotlight and by whom. For instance, Kacperczyk (2009: 261) found that "an exogenous increase in takeover protection leads to higher corporate attention to community and the natural environment but that this has no impact on corporate attention to employees, minorities, and customers". Similarly, "firms that increase their attention to stakeholders experience an increase in long-term shareholder value". On the other hand, Wang et al. (2009) found employees were reluctant to invest in specialised knowledge unless the organisation had established a trust relationship and/or provided other protections. Thus, value will be apportioned in line with the context. For instance, Zona (2012) found that boards that believe it is appropriate to innovate during a downturn are keen to use a number of mechanisms to stimulate innovation. Scherpereel (2008) found that the choice of a market, hybrid or firm governance structure was contingent on the level of option value being sought. Henisz et al. (2013) found that stakeholders positively value organisations after encouraging media reports about it are released.

A greater emphasis on meeting the needs of stakeholders rather than maximising shareholder value suggests three questions: (1) how is pledgeable income used when negotiating with important stakeholders, (2) how are deadlocks dealt with, and (3) is it possible to have a clear strategic mission when a stakeholder welfare approach is taken focus (Tirole, 2001)? Of course, it is important to make a distinction between market finance and intermediate finance or uninformed and informed capital.[5] It is also necessary to appreciate that starkly different governance characteristics may be used depending on the country or political environment under consideration (Shleifer & Vishny, 1997).

Corporate Governance and Organisational Decision-Making
If the shift to a stakeholder approach is to "induce or force management to internalise the welfare of stakeholders" (Tirole, 2001: 4), it follows that the decision-making processes evolved at an organisation are of critical importance too. Much of the research on decision oversight focused on exploring decision-making biases and other behavioural factors that could lead to efficiencies. As a result, how optimism bias, narcissism, overconfidence, escalation of commitment and excessive self-interest can creep into an organisation' decision-making processes were examined in some detail. In addition, it was found that capital allocation can be backward-looking (or overly improvement-oriented) instead

---

[5] "Market finance refers to issues of securities such as commercial paper and corporate bonds to a dispersed set of investors. Intermediated finance in contrast involves financing by a large investor (bank, large shareholder, venture capitalist, etc.) who monitors the firm. The distinction between intermediated and market finance is sometimes referred to as one between 'informed' and 'uninformed' capital" (Tirole, 2001: 8).

of forward-looking (or wealth-enhancing). This can lead to an overinvestment in business units with poor prospects and underinvestment in business units with strong prospects, and stronger performing units subsidising poorer performing units without any real justification (Arrfelt et al., 2013, 2015). It is also common for managers to use simple heuristics to allocate capital, for instance "[evenly] spread out allocations over all identified options" (Bardolet et al., 2011: 1478). The presence of slack has also been studied in a governance-decision-making context. For instance, slack was found to have both an up-and down-side. Slack may be necessary to be able to innovate. However, slack may also lead to managers acting self-interestedly, incompetently or apathetically (Nohria & Gulati, 1996).

Capital allocation efficiency may also be contingent on the levels of the hierarchy through which a project proposal must pass through to be approved (Burgelman, 1983) or the extent to which it is necessary to "substitute, to some extent, internal selection for external selection" to survive (Burgelman, 1996: 210). Similarly, the choice of organisational structure can be thought of as a problem of governance. For instance, Haier achieved greater levels of vertical and horizontal alignment after restructuring into 2000 microdivisions. The new structure allowed Haier to develop a more liberalised business case and approval process, which was enabled through the use of a platforms to achieve these ends. The problems normally associated with both centralised and decentralised decision-making were avoided as a result. All of these initiatives made it easier for Head Office to encourage innovation and ensure new ways of thinking could be embraced across the whole organisation when it was strategic to do so (Chen et al., 2021). Divisionalisation done well is about fostering "smarter investment behaviour", ensuring capabilities and knowledge are shared when appropriate (Natividad, 2013: 615).

The Theory of Organisational Design

Organisational design refers to how resources are deployed and used across the organisation and capabilities structured with the objective of achieving an organisation's strategic objectives. For instance, effective decision-making can be enabled by establishing an appropriate level of centralised versus decentralised decision-making (Chandler, 2001). The former enables forward-looking planning and reasoning while the latter is especially useful for dealing with emerging events and adapting the organisation over time. When a suitable balance is achieved between the two modes, it is more likely that an organisational culture will emerge where collaboration and learning are valued (Andersen, 2015).

The capabilities residing in an organisation's human resource base can be brought into play too by specifying employees' roles and the level of support employees will be given by the organisation's human resource function. The same applies to how an organisation's knowledge is accumulated, managed and then used. When particularised to ensure its optimal use, positive forms of learning, coordination and positive employee behaviours can be encouraged (Foss et al., 2013; Waddell et al., 2011; Weigelt & Miller, 2013). When thought is put into how the organisation's human resources are combined and used, it is more likely that the organisation can achieve its value creation and value appropriation objectives (Barney & Arikan, 2001; Nag et al., 2007; Porter, 1980, 1985, 1991; Prahalad & Hamel, 1990; Teece et al., 1997).

Since it is impossible to separate people from the institutional context, it follows that the organisational design adopted will reflect the external and internal institutional context. For instance, for-profits will adopt organisational designs devised to help them become profitable while not-for-profits will adopt designs devised to help them achieve their broader mission. This is because even though organisations need to operate viably or, in the great majority of cases, operate profitably, they are also required to comply with various institutions' regulatory, market, standard benchmark, reputational and/or societal expectations. Some of these will emanate from within the organisation itself, as institutions emerge within organisations too (Berrone et al., 2013; Campbell, 2007; Oliver, 1997; Peng et al., 2009; Scott, 1995). Of course, the design adopted will also be influenced by the level of isomorphism present in the country. Indeed, isomorphism is more likely to be more of a factor within a country rather than between countries (Chan et al., 2008; Fernhaber et al., 2009; Garcia-Canal & Guillen, 2008; Garcia-Pont & Nohria, 2002; Goerzen & Beamish, 2005; Makino et al., 2004; Meyer et al., 2009).

The Transformation: Human, Risk and Resource Capital

The preceding discussion demonstrates that the theories of corporate finance, corporate governance and organisational design have much in common. In short, they imply each other. For instance, it is impossible to discuss the theory of corporate finance without implying systems of corporate governance and how these are supported by certain organisational designs. Likewise, it is impossible to discuss corporate governance without discussing the different patterns of financing that are likely to advantage some stakeholders over others and, as a consequence, lead to the adoption of a certain organisation design. Neither is it possible to discuss organisational design without linking the concept to how different financing and governance objectives impelled the design in the first place. In each case, the institutional context will be a consideration (Stiglitz, 2012; Zubac, 2018). The inherently circular investment system plays an important role (Schumpeter, 1927, 1947).

At the heart of the matter is the fact that stakeholders play both a direct and indirect role in shaping an organisation's evolution (Zollo et al., 2017). The stakes they may have in an organisation may take many forms (Barney, 2018). These may or may not be formalised or be clear-cut. For instance, property rights theory has demonstrated that some internal stakeholders can appropriate rent by taking unified action or affecting or controlling critical forms of information (Amis et al., 2020). Thus, it becomes necessary for managers to structure and transform financial capital in ways that satisfies them or, more precisely, assures them.

The literature suggests this assurance is the result of building stocks of human, risk and resource capital. When this is done well, the organisation justifies its existence. The organisation will only have so much scope to grow too depending on how these stocks are built up and levered (Zubac et al., 2012).

Human Capital

Indeed, no matter what kind of organisation we are talking about—large or small, profit or not-for-profit, multi-divisional and global or not—the very act of organising to develop an organisation is impossible without some human input. It is for these reasons why it is so vital that human capital is built up prudently at an organisation. Research suggests that human capital is made up of two subtypes of capital, that is, knowledge and social capital. These two forms of human capital enable the organisation to interact within an institutionally thick environment; people are important because of the knowledge they possess and their ability to form relationships on behalf of the organisation. Indeed, it would be impossible to perform even the simplest of tasks as a worker without some knowledge and ability to interact with others. Of course, these principles only apply while the person in question is working for the organisation in some way. Once an individual leaves, any knowledge or social capital not transferred to the organisation in some appreciable way for the organisation to control and use, such as by documenting it or embedding into an organisational system will not be human capital from the point-of-view of the focal organisation (Zubac et al., 2012). It should also be kept in mind that internal stakeholders can appropriate value but may also incur costs themselves should they sever ties with the organisation before they are ready (Coff, 1999, 2010).

Knowledge Capital
In a modern organisation, it is important for there to be something unique about its human capital base. The human capital architecture used will be key here. This refers to the combinations and proportions of people at the organisation who have unique skills or knowledge as opposed to those who have more generic and easily transferable skills and knowledge (Lepak & Snell, 1999). The underlying human architecture developed will be contingent on how different people are deemed able to contribute to the organisation's exploration and/or exploitation activities (Kang et al., 2007). Of course, sometimes people need encouragement to use their skills and knowledge to advance the organisation's ends. Thus, the architecture will in part depend on the incentives put in place to encourage good behaviours (Kaplan & Henderson, 2005). Providing the right training and making it easy for employees to share knowledge is important if employees are to "simultaneously pursue exploratory and exploitative learning by building differentiated relationships within and across firm boundaries" (Riley et al., 2017: 251).

Social Capital
The human resource architecture also depends on social capital. Social capital is of value if it can advance an individual's objectives (Kwon & Adler, 2014). In general terms, it is the "the goodwill that is engendered by the fabric of social relations that can be mobilized to facilitate action" (Adler & Kwon, 2002: 17). It is greatly associated with the generation of sympathy without expecting anything in return (Robison et al., 2002). In an organisational context, it is "the capacity for people to lever their social connections to advantageously gain access to resources or better

use the firm's own resources" (Zubac et al., 2012: 1876). As this capacity evolves, the human capital architecture will evolve (Zollo et al., 2017). For instance, "the right mix of specialists and generalists" are those who are in a strong position to lever their social relationships at the present time in line with what they know (Byun et al., 2018). Similar principles apply to people's affiliations, as these can provide reputational advantages (Gubler & Cooper, 2019: 2287 and 2289). High quality relationships may also be particularly advantaging (Burt, 1997).

Social capital may be built through people's relationships, leading to improved cross-functional team performance and organisational learning. Strong inter-organisational relationships or being well-networked is also a source of social capital. Connections may also be built intra- or inter-organisationally by acting as a bridge or by forming bonds (Adler & Kwon, 2002; Burt & Merluzzi, 2016). Regardless, the building of social capital is contingent upon the institutional environment and the obligations and norms engendered by it (Portes, 1998).

Risk Capital

All organisations need to take some risks to implement their strategies (Reuefli et al., 1999). Naturally, investors prefer to invest in organisations that employ modern risk management methods (Chatterjee et al., 1999). A proactive approach to risk mitigation addresses investors' imperfect information concerns (Demsetz, 1997). Generally speaking, risk capital is "the means by which firms mitigate and underwrite their risks and protect their owners' ongoing interests". This is a definition that can be applied to for-profit and not-for-profit organisations alike (Zubac et al., 2012: 1877). However, there is very little in the strategic management literature or, for that matter, in the wider management literature which explains how risk capital is accumulated and managed at organisations. This is perplexing as it is not possible to fully understand how organisation's implement their strategies and change over time without appreciating the role risk capital management plays.

Notwithstanding, risk capital is a mature concept in corporate finance and in banking. In corporate finance, it is known as "the smallest amount that can be invested to insure the value of the firm's net assets against a loss in value relative to the risk-free investment of those net assets" (Merton & Perold, 1993: 17). In banking practice and consistent with

The Basel Accord,[6] it is defined as "the amount held … to underpin the risk of loss in value of exposures, businesses, etc. … [risk capital] acts as a buffer … leaving the bank room to recover or organise in an orderly winding down" (Matten, 2001: 17). It is of special concern for the governance of financial institutions because these institutions are essentially in the business of risk management and are heavily regulated. Financial institutions enable the efficient functioning of the credit system of money of which the economies of the world depend for their efficient functioning. The credit system of money must be safeguarded for obvious reasons, as the Global Financial Crisis of 2007–2008 demonstrated. In short, when a country's financial institutions possess an insufficient level of risk capital to act as a buffer should the worst occur, the whole economy is at risk. It may become necessary for a government to bail out the financial sector to restore health to the economy. Taxpayers' money may be diverted from initiatives that are designed to be of benefit to society and future generations. Global accords that specify how risk capital should be built up over time by financial institutions are necessary because the financial systems of the world are so interconnected; these accords and the rules and regulations they have stimulated protect the global economy (Ingham, 2008; Stiglitz, 2012).

A Clarifying Example
In addition, the calculation of risk capital at financial institutions is complex. Thus, it is not surprising that much more effort is expended on the calculation of risk capital at financial institutions as compared to other organisations. Indeed, there are a great many risks financial institutions, such as banks and insurers, etc. must shoulder to profitably extend credit, provide insurance coverage and operate as a going concern, etc. Consequently, the frameworks used for calculating and managing risk at financial institutions could serve as a useful base or template for understanding how risk capital could be defined or calculated at other organisations.

---

[6] The Basel Accord is the framework that is used globally by banks, as overseen by their respective country's regulators. It provides guidance for calculating the bank's capital adequacy level (Basel Committee on Banking Supervision, 2021). The objective of the accord is the ensure the integrity of a country's financial system through the management of risk capital and, consequently, helps to ensure the stability of the global financial system. It is different to what is normally done when protecting creditors in accounting (Matten, 2001).

The first step for calculating risk capital at a bank is to take an inventory of all of its risks. This is done so that it is possible to determine a suitable (or the mandated) capital adequacy ratio for the organisation, that is, the level of equity versus the computed risk weighted assets for the bank. Long-tailed distributions are usually used to profile, that is, determine suitable risk weightings for each of the key categories of risks. At one end of the continuum of risks, very high probability but very low impact risks are priced. At the other end, extremely low probability but potentially catastrophic risks are priced. Once all other risks are modelled and priced, it is then possible to gauge the level of risk capital that regulators require the financial institution to hold and how this could impact the strategy. The Basel Framework requires banks to hold three tiers of capital: Common equity Tier 1; Additional Tier 1; and Tier 2 capital. The Tier 1 categories are calculated to ensure a suitable ratio of equity to debt, that is, the capacity to pay creditors before all other claimants were the bank to experience liquidity problems. Tier 2 capital includes various categories of reserves that banks must hold. This is not technically working capital. This capital is held to ensure that if the bank gets into trouble, say, there was another global financial crisis, the losses can be absorbed sufficiently. The objective is to sufficiently protect depositors and creditors (Basel Committee on Banking Supervision, 2021; Matten, 2001).

The advantage of assuring depositors and creditors that their interests are protected is that it becomes much less likely that a run on the bank will occur, the bank collapses and/or, in the worst-case scenario, should very large banks or enough banks go under, the economy collapses. It is in this sense that Tier 1 and Tier 2 capital can be thought of as a form of insurance, albeit a regulatory form of insurance. If truth be told, bank risk capital is conceptually analogous to the general concept of "insurance". Insurance, as is generally understood, which all organisations can purchase (financial and non-financial alike) can also be thought of as corralled financial capital. Of course, providing fail safes and building redundancies across the organisation's systems are also analogous.

This means that it follows that just like insurance, as generally understood, of which it is desirable to purchase for low premiums, the less risk capital a financial institution or any organisation is required to hold or chooses to hold, the more financial capital that can be diverted to value creating activities, etc. Similar principles apply to providing fail safes and building redundancies across systems. In other words, just like it is always highly desirable to be charged low insurance premiums and have such robust systems fails safes and redundancies are not required, a bank will be better off if it is able to minimise the level of risk capital it must possess. A risk–benefit trade-off is implied. In short, it will not be possible to do this—hold optimal levels of risk capital—unless all risks are mitigated as much as it is possible and commercial decisions are made that reflect the bank's risk appetite. These ideas can be extended to all organisations even though their risk problems are likely to be very different to that of a bank.

Risk Mitigation and Risk Appetite
The bank example is again used to explain the risk-related differences across organisations. Banks are interesting because they must take risks to be profitable but they are also in the business of risk, albeit mostly in the business of credit, liquidity and market risk management (Central Bank Governance Group, 2009). Consequently, it will be impossible to implement commercially sound strategies at the bank unless its managers and those who govern it agree on what constitutes a suitable risk appetite for the bank. This can be defined as the level of risk the organisation is prepared to take on to achieve its strategic objectives while complying with its risk capital requirements. For many banks, it is a function of the credit rating to which the bank aspires to be given by the major credit agencies, such as by Moody's, S&P Global and Fitch and the risk culture. A positive risk culture is normally achieved by investing in governance mechanisms, such as incentives and targets that ensure risk is appropriately managed across the organisation on a daily basis:

> There are two fundamentally different ways that a bank's risk management can destroy value. First, risk management can fail to ensure that the bank has the right amount of risk. This failure can come about for a number of reasons .... risk management can fail to uncover bad risks that should be eliminated, ... mismeasure good risks, and it can fail ... to measure the firm's total risk. Second, risk management can be inappropriately inflexible, so that increases in risk are prevented even when they would be valuable to the institution. When risk management becomes too inflexible, it destroys value because the institution no longer has the ability to invest in valuable opportunities when they become available, and it also becomes less effective in making sure that the firm has the right amount of risk ... Striking the right balance ... is a critical challenge for risk management in any bank. (Stulz, 2016: 44)

It will be impossible to effectively govern and achieve a positive risk culture[7] unless a multi-stakeholder approach is taken, where cohorts of stakeholders (managers, board members, risk and other committee members, etc.) within the managerial hierarchy and governance structure can impartially advise about the risks that should be targeted (Van Greuning & Bratanovic, 2020). Much is at stake, all things considered (Stulz, 2016: 57). It is well-known that some bank decision-makers have focused on short-term gains to get large bonuses rather than on what was in the best interests of the bank and its key stakeholders (Stiglitz, 2012). To this end, it may be helpful to calculate a risk adjusted return on capital for the organisation.[8] This can be his is best done by keeping track of the various dynamic factors that could impact the organisation over time and by ensuring "a learning process that includes intuition, judgment, and discipline" (Guill, 2016: 29).

The preceding discussion confirms the logic that can be applied to all organisations. In summary, it is important to consider the organisation's risks carefully to be able to manage and govern it effectively and strategically.

Risk Management: Understanding the Different Categories of Risk in Order to Mitigate

Thus, it will be impossible to successfully achieve an organisation's strategy over time without good risk management. Generally, risk management is:

> A process of understanding and managing the risks that the entity is inevitably subject to in attempting to achieve its corporate objectives. For management purposes, risks are usually divided into categories such as operational, financial, legal compliance, information and personnel. One

---

[7] Risk culture is generally definable as "the set of shared attitudes, values and practices that characterise how an entity considers risk in its daily activities. Risk culture is mainly derived from an analysis of organisational practices, namely rewards or sanctions for risk-taking or risk-avoiding behaviour" (Harvey, 2008: 5).

[8] This is a profitability measure that is similar to return on equity since it is a profitability measure but the denominator is adjusted for risk. Indeed, different managers may be given targets that specify how they should contribute to achieve a risk adjusted return by managing risk and ensuring the organisation's risk appetite is appropriately reflected through its operations or when implementing strategic projects (Matten, 2001).

example of an integrated solution to risk management is enterprise risk management. (Harvey, 2008: 3)

However, risk is an umbrella term. It incorporates many other key concepts, such as expected outcome, variance and time. When discussing an organisation's risks, it will be a challenge to be precise about the nature of the risks confronting the organisation (Kallman, 2005). Nonetheless, the fact remains that it will not be possible to create or appropriate value as required or, for that matter, build risk capital sufficiently without having comprehensively and thoroughly managing risk first.

Using the bank example again, banks necessarily concentrate on the mitigation of their financial risks, for instance, much attention is given to the mitigation of credit risks at banks since these risks pose the biggest threat. However, this does not mean that other risks can be ignored. Regulators will not allow this and it is not possible to be truly strategic unless all other risks are considered. The majority of a bank's "other" risks will be operational risks. They are a smaller proportion of a financial institution's overall risks but still crucial to mitigate. However, at other (non-financial) organisations, the majority of risks are more likely to be overwhelmingly operational risks. Thus, processes for mitigating these risks will be key if the aim is to build up an adequate level of risk capital.

Operational risks (or business risks) are the risks that can arise due to the organisation's structure, systems, human resource base, products or processes. Project risk, reputational risk and strategic and/or policy risk are frequently included in this category of risk. However, so much depends upon the organisation. Some organisations consider risks such as strategic risk and policy risk as separate categories altogether (Basel Committee on Banking Supervision, 2021; Central Bank Governance Group, BIS, 2009; Matthews, 2008). Risk may also be specific to a country and the greater institutional context or be of a political, sociocultural, economic, technological, natural environment or legal nature. A risk may be a downside risk (the risk of something bad happening, such as an earthquake) or as an upside risk (the risk of something good not happening, such as a new product launch failing) (Harvey, 2008). Downside and upside risk are important concepts because they imply risk–benefit and choice. Consistent with concepts pertaining to risk appetite, some risk-taking involves rewarded risks while some risk-taking involves non-rewarded risks. For instance, providing services for a fee other organisations will not or cannot provide for risk-related reasons is a rewarded risk while developing a reputation for resilience during periods of adversity is a non-rewarded risk, that is, unless a way is found to ensure a reward (Elahi, 2013).

Because operational risk is such an important category of risk, including integral to calculating a suitable amount of risk capital to hold, the International Organization for Standardization introduced the ISO 31000 standard. The standard provides guidelines for objectively assessing, mitigating and controlling risks. Critically, the ISO 31000 standard provides a framework for communicating with and engaging stakeholders to define the risk context, identify the organisation's risks, conduct risk analyses, treat the identified risks and monitor and review risks periodically (International Organization for Standardization, 2018). This standard was so widely embraced, it actually informed the development of The Basel Framework (Basel Committee on Banking Supervision, 2021).

The main challenge of the ISO 31000 standard for managers is how the standard should be interpreted to address the organisation's unique requirements (Almeida et al., 2019). The problem is that this can be done superficially and risks end up being poorly and/or reactively mitigated. The standard can be especially problematic if it acts as a brake to innovation. The related IOS ERM framework was introduced to address some of these problems. This standard considers the risk pertaining to the life cycle of activities, projects and products. However, this standard is still very general. The risk and controls for understanding risks relationships and risk hierarchies over time are not specified, such as might occur when implementing a particular computer and information architecture (Lalonde & Boiral, 2012).

It may be necessary at some organisations to develop meta frameworks for mitigating risk that consider "major decisions and events, projects, and enterprise routines", and the role of time. That is, "temporal hierarchy as applied to enterprise risks are: first, changes at higher hierarchical levels are less frequent than at lower levels and second, higher levels cast the context and the boundary conditions within which the lower levels must exist and function" (Kmec, 2011: 1504, 1504–1505). It is increasingly evident too that risk velocity is yet to be fully addressed by most organisations. It will be difficult to truly understand the value of an opportunity if the speed by which the opportunity's respective upside and downside risks might be realised are ignored. Though models for understanding risk velocity do not exist as of yet, this does not stop managers from applying the concept intuitively (Ramamoorti et al., 2017).

Implementing Strategy and Risk

Thus, it is not surprising that so many organisations are using enterprise risk management (ERM) at their organisations, including as a platform. ERM "is an established management practice and is increasing in prominence as more firms spend substantial resources implementing ERM frameworks, partially induced by regulatory requirements" (Sax & Andersen, 2019: 719). ERM is best used strategically. For instance, when ERM is used to enhance how financial capital is allocated across the organisation, strategies are more likely to be implemented that reflect the organisation's risk appetite and the level of value that is desirable to put at risk (Ai et al., 2012).

Although there is much to be learned about ERM and how it can impact performance, the evidence so far is that it can make the strategy process easier to navigate. ERM has also been linked to improved profitability and financial leverage (Sax & Andersen, 2019). The problem is that it has traditionally been considered an anathema to innovation by non-risk managers. This is a concern because risk awareness should do the opposite. ERM is at its most useful when it encourages decision-makers to be forward-looking and not backward-looking, including when it helps employees to put intraorganisational politics aside. Nonetheless, people are people. Behavioural biases and the inability to appreciate the critical aspects of a strategic conundrum may lead the best of managers to misinterpret what the data discloses. Thus, ERM is of most value when it stimulates critical thinking:

> The Revealing Hand of risk management must be forceful and intrusive to allow individuals to activate "System 2" careful thinking about risk. It requires intrusive, interactive, and inquisitive processes to accomplish the following: (1) challenge existing assumptions about the world, internal and external to the organization; (2) communicate risk information, aided by tools such as risk maps, stress tests, and scenarios; (3) and draw attention to and help close gaps in the control of risks that other control functions (such as internal audit and other boundary controls) leave unaddressed, thereby complementing—though without displacing—existing management control practices. (Kaplan, 2016: 11)

Resource Capital

The extensive literature on resource-based theory in strategic management and as applied in other areas of management demonstrates its superiority for explaining high performance. From a variety of perspectives, it can explain how organisations coordinate but also create and appropriate value over time (Amit & Schoemaker, 1993; Barney & Arikan, 2001; McGahan & Porter, 1997; Penrose, 1959; Rumelt, 1991; Wernefelt, 1984). Thus, it provides a basis for explaining the concept of resource capital. Consistent with the arguments put forward so far, value accrues through this category of applied capital too. Resource capital with a capacity for growth through its effective management allows organisations to become attractive investment propositions. Of course, the value it represents may differ across stakeholders. For instance, it may represent future option value for some or a residual claim to others. It is for these reasons that resource capital is definable as "all the tangible and intangible assets, capabilities, and core competencies at the firm and any knowledge captured by it that allows the firm to operate and its managers to implement strategies" (Zubac et al., 2012). Resource capital enables managers to implement strategies that can attract new investors. It is capital as is commonly understood because it can be built up over time and be transferred beneficially (Arrow, 2000; Solow, 2000).

When resources are combined strategically, they may become more valuable and more so than if they were each valued separately. So much comes down to whether managers have been able to build up the resource base presciently or whether they just got lucky (Barney, 1986; Barney & Arikan, 2001). Likewise, resources used to complement the products and services of others may become valuable. However, it could be difficult to truly understand the nature of the "value added", including whether "a favourable asymmetry" between the organisation and its competitors has been achieved (Brandenburger & Stuart, 1996: 23). The orchestrating role managers at different levels play to ensure resources can be levered effectively throughout the organisation and over its life cycle is also of relevance here (Sirmon et al., 2011).

However, it is not possible to develop capabilities that are high on the hierarchy of capabilities, that is, dynamic capabilities without operational capabilities (Winter, 2003). For some organisations, just being able to operate effectively on a daily basis may be more than enough. It may not be necessary to outperform competitors, etc. through its resource base.

For instance, the priority for some family businesses is to ensure everyone in the family is able to earn a good living through the business. Strategy implementation may best be described as more like climbing Everest than like playing chess:

> Problems in business strategy are characterized by equifinality, randomness, and continuous interaction with external forces. In business competition, the range of strategic options is always constrained by external conditions and past choices, and executives seldom face a large number of feasible paths; in many cases, the actual number of feasible paths is one. In business strategy, good decisions sometimes fail, bad decisions succeed, margins for error are large, and the conditions of implementation can erase or reverse the core assumptions on which positioning decisions were based. Companies do not fail every time an executive chooses the wrong path, and it often happens that the human and economic conditions of competition—poor implementation of a bad decision, poor decisions by competitors, a favorable demand shift, a lucky change in government regulation, a corporate takeover—allow executives to profit from their own mistakes. (Powell, 2017: 165–166)

Exploration and Exploitation: Sensing, Seizing and Transforming
A resource base will also represent value because it enables both exploration and exploitation or, other words, allows the organisation to be ambidextrous. Although it may be more practicable for an organisation to focus on one or the other at different times, in the long-run, it could be difficult to remain competitive, relevant and/or a going concern unless the organisation can use its resource base to both explore and exploit opportunities. "Organizational ambidexterity refers to the ability of an organization to both explore and exploit—to compete in mature technologies and markets where efficiency, control and incremental improvements are prized and to also compete in new technologies and markets where flexibility, autonomy, and experimentation are needed". An appropriate trade-off between the two can be achieved by pursuing "simultaneous or structural ambidexterity" (exploring and exploiting simultaneously through separate units) or "contextual ambidexterity" (exploring and exploiting simultaneously or sequentially because people are behaviourally equipped to so). Either way, ambidexterity is best explained through a dynamic capability lens (O'Reilly & Tushman, 2013: 324, 328–329 and 332). When designing an ambidextrous organisation "execution appears to trump strategy". It is about the ability to

make hard choices at all stages of the strategy implementation process to ensure the different architectures across the organisation can be balanced (O'Reilly & Tushman, 2011: 18).

Teece's (2007) framework for explicating dynamic capabilities is essentially a means for articulating what is involved since its focus is on explaining the (sub)processes and cognitions that enable an organisation to remain competitive, relevant and/or a going concern. According to Teece, dynamic capabilities can be categorised according to what they are expected to enable allowing for the organisation's institutional context. All organisations will have three main objectives: (1) to sense and shape opportunities and understand threats, (2) to seize opportunities and mitigate threats/risks, and (3) to reconfigure or transform the organisation as is necessary. Organisations will develop dynamic capabilities in different ways to achieve either of these three objectives, that is, by combining enabling (sub)processes and cognitions to this end. Though dynamic capabilities can only be consciously developed through the input of the top management team, they are essentially an assemblage of the processes, systems and structures developed at the organisation in the past. Interestingly, although the Teece's influential 2007 paper is mainly concerned with explicating dynamic capabilities and not explaining how or in which ways financial capital is transformed, this objective is nevertheless implied. This means his arguments reinforce the arguments in this paper about circularity and why different forms of capital are essentially the means by which those with capital to invest in an organisation will do so.

CONCLUSION

This chapter uses a firm theoretic framework to explain the benefits of developing and implementing financial strategies that reflect the greater institutional environment with a particular emphasis on the underlying investment system. It does so by allowing for the fact that an organisation's external institutional environment will have been shaped by many stakeholders in a similar way to which the internal organisational landscape will have been shaped by internal stakeholders but also by the institutions that emerge at the organisation itself. It assumes the degrees of separation between some external and internal stakeholders at some organisations could be very short or the exact opposite or something in between. The same can be said about the degrees of separation between external stakeholders and the degrees of separation between internal stakeholders. The chapter also argues that a financial strategy is more likely to be efficacious and implementable if much thought is put into how financial capital should be acquired and transformed. Indeed, to effectively manage and govern an organisation it is important to regularly review the (sub)processes and cognitions employed across the organisation to acquire and transform capital. Continual improvement and adaptation of the organisation will not be possible otherwise. By the same token, even more thought needs to be put into how financial capital should be used to build human, risk and resource capital at organisations. If applied capital is built up satisfactorily, it is more likely that the organisation will remain an attractive investment proposition. Thus, it is also likely that its future strategies can be successfully implemented. The building of financial and non-financial capital (human, risk and resource capital) is important because ALL of these categories of capital reflect what it is key stakeholders want from the organisation.

However, people can be employed, risks balanced and resources levered at organisations in a great number of ways. This means the capital-centric transformations achieved at a particular organisation could be of value to different groups of key stakeholders in vastly different ways at times. It may be difficult to fully appreciate how value accrues to the organisation and determine how to share this information with others, especially since the value that accrues may not be fully reflected in the balance sheet, other such documents or via dashboards of performance. The arguments put forward about risk capital are particularly pertinent here. It is only a mature concept at some organisations and some management fields.

The implications of this chapter's arguments for further research and management practice are potentially immense. In summary, they point to eight broad questions: (1) how are the financial strategies at organisations of all types and sizes developed and implemented, (2) what is yet to be learned about the management of financial capital and its transformation into human, risk and resource capital, (3) what architectures are key for building human, risk and resource capital, (4) how are different organisations using the risk capital concept, (5) what is the relationship between applied capital and value creation, (6) what role do different internal and external stakeholders play in the building of applied capital, (7) how can a financial strategy be used to achieve greater levels of strategic vertical and horizontal alignment and (8) what are the implications for theory of the firm research?

References

Adler, P. S., & Kwon, S.-W. (2002). Social capital: Prospects for a new concept. *Academy of Management Review, 27*(1), 17–40.

Aguilera, R. V., Rupp, D. E., Williams, C. A., & Ganapathi, J. (2007). Putting the S back in corporate social responsibility: A multilevel theory of social change in organizations. *Academy of Management Review, 32*(3), 836–863.

Ai, J., Brockett, P. L., Cooper, W. W., & Golden, L. L. (2012). Enterprise risk management through strategic allocation of capital. *The Journal of Risk and Insurance, 79*(1), 29–55.

Almeida, R., Teixeira, J. M., da Silva, M. M., & Faroleiro, P. (2019). A conceptual model for enterprise risk management. *Journal of Enterprise Information Management, 32*(5), 843–868.

Amis, J., Barney, J., Mahoney, J. T., & Wang, H. (2020). Why we need a theory of stakeholder governance—And why this is a hard problem. *Academy of Management Review, 45*(3), 499–503.

Amit, R., & Schoemaker, P. J. H. (1993). Strategic assets and organizational rent. *Strategic Management Journal, 14*(1), 33–46.

Andersen, T. J. (2015). Interactive strategy-making: Combining central reasoning with ongoing learning from decentralised responses. *Journal of General Management, 40*(4), 69–88.

Arrfelt, M., Wiseman, R. M., & Hult, G. T. M. (2013). Looking backward instead of forward: Aspiration-driven influences on the efficiency of the capital allocation process. *Academy of Management Journal, 56*(4), 1081–1103.

Arrfelt, M., Wiseman, R. M., McNamara, G., & Hult, G. T. M. (2015). Examining a key corporate role: The influence of capital allocation competency on business unit performance. *Strategic Management Journal, 36*(7), 1017–1034.

Arrow, K. J. (2000). Observations of social capital. In P. Dasgupta & I. Serageldin (Eds.), *Social capital: A multifaceted perspective* (pp. 3–5). The World Bank.

Bardolet, D., Fox, C. R., & Lovallo, D. (2011). Corporate capital allocation: A behavioral perspective. *Strategic Management Journal, 32*(13), 1465–1483.

Barney, J. B. (1986). Strategic factor markets: Expectations, luck, and business strategy. *Management Science, 32*(10), 1231–1241.

Barney, J. B. (2018). Why resource-based theory's model of profit appropriation must incorporate a stakeholder perspective. *Strategic Management Journal, 39*(13), 3305–3325.

Barney, J. B., & Arikan, A. M. (2001). The resource-based view: Origins and implications. In M. A. Hitt, R. E. Freeman, & J. S. Harrison (Eds.), *The Blackwell handbook of strategic management* (pp. 124–188). Blackwell.

Barton, D. (2011, March). Capitalism for the long term. *Harvard Business Review*, 85–91.

Basel Committee on Banking Supervision. (2021). *The Basel framework*. Bank for International Settlements.

Bates, T. W., Kahle, K. M., & Stulz, R. M. (2009). Why do US firms hold so much more cash than they used to? *The Journal of Finance, 64*(5), 1985–2021.

Berrone, P., Fosfuri, A., Gelabert, L., & Gomez-Mejia, L. R. (2013). Necessity as the mother of 'green' inventions: Institutional pressures and environmental innovations. *Strategic Management Journal, 34*, 891–909.

Bettis, R. A. (1983). Modern financial theory, corporate strategy and public policy: Three conundrums. *Academy of Management Review, 8*(3), 406–415.

Bies, R. J., Bartunek, J. M., Fort, T. L., & Zald, M. N. (2007). Corporations as social change agents: Individual, interpersonal, institutional, and environmental dynamics. *Academy of Management Review, 32*(3), 788–793.

Bodie, Z., Kane, A., & Marcus, A. J. (2005). *Investments* (6th ed.). McGraw Hill.

Bonardi, J.-P., Hillman, A., & Keim, G. D. (2005). The attractiveness of political markets: Implications for firm strategy. *Academy of Management Review, 30*(2), 397–413.

Brandenburger, A. M., & Stuart, H. W. (1996). Value-based business strategy. *Journal of Economics & Management Strategy, 5*(1), 5–24.

Burgelman, R. A. (1983). A process model of internal corporate venturing in the diversified major firm. *Administrative Science Quarterly, 28*(2), 223–244.

Burgelman, R. A. (1996). A process model of strategic business exit: Implications for an evolutionary perspective on strategy. *Strategic Management Journal, 17*(S1), 193–214.

Burt, R. S. (1997). The contingent value of social capital. *Administrative Science Quarterly, 42*(2), 339–365.

Burt, R. S., & Merluzzi, J. (2016). Network oscillation. *Academy of Management Discoveries, 2*(4), 368–391.

Byun, H., Frake, J., & Agarwal, R. (2018). Leveraging who you know by what you know: Specialization and returns to relational capital. *Strategic Management Journal, 39*(7), 1803–1833.

Calandro, J., Gates, D., Madampath, A., & Ramette, F. (2015). A practical approach to business unit hurdle rates, portfolio analysis and strategic planning. *ACRN Journal of Finance and Risk Perspectives, 4*(2), 63–78.

Campbell, J. L. (2007). Why would corporations behave in socially responsible ways? An institutional theory of corporate social responsibility. *Academy of Management Review, 32*(3), 946–967.

Capron, L., & Guillen, M. (2009). National corporate governance institutions and post-acquisition target reorganization. *Strategic Management Journal, 30,* 803–833.

Central Bank Governance Group. (2009). *Issues in the governance of central banks*. Bank for International Settlements.

Chan, M. C., Isobe, T., & Makino, S. (2008). Which country matters? Institutional development and foreign affiliate performance. *Strategic Management Journal, 29,* 1179–1205.

Chandler, A. D. (2001, March–April). The enduring logic of industrial success. *Harvard Business Review,* 130–140.

Chatterjee, S., Lubatkin, M. H., & Schulze, W. S. (1999). Toward a strategic theory of risk premium: Moving beyond CAPM. *Academy of Management Review., 24,* 556–567.

Chen, R., Wang, L., Li, E., & Hu, G. (2021). Microdivisionalization as a way toward dynamic capability. *Management Decision, 59*(3), 506–523.

Christensen, C. M., & Bower, J. L. (1996). Customer power, strategic investment, and the failure of leading firms. *Strategic Management Journal, 17*(3), 197–218.

Coff, R. W. (1999). When competitive advantage doesn't lead to performance: The resource-based view and stakeholder bargaining power. *Organization Science, 10*(2), 119–133.

Coff, R. W. (2010). The coevolution of rent appropriation and capability development. *Strategic Management Journal, 31*(7), 711–733.

Cyert, R. M., & March, J. G. (1963). *A behavioural theory of the firm*. Prentice-Hall.

Demsetz, H. (1997). The firm in economic theory: A quiet revolution. *American Economic Review, 87,* 426–429.

Dickler, T. A., & Folta, T. B. (2020). Identifying internal markets for resource deployment. *Strategic Management Journal, 41*(13), 2341–2371.

Elahi, E. (2013). Risk management: The next source of competitive advantage. *Foresight, 15*(2), 117–131.

Ferguson, N. (2008). *The ascent of money: A financial history of the world*. Allen Lane.

Fernhaber, S. A., McDougall-Covin, P. P., & Shepherd, D. A. (2009). International entrepreneurship: Leveraging internal and external knowledge sources. *Strategic Entrepreneurship Journal, 3,* 297–320.

Foss, N. J., Lyngsie, J., & Zahra, S. A. (2013). The role of external knowledge sources and organizational design in the process of opportunity exploitation. *Strategic Management Journal, 34,* 1453–1471.

Garcia-Canal, E., & Guillen, M. F. (2008). Risk and strategy of foreign location choice in regulated industries. *Strategic Management Journal, 29,* 1097–1115.

Garcia-Pont, C., & Nohria, N. (2002). Local versus global mimetism: The dynamics of alliance formation on the automobile industry. *Strategic Management Journal, 23,* 307–321.

Garrouste, P., & Saussier, S. (2008). The theories of the firm. In E. Brousseau & J.-M. Glachant (Eds.), *New institutional economics: A guidebook* (pp. 23–36). Cambridge University Press.

Glaser, M., Lopez-De-Silanes, F., & Sautner, Z. (2013). Opening the black box: Internal capital markets and managerial power. *The Journal of Finance, 68*(4), 1577–1631.

Goerzen, A., & Beamish, P. W. (2005). The effect of alliance network diversity on multinational enterprise performance. *Strategic Management Journal, 26,* 333–354.

Goldstein, I., & Hackbarth, D. (2014). Corporate finance theory: Introduction to the special issue. *Journal of Corporate Finance.* https://doi.org/10.1016/j.jcorpfin.2014.10.018

Gubler, T., & Cooper, R. (2019). Socially advantaged? How social affiliations influence access to valuable service professional transactions. *Strategic Management Journal, 40*(13), 2287–2314.

Guill, G. D. (2016). Banker trust and the birth of modern risk management. *Journal of Applied Corporate Finance, 28*(1), 19–30.

Hall, P. A., & Soskice, D. (2001). *Varieties of capitalism: The institutional foundations of comparative advantage.* Oxford University Press.

Harris, M., & Raviv, A. (1991). The theory of capital structure. *The Journal of Finance, 46*(1), 297–355.

Harris, M., & Raviv, A. (2017). Why do firms sit on cash? An asymmetric information approach. *Review of Corporate Finance Studies, 6*(2), 141–173.

Hart, O. D. (1988). Incomplete contracts and the theory of the firm. *Journal of Law, Economics, and Organization, 4*(1), 119–139.

Hart, O. D. (2001). Financial contracting. *Journal of Economic Literature, 39*(4), 1079–1100.

Harvey, J. (2008). *Introduction to managing risk: Topic gateway series no. 28.* The Chartered Institute of Management Accountants.

Henisz, W. J., Dorobantu, S., & Nartey, L. J. (2013). Spinning gold: The financial returns to stakeholder engagement. *Strategic Management Journal.* https://doi.org/10.1002/smj.2180

Hodgson, G. M. (2006). What are institutions? *Journal of Economic Issues, 40,* 1–25.

Hoetker, G., & Mellewigt, T. (2009). Choice and performance of governance mechanisms: Matching alliance governance to asset type. *Strategic Management Journal, 30,* 1025–1044.

Ingham, G. (2008). *Capitalism*. Polity Press.
Kacperczyk, A. (2009). With greater power comes greater responsibility? Takeover protection and corporate attention to stakeholders. *Strategic Management Journal*, 30, 261–285.
Kallman, J. (2005). What is risk? *Risk Management*, 52(10), 57.
Kang, S.-C., Morris, S. S., & Snell, S. A. (2007). Relational archetypes, organizational learning, and value creation: Extending the human resource architecture. *Academy of Management Review*, 32(1), 236–256.
Kaplan, S., & Henderson, R. (2005). Inertia and incentives: Bridging organizational economics and organizational theory. *Organization Science*, 16(5), 509–521.
Kaplan, R. S. (2016). Risk management—The revealing hand. *Journal of Applied Corporate Finance*, 28(1), 8–18.
Kaplan, S. N., & Stromberg, P. (2002). Financial contracting. Theory meets the real world: An empirical analysis of venture capital contracts. *Review of Economic Studies*, 70(2), 281–315.
Kim, B., Burns, M. L., & Prescott, J. E. (2009). The strategic role of the board: The impact of board structure on top management team strategic action capability. *Corporate Governance: an International Review*, 17(6), 728–743.
Kim, B., & Prescott, J. E. (2005). Deregulatory forms, variations in the speed of governance adaptation, and firm performance. *Academy of Management Review*, 30(2), 414–425.
Kmec, P. (2011). Temporal hierarchy in enterprise risk identification. *Management Decision*, 49(9), 1489–1509.
Kwon, S.-W., & Adler, P. S. (2014). Social capital: Maturation of a field of research. *Academy of Management Review*, 39(4), 412–422.
International Organization for Standardization. (2018). *Risk management: ISO 31000*. ISO.
Lachmann, L. M. 1978[1956]. *Capital and its structure*. Sheed Andrews and McMeel.
Lalonde, C., & Boiral, O. (2012). Managing risks through ISO 31000: A critical analysis. *Risk Management*, 14(4), 272–300.
Langlois, R. N. (1985). Knowledge and rationality in the Austrian School: An analytical survey. *Eastern Economic Journal*, 9, 309–330.
Langlois, R. N. (2003). The vanishing hand: The changing dynamics of industrial capitalism. *Industrial and Corporate Change*, 12(2), 351–385.
Lepak, D. P., & Snell, S. A. (1999). The human resource architecture: Toward a theory of human capital allocation and development. *Academy of Management Review*, 24(1), 31–48.
Lewin, P. (1999). *Capital in disequilibrium*. Routledge.
Lewin, P. (2005). The capital idea and the scope of economics. *Review of Austrian Economics*, 18, 145–167.

Lovallo, D., Brown, A. L., Teece, D. J., & Bardolet, D. (2020). Resource reallocation capabilities in internal capital markets: The value of overcoming inertia. *Strategic Management Journal*, 41(8), 1365–1380.

Lovallo, D., & Kahneman, D. (2003, July). Delusions of success: How optimism undermines executives' decisions. *Harvard Business Review*, 56–63.

Mahoney, J. T. (2005). *Economic foundations of strategy, thousand Oaks*. Sage.

Makino, S., Isobe, T., & Chan, C. M. (2004). Does country matter? *Strategic Management Journal*, 1027–1043.

Matten, C. (2001). *Managing bank capital: Capital allocation and performance measurement*. John Wiley.

Matthews, H. (2008). *Operational risk: Topic gateway series no. 51*. The Chartered Institute of Management Accountants.

McGahan, A. M., & Porter, M. E. (1997). How much does industry matter, really? *Strategic Management Journal*, 18(SI), 15–30.

Merton, R. C., & Perold, A. (1993). Theory of risk capital in financial firms. *Journal of Applied Corporate Finance*, 6(3), 16–32.

Meyer, K. E., Estrin, S., Bhaumik, S. K., & Peng, M. W. (2009). Institutions, resources, and entry strategies in emerging economies. *Strategic Management Journal*, 30, 61–80.

Nag, R., Hambrick, D. C., & Chen, M.-J. (2007). What is strategic management, really? Inductive derivation of a consensus definition of the field. *Strategic Management Journal*, 28, 935–955.

Natividad, G. (2013). Multidivisional strategy and investment returns. *Journal of Economics & Management Strategy*, 22(3), 594–616.

Noda, T., & Bower, J. (1996). Strategy making as iterated processes of resource allocation. *Strategic Management Journal*, 17(S1), 159–192.

Nohria, N., & Gulati, R. (1996). Is slack good or bad for innovation? *Academy of Management Journal*, 39(5), 1245–1264.

North, D. C. (1994). Economic performance through time. *American Economic Review*, 84, 359–368.

Oliver, C. (1997). Sustainable competitive advantage: Combining institutional and resource-based views. *Strategic Management Journal*, 18, 697–713.

O'Reilly, C. A., & Tushman, M. L. (2011). Organizational ambidexterity in action: How managers explore and exploit. *California Management Review*, 53(4), 6–22.

O'Reilly, C. A., & Tushman, M. L. (2013). Organizational ambidexterity: Past, present, and future. *Academy of Management Perspectives*, 27(4), 324–338.

Peng, M. W., Sun, S. L., Pinkham, B., & Chen, H. (2009). The institution-based view as a third leg for a strategy tripod. *Academy of Management Perspectives*, 23(3), 63–81.

Penrose, E. T. (1959). *The theory of the growth of the firm*. John Wiley.

Porter, M. E. (1980). *Competitive strategy: Techniques for analyzing industries and competitors*. The Free Press.
Porter, M. E. (1985). *Competitive advantage: Creating and sustaining superior performance*. The Free Press.
Porter, M. E. (1991). Towards a dynamic theory of strategy. *Strategic Management Journal, 12*, 95–117.
Portes, A. (1998). Social capital: Its origins and applications in modern sociology. *Annual Review of Sociology, 24*, 1–24.
Powell, T. C. (2017). Strategy as diligence: Putting behavioral strategy into practice. *California Management Review, 59*(3), 162–190.
Prahalad, C. K., & Hamel, G. (1990). The core competence of the corporation. *Harvard Business Review, 68*, 79–92.
Rajan, R. G. (2012). The corporation in finance. *The Journal of Finance, 67*(4), 1173–1217.
Ramamoorti, S., Baskin, D. L., Epstein, B. J., & Wanserski, J. (2017, June). Managing risk at the speed of change. *The CPA Journal*, 6–9.
Reuefli, T. W., Collins, J. M., & Lacugna, J. R. (1999). Risk measures in strategic management research: Auld lang syne. *Strategic Management Journal, 20*, 167–194.
Riley, S. M., Michael, S. C., & Mahoney, J. T. (2017). Human capital matters: Market valuation of firm investments in training and the role of complementary assets. *Strategic Management Journal, 38*(9), 1895–1914.
Robins, J. A. (1992). Organizational considerations in the evaluation of capital assets: Toward a resource-based view of strategic investment by firms. *Organizational Science, 3*(4), 522–536.
Robison, L. J., Schmid, R. A. A., & Siles, M. E. (2002). Is social capital really capital? *Review of Social Economy, 60*, 1–21.
Rumelt, R. (1991). How much does industry matter? *Strategic Management Journal, 12*(3), 167–185.
Samuels, W. J. (1995). Critical survey: The present state of institutional economics. *Cambridge Journal of Economics, 19*, 569–590.
Sanders, W. M. G., & Boivie, S. (2004). Sorting things out: Valuation of new firms in uncertain markets. *Strategic Management Journal, 25*, 167–186.
Sax, J., & Andersen, T. J. (2019). Making risk management strategic: Integrating enterprise risk management with strategic planning. *European Management Review, 16*(3), 719–740.
Scherpereel, C. M. (2008). The option-creating institution: A real options perspective on economic organization. *Strategic Management Journal, 29*, 455–470.
Schumpeter, J. A. (1927). The explanation of the business cycle. *Econometrica, 21*, 286–311.

Schumpeter, J. A. (1947). The creative response in economic history. *The Journal of Economic History, 7*(2), 14–159.
Schumpeter, J. A. (1979 [1943]). *Capitalism, socialism and democracy* (5th ed.). George Allen & Unwin.
Scott, W. R. (1995). *Institutions and organizations.* Sage.
Sengul, M., Costa, A. A., & Gimeno, J. (2019). The allocation of capital within firms. *Academy of Management Annals, 13*(1), 43–83.
Shleifer, A., & Vishny, R. W. (1991). Takeovers in the 60's and the 80's: Evidence and implications. *Strategic Management Journal, 12,* 51–59.
Shleifer, A., & Vishny, R. W. (1997). A survey of corporate governance. *The Journal of Finance, 52*(2), 737–783.
Simerly, R. L., & Li, M. (2000). Environmental dynamism, capital structure and performance: A theoretical integration and an empirical test. *Strategic Management Journal, 21*(1), 31–49.
Sirmon, D. G., Hitt, M. A., Ireland, R. D., & Gilbert, B. A. (2011). Resource orchestration to create competitive advantage: Breadth, depth, and life cycle effects. *Journal of Management, 37*(5), 1390–1412.
Solow, R. M. (2000). Notes on social capital and economic performance. In P. Dasgupta & I. Serageldin (Eds.), *Social capital: A multifaceted perspective* (pp. 6–12). The World Bank.
Stein, J. C. (1997). Internal capital markets and the competition for corporate resources. *Journal of Finance, 52*(1), 111–133.
Stiglitz, J. E. (2001). Information and the change in the paradigm of economics. *(Nobel) Prize Lecture, 472–*540. https://www.nobelprize.org/upl oads/2018/06/stiglitz-lecture.pdf
Stiglitz, J. E. (2010). *Freefall: America, free markets, and the sinking of the world economy.* WW Norton & Company.
Stiglitz, J. E. (2012). *The price of inequality: How today's divided society endangers our future.* WW Norton & Company.
Stulz, R. M. (2016, August). Risk management, governance, culture, and risk taking in banks. *FRBNY Economic Policy Review,* 43–59.
Teece, D. J. (2007). Explicating dynamic capabilities: The nature and micro-foundations of (sustainable) enterprise performance. *Strategic Management Journal, 28,* 1319–1350.
Teece, D. J., Pisano, G., & Shuen, A. (1997). Dynamic capabilities and strategic management. *Strategic Management Journal, 18,* 509–533.
Tirole, J. (2001). Corporate governance. *Econometrica, 69*(1), 1–35.
Tirole, J. (2006). *Theory of corporate finance.* Princeton University Press.
Van Greuning, H., & Bratanovic, S. B. (2020). *Analyzing banking risk: A framework for assessing corporate governance and risk management* (4th ed.). International Bank for Reconstruction and Development/The World Bank.

Waddell, D. M., Cummings, T. G., & Worley, C. G. (2011). *Organizational change: Development and transformation* (4th ed.). Cengage Learning.

Wang, H. C., He, J., & Mahoney, J. T. (2009). Firm-specific knowledge resources and competitive advantage: The roles of economic-and relationship-based employee governance mechanisms. *Strategic Management Journal, 30*, 1265–1285.

Weigelt, C., & Miller, D. J. (2013). Implications of internal organization structure for firm boundaries. *Strategic Management Journal, 34*, 1411–1434.

Wernefelt, B. (1984). A resource-based view of the firm. *Strategic Management Journal, 5*(2), 171–180.

Williamson, O. E. (2010). Transaction cost economics: The natural progression. *American Economic Review, 100*(3), 673–690.

Winter, S. G. (2003). Understanding dynamic capabilities. *Strategic Management Journal, 24*(10), 991–995.

Zambon, S., & Zan, L. (2000). Accounting relativism: The unstable relationship between income measurement and theories of the firm. *Accounting, Organizations and Society, 25*(8), 799–822.

Zingales, L. (2000). In search of new foundations. *The Journal of Finance, 55*(4), 1623–1653.

Zollo, M., Minoja, M., & Coda, V. (2017). Toward an integrated theory of strategy. *Strategic Management Journal, 39*(6), 1753–1778.

Zona, F. (2012). Corporate investing as a response to economic downturn: Prospect theory, the behavioural agency model and the role of financial slack. *British Journal of Management, 23*, S42–S57.

Zubac, A., Hubbard, G., & Johnson, L. (2012). Extending resource-based logic: Applying the resource-investment concept to the firm from a payments perspective. *Journal of Management, 38*(6), 1867–1891.

Zubac, Z. (2018). Capitalism as discourse: How can strategic management scholars contribute new insights and refocus debate? *Journal of Management & Organization, 24*(2), 189–208.

CHAPTER 8

An Evolution: Turning Management Accounting into a Strategic Function

Mark Pickering ⓘ

INTRODUCTION

While the stereotype of the "bean counter" role of the management accountant persists for some (Christensen & Rocher, 2020; Friedman & Lyne, 2001), the role of management accounting has evolved substantially over the past half century (de Lautour, 2018). Management accounting-related activities and the role of management accountants differ across geographies (Goretzki & Strauss, 2018), industries, organisations and business units (de Lautour, 2018). While the magnitude of change may vary, there has been substantial evolution away from an almost clerical role of collecting, collating and reporting financial information for costing, budgeting and management reporting purposes with some provision of ad hoc decision support to a much more central role in management decision-making and control (IMA, 2008). Management accounting is now fundamental to strategy formulation, evaluation and

---

M. Pickering (✉)
Swinburne University of Technology, Hawthorn, VIC, Australia
e-mail: mpickering@swin.edu.au

© The Author(s), under exclusive license to Springer Nature Singapore Pte Ltd. 2022
A. Zubac et al. (eds.), *Effective Implementation of Transformation Strategies*, https://doi.org/10.1007/978-981-19-2336-4_8

implementation, playing a crucial role in tying strategy and operations together (IMA, 2008).

Management accounting has broadened in scope within organisations, its importance has grown across industries and reporting has expanded from mainly financial measures. Fifty years ago, management accountants produced periodic (usually monthly) management reports of financial performance in most companies, significantly more effort was placed in costing and monitoring performance on the factory floor in manufacturing firms (Johnson & Kaplan, 1987). Costing has now expanded across the whole value chain in manufacturing and has become an important exercise in strategic and operational decision-making, implementation and control across many other industries including services, government and not for profit organisations (Kaplan & Cooper, 1998). Management reports are no longer limited to financial data but also communicate strategic non-financial performance measures often in a Balanced Scorecard framework (Kaplan & Norton, 1996b). Rather than spending all of their time producing management reports, a large portion of management accounting time is spent performing analysis on reports produced and ad hoc financial analysis to assist executive and managers with strategic decisions (IMA, 2008).

This chapter explores this evolution of management accounting becoming a strategic function. It traces the new management accounting methods that contribute to strategic decisions and the implementation of those decisions. Observations are drawn from the literature and from the author's experience of the changes in a career of over 30 years in the accounting and management consulting industries and periodic involvement in accounting and strategic management education over that same time. The chapter begins by defining management accounting and the traditional role of management accounting in organisations. It then discusses the current more strategic role of management accounting and provides an outline of the management accounting tools and techniques that have emerged over the past few decades to link strategic, operational and the financial aspects of organisations. Last, how strategic management accounting (SMA) informs management decision-making and strategy implementation is outlined.

WHAT IS MANAGEMENT ACCOUNTING?

The Institute of Management Accountants (IMA) highlights the important role that management accountants play in strategy formulation and implementation with a contemporary definition of management accounting as:

> Management accounting is a profession that involves partnering in management decision making, devising planning and performance management systems, and providing expertise in financial reporting and control to assist management in the formulation and implementation of an organization's strategy. (IMA, 2008)

This focus on assisting with the formulation and implementation of strategy is consistent with the view of the Chartered Institute of Management Accountants, who indicate that:

> Management accountants analyse information to advise strategy and drive sustainable business success (CIMA).

These recent and strategic focused definitions of management accounting reflect a significant departure from the view of management accounting from 40 years ago. Contrast the above definitions with IMA definition of management accounting in 1981:

> ...the process of identification, measurement, accumulation, analysis, preparation, interpretation, and communication of financial information used by management to plan, evaluate, and control an organization and to assure appropriate use of and accountability for its resources. Management accounting also comprises the preparation of financial reports for non-management groups such as shareholders, creditors, regulatory agencies, and tax authorities. (IMA, 2008)

The traditional role of management accounting, common 40 years, and still in place in some organisations now, is discussed next followed by limitations of traditional management accounting.

Traditional Management Accounting Roles and Activities

Management accounting has traditionally contributed to the strategy development process through providing financial analysis of the performance of the prior strategy and the quantification of planned actions into the annual capital investment, operating and cash flow budgets (Bird et al., 1982; Eldenburg et al., 2020). These budgets are a component of strategy implementation by communicating priorities and allocating limited resources for the coming year. Management accounting has also been used to perform financial analysis to support various tactical or operation decisions required for implementation of the strategy and to respond to ad-hoc issues and opportunities that emerged during the period. Traditional management accounting played an important control role in monitoring financial performance against the strategic plan and operational performance against pre-established standards to identify out of control situations requiring management attention.

Traditional management accounting consists of four main activities that contribute to strategy development, its communication, implementation and the control cycle. These are costing, financial budgeting, management reporting and financial analysis (Bird et al., 1982). Management accounting had not changed much in the 75 years prior to the 1980s (Johnson & Kaplan, 1987) leading some to characterise the period as the "dark ages" of management accounting (Krumweide & Lawson, 2019).

Limitations of Traditional Management Accounting

Since the 1980s there has been significant criticism of the main traditional management accounting activities, including that these activities are resource intensive, provide little value to management decision-making and, in some cases, lead to value destroying decisions being implemented (e.g. Hope & Fraser, 2003; Johnson & Kaplan, 1987; Kaplan & Norton, 1992). The following are criticisms of costing, budgeting, performance reporting and financial analysis.

Costing

Traditionally, costing was primarily performed in manufacturing and engineering organisations and limited to the factory. Costing can potentially perform four functions: (1) valuing inventory to enable production costs to be allocated between inventory and cost of goods sold in the financial statements, (2) facilitating process control and evaluation of firm and functional managers performance by comparing actual manufacturing costs against predetermined cost standards, (3) provide product cost information to inform decision-making and (4) provide cost data for ad-hoc special studies (Johnson & Kaplan, 1987). A primary driver of costing was accounting standards, which determine costs to be included in year-end inventory in the external financial reports. Product costs in standard costing and job costing systems usually included three components—direct labour costs and direct material costs that could be traced directly to a product and overhead costs, which were indirect costs required to run the factory but not easily directly related to a product. Until the 1980s, and indeed still in some organisations, management accounting consolidated overhead costs into a cost "bucket" and then allocated across products produced in an arbitrary manner such as number of direct labour hours costs required to produce each product.

Much criticism was raised against traditional costing during the 1980s. The main issues raised were (Johnson & Kaplan, 1987):

- Product costs produced by the costing processes provided information of little value for strategic management decisions. Global competition had increased resulting in the need for accurate cost information. Increasing automation in factories and therefore growing overhead costs were being allocated in an arbitrary manner across an increasingly diverse number of products, reducing the accuracy of costs. Costs included in the costing systems only included the manufacturing costs allowed for financial reporting and did not include the costs of developing, selling, delivering or servicing products and therefore did not enable analysis of the overall profitability of products. In extreme cases, companies could be generating significant financial losses while the costing system indicated that all products were profitable. The need to identify all costs related to a product was raised by Porter (1985).

- Maintaining the costing system and reporting and investigating variances is resource intensive with many non-accountants in the business struggling to understand and action findings.
- The costing system encouraged manufacturing managers to run large batches of products and manufacture products to store in inventory (see also Goldratt & Cox, 1984). This resulted in increased investment in inventory and warehouses, increased obsolescence and damage to inventory and reduced ability to manufacture flexibly to customer demand.
- The costing systems were product focused and provided little information on the costs and profitability of customers.
- The systems provided little information on the causes of costs incurred or behaviour of costs, such as which costs were fixed or variable or capacity utilisation of existing resources.

Budgeting

Over the past two decades, the traditional annual budget cycle has received substantial criticism (e.g. Hope & Fraser, 2003) with limitations raised including:

- It is resource intensive to develop requiring up to thousands of manager and management accounting hours and often not complete until a few months into the new period.
- During the long and iterative process of budget development the connection between the strategy and the final budget produced may be broken.
- Due to the workload in budget development, some budgeted functions or costs may be calculated in a mechanical manner by incrementing prior year expenditure or budgets by a simple percentage with little consideration of changes in strategy or efficiency or effectiveness of operations.
- Development of the budget can involve substantial dysfunctional behaviour, such as padding the budget, particularly when managers will be rewarded based on performance against budget.
- The budget is often based on assumptions made sometimes months before the start of the budget year and is often out-of-date within

months of the commencement of the budget period. While flexible budgets adjust somewhat for changes in sales and production volumes, the budget can quickly become meaningless. Spending time and effort reporting and analysing performance against an out-of-date budget provides little value and managers may be restricted from responding to a changing environment due to commitment to an out-of-date budget.
- The budget may drive dysfunctional management decisions and/or reward or punish managers due to changes in the environment rather than performance issues.

Performance Reporting

Traditional management accounting produced management performance reports on a monthly basis as a control mechanism to monitor performance against plan, typically by comparing performance to the budget. Criticisms of the approach include (Johnson & Kaplan, 1987; Kaplan & Norton, 1992, 1996a, 1996b):

- Monthly management reporting has traditionally been financially focused. Financial measures are lagging indicators of performance, focused on how the firm has performed in the past. These measures provide limited information on why the firm performed as it did, how it can improve and how it is likely to perform in future (Kaplan & Norton, 1992, 1996a, 1996b).
- Actions such as cutting investment in research and development or marketing expenses could result in organisations reporting higher current period profitability but negatively impact on the firm's future performance (Stewart, 1991). Use of popular financial performance measures, such as Return on Investment (ROI) can contribute to dysfunctional management decisions on investments (Eldenburg et al., 2020). For example, where managers are rewarded based on the ROI of their business unit they are likely to reject a project that has an ROI above the company investment hurdle rate but below the business unit's current ROI. While the potential investment is attractive for the company, accepting it will bring down the business unit's ROI and negatively impact manager bonuses.

- The budget can be quickly obsolete because it is often established on assumptions made before the start of the year and changes to the environment or internal performance can make these assumptions and the resulting budget invalid. Reporting and analysing performance against an out-of-date budget provides limited insight on performance (Hope & Fraser, 2003).
- Producing management reports can require substantial resources, time and effort. In some cases, the management reports are provided to key decision-makers weeks after the end of the month. This can result in delays in decision-makers becoming aware of issues and could therefore reduce the value of the information provided (Johnson & Kaplan, 1987).

Financial Analysis

Traditional management accounting provides useful tools, such as net present value (NPV) analysis of investment options and cost volume profit analysis, to support management decisions such as whether to invest in new facilities or equipment, accept a special order or outsource a process or the production of a component (Eldenburg et al., 2020). Criticisms of the role of management accounting in performing and supporting financial analysis include the lack of appropriate cost data to inform decisions (Johnson & Kaplan, 1987), limited time with management accountants bogged in data collection and report generation and limited management accountant understanding of the operations of the business and the markets in which it operates (Friedman & Lyne, 2001). The use of ROI to assess investment opportunities can result in the rejection of attractive projects that are forecast to achieve returns above corporate targets but below the average ROI in a division (Eldenburg et al., 2020).

Traditional management accounting has been criticised for being too inwardly orientated, providing historically focused information focused on the short term, emphasising efficiency and being of limited value to managers for strategic decision-making. These issues have affected the image of management accountants with the use of the derogative term "bean counters" (Christensen & Rocher, 2020; Friedman & Lyne, 2001).

Strategic Management Accounting—Evolution of Tools and Techniques

The past 40 years have seen an evolution of management accounting that has seen it develop the potential to be a truly strategic function. This has been through the development of management accounting techniques and tools that are broader, externally and future focused, enabled by technology advancements. Many of these new techniques and tools emerged during the late 1980s and through the 1990s, a period considered the "golden age" of management accounting (Shank, 2007). Simmonds (1981: 26) first described "strategic management accounting" as "the provision and analysis of management accounting data about a business and its competitors for use in developing and monitoring the business strategy". During the 1980s, the term "strategic cost management" emerged in the United States to describe the combining of financial analysis themes with those from strategic management (Shank & Govindarajan, 1994). Management accounting tools and techniques have generally been classified by researchers as SMA if they are focused on the long term, typically over one year into the future, and externally focused (Cadez & Guilding, 2008).

Numerous studies of SMA over two decades have identified a number of different management accounting tools and techniques as SMA (e.g. Cadez & Guilding, 2007; Cescon et al, 2019; Cinquini & Tenucci, 2010; Cravens & Guilding, 2001; Guilding et al., 2000; Rashid et al, 2020). The following sub-sections give a brief description of these SMA tools and techniques as well as adding management accounting techniques that enable greater linkage to operations, such as zero based budgeting, and linkages between strategy, finance and operations, such as Strategy Maps. Performance measurement has moved beyond financial information to include non-financial performance measures and the information produced is now more closely connected to operations and strategy. This section looks at evolution in costing, the move to analysis of competitors and customers, changes in performance measurement and changes in the way some organisations budget. It is important to note that these emerging "management accounting" tools and techniques have been implemented to varying degrees across organisations with few, if any, organisations having implemented all of these (Nixon & Burns, 2012). While these evolving approaches are management accounting related, in some organisations the tools and techniques are used by managers in business operations rather than being applied and managed by management accountants in the finance department (Langfield-Smith, 2008).

Evolution in Costing

Since the 1980s costing techniques have emerged which have facilitated a much greater engagement with staff outside of the finance function, have provided a greater link between finance and operations and produced information that provides cost and profitability information that supports strategic decision-making. Some of the costing techniques also take a future view of costs rather that consolidating and reporting historic cost data. This section will touch briefly on activity-based costing, value chain costing, target costing, lifecycle costing, attribute costing and quality costing. Customer and competitor costing is considered in later sections.

Activity Based Costing (ABC): The underlying logic behind ABC is that organisations spend money to acquire resources which are used to perform activities in order to produce products or services for customers (see Kaplan & Cooper, 1998). Financial costs are allocated to resources and then to the activities performed in the organisation on a causal basis. The cost of these activities are then assigned to the products produced and customers served, also on a causal basis. ABC can improve the accuracy of traditional costing by breaking the large factory overhead cost bucket down into activities, such as "issuing raw materials", and assigning these activity costs to products based on the volume of each activity performed for each product. ABC can go much further and is used beyond the factory within manufacturing organisations and used to cost services in other industries such as banks, health care and government.

Implementing ABC brings management accountants much closer to operations as they need to identify activities performed throughout the organisation, the resources used to perform these activities and the causal drivers of the activities. This activity-related information enables activity analysis to improve efficiency by identifying and taking actions to reduce non-value adding activities. Improvements can also be realised by implementing best practices identified by comparing activity information across various locations in the organisation or benchmarking with other organisations. As discussed below ABC can be used in quality costing by identifying and tagging quality-related activities and associated costs.

Time driven ABC (TDABC) is an evolution of ABC that simplifies cost allocation and enables the identification of costs associated with spare capacity of resources (Kaplan & Anderson, 2003, 2007). ABC information enables the management of activities and their causal drivers (activity based management) and improvements in budgeting by using the causal drivers of the activities in calculating budgeted costs (activity based budgeting).

ABC can provide a much more complete understanding of how profits are generated in the business providing a valuable input into strategy development. By going beyond the factory floor, ABC can be used to assign selling, administration, customer service and distribution costs to the products and/or customers that are generating these activities for a more complete view of product or customer or even channel profitability. This is valuable information for strategic decisions such as which customers should the firm target with which products in which markets and through which channels. This information can also be used to inform marketing and pricing decisions.

Value Chain Costing: This involves determining the cost of performing various activities throughout the value chain, often using ABC. Leveraging Porter's value chain concepts (Porter, 1985), the analysis can be used to determine activities within the company and industry value chains that the company may have or is pursuing a competitive advantage in, potential duplication or issues between different components of the value chain and activities that may be appropriately outsourced. Value chain costing enables examination of the cost of activities performed to determine whether customers are willing to pay for differentiation or whether a cost strategy is appropriate.

Target Costing: While traditional costing allocates past costs to products, target costing involves proactively developing products that can meet a need in the market at a cost that enables the company to make its target profit (Cooper & Chew, 1996). Management accountants work in development teams with product development, engineering and marketing staff. Market positioning, including attributes and pricing, of a potential product is identified through investigation of customer needs and competitor offerings. The required profit margin for the product is subtracted from the planned selling price to calculate the target cost for the product. The target cost is allocated to the different components of the product and engineers work to develop each component at the required cost. This approach builds relationships between management accountants and other functions, puts costing in a proactive rather than historic form and increases the links between costs, operations and the market.

Lifecycle Costing: This approach takes a much longer view of costs reflecting an examination of product costs over the expected life of a product. This includes development costs, costs through various stages of the lifecycle (introduction, growth, maturity and decline) and any end-of-life costs (Guilding et al., 2000).

Attribute Costing: Attributes or characteristics provided to customers by products are costed and reported against those provided by current competitors or competitors likely to enter the market in future (Langfield-Smith, 2008). Companies must continue to produce and offer competitive products to deliver the customers' desired bundle of attributes. Where attributes or characteristics of the overall offering are used to implement a differentiation strategy, understanding the cost of each attribute enables evaluation as to whether customers are willing to pay more than the cost of providing this differentiation. This approach requires accountants to engage with strategic market information as well as cost information.

Quality Costing: Quality costing emerged to support the total quality management (TQM) movement. Improving quality reduces rework and rectification issues. Quality costing involved identifying and costing different types of quality activities including prevention, inspection, internal failure and external failure (Guilding et al., 2000). This is typically done through using ABC and tagging appropriate activities. The objective is to put greater resources into earlier stage quality assurance activities to reduce much greater costs associated with failure.

Analysis of Customers

Costing analysis has moved beyond the predominantly product focus of traditional costing to analyse the economics of different customers or customer segments to the firm.

Customer Profitability Analysis: Customer costing and customer profitability analysis takes into account that different customers or customer segments often pay different prices for the services and products that they buy, buy in different ways through different channels, require different levels of customer service and receive different levels and frequency of distribution of products (Johnson & Kaplan, 1987; Kaplan & Cooper, 1998). ABC is used to calculate the cost of each of these various customer-related activities for each customer segment or individual customer. The profitability of customer segments or individual customers is calculated by subtracting the cost to serve from gross margin made on products/services purchased by those customers (Kaplan & Cooper, 1998). The gross margin used takes into account the price paid by those customers (net of discounts), which can vary substantially across customer segments.

Understanding the profitability of different types of customers and the drivers of profitability of each group can provide important input into management decisions such as which customers segments should our marketing and sales force target? How can we most efficiently target different customers? Should we renegotiate service terms or price? In extreme cases, should we exit unprofitable customers or customer segments?

Customer Lifetime Value (CLV): CLV looks at the value to a firm of customer relationships (Reichheld, 1996). It treats customers as assets that have costs to acquire and generate profits for the firm over the period of the relationships. CLV is modelled over the expected period of the relationship and a discount rate is applied to determine the current value. Using CLV highlights the importance of retaining existing customers and can result in an increased focus on customer service and customer satisfaction from an over-emphasis on finding new customers. Where customer acquisition costs are high, rapid customer churn can mean that investment in customer acquisition activities may never earn a return. As customers may change over time, for example, small companies grow and consumers may earn higher salaries in future, the current profitability of customers may not be reflective of their value to the firm. CLV can be an important technique for identifying and targeting valuable customer segments, determining methods to improve lower value segments and increasing the focus on customer retention-related performance measures.

Competitor Analysis

Management accounting techniques used to analyse competitors include analysis and monitoring of competitors' cost base, their competitive positioning and quantitative analysis of their published financial statements to identify potential sources of competitive advantage (Guilding et al., 2000).

Cost base analysis involves regularly collecting external data on competitors' resources and analysing the potential implications on costs. This can include physical facilities, technologies utilised in production and within products, relationships with suppliers and economies of scale. Potential sources of data include discussions with mutual customers and suppliers and ex-employees, direct observation and publicly available information, such as company announcements and annual reports.

Competitor Analysis: Analysis of the industry and competitor positions within it involves analysing trends in competitor sales, market share, pricing, unit costs and profitability. This analysis provides insights into the competitive strategy of competitors.

Performance Measurement

Major innovations have been developed in performance measurement since the 1980s including the Balanced Scorecard, Strategy Maps and Economic Value Added (EVA®).

The Balanced Scorecard: Major improvements in performance measurement include the introduction of non-financial performance measures, which link financial measures to the firm's strategy and operations and are leading indicators of future financial performance (Kaplan & Norton, 1992, 1996a, 1996b). The Balanced Scorecard links innovation and growth activities of continuous improvement of organisational products and capabilities, effective and efficient internal processes, creating customer value and financial performance (Kaplan & Norton, 1996a, 1996b). Measures are developed from the strategy, communicating the strategy to staff, with implementation of the strategy requiring the identification of operational activities to achieve targets for each of the measures. Regular reporting of the measures enables monitoring/controls of the strategy.

Strategy Maps: Strategy Maps emerged as an important strategic management accounting tool in the early 2000's through an evolution in the use of the Balanced Scorecard (Kaplan & Norton, 2001, 2004). Strategy Maps involve documenting in graphical form the cause and effect relationships between elements and measures in the Balanced Scorecard. This enables a comprehensive description of the strategy to communicate to managers and employees, enables shared understanding and alignment of measures and actions with the strategy and supports the implementation of new strategies in a changing environment with global competition, increasing deregulation, increased customer focus and emerging technologies (Kaplan & Norton, 2004).

Economic Value Added (EVA®): EVA® was developed by Stern Stewart and Co in the 1980s to address issues with traditional financial performance measures and capital allocation tools, such as ROI (Stewart, 1991). The approach involves adjusting net income after taxation to treat some period expenses as assets and applies a capital charge to the division to determine the Economic Value Added for the period.

Budgeting

A number of approaches have evolved to address issues with the traditional approach to budgeting identified earlier. These include driver-based budgeting (including activity based budgeting), zero based budgeting, Beyond Budgeting and scenario planning.

Driver Based Budgeting: involves understanding the causes or drivers of costs and calculating budgeted costs by applying the unit costs based on planned outputs (Kaplan & Cooper, 1998). Many manufacturing organisations utilise this approach to budget direct manufacturing costs, such as direct labour and direct materials with the traditional budgeting approach. For example, direct labour hours per unit are multiplied by expected cost per hour and by number of planned units to budget total labour costs. Driver based budgeting extends this to other operations with forecast sales volume or other factors used to calculate estimated activity, such as number of customer service calls, and the budgeted cost for customer service calls estimated based on the cost per call.

Zero Based Budgeting: emerged in the 1970s but lost favour due to the significant resources required to implement and maintain it (see Deloitte, 2015; McKinsey, 2014). The approach has increased in popularity in recent years. Traditional budgeting uses the prior year costs as a starting point and increments the budget for expected changes in volumes and/or agreed new activities (McKinsey, 2014). This can result in costs built into the previous budgets remaining in future budgets when the projects or activities budgeted are no longer relevant or no longer a strategic priority. ZBB involves starting the budget for each cost at zero each year and building up budgeted costs based on the current strategy (McKinsey, 2014). This requires a strong understanding of the operations of the business and the links between operations and the strategy and operations and finances. ZBB is more resource intensive than the traditional approach and is therefore not always performed every year or is rotated through different parts of the business through a number of budget cycles (Deloitte, 2015).

Beyond Budgeting: is to some degree the opposite of ZBB. Under this approach, the detailed annual budget is discontinued and replaced with more frequent, higher level financial forecasts and an increased reliance on key performance indicators (Hope & Fraser, 2003). Executives are no longer rewarded based on achievement of the budget but on firm performance in comparison to peer competitors.

Management Accounting Tools and Techniques and Sustainability

The impact of organisations on society and the environment is increasingly becoming a concern for governments, society, investors and society and therefore for managers of organisations. There have been increasing requirements for organisations to report the impact of their organisations on society and the environment as well as the historic financial measures (Adams & Abhayawansa, 2022) in a triple bottom line report (Elkington, 1998). Scarce resources, increasing regulation, more visibility into the consequence of organisational activities and a growing customer and investor preference for less socially and environmentally damaging products require managers to have a greater understanding of resources utilised and waste outputs produced (Eldenburg et al., 2020). As well as improving outcomes for society and the environment, improved corporate sustainability can have strategic and operational benefits for organisations that can differentiate the sustainability of their products and reduce costs of natural resource inputs, waste disposal and regulatory failures.

Some of the management accounting tools mentioned earlier are being used to measure, report and manage and reduce the use of scarce resources and output of waste and improve the implications of corporate actions on society (Eldenberg et al., 2020). The Balanced Scorecard is used by some organisations to develop targets, action plans and measure and report sustainability performance either in a fifth "Sustainability" dimension or by embedding sustainability measures in the existing dimensions. ABC is being used to identify sustainability costs, the physical flow of scarce natural resources and wastes created through the value chain and to allocate these to company products to understand the environmental impacts of activities and products. Environmental-related costs can be identified and analysed using TQM concepts highlighting the high costs of failures, such as fines and clean-up costs for pollution, and economic benefits of prevention-related activities. Lifecycle costing is important to consider the whole of life costs of products to the company and society, including end-of-life disposal or rectification costs. While management accounting has traditionally provided only the financial aspects of information required for management decisions, such as whether to introduce a new product, buy a new machine or where to locate a new plant, management accounting tools are increasingly being used to provide other social and environmental information relevant to decisions. Increasing stakeholder concerns on sustainability and greater regulation, including disclosure requirements, is likely to increase the use of management accounting tools to support management decisions and management reporting in these non-financial areas.

STRATEGIC MANAGEMENT ACCOUNTING AS A STRATEGIC FUNCTION—SUPPORTING MANAGEMENT DECISIONS

The recent evolution of management accounting tools and techniques enables the function to become strategic providing financial and non-financial information to help managers make strategic management, operational management, organisational design, financial and capital management decisions.

Strategic Management Decisions

SMA provides valuable information that supports major strategic management decisions such as:

- Which products/services should we produce?
- Which customer segments should we target through what channels?
- Which markets should we focus on?
- What are our sources of competitive advantage?
- What should our competitive position be?
- What scope of activities should we perform within the organisation?

Costing techniques, such as ABC, product lifecycle costing and customer profitability and customer lifetime value analysis, provide a full view of the economics of the business. This provides an understanding of which products and customer segments are generating long-term profits and have the most potential value.

Value chain costing, attribute costing and competitor analysis provide input into the identification and monitoring of relative competitive position and perceived or potential sources of competitive advantage. Attribute costing assists in determining whether differentiated characteristics of products generate revenues above their costs. Value chain costing and competitor analysis provides input into the identification of the activities that the firm performs that provide competitive advantage through low cost or differentiation. This informs strategic decisions on the boundaries of the organisation including which activities to keep in-house and which to outsource. Developing Balanced Scorecards and Strategy Maps can assist to identify potential actions in developing the strategic plan. These tools and techniques can also be used to include sustainability into strategy development.

As can be seen in the following section, management accounting tools and techniques can support the implementation of strategic decisions. This includes providing information and analysis to support management decisions in operations, organisational design, finance and capital management in order to achieve strategic objectives.

STRATEGIC MANAGEMENT ACCOUNTING—ENABLING STRATEGY IMPLEMENTATION

As mentioned above, SMA can provide valuable information on the economics of the business, its products, customers, value chain and competitors, to inform strategic management decisions in the development of the strategy. SMA can provide support for operational management, organisational design and capital management decisions enabling the implementation of the strategy. SMA can support strategy implementation by providing frameworks and tools to (1) communicate the strategy; (2) develop performance measures, targets and actions and rewards aligned with the strategy; (3) monitor implementation of the strategy and ongoing environmental fit. These are discussed below.

1. *Communicating the Strategy*

Traditional management accounting provided some communication of the strategy through the allocation of resources in the operating and capital budgets (Eldenburg et al., 2020). It could be inferred that business units and projects that were allocated an increased level of resources were a higher strategic priority than those that were not. Of course, not all staff were privy to the budget and the budget did not necessarily disclose actions to be taken and why. The Balanced Scorecard and Strategy Maps can make the strategy explicit and clear to all by showing objectives, performance measures and targets across the four dimensions of the Scorecard: learning and growth, internal processes, customers and financial (Kaplan & Norton, 1996b, 2004). The map demonstrates the relationship between these measures enabling managers to make decisions that benefit the whole organisation and achievement of the strategy rather than optimising their own function (Kaplan & Norton, 2004). Aligning rewards with these measures and targets further communicates the priorities and motivates managers and staff towards their achievement (Kaplan & Norton, 1996b).

2. Develop Action Plans and Support Management Decisions to Achieve Strategic Targets

The development of Balanced Scorecards and Strategy Maps that are aligned to the strategy may provide a framework for the development of action plans designed to move key performance measures towards the targets and achievement of the strategy (Kaplan & Norton, 2004). Management accounting tools and techniques provide information and analysis to support management decisions aligned with achieving the corporate strategies and objectives. This includes decisions anticipated in the planning phase but also those that emerge through changing circumstances. The types of decisions supported include those related to operations, organisational design and finance and capital management as discussed below.

2a. Operational Management Decisions

Traditional management accounting techniques and tools, such as NPV, payback period, ROI, cost volume profit analysis have been, and still are, used to support management decisions on investing in plant and equipment, evaluating special customer orders or options to outsource operations (Eldenburg et al., 2020). SMA advancements provide greater support for operational decisions. Balanced Scorecards and Strategy Maps assist in identifying and prioritising operational actions required to achieve strategic objectives (Hope & Fraser, 2003). Such activities can further enhance operations performance of the organisation through successful implementation of projects that support the organisation's strategy.

The understanding of activities and their relationship to costs and causes or drivers of activities developed through ABC provides information to analyse costs but also manage underlying activities (Kaplan & Cooper, 1998). Insights on the potential implications of operational decisions can be provided by forward-looking costing approaches such as target costing (Cooper & Chew, 1996) and lifecycle costing (Guilding et al., 2000). An increasing understanding of environmental costs enables the identification of actions to reduce these costs. Embedding management accountants in design teams enable the development of products that meet strategic positioning and can be produced at a target cost to achieve planned profit margins. Advances in budgeting provide greater visibility into costs and their causes, providing information to assist in efficiency improvement as well as continuing to flag out of control areas requiring management attention.

2b. Organisational Design Decisions

The understanding of activities, and associated costs, performed throughout the organisation provided by ABC and the understanding of activities that provide competitive advantage, informed by value chain costing and competitor analysis, provide information that supports organisational design decisions (Kaplan & Cooper, 1998). This includes potential opportunities to consolidate duplicated or fragmented support activities performed around the organisation into shared service organisations to develop greater expertise and/or reduce costs. It also includes opportunities to outsource activities that do not provide competitive advantage and may be performed more effectively and/or more efficiently by an external organisation.

While SMA has been an input into these organisational design changes, the function has also been impacted by them (Seal, 2018). Many large organisations have split the transaction process and management reporting roles of management accounting from the analytical decision support areas and placed them in global shared service centres. Management accountants remain in business units in business partner roles providing decision support to managers.

Management accounting has continued to evolve performance measures to determine the performance of departments or business units of large, complex business and to motivate optimal economic interaction between units (Kaplan & Cooper, 1998). This includes evolving performance measurement techniques, such as EVA® (Stewart, 1991) and charge-backs from shared service centres to business unit "clients" and transfer pricing between business units (Kaplan & Cooper, 1998).

2c. Financial and Capital Management Decisions

Financial and capital management decisions are integrated with the strategic, operation management and organisational design decisions discussed previously to allocate scarce resources. The budget process is used to project the financial and cash flow implications of operational plans and to develop the capital budget that reflects the prioritisation of potential projects. This process can be improved through strategic management accounting due to the explicit linkage between proposed investments and strategic objectives established in the Balanced Scorecard and the Strategy Map. Improved insights into the activities performed in the organisation and their costs and causes gained through activity-based costing can enable improved business cases for investment decisions. Finally, use of performance measures, such as EVA® can improve the evaluation of, and allocation of capital to business units.

3. *Monitor Implementation and Ongoing Environmental Fit*

The Balanced Scorecard enables implementation of the strategy to be monitored and areas requiring management attention to be identified (Kaplan & Norton, 1996b, 2004). Progress towards targets for each measure is monitored regularly. Careful attention is paid to the linkages between measures to learn more about cause and effect relationships. For example, the strategy may have called for improvements to customer service processes with expectations that this would flow through to increased customer satisfaction and then sales growth. This expected relationship can be tested to see if it holds. Performance against budget provides information of the implementation of the strategy and potential out of control areas. Ongoing competitor analysis enables ongoing monitoring of competitor capabilities, cost structures and offerings to discover changes to the competitive environment on a timely basis (Guilding et al., 2000). This ongoing monitoring identifies areas requiring attention or potentially flags the need to revisit the strategy and its assumptions.

Conclusions

Management accounting has evolved over the past four decades with the emergence of tools and techniques that are externally focused, forward-looking and link strategic, financial and operational aspects of the organisation. Use of these tools goes beyond the accounting department. Management accounting tools now exist to achieve greater horizontal and vertical alignment throughout the organisation. The customer value creation strategy can be enhanced through the use of cost analysis tools that assist to develop a strong understanding of the economics of the business including its activities, products and customers and of the linkages between different non-financial aspects and performance. Refined costing, budgeting, capital expenditure evaluation and performance measurement processes assist in developing the resource strategy required to implement the customer value creation strategy. Tools such as triple bottom line reporting and the Balanced Scorecard can be an integral component of developing the customer value creation strategy but also non-market strategies addressing the requirements of all stakeholders. These tools and techniques can be used to inform management decision-making throughout the organisation and to support strategy implementation moving management accounting to a truly strategic function.

References

Adams, C., & Abhayawansa, S. (2022). Connecting the COVID-19 pandemic, environmental, social and governance (ESG) investing and calls for 'harmonisation' of sustainability reporting. *Critical Perspectives on Accounting*, Vol. 82 January. https://doi.org/10.1016/j.cpa.2021.102309

Bird, R. G., McDonald, M. G., & McHugh, A. J. (1982). *Management Accounting: Processing, evaluating, and using cost data*. Butterworths Publishing.

Cadez, S., & Guilding, C. (2007). Benchmarking the incidence of strategic management accounting in Slovenia. *Journal of Accounting and Organizational Change, 3*(2), 126–146.
Cadez, S., & Guilding, C. (2008). An exploratory investigation of an integrated contingency model of strategic management accounting. *Accounting, Organizations and Society, 33*(7/8), 836–863.
Cescon, F., Costantini, A., & Grassetti, L. (2019). Strategic choices and strategic management accounting in large manufacturing firms. *Journal of Management and Governance, 23*(3), 605–636.
Christensen, M., & Rocher, S. (2020). The persistence of accountant beancounter images in popular culture. *Accounting, Auditing & Accountability Journal, 33*(6), 1395–1422.
CIMA, Chartered Institute of Management Accountants, website https://www.cimaglobal.com/ Sighted 7 March 2021.
Cinquini, L., & Tenucci, A. (2010). Strategic management accounting and business strategy: A loose coupling? *Journal of Accounting and Organizational Change, 6*(2), 228–259.
Cooper, R., & Chew, W. B. (1996, January–February). Control tomorrow's costs through today's designs. *Harvard Business Review*, 88–97.
Cravens, K. S., & Guilding, C. (2001). An empirical study of the application of strategic management accounting techniques. *Advances in Management Accounting, 10*, 95–124.
de Lautour, V. J. (2018). *Strategic management accounting, volume 1: Aligning strategy, operations and finance.* Palgrave Macmillan.
Deloitte. (2015). *Zero based budgeting zero or hero.* Deloitte UK. Sighted 12 June 2021. https://www2.deloitte.com/content/dam/Deloitte/global/Documents/Process-and-Operations/gx-us-operations-cons-zero-based-budgeting.pdf
Eldenburg, L. G., Brooks, A., Oliver, J., Vesty, G., Dormer, R., Murphy, V., & Pawsey, N. (2020). *Management accounting.* Wiley Gabriola Island, New Society Publishers.
Elkington, J. (1998). *Cannibals with forks: The triple bottom line of 21 century business.* New Society Publishers.
Friedman, A. L., & Lyne, S. R. (2001). The beancounter stereotype: Towards a general model of stereotype generation. *Critical Perspectives of Accounting, 12*(4), 423–445.
Goldratt, E., & Cox, J. (1984). *The goal.* Gower.
Goretzki, L., & Strauss, E. (2018). *The role of the management accountant: Local variations and global influences.* ProQuest (Firm), Routledge.
Guilding, C., Cravens, K. S., & Tayles, M. (2000). An international comparison of strategic management accounting techniques. *Management Accounting Research, 11*(1), 113–135.

Hope, J., & Fraser, R. (2003). *Beyond budgeting: How managers can break free from the annual performance trap*. Harvard Business School Press.
IMA. (2008). *Statements on management accounting: Definition of management accounting*. Institute of Management Accountants.
Johnson, H. T., & Kaplan, R. S. (1987). *Relevance lost: The rise and fall of management accounting*. Harvard Business School Press.
Kaplan, R. S., & Anderson, S. R. (2003, November). *Time-driven activity-based costing*. Available at SSRN: https://ssrn.com/abstract=485443 or http://dx.doi.org/10.2139/ssrn.485443
Kaplan, R. S., & Anderson, S. R. (2007). *Time-driven activity-based costing: A simple and more powerful approach to higher profits*. Harvard Business School Press.
Kaplan, R. S., & Cooper, R. (1998). *Cost & effect: Using integrated cost systems to drive profitability and performance*. Harvard Business School Press.
Kaplan, R. S., & Norton, D. (1992). The balanced scorecard: Measures that drive performance. *Harvard Business Review, 1*(1), 71–79.
Kaplan, R. S., & Norton, D. (1996a). The balanced scorecard as a strategic management system. *Harvard Business Review, 4*(1), 75–85.
Kaplan, R. S., & Norton, D. (1996b). *The balanced scorecard: Translating strategy into action*. Harvard Business School Press.
Kaplan, R. S., & Norton, D. (2001). Having trouble with your strategy? Then map it. *Harvard Business Review, 78*(5), 167–202.
Kaplan, R. S., & Norton, D. (2004). *Strategy maps: Converting intangible assets into tangible outcomes*. Harvard Business School Press.
Krumweide, K., & Lawson. R. (2019). Management accountants in the United States evolving to meet the changing needs of practice. In L. Goretzki, & E. Strauss (1982) (Eds.), *The role of the management accountant: Local variations and global influences* (p. 198 to 212). ProQuest (Firm), Routledge, 2018.
Langfield-Smith, K. (2008). Strategic management accounting: How far have we come in 25 years? *Accounting, Auditing & Accountability Journal, 21*(2), 204–228.
McKinsey. (2014). *Five myths (and realities) about zero-based budgeting*. McKinsey Insights. Sighted 12 June 2021 https://www.mckinsey.com/business-functions/strategy-and-corporate-finance/our-insights/five-myths-and-realities-about-zero-based-budgeting
Nixon, B., & Burns, J. (2012). The paradox of strategic management accounting. *Management Accounting Research, 23*(4), 229–244.
Porter, M. (1985). *Competitive advantage*. Free Press.
Rashid, M. M., Ail, M. M., & Hossain, D. W. (2020). Strategic management accounting practices and opportunities for further research. *Asian Journal of Accounting Research, 6*(1), 109–132.

Reichheld, F. F. (1996). *The loyalty effect: the hidden force behind growth, profits, and lasting value*. Harvard Business School Press.

Seal, W. (2018). Agent or victim? Shared services and management accounting. In L. Goretzki, & E. Strauss (1982) (Eds.), *The role of the management accountant: Local variations and global influences* (p. 225 to 235). ProQuest (Firm), Routledge, 2018.

Shank, J. K. (2007). Strategic cost management: Upsizing, downsizing, and right (?) sizing. In A. Bhimani (Ed.), *Contemporary issues in management accounting* (pp. 355–379). Oxford University Press.

Shank, J. K., & Govindarajan, V. (1994). *Strategic cost management—The new tool for competitive advantage*. The Free Press.

Simmonds, K. (1981). Strategic management accounting. *Management Accounting, 59*(4), 26–30.

Stewart, G. B. (1991). *The quest for value*. Harper Collins.

PART III

The Customer Value Creation Strategy

CHAPTER 9

Introduction: The Customer Value Creation Strategy

Angelina Zubac, Danielle Tucker, Ofer Zwikael, Kate Hughes, and Shelley Kirkpatrick

The three chapters in this section shed light on the different problems managers need to solve when they develop and implement their organisation's customer value creation strategies. More to the point, they demonstrate that customer value cannot be created successfully, including

---

A. Zubac (✉)
University of Queensland, Brisbane, QLD, Australia
e-mail: a.zubac@business.uq.edu.au; angelina.zubac@aim.com.au; az@strategylink.com.au

D. Tucker
University of Essex, Colchester, UK
e-mail: dtucker@essex.ac.uk

O. Zwikael
Australian National University, Canberra, ACT, Australia
e-mail: ofer.zwikael@anu.edu.au

K. Hughes
Technological University Dublin, Dublin, Ireland

© The Author(s), under exclusive license to Springer Nature Singapore Pte Ltd. 2022
A. Zubac et al. (eds.), *Effective Implementation of Transformation Strategies*, https://doi.org/10.1007/978-981-19-2336-4_9

systematically over time unless the organisation's customer value creation internal and external contexts are understood. Chapter 10 by Lenore Pennington demonstrates this by making it clear that in a world where all organisations are now required to be more sustainable and play their part in tackling climate change and other global megaproblems, success is now tied to how well the organisation adapts its business model to better reflect customers' sustainability concerns. Chapter 11 by Angelina Zubac explains that some customer value definitions are just much more suited to solving some customer value creation related dilemmas than others. Chapter 12 by Wojciech Dyduch, which is an empirical study, demonstrates that organisations operating in emerging market economies often struggle to achieve a suitable balance between value creation and value appropriation because they are resource constrained.

Thus, all of the chapters provide insight into how critical it is for the customer value creation strategy to reflect the organisation's internal and external contexts. This can be achieved by ensuring the customer value strategy aligns with the financial, resource and non-market strategies, as they enable the organisation to achieve its corporate strategic objectives. This is depicted in Fig. 9.1. As one can see by examining Fig. 9.1, there are many external market and non-market related factors that constrain or promote an organisation's growth. They determine what the organisation can achieve overall through its financial, resource, non-market and customer value creation strategies. There are also many (sub)processes and cognitions that may need to be rationalised over time to build the (dynamic) capabilities required to allow the organisation to implement strategies that are soundly aligned. For instance, it may be necessary to invest in capabilities that allow the organisation to achieve both its efficiency and sustainability objectives at the same time.

These ideas are demonstrated in the first chapter in this section by Lenore Pennington, *Business models for sustainability*, which argues that organisations can create customer value by delivering on customers' sustainability concerns. To do this, organisations must review their

---

e-mail: kate.hughes@hughes-scm.com

S. Kirkpatrick
The MITRE Corporation, McLean, VA, USA
e-mail: skirkpatrick@mitre.org

9 INTRODUCTION: THE CUSTOMER VALUE CREATION STRATEGY

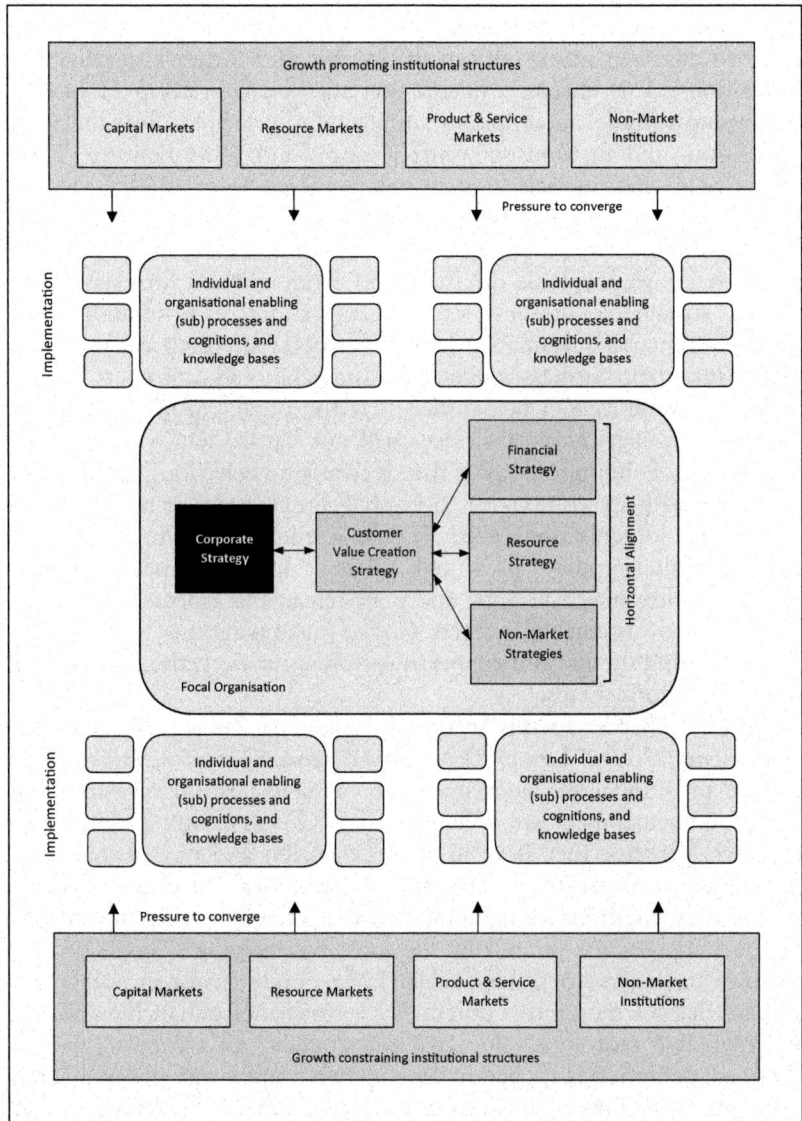

Fig. 9.1 Implementing strategy and organisational change: a customer value creation strategy focus

entire business model, and devise and implement a sustainable business model to ensure it meets customers' and broader society's sustainability expectations. This chapter explains that the strongest form of sustainable business model incorporates sustainability principles into the value proposition, and methods of value creation and value delivery. These innovative business models consider stakeholders, society and the environment. As opposed to the "traditional" business model with its focus on achieving competitive advantage and ensuring the organisation's products and/services are profitable due to sound economic and financial fundamentals, sustainable business models are broader, incorporating social and environmental sustainability fundamentals. Only then can organisations ensure their business is operated sustainably, and customers and the broader community can be satisfied that the organisation's operational processes, products and/or services will not harm them, others or the environment. Pennington argues that as corporate behaviour and thinking is coupled with its culture, to successfully implement sustainable business models, organisations need to change their underlying culture. A detailed cultural model is presented. While adopting an enabling organisational culture may take time and persistence, this culture change will support more sustainable business models and operations, which themselves will bring significant benefits to customers, society, the environment and organisations themselves.

The next chapter in this section by Angelina Zubac, *The Customer Value Concept: How Best to Define and Create Customer Value*, examines the pros and cons associated with defining customer value as (1) the amount customers are willing to pay, (2) an equity position that customers perceive they have in an organisation and (3) an inherently multidimensional construct. The chapter concludes that even though all three of these methods for defining customer value have their advantages, the third approach is potentially the most advantaging. This is because it allows managers to systematically learn about customer value, and translate that learning into a potentially performance-enhancing and very implementable customer value creation strategy. An exemplar multidimensional definition is applied to develop two frameworks to demonstrate this point. Both frameworks can be used to build a boundary-spanning, customer value learning, co-creation and co-delivery (platform-based) system as an active participant within an institutional complex ecosystem. Were such a system to be built, it should be possible to create new forms of customer value.

9 INTRODUCTION: THE CUSTOMER VALUE CREATION STRATEGY

The ideas in this chapter are also consistent with the idea that by being customer-centric, the organisation can become more strategically aligned. This is generally depicted in Fig. 9.2. As one can see by comparing "A" to "B" and "C", by investing in customer value creating managerial, technical and marketing dynamic capabilities the organisation cannot only build a satisfied customer base but can more adeptly reinvest in itself for the future. All going well, these customer-centric resource investments will lead to a corresponding reconfiguration of the organisation's (activity-based) value chain, as illustrated in "D" of Fig. 9.2, albeit illustrated as such in a highly stylised manner.

The investment in customer-centric dynamic capabilities can also be thought of as the means by which the organisation and its people can learn about customers' values over time, as well as become sensitive to changes in customers' values when co-creating and co-delivering value with partners. As Fig. 9.3 illustrates, these dynamic capabilities may evolve into platforms designed to enable mutual learning and resource sharing. In the top part of the Fig. 9.3, it can be observed that when the environment becomes more complex, that is, the emphasis moves from developing the organisation's own internal systems, as well as developing shared systems with customers, the widespread sharing of systems within the ecosystem is likely to occur. This reflects the fact that in most ecosystem environments many parties must work together. When many parties work together, this stimulates creativity. The different parties can create new forms of customer value through the very act of interacting cooperatively. Although dyadic relationships are still possible and even desirable, at the other end of the extreme, everyone within the ecosystem shares knowledge to create customer value.

Thus, Fig. 9.3 demonstrates how as the environment becomes more complex, it becomes increasingly necessary for organisations to become correspondingly customer-centric. In the bottom part of the Fig. 9.3, similar principles are reflected. However, this is from the perspective that all industries have value chains. As can be observed, as an environment becomes more complex and organisationally diverse, as one would expect in the ecosystems of today, co-learning, co-creating and co-delivery activities are increasingly required. The focal organisation's industry value chain and the value chains of complementors will also need to change. Logic also suggests the institutions that can impact these industry value chains will also be required to change to stimulate new forms of isomorphic (or homogenising) change across the industries in question. This is in contrast

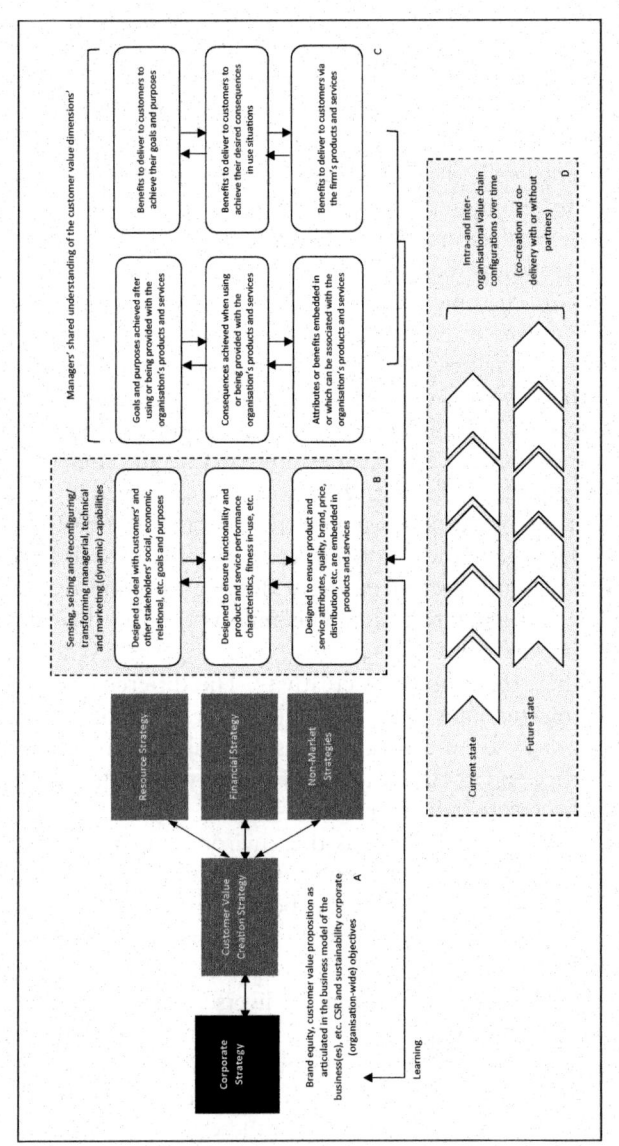

Fig. 9.2 Strategic customer value creation

9 INTRODUCTION: THE CUSTOMER VALUE CREATION STRATEGY 211

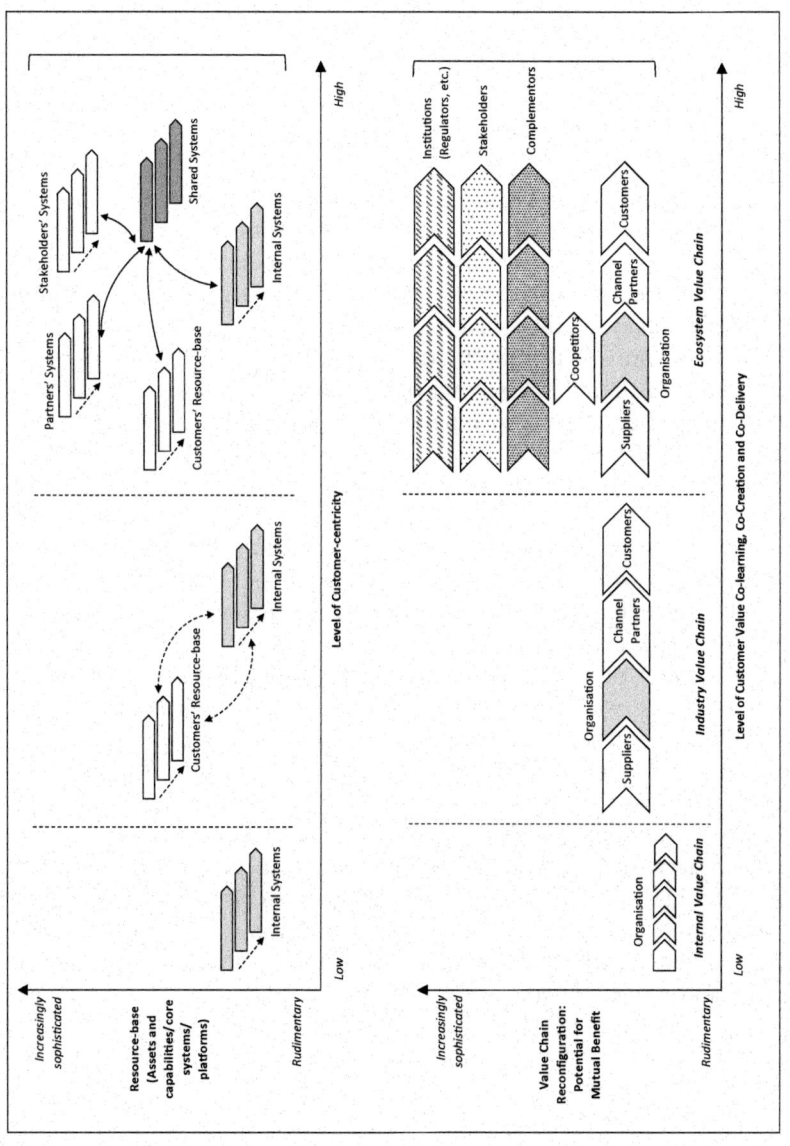

Fig. 9.3 Building a sustainable comprehensive customer value co-learning, co-creation and co-delivery system

to the far-left side of Fig. 9.3, where despite being part of an industry, there are no real opportunities in place yet to co-learn about customer value or co-create and co-deliver customer value with other parties.

The final chapter in this part by Wojciech Dyduch demonstrates what may be involved in practice. This chapter, *Strategic Mechanism of Value Creation and Value Capture: Some Insights from Business Organisations in Poland*, takes it as a given that in an emerging economy customer value creation and value creation are interchangeable concepts, that is, they are essentially the same thing in an emerging market system because competing to earn profits is still a relatively new concept. As the chapter suggests, in an emerging market economy, many organisations struggle at the early stages of their lifecycle. This is illustrated theoretically in the middle section of the lower part of Fig. 9.3. As can be observed, organisations in the middle section of the lower part of Fig. 9.3 are still transitioning; they are still grappling with how best to operate within their own industry with the view to operate profitably. Presumably, this is because the innovation system within the country is still not mature enough. Organisations are yet to evolve to aggressively partner and commit to the widespread sharing of resources and the co-development of complementary products even though this could help them become more profitable. The fact that strategic and market leadership potential, the control of unique resources, the ability to observe and imitate competitors, the quality of stakeholder relations and the ability to appropriate the value created were found to be important differentiators suggests as much. However, when organisations become good at cooperating with their customers, partners and other key stakeholders, their higher levels of relative success can be attributed to the investment in mechanisms to appropriate value but also the maturity of these mechanisms.

In summary, these chapters demonstrate that organisations are more likely to be high-performing if their managers become good at creating and delivering value to customers by proactively and constructively learning about the context by which all customer-related decisions should be made and implemented.

CHAPTER 10

Business Models for Sustainability

Lenore K. Pennington

INTRODUCTION

By producing goods and services, providing employment, and generating income and profits, organisations are recognised to be the mainstay of society's economic activities. However, this same economic and industrial activity is long understood to cause pollution problems; is exhausting the worlds resources; is causing significant damage to the world's ecology; and is impacting social structures (Benn et al., 2018; Conceição, 2020).

A sevenfold growth in population since 1800 (World Wide Fund for Nature, 2018: 22), and unparalleled, increasing rates of economic growth, as shown by rising countries' Gross Domestic Product (GDP) (Ioannou & Hawn, 2019), have generated an unprecedented demand for land, non-renewable resources, energy and water. This in turn, has interfered with the Earth's natural systems. As reported by the World

---

L. K. Pennington (✉)
University of Wollongong, Wollongong, NSW, Australia
e-mail: lenorekp@wyreepi.com

© The Author(s), under exclusive license to Springer Nature Singapore Pte Ltd. 2022
A. Zubac et al. (eds.), *Effective Implementation of Transformation Strategies*, https://doi.org/10.1007/978-981-19-2336-4_10

Wide Fund for Nature (2020: 56) the world population's Ecological Footprint[1] has increased by about 173% over the past 60 years, and human activities are using 1.56 times more than Earth can renew; equivalent to consuming the resources of 1.56 Earths.

Research by Steffen et al. (2015: 738) has found that human activity now has breached four of the nine natural planetary boundaries, which "define a safe operating space for humanity based on the intrinsic biophysical processes that regulate the stability of the Earth system". Climate change, loss of biosphere[2] integrity; flows of nitrogen and phosphorus to the biosphere and oceans; and destruction of forests, grasslands, and wetlands for agriculture and urban development, have all exceeded safe limits (Ripple et al., 2020; Steffen et al., 2015). Climate change and ocean acidification caused by atmospheric greenhouse gases have risen to their highest recorded levels (Butler & Montzka, 2019: 2; Nisbet et al., 2019; Peters et al., 2020; World Meteorological Organization, 2019a: 2). Consequently, it is believed the world has entered a new geological epoch, the Anthropocene era, which has replaced the 12,000 year long post ice age Holocene era, and marks the significant ways human activity has altered the planet (Conceição, 2020; Lewis & Maslin, 2015).

Debates about the escalating damage to both the environment and people are focused on the rapidly expanding population, which, combined with rising wealth have generated increasing societal and organisation demands for limited and non-renewable resources (Conceição, 2020). Consequences of these demands include resources shortages; water and food scarcity; poverty; global warming and related climate changes; land degradation; loss of biodiversity; extinction of species; air and water pollution; and growing signs of toxic chemicals in humans and animals (Benn et al., 2018; Henderson et al., 2018; Intergovernmental Panel on Climate Change, 2019, 2021; Rauter et al., 2017; World Meteorological Organization, 2019b). There are many predictions of increasing economic

---

[1] The Ecological Footprint is an established measure of sustainability. It measures how much of the Earth's biological capacity is used in the consumption of resources and the production of goods and services. It also identifies the direct and indirect impacts of production and consumption activities on the environment to support a preferred lifestyle (Destek et al., 2018: 29388; Jóhannesson et al., 2020: 2).

[2] The Biosphere is part of the Earth's system. It is comprised of all ecosystems and living organisms, whether in the atmosphere, on land (terrestrial biosphere) or in the oceans (marine biosphere). It also includes dead organic matter, such as litter, soil organic matter and oceanic debris (Intergovernmental Panel on Climate Change [IPCC], 2007).

instability and social unrest, depleted resources and potentially irreparable environmental damage (Arnell et al., 2016; Hsiang et al., 2017; Johnson et al., 2021; von Weizsacker & Wijkman, 2017).

Further to these planetary changes, globally there are serious social issues, including: widening wealth and income disparity within and between countries; increasing unemployment and underemployment; social immobility; extreme poverty and human rights abuses (Conceição, 2020; Ioannou & Hawn, 2019: 453). This growing inequity and sense of unfairness has led to an increasing sense of injustice and declining trust in the competence and ethical behaviour of institutions across both developed and lesser developed nations, with governments and societal leaders least trusted (Edelman, 2020, 2021). The novel coronavirus (COVID-19) pandemic, which took hold in 2020 and has caused the largest, economic and social crisis since the Great Depression of 1929–1939,[3] has further revealed these wealth inequities and ecosystem destruction (United Nations, 2020; Ward et al., 2020).

Therefore, as stated in the Intergovernmental Panel on Climate Change's 2018 report, globally the challenge is how to conserve natural resources and reduce pressure on the environment, while also meeting the economic and social needs of the global population.

Sustainable Development

Increasing fears about the consequences of these major problems led to demands for a more sustainable economy and society (Adams et al., 2016: 268). In 1983 in response to global pressures, the United Nations established the Commission on Environment and Development (WCED). Its 1987 report established the term Sustainable Development (Bansal, 2019), with its landmark definition: "development that allows the present generation to meet our current needs, without compromising the ability of future generations to meet their needs" (Brundtland & Khalid, 1987: 47).

While the earlier discussions about sustainability focused on protecting the natural environment and the Earth's non-renewable resources, the WCED's definition of sustainable development encompasses three areas:

---

[3] The Great Depression was the longest and most severe economic depression in the industrialised Western world (Romer & Pells, 2021. https://www.britannica.com/event/Great-Depression).

economic development and prosperity (Kok et al., 2019); maintaining environmental protection and managing resources limits (water, land, air, raw materials and energy); and ensuring social equity and justice for current and future generations (i.e. inter- and intra-generational fairness) (Eskerod & Huemann, 2013; Stubbs & Cocklin, 2008). Key to this is a future oriented, long-term perspective, together with the interconnection of all three dimensions which both influence each other and need to be carefully and equitably balanced (Eskerod & Huemann, 2013). Of all sustainability definitions, the WCED's remains the most widely accepted (Edwards et al., 2017).

Organisational Sustainability

Organisational sustainability evolved from the broader concepts of sustainability and sustainable development. For organisations, sustainability implies organisations should simultaneously improve social and human welfare while reducing their ecological impact and ensuring the effective achievement of organisational objectives (Pennington, 2015). Therefore, organisational sustainability often is defined as managing the Triple Bottom Line (TBL), which also is described as the "3Ps" of people, planet, and profit. The TBL is a process to assist organisations manage their financial, social and environmental risks, obligations and opportunities (Elkington, 1997). Some have added a fourth factor, corporate governance, which incorporates aspects characteristics such as organisational transparency and accountability (Haffar & Searcy, 2019).

While it has been widely accepted and applied by organisations (Svensson et al., 2018), the TBL has been criticised. For example, Milne and Gray (2013) argue that while the TBL is a good first step towards organisational sustainability, it is an incomplete measure, as it focuses on profit and financial capital and ignores the scientific limits of Earth's natural capital. Too often organisations associate sustainability with economic advantages for the organisation itself (Howard-Grenville, 2017). Elkington (2018) himself is disappointed that "the TBL concept has been captured and diluted by accountants and reporting consultants", and believes many organisations' leadership teams continue to emphasise profit targets, and give less attention to people and planet targets.

Organisational sustainability has a range of other understandings and definitions (Antolín-Lopez et al., 2016; Bansal & Song, 2017; Lankoski, 2016). These interpretations of organisational sustainability include corporate social responsibility (CSR) (Bansal et al., 2014; Cheng et al., 2011); corporate sustainable development (Bansal & Song, 2017); corporate responsibility (Lozano, 2015); corporate social performance (Linnenluecke & Griffiths, 2013); strategic CSR (Bansal et al., 2015); corporate citizenship (Matten & Moon, 2008); environmental, social and governance performance (Auer & Schuhmacher, 2016; Montiel, 2008); environmental CSR (Flammer, 2013; Montiel & Delgado-Ceballos, 2014); environmental management or corporate environmental sustainability, where the focus is on the environmental aspects; green- eco- or ecological-innovation (Adams et al., 2016); and shared value creation (Porter & Kramer, 2011).

Many of these definitions have a common theme: to become sustainable, organisations need to emphasise three objectives, financial (economic), environmental and social, all of which are essential and of equal importance (Bondy et al., 2012). If the WCED definition is applied, organisational sustainability can be defined as "the ability of organisations to respond to their short-term financial needs as well as the needs of their stakeholders[4] without compromising their ability to meet the needs of future stakeholders" (Dyllick & Hockerts, 2002: 131). This implies that organisations should both fulfil their stakeholders' expectations and needs, and enable future generations to meet their needs (Garvare & Johansson, 2010: 741).

Bansal (2005: 198–200) created the term Corporate Sustainable Development (CSD), basing it on three principles:

1. economic prosperity through value creation;
2. environmental integrity through corporate environmental management; and
3. social equity through corporate social responsibility.

A widely accepted interpretation of organisational sustainability is that sustainable organisations accept, adopt, and are committed to all aspects of sustainable development. From this, Linnenluecke and Griffiths (2010) identified four perspectives on organisation sustainability, in that sustainable organisations:

---

[4] Stakeholders are discussed in more detail later in this chapter.

1. continue to focus on long-term economic performance;
2. adopt responsibility for minimising or even mitigating ecological and environmental outcomes of their activities;
3. give attention to stakeholder groups, including employees and the local and global communities which they impact; and
4. take a holistic approach, in which sustainability incorporates all three of the above perspectives.

It generally is agreed that truly sustainable organisations understand how they can positively impact society and the planet, and have a deep understanding of their external environment (Dyllick & Muff, 2016: 165–166). They also create environmentally and socially beneficial outcomes while continuing to maintain financial viability (Stubbs & Cocklin, 2008); and act to increase the sustainability of the economy, environment and society (Schaltegger et al., 2016a).

Organisations' Role in Sustainable Development

There is escalating support for the view that organisations, as the engines of the economy and a principal way economy activity occurs, have played and continue to play a significant part in creating the environmental, resources shortages and social problems now facing the world, including significantly contributing to the destruction of the ecosystem; the increasing levels of greenhouse gases; and the consequent changing climate (Benn et al., 2018; Henderson et al., 2018; Schaltegger et al., 2016a; Shrivastava, 2018; Wright & Nyberg, 2017).

Welford (1997: 4) put this compellingly, when he wrote:

> Business has to accept a very large share of the responsibility for this devastation and crises. Businesses are central to a system which is destroying life on Earth and if we continue with this path not one area of wilderness, indigenous culture, endangered species, or uncontaminated water supply will survive the global market economy.

Therefore, organisations are being challenged to understand and respect planetary boundaries (Winn & Pogutz, 2013); adhere to sustainable development principles (Benn et al., 2018; Shrivastava, 2018); and actively reduce their environmental and social impacts (Schaltegger & Horisch, 2017), by changing their business and operational practices to more sustainable ones. To quote H. E. António Guterres, Secretary-General, United Nations:

> We have to mobilize the private sector, it is 75% of the global GDP. Moving forward, collaboration with business - and the key CEOs in the world - is crucial when it comes to fighting climate change; but also, to meet sustainable development goals, eradicate all extreme poverty by 2030, and we're not on track on this. (Gupta et al., 2019: 3)

Therefore, to achieve organisational sustainability, organisations need to consider and address a wide and varied range of environmental and social objectives beyond the organisation itself, and embed these into their strategy (Hahn et al., 2017). Some organisations are endeavouring to demonstrate they are responsible corporate citizens, by developing a sustainability strategy (Edgecliffe-Johnson, 2019; Khan et al., 2016; Searcy, 2016). However, a number of their actions are reactive rather than strategic, and sustainability efforts vary across industry, organisation size and geography (Kiron et al., 2017). Consequently, to date globally their intentions have shown little improvement in social or environmental sustainability (Dyllick & Muff, 2016; Landrum, 2018).

Research has identified that in many organisations, sustainable business thinking has not yet become embedded into day-to-day decisions and operations (Bocken & van Bogaert, 2016), and many companies have little or no strategy for integrating sustainability into their business (Engert et al., 2016; Kiron et al., 2017; Pinelli & Maiolin, 2017). This may be due to the complexities of combining societal, environmental, and economic factors into all elements of their business (Dyllick & Hockerts, 2002). Another factor is that in response to pressures from the financial markets, organisations' planning horizons have significantly decreased (Dyllick & Muff, 2016). As organisations are more likely to focus on short-term profits, rather than on longer-term strategic actions and value creation, sustainability either is pushed aside, or it is not considered at all (Howard-Grenville et al., 2014; McKinsey & Company, 2014; Slawinski et al., 2017; Wright & Nyberg, 2017). The increasing emphasis on short-term maximisation of financial returns is reinforced by neo-liberal values which came to prominence in the 1970s, and subsequently have driven government policy and organisations' practices (Burnes, 2017; Stiglitz, 2016: 336). Further, as the varied and conflicting definitions and interpretations of "sustainable development" and "sustainability" between, and even within organisations and among external stakeholders are confusing and vague, this can inhibit discussion, planning and progress towards organisational sustainability (Lankoski, 2016).

Organisations tend to focus on economic value, and overlook the social and environmental harm caused by their activities (Kurucz et al., 2017). One reason is the current market system, unchanged since the establishment of classical economics, regards natural resources as cost free to the organisation, while the negative externalities (i.e. the costs of economic activities to society or the costs caused by these activities' environmental damage) are ignored (Brozovic, 2020). This has been described as the "Tragedy of the Commons" (Hardin, 1968), or the "free-rider problem". As the natural environment, the oceans, water and air are public goods, and the improvement from one organisation cleaning up their own pollution or taking action to prevent pollution is marginal, no single organisation has an incentive to pay the costs involved.

While there is focus on large corporations causing environmental and social problems, small and medium enterprises (SMEs) also should be considered as they are significant contributors to these issues. In the European Union for example, SMEs employ 99.8% of all workers, create 56–60% of value added, and generate 60–70% of Europe's industrial pollution (Cantele & Zardini, 2020). Similarly, among the Organisation for Economic Co-operation and Development (OECD) member nations, SMEs comprise 99% of all businesses and generate between 50 and 60% of value added (OECD, 2019: 3). SMEs are substantial suppliers to larger organisations and have a high environmental footprint. In the manufacturing sector in particular, they have a large share of global resource consumption, pollution, and waste generation (Koirala, 2019: 5).

Business Models

Business models (BMs) reflect organisations' strategies and detail how organisations intend to generate revenue by providing products and services to customers (Boons & Lüdeke-Freund, 2013: 9). Business models are not a strategy, as a business strategy is that business model which an organisation chooses to take to the market (Casadesus-Masanell & Ricart, 2010). These models are the blueprint for how an organisation conducts its business and how it functions, and provide the data and evidence which underlies expected operating costs and revenue (Osterwalder et al., 2005: 2). Most often, the focus of business models is customers and maintaining and growing markets (Pedersen et al., 2018), but they also may consider other groups, including suppliers and distributors, business partners, shareholders and owners (Brozovic, 2020).

Initially conceived for commercial, for-profit organisations, business models' primary purpose was to describe customers' needs and their ability to pay. They were intended to create a sustainable competitive advantage for organisations within their markets, and to generate profitable and ongoing revenue streams (DaSilva & Trkman, 2014). To achieve this, business models describe the actions taken to respond to customers' needs and to deliver value to these customers; how to entice customers to pay for this value; and to ensure payments are converted to profit by properly designing and operating the various stages in the value chain (Schaltegger et al., 2016a: 4–5). Therefore, the key principle underlying business models is value which, in turn, requires that BMs include descriptions of the products or services to be offered, the target market segments, and the value of these products or services (Al-debei & Avison, 2010).

Value has several different aspects. From an economic perspective, value is defined as the end customers' willingness to pay for a product/service (Brandenburger & Stuart Jr., 1996). A core concept is *value creation*, which itself has three main components. Firstly, s*hareholder value creation* refers to actions that increase value and is the value accrued by the organisations' owners/shareholders. Secondly, *total value* creation is accrued by all the organisation's stakeholders, both internal and external to the organisation (Biloshapka & Osiyevskyy, 2018; Garcia-Castro & Aguilera, 2015: 138). The total value created is determined by the price paid by customers less all production costs. In this context stakeholders are all groups or individual who create and capture economic value in their interaction with the organisation, and includes employees, customers and society at large (Barsky et al., 1999). The third key concept is *customer value* which is defined by Woodruff (1997: 142) as "a customer's perceived preference for and evaluation of those product attributes, attribute performances, and consequences arising from use that facilitate (or block) achieving the customer's goals and purposes in use situations". More simply, it is the production of goods or services that a consumer is willing to buy (Bapuji et al., 2018).

Customer value creation is described in a range of ways, including Customer Value Proposition (CVP), value object, value offering, and customer benefit. The CVP is designed from customers' perspectives. It describes the *intended benefits (value proposition)* that products/services will provide to existing and future customers; how this promise will be communicated to customers; and whether these meet customers' needs (Ballantyne et al., 2011). CVPs can have one or more of four types of value for the customer: economic value, functional value, emotional value and symbolic value (Payne et al., 2017: 469). *Value creation* is achieved by identifying and developing new business opportunities, new markets and new revenue streams (Bocken et al., 2014). *Value delivery* is comprised of the resources, infrastructure and activities needed to deliver customer value. Finally, *value appropriation* also known as value capture, value claiming or value sharing, is the revenue and profit, or economic value, derived from providing goods and services to users and customers (Teece, 2010). It is related closely to value creation: organisations create value from their relationships with customers and suppliers, and to remain competitive they appropriate some of this value for themselves. In so doing, organisations retain the resources they need to invest in future value creation (Ellegaard et al., 2014).

From an organisational sustainability perspective, there are several criticisms of business models, sometime referred to as traditional business models (TBMs). In line with strategy theory, as organisations are market- and profit-driven and are focused on their product or services delivering a distinctive value proposition to customers, and on creating shareholder wealth, their attention is on the economy and economic value (Porter & Kramer, 2011). Therefore, they overlook the harm their activities cause to the well-being of the broader population or on future generations (Kurucz et al., 2017). They also disregard their impact on the Earth's ecosystems[5] (Brozovic, 2020: 764).

Porter and Kramer (2011) sought to address issues of societal harm with their popular Creating Shared Value (CSV) model in which organisations, by innovatively addressing social issues and harm caused by their production methods or the products themselves, could increase productivity, expand markets and achieve greater financial success. While praised for highlighting the need for organisations to address their harm to

---

[5] An ecosystem includes all the living things (plants, animals and organisms) their non-living environments (weather, earth, sun, soil, climate, atmosphere) (Murray, 2018).

society, CSV is criticised for using harm reduction to increase profits for individual organisations and their owners, rather than to improve social and environmental well-being (Crane et al., 2014).

Overall, short-term pressures from investors and demands to maintain high share prices have let to myopic, short-term thinking, and have contributed to cost-cutting, under investment in research and development, and less innovative thinking, accompanied by a narrow view and approach to business strategy and business models (Kurzback & Timmer, 2019). With their emphasis on profit and value, TBMs are short-term focused, whereas problems such as increasing resources shortages, environment damage, and climate change and its impacts, all require a long-term perspective (Dyllick & Muff, 2016; Starik et al., 2016). Overall from a sustainability perspective, the focus of TBMs is too narrow to assist organisations generate "sustainable value" (Bocken et al., 2015).

Sustainable Business Models

To transform their business purpose and significantly change their operations to become more sustainable, it is recommended organisations should integrate sustainability into their strategy, business models and operations (Bocken et al., 2015; Bocken & Geradts, 2020; Breuer et al., 2018 #4686). Further, their business models should include social, environmental and economic principles, with environmental and social concerns regarded as important as profits (Bocken et al., 2019; Massa et al., 2017). Therefore, from a sustainability perspective, the focus of TBMs is too narrow to assist organisations generate 'sustainable value' (Bocken et al., 2015).

Sustainable Business Models (SBMs) extend TBMs by integrating organisational sustainability into business models, so they contribute to the sustainable development of the environment, society, and economy. The SBM has been defined as "a promise on the economic, environmental and social benefits that an organisation's offering delivers to customers and society at large, considering both short-term profits and long-term sustainability" (Patala et al., 2016: 144). SBMs also require developing a sustainable value proposition which is broader than the traditional customer value proposition, and balances the needs of customers, society and the environment. Thus, they create ecological and social value that are valued by customers, which in turn, can create a competitive advantage (Freudenreich et al., 2020).

To achieve this, SBMs have four main characteristics. Firstly, they explicitly focus on environmental, social and economic sustainability (Bocken et al., 2014); and secondly, they question and extend the traditional understanding of value and value creation (Kurucz et al., 2017). Thirdly, they focus on a wider set of stakeholders to address potential sustainability impacts (Baldassarre et al., 2017; Bocken et al., 2014; Stubbs & Cocklin, 2008). Finally, they focus on the wider system in which the organisation and, therefore, the SBM is embedded. This can include advocating for changes in legislation and regulations; and developing collaboration with and between stakeholders, including other organisations, competitors, industry associations, governments, interest groups and the media (Stubbs, 2017: 303). Thus, SBMs require that organisations widen their identified stakeholders from customers and shareholders, and include all other stakeholders who might be directly or indirectly affected by the organisation's activities, such as the broader society and the ecosystem (Lüdeke-Freund et al., 2018: 147).

SBMs are delineated as "...describing, analysing, managing and communicating (i) a company's sustainable value proposition to its customers and all other stakeholders, (ii) how it creates and delivers this value, (iii) and how it captures economic value while maintaining or regenerating natural, social and economic capital beyond its organisational boundaries". (Schaltegger et al., 2016b: 268). This sustainable value integrates environmental, social and economic value into a new form of value (Evans et al., 2017: 607). Further, when an organisation determines the value to be created, it must ensure this value both benefits the organisation itself, and is aligned with its stakeholders' responsibilities and needs (Evans et al., 2017).

Therefore, organisations intending to develop and implement SBMs need to move beyond their economic paradigm, and significantly change their orientation from solely on from profit generation to also resolving social and environmental issues (Freudenreich et al., 2020). This requires organisations to entrench sustainability principles into all their goals and objectives; products or services; processes and operations; governance; organisational structures; and reporting systems (Adams et al., 2016). In particular, SBMs integrate the ecological and social impact of their activities into their understanding and intent of value creation (Freudenreich et al., 2020). This is achieved through innovating their business models by changing the customer value proposition, and changing the ways the organisation creates, delivers and captures value (Bocken et al.,

2014: 44). This value can be in the form of social or ecological value, such as supporting marginalised groups in society, supporting NGO's, reduced use of resources, or lower emissions (Freudenreich et al., 2020). Overall, SBMs need to ensure that sustainable value flows to multiple stakeholders including the natural environment and society (Evans et al., 2017). Figure 10.1 demonstrates how all three components of organisational sustainability influence sustainable value.

Lüdeke-Freund (2010: 18) suggests that for SBMs and their customer value propositions to be authentic, as customer value is a core component of business models, "customer" should be extended to include the general public, with public benefits including positive social and environmental outcomes to be designated as "public customer value".

With the general population, and organisations' customers becoming increasingly concerned about social and environmental sustainability issues, successfully integrating sustainability principles and goals into business strategies and business models can enhance their reputation and customers' perception of the value proposition (Kreiss et al., 2016).

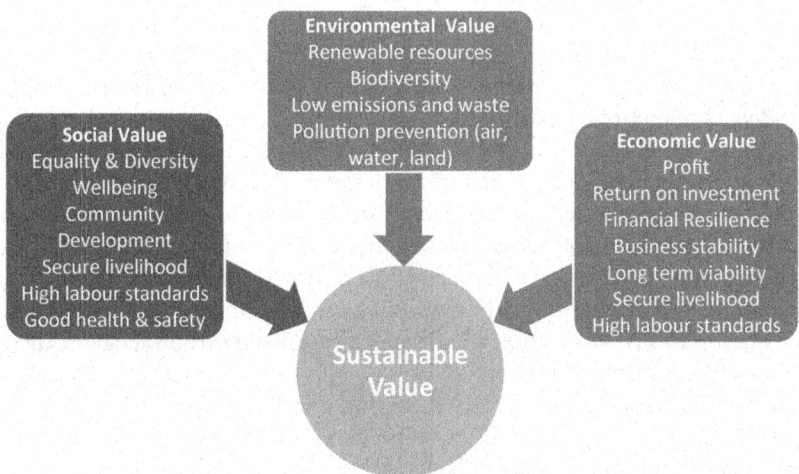

Fig. 10.1 Sustainable value (*Source* Adapted from Evans et al. [2017: 600])

Stakeholders and Business Models

Strategic management theory suggests that organisations' ability to create value is dependent on their stakeholders' needs and expectations (Shams et al., 2020: 2).

Stakeholder theory, which has become embedded in management theory, explains the relationship between organisations and various groups in society, and identifies those groups to which organisations have responsibility (Maon et al., 2008). The term "stakeholder" was first used in business context in 1963 by the Stanford Research Institute (now SRI International, Inc.), and emphasised that organisations need to focus only on the needs of shareholders (Freeman, 1984: 32). Over time the definition of stakeholders has broadened, as shown in Table 10.1.

Freeman (2010: 7) emphasised that, according to stakeholder theory, "business is about how customers, suppliers, employees, financiers (stockholders, bondholders, banks), communities and managers interact and create value". Consequently, stakeholder management often is linked to organisations' financial performance (Parmar et al., 2010), and to how stakeholders support organisations' financial success. Further, while stakeholders benefit from organisations' activities, they also supply resources to organisations and can influence business environments. Therefore, organisations' stakeholders underlie value creation and underpin their business models (Freudenreich et al., 2020).

Today, stakeholder theory increasingly is linked to organisations' social and environmental management (Hörisch et al., 2014). With organisations increasingly asked to take responsibility for the environmental and social impacts of their activities, stakeholders play an important role in encouraging them to give sufficient attention to managing, measuring, and reporting their sustainability strategies. This means it is important for organisations seeking to operate more sustainably to understand their stakeholders (Lindgreen et al., 2012).

Should organisations disregard secondary stakeholders' expectations and requirements, secondary stakeholders can apply pressure to the organisation and its primary stakeholders (Garvare & Johansson, 2010). For example, by acting as intermediaries for often marginalised groups and speaking for nature, societal stakeholders such as NGOs contribute to value creation, and can influence organisations to consider the ecological and social impacts of their activities (Stubbs & Cocklin, 2008). Secondary stakeholders also influence broader societal opinions about organisations

Table 10.1 Stakeholder definitions

Definition	Source
A stakeholder is any group or individual who "can affect or is affected by the achievement of an organisation's objectives"	Freeman (1984: 46)
Stakeholders are "groups and individuals who benefit or are harmed by, and whose rights are violated or respected by corporate actions"	Freeman (2014: 186)
Internal/Primary stakeholders Have a direct economic stake in the organisation Includes: Shareholders; financiers and other investors; customers; employees; suppliers	Freeman (1984)
External/secondary stakeholders/aka societal stakeholders Are outside the organisation Those "who influence or affect or are influenced or affected by the organisation but … are not engaged in transactions with the organisation and are not essential for its survival" Includes: Competitors; governments and regulators; non-government organisations (NGOs); fair trade bodies; consumer advocates; environmentalists; special interest groups; the press and other media	Clarkson (1995: 107) Bocken et al. (2019) Darnall et al. (2010)
Additional secondary stakeholders Incudes: Society; the environment, ecosystems and nature; future generations	Geissdoerfer et al. (2016) Lüdeke-Freund et al. (2018) McGrath and Whitty (2017) Stubbs (2017) Stubbs and Cocklin (2008)

and their actions, through public protests or campaigns, boycotts, strikes, and mass social media (Ferrón Vilchez et al., 2017). Consequently, organisations' attitudes to the social, ethical and environmental consequences of their business operations can be shaped by stakeholders' political, social or economic pressures (Ferrón Vilchez et al., 2017).

There is debate as to whether nature and the environment can be considered a stakeholder. One argument is that organisations actively addressing environmental sustainability problems and seeking to create positive societal and environmental value should include nature and the environment as a stakeholder. A second approach regards human beings, groups, and organisations as stakeholders who represent the interests of nature and the environment, and intercede between nature and the environment, and organisations (Hörisch et al., 2014: 336).

Despite the pressure from these additional stakeholders, most often TBMs continue to focus on customers and shareholders as their key stakeholders, on maintaining and growing markets, and increasing financial value, resulting in organisations continuing to overexploit natural resources (Pedersen et al., 2018). Frequently they give the other stakeholders lower priority (Freudenreich et al., 2020), which limits their ability to address social and environmental issues (Brozovic, 2020). Larger organisations also are likely to have sufficient resources to resist pressures to become more environmentally and socially sustainable, and to lobby against the needed changes (Darnall et al., 2010).

Consequently, as found by the 2019 United Nations Global Compact/Accenture Strategy CEO Study on Sustainability, companies, industries and business as a whole are not doing enough to achieve the 2030 UN Global Sustainability Goals, and commitment of the largest organisations to the climate targets established at the 2015 Paris has declined (Gupta et al., 2019).

ORGANISATIONAL CULTURE AND SUSTAINABILITY

Shifting organisations' focus from organisational and shareholder profit objectives to incorporate sustainability goals requires changes to their behaviour. As this behaviour is underpinned by organisations' culture, changing their culture is equally important (Benn et al., 2018; Engert & Baumgartner, 2016; Kiesnere & Baumgartner, 2019; Linnenluecke et al., 2009).

Originally, interest in organisational culture was focused on its influence on an organisation's effectiveness (O'Reilly et al., 2017). Schein's (1986) organisational culture framework is one basis for understanding organisational culture. Schein's framework and definition are one of the most widely accepted and, therefore, in this chapter, Schein's oft-cited classic definition (Schein, 1986: 3; Schein & Schein, 2017: 6) is used:

> ... the pattern of basic assumptions that a given group has invented, discovered, or developed in learning to cope with its problems of external and internal integration and that have worked well enough to be considered valid and therefore is to be taught to new members as the correct way to perceive, think and feel in relation to these problems.

In 2017 Schein and Schein (p. 6) added the following words:

This accumulated learning is a pattern or system of beliefs, values and behavioural norms that come to be taken for granted as basic assumptions and eventually drop out of awareness.

Therefore, culture is found in the deep-seated shared beliefs, behaviours, values and unchallengeable assumptions of a group of people, and generally is experienced through groups' unwritten rules, also known as norms and expectations. Culture often is described as being comprised of three levels. The surface or visible level of culture, referred to as artefacts, include the physical setting (architecture, office layouts and logos); dress codes; organisational structures; rules, procedures and systems; and ceremonies (Smircich, 1983). Other symbols can be organisation-specific language and acronyms; which aspects of performance are measured; and what is rewarded. These symbols convey complex meanings and are used by individual members to understand their work environment and make judgements, decisions and underlay strategy design (Howard-Grenville et al., 2003).

The second culture level is expressed values; that is, consciously held convictions, clearly stated or practised, which influence the behaviour of group members. These values are "the defining elements of a culture" (Chatman & Jehn, 1994: 524), and the bedrock of organisational culture (Detert et al., 2000; Posner et al., 1985: 298; Quinn & Rohrbaugh, 1981, 1983). Also described as "principles", "philosophies", "ideals" (Sull et al. 2020) or "dimensions" (Pennington, 2015), organisations' values are pervasive standards that influence moral and ethical judgements; and underpin all organisational decisions, objectives and activities (Posner et al., 1985: 294; Vandenberghe & Peiro, 1999: 572). Many organisations name and list their values, and may have between three and seven stated values, with five being the most common number (Sull et al., 2020).

The third and deepest level of culture is comprised of embedded, taken for granted beliefs, thoughts & feelings, and are the ultimate source of peoples' values and actions (Baumgartner, 2009). Hawkins (1997: 429) describes this third level as "unconscious culture – the unthought known that is collectively experienced, but unnoticed by conscious reflection and not able to be verbalized". These unconscious basic assumptions form the essence of culture, and are difficult to identify or change (Alvesson & Sveningsson, 2016; Schein & Schein, 2017).

The shared values, ethics and norms underpinning an organisation's culture influence how its leaders and employees identify and interact both with others in the organisation and with the organisation's environment (Schein & Schein, 2017). An organisation's culture exists at all organisational levels, and guides leaders' and employees' thoughts, decisions and actions. It has been described as a "kind of silent language" (Groysberg et al., 2018: 46), which can determine what is considered important and what will be disregarded. These values, beliefs and norms underpin an organisation's philosophy and ideology (Alvesson & Berg, 1992), and influence how specific situations are interpreted, and provides a decision making framework for senior management (Howard-Grenville et al., 2003). Culture also forms an organisation's identity, character or image, and can be used to gain external recognition and approval (Alvesson & Berg, 1992).

As an organisation's values and ethical principles are embodied in its culture, it can either support or inhibit the adoption of sustainable principles and practices (Kok et al., 2019); and is fundamental to promoting and achieving sustainability (Dyllick & Muff, 2016; Eccles et al., 2012a; Engert & Baumgartner, 2016; Engert et al., 2016; Sroufe, 2017). An organisation's culture also underpins its ability to successfully develop a sustainability strategy and business model (Amui et al., 2017; Pedersen et al., 2018; Rauter et al., 2017; Starik et al., 2016). It is suggested that the differences in culture between organisations may contribute to their differing sustainability strategies (Baird et al., 2018).

Culture's significance led Dunphy (2011: 8–9) to declare:

> The foremost issue in shifting to the post-carbon sustainable economy is to create the cultural change needed to move the multitude of organisations that make up the economy to a more sustainable operational model.

Thus, organisations intending to become sustainable, also must address their organisational culture, and adopt new values, beliefs and behaviours (Benn et al., 2018). Their underlying philosophy, attitudes, behaviours and values all need to be changed to align with sustainability (Adams et al., 2016; Dyllick & Muff, 2016; Kiesnere & Baumgartner, 2019;

Linnenluecke & Griffiths, 2010). Stubbs and Cocklin (2008) also advocate that environmental, social and economic principles and values be embedded in organisations' vision and mission.

Recommendations range from the importance of integrating sustainability principles into organisations' values and culture, so they are deeply entrenched (Engert & Baumgartner, 2016; Rauter et al., 2017); to requiring "a complete moral transformation"; and a "radical overhaul of business culture" and values (Crane, 2000: 674). According to Kiesnere and Baumgartner (2019: 2), to become sustainable, organisations must embed sustainability across all departments and at all levels, and change their culture.

A sustainability culture with clearly specified values and beliefs is likely to be a competitive advantage (Eccles et al. 2011, 2012c). As this culture shapes employees' individual and group behaviour, it can influence their own commitment to sustainability (Howard-Grenville et al., 2014: 258). Therefore, organisations aiming to become sustainable and for their SBM to be achieved, also need to ensure their cultural characteristics will support and enable this.

Characteristics of a Sustainability Culture

The organisational sustainability literature reveals a variety of different values, attitudes, behaviours, and cultural dimensions which researchers consider important to organisational sustainability. The underlying principles of a SBM include environmental stewardship; including nature as a stakeholder; and sharing resources (people, profits, time) with stakeholders (Ritala et al., 2018).

Importantly, SBMs take a longer-term perspective, with the long-term and short-term given equal weight (Brozovic, 2020; Dyllick & Muff, 2016). As SBMs are based on the conviction that there is a higher purpose to business than short-term profit maximisation, profit is a means, not an end in itself (Stubbs, 2017).

Benn et al. (2006) proposed a sustainability culture is characterised by questioning, challenging, extending to open dissent; innovation; learning; respect; trust; transparency and candour, as essential cultural dimensions, along with empowerment, teamwork and continuous learning. Following on from this, collaboration with stakeholders is an important cultural dimension for all organisations and is especially important for those organisations endeavouring to become sustainable (Adams et al., 2016; Bocken et al., 2015; Geradts & Bocken, 2019).

Sharma and Kearins (2011: 194) also revealed the importance and complexities of collaboration between organisations, and noted the contribution which shared ideas, and new approaches can make to the achievement of sustainability goals. Eccles et al. (2012a) found, when compared with "Low Sustainability" companies, "High Sustainability" companies were more likely to have formal stakeholder engagement processes; build long-term relationships with key stakeholders based on mutual respect, trust and cooperation; measure and disclose non-financial information, such as environmental, social, and corporate governance data. Stubbs and Cocklin (2008), Dybdahl (2019) and Evans et al. (2017) also argue that to achieve sustainability, organisations need to build strong relationships and collaborate with key stakeholders.

Rauter et al. (2017) concluded sustainable organisations require an "open" and transparent organisational culture in which there is open communication, transparency and participative decision-making. Similarly, Freudenreich et al. (2020) emphasise that SBMs require transparency to ensure stakeholder groups' interests are considered and included. This aligns with the findings of Eccles et al. (2012a) that "High Sustainability" companies also are more likely to measure and disclose non-financial information, such as environmental, social corporate governance data.

According to Roome and Louche (2016), in sustainable organisations, key cultural values include employee empowerment and participation; listening; transparency; strong business values; accountability; teamwork; challenging and questioning; and learning. Other dimensions highlighted by researchers discussing SBMs include empowerment and inclusiveness (Roome & Louche, 2016); innovation and creativity (e.g. Rauter et al., 2017); innovation (Kaplan & McMillan, 2020); integrity and fairness/equity (e.g. Stubbs & Cocklin, 2008; Van Bommel et al., 2020); teamwork, which is embodied by internal cooperation (Roome & Louche, 2016); and systems thinking (Adams et al., 2016; Bocken & van Bogaert, 2016; Geradts & Bocken, 2019; Schaltegger et al., 2016b; Starik et al., 2016).

A long-term perspective is important for organisations seeking financial longevity (Kurzback & Timmer, 2019). For sustainable organisations, a long-term perspective is even more critical for organisations, as it enables them to balance both the long-term and the short-term; and to stop

Table 10.2 Cultural values for SBMs

- Collaboration with stakeholders
- Connectedness
- Cooperation (internal)
- Empowerment and inclusiveness
- Fairness/equity
- Innovation and creativity
- Integrity
- Knowledge sharing/open communication with all stakeholders
- Long-term perspective
- Responsibility
- Systems thinking
- Transparency and openness/trust

Source Pennington (2015)

sacrificing long-term sustainable value creation to achieve short-term financial value (Bansal & DesJardine, 2014; Brozovic, 2020; Durach & Wiengarten, 2017; Dyllick & Muff, 2016; Evans et al., 2017).

In a study of the organisational sustainability and organisational culture literature from the past 30 years, Pennington (2015) identified 18 different cultural dimensions (values) related to organisational sustainability. Of these, 12 values are discussed in the SBM literature (see Table 10.2. For detailed definitions refer to Appendix A).

Given most organisations have between three and seven cultural values, when building a culture which supports sustainability, it is important to prioritise which cultural values to adopt. As illustrated in Appendix A, collaboration with stakeholders is highlighted as an important cultural dimension underpinning SBMs, as are a long-term perspective, systems thinking, and innovation and creativity, with the latter needed to innovate strategy and TBMs, and to adopt SBMs and sustainable practices.

Changing Organisational Culture

Organisation Culture Change Barriers

An organisation's culture evolves over a number of years and is based on collective traditions and deeply entrenched values, and therefore it can be difficult to change (Hansen & Schaltegger, 2016; Ostroff et al., 2013). Culture change, or culture evolution as Schein (2009) describes it, can take years and will meet resistance from within the organisation (Ostroff et al., 2013). As existing cultural values are a significant factor in an organisation's success and its competitive advantage, it is hard to convince people that these need to change (Lozano & von Haartman, 2018; Sarros et al., 2008; Schein, 2010). Additionally, most employees identify and feel comfortable with the existing culture, and are likely to oppose any changes. With many employees' sense of self and personal identity linked to their job and the organisation where they work, changes in the organisation's culture can be seen as a threat to individuals' personal identity (Jacobs et al., 2013). Culture change can jeopardise employees' familiar organisational lifestyles, causing them to become defensive and lose trust in the organisation and its leaders (Stoughton & Ludema, 2012).

Although an organisation's leaders may not recognise it, their fundamental underlying beliefs and values are a factor in determining the vision, mission and strategy. For example, while leaders may understand the organisation needs to act sustainably, their experience, thinking and values, including a commitment to free markets, cause them to continue focusing on maximising profits and financial rewards for the organisation and its shareholders (Stiglitz, 2016). The prevailing short-term pressures to maximise financial returns also can take priority over long-term sustainability (Burnes, 2017). Achieving organisational sustainability requires leaders whose values enable them to balance environmental, social and profit requirements.

Organisational subcultures are another impediment to culture change. Typically, organisations have a defining predominant culture which is shared across the organisation, and a number of subcultures. These arise because employees and leaders in any organisation hold many and diverse values and assumptions. Organisational subgroups form due to the different functional areas, hierarchical levels, work roles and responsibilities, and geographic locations. These groups develop their own subcultures which hold peripheral values (e.g. Howard-Grenville, 2006; Martin, 2002). Other factors leading to cultural fragmentation include occupational group, gender and generational differences (Alvesson & Sveningsson, 2016). These diverse subgroups can hold different beliefs and values about sustainability (Stoughton & Ludema, 2012), with some perceiving any sustainability-related changes as a threat to the business (Howard-Grenville et al., 2014). Therefore, cultural change needs to be addressed at the subgroup level, and changes can occur at different rates through the organisation, which may impede organisations' sustainability endeavours (Howard-Grenville et al., 2014; Pennington, 2015).

Culture Change Steps

Despite these challenges, organisational culture change is feasible, even though it can take a long time, possibly years, and requires patience and persistence (Alvesson & Sveningsson, 2016; DeWitte & van Muijen, 1999; Ostroff et al., 2013). Organisations can take several steps to change their culture to one which embeds the most important cultural values for SBMs. These include: creating a vision for the new culture; ensuring leaders' and managers' actions are aligned with the new culture; involving employees; underpinning planning and resource allocation decisions with the new cultural values; and reviewing and updating the human resources systems and processes.

Initially, it is important to create a vision for the intended new culture, along with a road map for introducing it. Before attempting to change the culture, organisations should analyse their current culture, including the values underlying the various subcultures (Linnenluecke & Griffiths, 2010). Only then can they ascertain which existing cultural dimensions are effective and should remain; those which are no longer relevant or appropriate; those which may need to be modified or removed; and what new dimensions should be introduced. In this way, the culture change can be a culture adaptation rather than a complete change. Then the organisation's vision and mission can be updated to incorporate the new cultural values and remove any values which are no longer appropriate (Cummings & Worley, 2015).

Leaders shape attitudes to towards culture and one of the most important influences on culture change is senior leaders' and managers' actions (Howard-Grenville et al., 2014; Rauter et al., 2017). They influence culture through their values, leadership style, behaviours and their business strategies, with top level leaders having the most significant impact (Warrick, 2017).

"Walking the talk", as it is commonly known, is extremely important, as an organisation's employees and broader stakeholders pay more attention to leaders' actions than to what they say (Schein, 2009, 2010; Sull et al., 2020). According to Bass (1999: 16) and Schein (2010), top level leaders' behaviours are symbols of an organisation's culture; and their visible behaviours and actions convey clear messages about their values and beliefs to employees. What leaders ignore also reveals their fundamental values and beliefs. Therefore, employees need to see people at higher levels in the organisation modelling the new behaviours and attitudes.

Some leaders may be psychologically committed to continuing the organisation as is, and may resist change (Sannino et al., 2020). As culture change starts with an organisation's leadership team, it may be necessary to terminate those leaders or other employees whose values and behaviours are antithetical to the desired new culture, and employ new leaders or employees (Alvesson & Sveningsson, 2016; Benn et al., 2018; Cummings & Worley, 2015). A new leadership team needs to remain for an extended time period to ensure stability and achieve culture change (Burnes, 2017: 345).

When leaders communicate clearly the reasons for changing the existing culture, and involve employees in the design and implementation of the new cultural values, employees are more likely to accept the new values, and encourage their peers also to accept the new culture (Alvesson & Sveningsson, 2016; Burnes, 2017).

Planning, designing and implementing business models, budgets, their content, and where resources are allocated, all demonstrate leaders' values, and their underlying assumptions and beliefs. Therefore, the criteria used during planning processes to determine BMs and budgets should include the intended cultural values (Schein, 2010).

Recruitment and selection criteria and processes, employee and manager training and development programmes, and performance management systems all need to be reviewed.

Along with job specific skills and competencies, new recruitment and selection criteria linked to the cultural values need to be agreed and implemented so newly hired employees' values are aligned with the intended cultural values (Alvesson & Sveningsson, 2016; Schein, 2010).

Individual and team training programmes provide an opportunity to communicate the cultural values. Cultural values and their importance can be included in induction, orientation and training programmes for new employees (Ramus, 2002), as well as in other programmes such as management, leadership and team skills.

Rewards, praise, pay increases, promotions and praise signal the values and behaviours needed to succeed, and communicate these to others in the organisation and should reflect both required behaviours and results. Therefore, the current performance management and appraisal system needs to be reviewed and a new system developed which includes, encourages and rewards behaviours aligned with the new cultural values (Alvesson & Sveningsson, 2016; Ramus, 2002).

EMBEDDING SUSTAINABILITY

While Integrating sustainability culture dimensions into an organisation's culture supports sustainability, there are other specific ways organisations can embed sustainability.

Leader's and Manager's Commitment to Sustainability

An organisation's leadership team plays a significant role in disseminating and implementing sustainability principle and actions (Rauter et al., 2017). Depending on their own values, understanding of sustainability, and experience, an organisation's leaders can either present sustainability issues as a threat to the organisation, or as a business opportunity, with the latter approach encouraging the adoption of sustainability principles (Howard-Grenville et al., 2014). When an organisation's senior and line managers value and communicate their commitment to sustainability, employees are more likely to increase their own commitment to sustainable business practices and their implementation (Pellegrini et al., 2018; Raineri & Paillé, 2016).

Those organisations' leaders who are change averse can be reluctant to introduce a sustainability strategy and the related SBM. Researchers propose a number of reasons for this. When organisations are performing successfully, their leaders also are perceived to be successful, and see no need to make changes. The longer an organisation has been successful, the less likely leaders will see any need for change. Leaders' previous experience, personal values and political ideology also can influence their attitudes towards environmental and/or social sustainability, and whether these are included in business strategy and business models (Chin et al., 2013; Sannino et al., 2020). Finally, strategic decisions to transition organisations to environmental and social sustainability can be influenced by leaders', and particularly the CEO's, salary and financial (e.g. bonuses and shares options) and non-financial incentives (e.g. status and career) (Walls & Berrone, 2017). Therefore, as with organisational culture change, organisations may need to replace current leaders with people who understand and value environmental and social sustainability and can motivate others to achieve a sustainability vision and strategy.

Sustainability Communication

Leaders' sustainability commitment is reflected in a well-developed and clearly communicated business model, sustainability strategies, formal policies and procedures, and related management systems and practices. When these policies are written and disseminated throughout the organisation, they demonstrate the organisation is serious about sustainability (Dumont et al., 2017; Ramus, 2002). In turn, they encourage both employees' task-related and proactive, innovative sustainability-related behaviour (Birou et al., 2019; Norton et al., 2014).

Employee Involvement

Similar to employee involvement with culture change, involving employees in sustainability fosters their commitment to the organisation's sustainability objectives. This involvement can include encouraging employees to use their sustainability knowledge together with their knowledge of existing processes; inviting employees to contribute to designing and implementing sustainability programmes; and asking employees to make suggestions for improving the organisation's sustainability activities (Pinzone et al., 2016; Zibarras & Coan, 2015).

Sustainability Reporting

Sustainability reporting can show an organisation's willingness to be transparent about their sustainability activities and results. Voluntary standards programmes such as ISO 14001,[6] an environmental management system; ISO 26000,[7] which measures performance and improvement in socially responsible behaviour; SA 8000 which focuses on socially accepted workplace standards; or the Global Reporting Initiative's (GRI) sustainability reporting framework, include guidelines, and recommended actions and processes for improving sustainability performance (Schaltegger et al., 2012). These reports require organisations to pay attention to their sustainability activities, measure progress, and communicate these

---

[6] ISO 140001 is the international standard for an effective environmental management system (EMS). It specifies organisational guidelines for good environmental practices.

[7] ISO 26000 measures performance areas such as such as human rights; labour practices; community involvement and development; fair operating practises; and consumer issues.

to employees and other stakeholders; show the organisation's sustainability commitment and intentions; and increase employees' awareness of and commitment to the issues (Bebbington et al., 2009; Raineri & Paillé, 2016). Including sustainability issues, activities and progress in published annual reports also signals an organisation's focus on sustainability.

> While widely used by some of the world's largest companies, there are strong criticisms of the veracity and reliability of sustainability reports, including the GRI (Boiral et al., 2019). There is a wide range of reporting frameworks and many of these, including the GRI, allow organisations to select which aspects of sustainability they will report on (Roca & Searcy, 2012). Therefore, these reports can be incomplete and lack quantitative data and it is difficult to compare reports year on year, or across organisations (Delmas et al., 2013). They also are criticised as being statements of policies and intentions, rather than communicating sustainability achievements, and for being marketing impression management tools which emphasise good news and conceal bad news in order to maintain a positive reputation and maintain brand equity (Cho et al., 2012; Eccles et al., 2012b). Other issues include a lack of balance, timeliness, precision, clarity and reliability in the information provided, and often do not provide the information sought by their stakeholders (Diouf & Boiral, 2017; Silva et al., 2019).
> Despite these criticisms, the advantage of these reports is they encourage organisations to pay attention to their sustainability activities, measure progress, and communicate these to employees and other stakeholders (Bebbington et al., 2009).

Sustainability Education and Awareness Training

Sustainability education and awareness training is an important tool which enables employees to gain sustainability related knowledge, ideas and skills, helps them develop sustainability mindsets, and encourages them to consider sustainability in their decisions and actions (Baumgartner & Winter, 2014; Birou et al., 2019; Law et al., 2017). This training, which needs to be aligned with, and explains the organisation's sustainability strategy and objectives, can give employees a comprehensive understanding of the organisation's reasons and purposes for sustainability management, and of the sustainability objectives, measures, policies and procedures (Pham et al., 2019; Tung et al., 2014).

Sustainability training should be provided to all employees and managers, and can be in various forms, from formal structured classroom training to on-line modules and one-on-one mentoring or coaching (Baumgartner & Ebner, 2010). Other training and learning opportunities include visits to other organisations which have implemented sustainability projects successfully (Haugh & Talwar, 2010).

This training can shape and influence employees' attitudes towards sustainability, enable them to recognise sustainability issues and improve their decision-making. The training also supports efforts to establish a sustainability culture and can lead to employees personally adopting the desired sustainability values, and motivate employees to commit to their organisation's sustainability vision and strategy (Birou et al., 2019; Xie & Zhu, 2020).

Employee Performance Measures, Rewards and Incentives

Including employee performance measures in the organisation's performance management system, and appraising these so employees receive feedback on their sustainability-related activities, encourages their sustainability efforts. This sends a clear message about an organisation's business priorities (Dumont et al., 2017).

It also is important to design a new reward system for leaders and employees which incorporates the organisation's sustainability objectives. These rewards or incentives need to be clearly linked to achievement of well-defined sustainability targets and related key performance indicators (KPIs) (Kiesnere & Baumgartner, 2019). Incentives can be monetary or non-monetary (such as praise or recognition awards), and should apply to all hierarchical levels of the organisation. Research has shown that non-monetary incentives are more effective for encouraging social sustainability behaviours, while monetary incentives are more successful in motivating achievement of environmental targets and changing organisational cultures (Dahlmann et al., 2017).

CONCLUSION

This chapter discusses current research that analyses organisational sustainability. The aim was to demonstrate the linkages between sustainable development and organisations' contributions to the world's current environmental and social crises. Business models and their purposes were examined, and the focus of these on economic value was highlighted as limiting organisations' capabilities to contribute to both the social wellbeing of the general population and to reduce their destructive impact on the environment and climate. It identifies that, to become more environmentally and socially sustainable, organisations need to review and innovate their current more traditional business models, and transform them into SBMs. In so doing, they will develop broader value propositions to encompass social and ecological value, which are of increasing importance to their stakeholders. These SBMs reconceptualise the traditional customer value proposition and adopt a broader sustainable customer value proposition, which adds social value and significantly reduces the organisation's negative environmental and ecological impacts. This also can create a competitive advantage and increase value appropriation.

It is explained that organisations need to extend relationships with stakeholders beyond the conventionally accepted group of shareholders, financiers, customers, suppliers and employees to numerous stakeholder groups, and to consider the expectations of any stakeholders who are likely to be affected, either directly or indirectly, by the organisation's activities.

An organisation's culture has a strong influence on its ability to successfully develop and implement a sustainability strategy and SBM. Therefore, this chapter presents a set of cultural values which researchers have identified are important for a successful transition to sustainability. It introduces actions organisations can take to successfully adopt new and requisite cultural values and behaviours which will support transition to a sustainable business model. These include ensuring leaders behaviours reflect the desired cultural values and replacing leaders who are not aligned with the desired culture; introducing a new performance appraisal and reward system; ensuring the recruitment process and selection criteria include the desired cultural values; and embedding the new cultural values into training and development programmes.

Finally, the chapter provides some steps organisations can take to adopt the social and environmentally sustainable principles and behaviours which are necessary to successfully execute the SBM; produce the intended sustainable customer value propositions for customers; generate sustainability-linked value for stakeholders; and ensure value appropriation for the organisation. Some of these are: develop and disseminate environmental and social sustainability policies and procedures which support the sustainability strategy; include sustainability measures in the performance management system; develop and introduce appropriate rewards; introduce a sustainability reporting system; and conduct sustainability education and awareness training.

In summary, today's organisations are asked to recognise their role in today's environmental and social issues and change the way they operate. Those organisations intending to increase their environmental and/or social sustainability need to understand the links between organisational sustainability, stakeholders and business models; and to recognise the important role their cultural values play in these changes.

Appendix A

Cultural Values for Sustainable Business Models

Cultural value	Summary definition
Collaboration with Stakeholders	Building relationships, strategic networks, alliances and partnerships and multi-way dialogue with internal and external stakeholders, including all sectors of society. Seeking and sharing information and knowledge to develop wider perspectives and visions for sustainability
Connectedness	Understanding and respecting the interconnectedness and interdependence of the environment and ecology, human and societal welfare, and the economy. Recognising that activities which damage any part of these will impact the long-term viability of organisations, nations, populations and the planet

(continued)

(continued)

Cultural value	Summary definition
Cooperation (internal)	Working cooperatively internally, coordinating together and readily resolving conflict, reduces barriers and facilitates resolution of complex and difficult sustainability challenges
Empowerment and inclusiveness	Empowering employees and encouraging their involvement in planning and implementing organisational sustainability activities
Environmental stewardship	Responsible management practices which pursue a triple bottom-line of economic, social and environmental performance in business. The responsible use of resources that takes into account the well-being of society and ecological systems and future generations
Fairness/equity	Carefully managing the scale and impact of activity, and appropriately using environmental and ecological, human and social resources. Fairly distributing resources and property rights, within and between generations
Innovation and creativity	Fostering creativity, ingenuity and innovation to modify existing or develop new products, services and technologies which integrate and support the various elements of sustainability
Integrity	Considering sustainability and making sustainability-based decisions in strategic planning and implementation of the business
Knowledge sharing/open communication with all stakeholders	Seeking and sharing knowledge, information, ideas and success stories within the organisation and with stakeholders and competitors
Long-term perspective	Emphasising long-term goals which incorporate environmental, social, and financial sustainability, sustainable products and services, and long-term relationships with stakeholders
Responsibility	Accepting responsibility for decreasing and eliminating the environmental, ecological and social impact of the entire lifecycle of products and services

(continued)

(continued)

Cultural value	Summary definition
Systems thinking	Creating an integrated systems perspective by recognising the organisation operates in an open system—diverse cultures, constraints and opportunities between the internal and external
Transparency and openness/trust	Developing trust by communicating openly, honestly and consistently to all internal and external stakeholders concerning environmental, social and financial performance and impacts on all stakeholders

Source Pennington (2015)

REFERENCES

Adams, R., Jeanrenaud, S., Bessant, J., Denyer, D., & Overy, P. (2016). Sustainability-oriented innovation: A systematic review. *International Journal of Management Reviews, 18*(2), 180–205.

Agyeman, J., Bullard, R. D., & Evans, B. (2002). Exploring the nexus: Bringing together sustainability, environmental justice and equity. *Space and Polity, 6*(1), 77–90.

Al-debei, M. M., & Avison, D. (2010). Developing a unified framework of the business model concept. *European Journal of Information Systems, 19*(3), 359–376.

Alvesson, M., & Berg, P. O. (1992). *Corporate culture and organizational symbolism*. Walter de Gruyter.

Alvesson, M., & Sveningsson, S. (2016). *Changing organizational culture: Cultural change work in progress* (2nd ed.). Routledge.

Amui, L. B. L., Jabbour, C. J. C., Beatriz, A., Jabbour, L. d. S., & Devika, K. (2017). Sustainability as a dynamic organizational capability: A systematic review and a future agenda toward a sustainable transition. *Journal of Cleaner Production, 142*(Part 1), 308–322.

Antolín-Lopez, R., Delgado-Ceballos, J., & Montiel, I. (2016). Deconstructing corporate sustainability: A comparison of different stakeholder metrics. *Journal of Cleaner Production, 136*, 5–17.

Arnell, N. W., Brown, S., Gosling, S. N., Hinkel, J., Huntingford, C., Lloyd-Hughes, B., Lowe, J. A., Nicholls, R. J., Osborn, T. J., Osborn, T. M., Rose, G. A., Smith, P., Wheeler, T. R., & Zelazowski, P. (2016). The impacts

of climate change across the globe: A multi-sectoral assessment. *Climatic Change*, *134*(3), 457–474.
Auer, B. R., & Schuhmacher, F. (2016). Do socially (ir)responsible investments pay? New evidence from international ESG data. *The Quarterly Review of Economics and Finance*, *59*, 51–62.
Baird, K., Su, S., & Tung, A. (2018). Organizational culture and environmental activity management. *Business Strategy and the Environment*, *27*(3), 403–414.
Baldassarre, B., Calabretta, G., Bocken, N. M. P., & Jaskiewicz, T. (2017). Bridging sustainable business model innovation and user-driven innovation: A process for sustainable value proposition design. *Journal of Cleaner Production*, *147*, 175–186.
Ballantyne, D., Frow, P., Varey, R. J., & Payne, A. (2011). Value propositions as communication practice: Taking a wider view. *Industrial Marketing Management*, *40*(2), 202–210.
Bansal, P. (2005). Evolving sustainably: A longitudinal study of corporate sustainable development. *Strategic Management Journal*, *26*(3), 197–218.
Bansal, P. (2019). Sustainable development in an age of disruption. *Academy of Management Discoveries*, *5*(1), 8–12.
Bansal, P., & DesJardine, M. R. (2014). Business sustainability: It is about time. *Strategic Organization*, *12*(1), 70–78.
Bansal, P., Gao, J., & Qureshi, I. (2014). The extensiveness of corporate social and environmental commitment across firms over time. *Organization Studies*, *35*(7), 949–966.
Bansal, P., Jiang, G. F., & Jung, J. C. (2015). Managing responsibly in tough economic times: Strategic and tactical CSR during the 2008–2009 global recession. *Long Range Planning*, *48*(2), 69–79.
Bansal, P., & Song, H.-C. (2017). Similar but not the same: Differentiating corporate sustainability from corporate responsibility. *Academy of Management Annals*, *11*(1), 105–149.
Bapuji, H., Husted, B. W., Lu, J., & Mir, R. (2018). Value creation, appropriation and distribution: How firms contribute to societal economic inequality. *Business and Society Review*, *57*(6), 983–1009.
Barsky, N. P., Hussein, M. E., & Jablonsky, S. F. (1999). Shareholder and stakeholder value in corporate downsizing–The case of United Technologies Corporation. *Accounting, Auditing & Accountability Journal*, *12*, 583–604.
Bass, B. M. (1999). Two decades of research and development in transformational leadership. *European Journal of Work and Organizational Psychology*, *8*(1), 9–32.
Baumgartner, R. J. (2009). Organizational culture and leadership: Preconditions for the development of a sustainable corporation. *Sustainable Development*, *17*(2), 102–113.

Baumgartner, R. J., & Ebner, D. (2010). Corporate sustainability strategies: Sustainability profiles and maturity levels. *Sustainable Development, 18*(2), 76–89.

Baumgartner, R. J., & Winter, T. (2014). The sustainability manager: A tool for education and training on sustainability management. *Corporate Social Responsibility and Environmental Management, 21*(3), 167–174.

Bebbington, J., Higgins, C., & Frame, B. (2009). Initiating sustainable development reporting: Evidence from New Zealand. *Accounting, Auditing & Accountability Journal, 22*(4), 588–625.

Benn, S., Dunphy, D., & Griffiths, A. (2006). Enabling change for corporate sustainability: An integrated perspective. *Australasian Journal of Environmental Management, 13*(3), 156–165.

Benn, S., Edwards, M., & Williams, T. (2018). *Organizational change for corporate sustainability* (4th ed.). Routledge.

Biloshapka, V., & Osiyevskyy, O. (2018). Value creation mechanisms of business models: Proposition, targeting, appropriation, and delivery. *The International Journal of Entrepreneurship and Innovation, 19*(3), 166–176.

Birou, L. M., Green, K. W., & Inman, R. A. (2019). Sustainability knowledge and training: Outcomes and firm performance. *Journal of Manufacturing Technology Management, 31*(2), 294–311.

Bocken, N. M. P., Boons, F., & Baldassarre, B. (2019). Sustainable business model experimentation by understanding ecologies of business models. *Journal of Cleaner Production, 208*, 1498–1512.

Bocken, N. M. P., & Geradts, T. H. J. (2020). Barriers and drivers to sustainable business model innovation: Organization design and dynamic capabilities. *Long Range Planning, 53*, 101950

Bocken, N. M. P., Rana, P., & Short, S. W. (2015). Value mapping for sustainable business thinking. *Journal of Industrial and Production Engineering, 32*(1), 67–81.

Bocken, N. M. P., Short, S. W., Rana, P., & Evans, S. (2014). A literature and practice review to develop sustainable business model archetypes. *Journal of Cleaner Production, 65*, 42–56.

Bocken, N. M. P., & van Bogaert, A. (2016). Sustainable business model innovation for positive societal and environmental impact. In R. Cörvers, J. de Kraker, R. Kemp, P. Martens, & H. van Lente (Eds.), *Sustainable development research at ICIS: Taking stock and looking ahead* (pp. 107–119). ICIS, Maastricht University.

Boiral, O., Heras-Saizarbitoria, I., & Brotherton, M.-C. (2019). Assessing and improving the quality of sustainability reports: The auditors' perspective. *JBE: Journal of Business Ethics, 155*(3), 703–721.

Bondy, K., Moon, J., & Matten, D. (2012). An institution of corporate social responsibility (CSR) in multi-national corporations (MNCs): Form and implications. *Journal of Business Ethics, 111*(2), 281–299.

Boons, F., & Lüdeke-Freund, F. (2013). Business models for sustainable innovation: State-of-the-art and steps towards a research agenda. *Journal of Cleaner Production, 45*, 9–19.

Brandenburger, A. M., & Stuart, H. W., Jr. (1996). Value-based business strategy. *Journal of Economics & Management Strategy, 5*(1), 5–24.

Breuer, H., Fichter, K., Ludeke-Freund, F., & Tiemann, I. (2018). Sustainability-oriented business model development: Principles, criteria and tools. *International Journal of Entrepreneurial Venturing, 10*(2), 256–286.

Brozovic, D. (2020). Business model based on strong sustainability: Insights from an empirical study. *Business Strategy and the Environment, 29*(2), 763–778.

Brundtland, G. H., & Khalid, M. (1987). *Our common future: Brundtland Commission (WCED) report*. Oxford University Press.

Burnes, B. (2017). After Paris: Changing corporate behaviour to achieve sustainability. *Social Business, 7*(3/4), 333–357.

Butler, J. H., & Montzka, S. A. (2019). *The NOAA Annual Greenhouse Gas Index (AGGI)* (pp. 1–7). National Oceanic & Atmospheric Administration Earth System Research Laboratory.

Cantele, S., & Zardini, A. (2020). What drives small and medium enterprises towards sustainability? Role of interactions between pressures, barriers, and benefits. *Corporate Social Responsibility and Environmental Management, 27*(1), 126–136.

Casadesus-Masanell, R., & Ricart, J. E. (2010). From strategy to business models and onto tactics. *Long Range Planning, 43*(2), 195–215.

Chatman, J. A., & Jehn, K. A. (1994). Assessing the relationship between industry characteristics and organizational culture: How different can you be? *Academy of Management Journal, 37*(3), 522–553.

Cheng, B., Ioannou, I., & Serafeim, G. (2011). Corporate social responsibility and access to finance. *Strategic Management Journal, 35*(1), 1–23.

Chin, M. K., Hambrick, D. C., & Treviño, L. K. (2013). Political ideologies of CEOs: The influence of executives' values on corporate social responsibility. *Administrative Science Quarterly, 58*(2), 197–232.

Cho, C. H., Guidry, R. P., Hageman, A. M., & Patten, D. M. (2012). Do actions speak louder than words? An empirical investigation of corporate environmental reputation. *Accounting, Organizations and Society, 37*(1), 14–25.

Clarkson, M. B. E. (1995). A stakeholder framework for analyzing and evaluating corporate social performance. *The Academy of Management Review, 20*(1), 92–117.

Conceição, P. (2020). *Human Development Report 2020: The next frontier—Human development and the Anthropocene* (pp. 1–412). Human Development Report. United Nations Development Program. http://hdr.undp.org/sites/default/files/hdr2020.pdf

Crane, A. (2000). Corporate greening as amoralization. *Organization Studies, 21*(4), 673–696.

Crane, A., Palazzo, G., Spence, L. J., & Matten, D. (2014). Contesting the value of "creating shared value". *California Management Review, 56*(2), 130–153.

Cummings, T. G., & Worley, C. G. (2015). *Organization development and change* (10th ed.). Cengage Learning.

Dahlmann, F., Branicki, L., & Brammer, S. (2017). 'Carrots for corporate sustainability': Impacts of incentive inclusiveness and variety on environmental performance. *Business Strategy and the Environment, 26*(8), 1110–1131.

Darnall, N., Henriques, I., & Sadorsky, P. (2010). Adopting proactive environmental strategy: The influence of stakeholders and firm size. *Journal of Management Studies, 47*(6), 1072–1094.

DaSilva, C. M., & Trkman, P. (2014). Business model: What it is and what it is not. *Long Range Planning, 47*(6), 379–389.

Delmas, M. A., Etzion, D., & Nairn-Birch, N. (2013). Triangulating environmental performance: What do corporate social responsibility ratings really capture? *Academy of Management Perspectives, 27*(3), 255–267.

Destek, M. A., Ulucak, R., & Dogan, E. (2018). Analyzing the environmental Kuznets curve for the EU countries: The role of ecological footprint. *Environmental Science and Pollution Research International, 25*(29), 29387–29396.

Detert, J. R., Schroeder, R. G., & Mauriel, J. J. (2000). A framework for linking culture and improvement initiatives in organizations. *Academy of Management Review, 25*(4), 850–863.

DeWitte, K. D., & van Muijen, J. J. (1999). Organizational culture. *European Journal of Work & Organizational Psychology, 8*(4), 497–502.

Diouf, D., & Boiral, O. (2017). The quality of sustainability reports and impression management: A stakeholder perspective. *Accounting, Auditing & Accountability Journal, 30*(3), 643–667.

Dumont, J., Shen, J., & Deng, X. (2017). Effects of green HRM practices on employee workplace green behavior: The role of psychological green climate and employee green values. *Human Resource Management, 56*(4), 613–627.

Dunphy, D. (2011). Conceptualizing sustainability: The business opportunity. In G. Eweje & M. Perry (Eds.), *Business and sustainability: Concepts, strategies and changes* (pp. 3–24). Emerald Publishing Group Limited.

Durach, C. F., & Wiengarten, F. (2017, November). Environmental management: The impact of national and organisational long-term orientation on plants' environmental practices and performance efficacy. *Journal of Cleaner Production, 167*, 749–758.

Dybdahl, L. M. (2019). Business model innovation for sustainability through localism. In N. M. P. Bocken, P. Ritala, L. Albareda, & R. Verberg (Eds.), *Innovation for sustainability* (pp. 193–211). Palgrave Macmillan.
Dyllick, T., & Hockerts, K. (2002). Beyond the business case for corporate sustainability. *Business Strategy and the Environment, 11*, 130–141.
Dyllick, T., & Muff, K. (2016). Clarifying the meaning of sustainable business: Introducing a typology from business-as-usual to true business sustainability. *Organization & Environment, 29*(2), 156–174.
Eccles, R. G., Ioannou, I., & Serafeim, G. (2011). The impact of a corporate culture of sustainability on corporate behavior and performance (H. B. School, Ed., pp. 1–56). Working Paper 12-035.
Eccles, R. G., Ioannou, I., & Serafeim, G. (2012a). The impact of a corporate culture of sustainability on corporate behavior and performance. National Bureau of Economic Research.
Eccles, R. G., Krzus, M. P., Rogers, J., & Serafeim, G. (2012b). The need for sector-specific materiality and sustainability reporting standards. *Journal of Applied Corporate Finance, 24*(2), 65–71.
Eccles, R. G., Perkins, K. M., & Serafeim, G. (2012c, Summer). How to become a sustainable company. *MIT Sloan Management Review*, 43–50.
Edelman. (2020). Edelman trust barometer 2020: Global report. In J. Tropiano (Ed.), *Edelman trust barometer* (pp. 1–78). Edelman. https://www.edelman.com/trust/2020-trust-barometer.
Edelman. (2021). Edelman trust barometer 2021: Global report. In *Edelman trust barometer*. https://www.edelman.com/sites/g/files/aatuss191/files/2021-01/2021%20Edelman%20Trust%20Barometer_Final.pdf.
Edgecliffe-Johnson, A. (2019). Should business put purpose before profits? Companies are starting to think so. *The Australian Financial Review*.
Edwards, M., Benn, S., & Starik, M. (2017). Business cases for sustainability-integrated management education. In J. A. Arevalo & S. Mitchell, F. (Eds.), *Handbook of sustainability in management education* (pp. 45–66). Edward Elgar Publishing.
Elkington, J. (1997). *Cannibals with forks: The triple bottom line of twenty-first century business*. Capstone.
Elkington, J. (2018, June 25). 25 years ago I coined the phrase "triple bottom line." Here's why it's time to rethink it. *Harvard Business Review*. Reprint H04E7P. https://hbr.org/2018/06/25-years-ago-i-coined-the-phrase-triple-bottom-line-heres-why-im-giving-up-on-it
Ellegaard, C., Medlin, C. J., & Geersbro, J. (2014). Value appropriation in business exchange: Literature review and future research opportunities. *Journal of Business & Industrial Marketing, 29*(3), 185–198.

Engert, S., & Baumgartner, R. J. (2016, February). Corporate sustainability strategy—Bridging the gap between formulation and implementation. *Journal of Cleaner Production, 113*, 822–834.

Engert, S., Rauter, R., & Baumgartner, R. J. (2016). Exploring the integration of corporate sustainability into strategic management: A literature review. *Journal of Cleaner Production, 112*(Part 4), 2833–2850.

Eskerod, P., & Huemann, M. (2013). Sustainable development and project stakeholder management: What standards say. *International Journal of Managing Projects in Business, 6*(1), 36–50.

Evans, S., Vladimirova, D., Holgado, M., Van Fossen, K., Yang, M., Silva, E. A., & Barlow, C. Y. (2017). Business model innovation for sustainability: Towards a unified perspective for creation of sustainable business models. *Business Strategy and the Environment, 26*(5), 597–608.

Ferrón Vilchez, V., Darnall, N., & Aragón Correa, J. A. (2017). Stakeholder influences on the design of firms' environmental practices. *Journal of Cleaner Production, 142*, 3370–3381.

Flammer, C. (2013). Corporate social responsibility and shareholder reaction: The environmental awareness of investors. *The Academy of Management Journal, 56*(3), 758–781.

Freeman, R. E. (1984). *Strategic management: A stakeholder approach*. Pitman-Ballinger.

Freeman, R. E. (2010). Managing for stakeholders: Trade-offs or value creation. *Journal of Business Ethics, 96*, 7–9.

Freeman, R. E. (2014). Stakeholder theory of the modern corporation. In W. M. Hoffman, R. E. Frederick, & M. S. Schwartz (Eds.), *Business ethics: Readings and cases in corporate morality* (pp. 184–191). Wiley.

Freudenreich, B., Lüdeke-Freund, F., & Schaltegger, S. (2020). A stakeholder theory perspective on business models: Value creation for sustainability. *Journal of Business Ethics, 166*(1), 3–18.

Garcia-Castro, R., & Aguilera, R. V. (2015). Incremental value creation and appropriation in a world with multiple stakeholders. *Strategic Management Journal, 36*(1), 137–147.

Garvare, R., & Johansson, P. (2010). Management for sustainability—A stakeholder theory. *Total Quality Management & Business Excellence, 21*(7), 737–744.

Geissdoerfer, M., Bocken, N. M. P., & Hultink, E. J. (2016). Design thinking to enhance the sustainable business modelling process—A workshop based on a value mapping process. *Journal of Cleaner Production, 135*, 1218–1232.

Geradts, T. H. J., & Bocken, N. M. P. (2019). Driving sustainability-oriented innovation. *MIT Sloan Management Review, 60*(2).

Groysberg, B., Lee, J., Price, J., & Cheng, J.Y.-J. (2018). The leader's guide to corporate culture. *Harvard Business Review, 96*(1), 44–52.

Gupta, A., Raghunath, A., Gula, L., Rheinbay, L., & Hart, M. (2019). *The decade to deliver: A call to business action* (p. 43). The 2019 United Nations Global Compact/Accenture Strategy CEO Study on Sustainability. https://www.unglobalcompact.org/library/5715.

Haffar, M., & Searcy, C. (2019). How organizational logics shape trade-off decision-making in sustainability. *Long Range Planning, 52*(6), 101912.

Hahn, T., Figge, F., Aragón-Correa, J. A., & Sharma, S. (2017). Advancing research on corporate sustainability: Off to pastures new or back to the roots? *Business & Society, 56*(2), 155–185.

Hansen, E. G., & Schaltegger, S. (2016). The sustainability balanced scorecard: A systematic review of architectures. *Journal of Business Ethics, 133*(2), 193–221.

Hardin, G. (1968). The tragedy of the commons. *Science, 162*(3859), 1243–1248.

Haugh, H. M., & Talwar, A. (2010). How do corporations embed sustainability across the organization? *Academy of Management Learning & Education, 9*(3), 384–396.

Hawkins, P. (1997). Organizational culture: Sailing between evangelism and complexity. *Human Relations, 50*(4), 417–440.

Henderson, R. M., Reinert, S. A., Dekhtyar, P., & Migdal, A. (2018). *Climate change in 2018: Implications for business*. Harvard University.

Hörisch, J., Freeman, R. E., & Schaltegger, S. (2014). Applying stakeholder theory in sustainability management: Links, similarities, dissimilarities, and a conceptual framework. *Organization & Environment, 27*(4), 328–346.

Howard-Grenville, J. A., Bertels, S., & Lahneman, B. (2014). Sustainability: How it shapes organizational culture and climate. In B. Schneider, & K. M. Barbera (Eds.), *The Oxford handbook of organizational climate and culture* (pp. 257–275). Oxford University Press.

Howard-Grenville, J. A. (2006). Inside the "black box": How organizational culture and subcultures inform interpretations and actions on environmental issues. *Organization & Environment, 19*(1), 46–73.

Howard-Grenville, J. A. (2017). Sustainable development for a better world: Contributions of leadership, management and organizations: Special issue call for submissions. *Academy of Management Discoveries, 3*(1), 107–110.

Howard-Grenville, J. A., Hoffman, A. J., & Wirtenberg, J. (2003). The importance of cultural framing to the success of social initiatives in business [and executive commentary]. *The Academy of Management Executive (1993–2005), 17*(2), 70–86.

Hsiang, S. M., Kopp, R., Jina, A., Rising, J., Delgado, M., Mohan, S., Rasmussen, D. J., Muir-Wood, R., Wilson, P., Michael, O., Larsen, K., & Houser, T. (2017). Estimating economic damage from climate change in the United States. *Science, 356*, 1132–1369.

Intergovernmental Panel on Climate Change (IPCC). (2007). Summary for policymakers. In M. L. Parry, O. F. Canziani, J. P. Palutikof, P. J. Van Der Linden, & C. E. Hanson (Eds.), *Climate change 2007: Impacts, adaptation and vulnerability. Contribution of working group II to the fourth assessment report of the intergovernmental panel on climate change*. Cambridge University Press.

Intergovernmental Panel on Climate Change. (2018). *Global warming of 1.5°C: An IPCC special report on the impacts of global warming of 1.5°C above pre-industrial levels and related global greenhouse gas emission pathways, in the context of strengthening the global response to the threat of climate change, sustainable development, and efforts to eradicate poverty*. Intergovernmental Panel on Climate Change.

Intergovernmental Panel on Climate Change. (2019). *Climate change and land. An IPCC special report on climate change, desertification, land degradation, sustainable land management, food security, and greenhouse gas fluxes in terrestrial ecosystems*. Summary for Policymakers. Intergovernmental Panel on Climate Change. https://www.ipcc.ch/site/assets/uploads/2019/08/4.-SPM_Approved_Microsite_FINAL.pdf

Intergovernmental Panel on Climate Change (IPCC). (2021). Summary for policymakers. In V. Masson-Delmotte, P. Zhai, A. Pirani, S. L. Connors, C. Péan, S. Berger, N. Caud, Y. Chen, L. Goldfarb, M. I. Gomis, M. Huang, K. Leitzell, E. Lonnoy, J. B. R. Matthews, T. K. Maycock, T. Waterfield, O. Yelekçi, R. Yu & B. Zhou (Eds.), *Climate change 2021: The physical science basis. Contribution of working group I to the sixth assessment report of the intergovernmental panel on climate change* (pp. 3–32). Cambridge University Press.

Ioannou, I., & Hawn, O. V. (2019). Redefining the strategy field in the age of sustainability. In A. McWilliams, D. E. Rupp, D. S. Siegel, G. K. Stahl, & D. A. Waldman (Eds.), *The Oxford handbook of corporate social responsibility: Psychological and organizational perspectives* (pp. 452–489). Oxford University Press.

Jacobs, G., van Witteloostuijn, A., & Christe-Zeyse, J. (2013). A theoretical framework of organizational change. *Journal of Organizational Change Management, 26*(5), 772–792.

Jóhannesson, S. E., Heinonen, J., & Davíðsdóttir, B. (2020, April). Data accuracy in Ecological Footprint's carbon footprint. *Ecological Indicators, 111*, 105983.

Johnson, J. A., Ruta, G., Baldo, U., Cervigni, R., Chonabayashi, S., Corong, E., ... & Polasky, S. (2021). *Economic case for nature: A global earth-economy model to assess development policy pathways*. International Bank for Reconstruction and Development: The World Bank.

Kaplan, R. S., & McMillan, D. (2020). *Updating the balanced scorecard for triple bottom line strategies.* Harvard Business School Accounting & Management Unit. https://doi.org/10.2139/ssrn.3682788

Khan, M., Serafeim, G., & Yoon, A. (2016). Corporate sustainability: First evidence on materiality. *The Accounting Review, 91*(6), 1697–1724.

Kiesnere, A. L., & Baumgartner, R. J. (2019, January). Sustainability management in practice: Organizational change for sustainability in smaller large-sized companies in Austria. *Sustainability, 11,* 572.

Kiron, D., Unruh, G., Kruschwitz, N., Reeves, M., Unruh, G., Rubel, H., & Meyer Zum Felde, A. (2017, Summer). Corporate sustainability at a crossroads: Progress towards our common future in uncertain times. Summary Findings from the Sustainability Global Executive Studies, 2009–2016. *MIT Sloan Management Review, 58*(4).

Koirala, S. (2019). *SMEs: Key drivers of green and inclusive growth* (OECD Green Growth Papers, No. 2019/03). OECD Publishing. https://doi.org/10.1787/8a51fc0c-en

Kok, A. M., De Bakker, F. G. A., & Groenewegen, P. (2019). Sustainability struggles: Conflicting cultures and incompatible logics. *Business & Society, 58*(8), 1496–1532.

Kreiss, C., Nasr, N., & Kashmanian, R. (2016). Making the business case for sustainability: How to account for intangible benefits—A case study approach. *Environmental Quality Management, 26*(1), 5–24.

Kurucz, E. C., Colbert, B. A., Lüdeke-Freund, F., Upward, A., & Willard, B. (2017). Relational leadership for strategic sustainability: Practices and capabilities to advance the design and assessment of sustainable business models. *Journal of Cleaner Production, 140,* 189–204.

Kurzback, L., & Timmer, R. (2019). *Winning strategies for the long term: How to create value and enhance competitiveness in the age of disruption and short-termism.* KPMG International. https://home.kpmg/xx/en/home/insights/2019/04/winning-strategies-for-the-long-term.html

Landrum, N. E. (2018). Stages of corporate sustainability: Integrating the strong sustainability worldview. *Organization & Environment, 31*(4), 287–313.

Lankoski, L. (2016). Alternative conceptions of sustainability in a business context. *Journal of Cleaner Production, 139,* 847–857.

Law, M. M. S., Hills, P., & Hau, B. C. H. (2017). Engaging employees in sustainable development—A case study of environmental education and awareness training in Hong Kong. *Business Strategy and the Environment, 26*(1), 84–97.

Lewis, S. L., & Maslin, M. A. (2015). Defining the anthropocene. *Nature, 519,* 171–180.

Lindgreen, A., Xu, Y., Maon, F., & Wilcock, J. (2012). Corporate social responsibility brand leadership: A multiple case study. *European Journal of Marketing*, *46*(7/8), 965–993.

Linnenluecke, M. K., & Griffiths, A. (2010). Corporate sustainability and organizational culture. *Journal of World Business*, *45*(4), 357–366.

Linnenluecke, M. K., & Griffiths, A. (2013). Firms and sustainability: Mapping the intellectual origins and structure of the corporate sustainability field. *Global Environmental Change*, *23*(1), 382–391.

Linnenluecke, M. K., Russell, S. V., & Griffiths, A. (2009). Subcultures and sustainability practices: The impact on understanding corporate sustainability. *Business Strategy and the Environment*, *18*(7), 432–452.

Lozano, R. (2015). A holistic perspective on corporate sustainability drivers. *Corporate Social Responsibility and Environmental Management*, *22*(1), 32–34.

Lozano, R., & von Haartman, R. (2018). Reinforcing the holistic perspective of sustainability: Analysis of the importance of sustainability drivers in organizations. *Corporate Social Responsibility and Environmental Management*, *25*(4), 508–522.

Lüdeke-Freund, F. (2010). Towards a conceptual framework of 'business models for sustainability'. In R. R. Wever, J. Quist, A. Tukker, J. Woudstra, F. Boons, & N. Beute (Eds.), *ERSCP-EMSU conference*. Knowledge Collaboration & Learning for Sustainable Innovation, The Netherlands.

Lüdeke-Freund, F., Carroux, S., Joyce, A., Massa, L., & Breuer, H. (2018). The sustainable business model pattern taxonomy—45 patterns to support sustainability-oriented business model innovation. *Sustainable Production and Consumption*, *15*, 145–162.

Maon, F., Lindgreen, A., & Swaen, V. (2008). Thinking of the organization as a system: The role of managerial perceptions in developing a corporate social responsibility strategic agenda. *Systems Research and Behavioral Science*, *25*(3), 413–426.

Martin, J. (2002). *Organizational culture: Mapping the terrain*. Sage.

Massa, L., Tucci, C. L., & Afuah, A. (2017). A critical assessment of business model research. *Academy of Management Annals*, *11*(1), 73–104.

Matten, D., & Moon, J. (2008). "Implicit" and "explicit" CSR: A conceptual framework for a comparative understanding of corporate social responsibility. *Academy of Management Review*, *33*(2), 404–424.

McGrath, S. K., & Whitty, J. (2017). Stakeholder defined. *International Journal of Managing Projects in Business*, *10*(4), 721–748.

McKinsey & Company. (2014). *McKinsey global survey results: Sustainability's strategic worth*. McKinsey & Company.

Milne, M. J., & Gray, R. (2013). W(h)ither ecology? The triple bottom line, the Global Reporting Initiative and corporate sustainability reporting. *Journal of Business Ethics, 118*(1), 13–29.

Montiel, I. (2008). Corporate social responsibility and corporate sustainability: Separate pasts, common futures. *Organization & Environment, 21*(3), 245–269.

Montiel, I., & Delgado-Ceballos, J. (2014). Defining and measuring corporate sustainability: Are we there yet? *Organization and Environment, 27*(2), 113–139.

Murray, M. (2018). *What is an ecosystem?* [Online]. Australian Museum. Retrieved January 23, 2021, from https://australian.museum/learn/species-identification/ask-an-expert/what-is-an-ecosystem/

Nisbet, E. G., Manning, M. R., Dlugokencky, E. J., Fisher, R. E., Lowry, D., & Michel, S. E. (2019, April). Very strong atmospheric methane growth in the 4 years 2014–2017: Implications for the Paris Agreement. *Global Biogeochemical Cycles, 33*(4), 318–342.

Norton, T. A., Zacher, H., & Ashkanasy, N. M. (2014). Organisational sustainability policies and employee green behaviour: The mediating role of work climate perceptions. *Journal of Environmental Psychology, 38*(Suppl. C).

OECD. (2019). *OECD SME and entrepreneurship outlook 2019: Policy highlights* (pp. 1–18). OECD. https://www.oecd.org/industry/smes/SME-Outlook-Highlights-FINAL.pdf

Osterwalder, A., Pigneur, Y., & Tucci, C. L. (2005). Clarifying business models: Origins, present, and future of the concept. *Communications of the Association for Information Systems, 16*, 1–28. https://doi.org/10.17705/1CAIS.01601

O'Reilly, C. A., Caldwell, D. F., Chatman, J. A., & Doerr, B. (2017). The promise and problems of organizational culture: CEO personality, culture, and firm performance. *Group & Organization Management, 39*(6), 595–625.

Ostroff, C., Kinicki, A. J., & Muhammad, R. S. (2013). Organizational culture and climate. In I. B. Weiner (Ed.), *Handbook of psychology* (2nd ed., pp. 643–676). Wiley.

Parmar, B., Freeman, R. E., Harrison, J. S., Wicks, A. C., De Colle, S., & Purnell, L. (2010). *Stakeholder theory: The state of the art*. UR Scholarship Repository, University of Richmond. https://scholarship.richmond.edu/cgi/viewcontent.cgi?article=1098&context=management-faculty-publications

Patala, S., Jalkala, A., Keränen, J., Väisänen, S., Tuominen, V., & Soukka, R. (2016). Sustainable value propositions: Framework and implications for technology suppliers. *Industrial Marketing Management, 59*, 144–156.

Payne, A., Frow, P., & Eggart, A. (2017). The customer value proposition: Evolution, development, and application in marketing. *Journal of the Academy of Marketing Science, 45*, 467–489.

Pedersen, E. R. G., Gwozdz, W., & Hvass, K. K. (2018). Exploring the relationship between business model innovation, corporate sustainability, and organisational values within the fashion industry. *Journal of Business Ethics, 149*(2), 267–284.

Pellegrini, C., Rizzi, F., & Frey, M. (2018). The role of sustainable human resource practices in influencing employee behavior for corporate sustainability. *Business Strategy and the Environment, 27*(8), 1221–1232.

Pennington, L. K. (2015). *Impact of organizational culture on sustainability endeavours: The real story of sustainability*. Macquarie University.

Peters, G. P., Andrew, R. M., Canadell, J. G., Friedlingstein, P., Jackson, R. B., Korsbakken, J. I., Le Quéré, C., & Peregon, A. (2020, January). Carbon dioxide emissions continue to grow amidst slowly emerging climate policies. *Nature Climate Change, 10*, 3–6.

Pham, N. T., Tučková, Z., & Phan, Q. P. T. (2019). Greening human resource management and employee commitment toward the environment: An interaction model. *Journal of Business Economics and Management, 20*(3), 446–465.

Pinelli, M., & Maiolin, R. (2017). Strategies for sustainable development: Organizational motivations, stakeholders' expectations and sustainability agendas. *Sustainable Development, 25*(4), 288–298.

Pinzone, M., Guerci, M., Lettieri, E., & Redman, T. (2016). Progressing in the change journey towards sustainability in healthcare: The role of 'Green' HRM. *Journal of Cleaner Production, 122*, 201–211.

Porter, M. E., & Kramer, M. R. (2011). Creating shared value: How to reinvent capitalism—And unleash a wave of innovation and growth. *Harvard Business Review, 89*(1/2), 62–77.

Posner, B. Z., Kouzes, J. M., & Schmidt, W. H. (1985). Shared values make a difference: An empirical test of corporate culture. *Human Resource Management, 24*(3), 293–309.

Quinn, R. E., & Rohrbaugh, J. (1981, June). A competing values approach to organizational effectiveness. *Public Productivity Review, 5*(2): 122–140.

Quinn, R. E., & Rohrbaugh, J. (1983). A spatial model of effectiveness criteria: Towards a competing values approach to organizational analysis. *Management Science, 29*(3), 363–377.

Raineri, N., & Paillé, P. (2016). Linking corporate policy and supervisory support with environmental citizenship behaviors: The role of employee environmental beliefs and commitment. *Journal of Business Ethics, 137*(1), 129–148.

Ramus, C. A. (2002). Encouraging innovative environmental actions: What companies and managers must do. *Journal of World Business, 37*(2), 151–164.

Rauter, R., Jonker, J., & Baumgartner, R. J. (2017). Going one's own way: Drivers in developing business models for sustainability. *Journal of Cleaner Production, 120*, 144–154.

Ripple, W. J., Wolf, C., Newsome, T. M., Barnard, P., Moomaw, W. R., Grandcolas, P., & and 11258 Scientist Signatories from 153 Countries. (2020, January). World scientists' warning of a climate emergency. *Bioscience, 70*(1), 8–12.
Ritala, P., Huotari, P., Bocken, N., Albareda, L., & Puumalainen, K. (2018). Sustainable business model adoption among S&P 500 firms: A longitudinal content analysis study. *Journal of Cleaner Production, 170*, 216–226.
Roca, L. C., & Searcy, C. (2012). An analysis of indicators disclosed in corporate sustainability reports. *Journal of Cleaner Production, 20*(1), 103–118.
Romer, C. D., & Pells, R. H. (2021). *Great Depression*. Encyclopedia Britannica. https://www.britannica.com/event/Great-Depression
Roome, N., & Louche, C. (2016). Journeying toward business models for sustainability: A conceptual model found inside the black box of organisational transformation. *Organization & Environment, 29*(1), 11–35.
Sannino, G., Di Carlo, F., & Lucchese, M. (2020). CEO characteristics and sustainability business model in financial technologies firms: Primary evidence from the utilization of innovative platforms. *Management Decision, 58*(8), 1779–1799.
Sarros, J. C., Cooper, B. K., & Santora, J. C. (2008). Building a climate for innovation through transformational leadership and organizational culture. *Journal of Leadership & Organizational Studies, 15*(2), 145–158.
Schaltegger, S., Hansen, E. G., & Lüdeke-Freund, F. (2016a). Business models for sustainability: Origins, present research, and future avenues. *Organization and Environment, 29*(1), 3–10.
Schaltegger, S., & Horisch, J. (2017). In search of the dominant rationale in sustainability management: Legitimacy- or profit-seeking? *Journal of Business Ethics, 145*, 259–276.
Schaltegger, S., Lüdeke-Freund, F., & Hansen, E. G. (2016b). Business models for sustainability: A co-evolutionary analysis of sustainable entrepreneurship, innovation, and transformation. *Organization & Environment, 29*(3), 264–289.
Schaltegger, S., Windolph, S. E., & Herzig, C. (2012). A longitudinal analysis of the knowledge and application of sustainability management tools in large German companies. *Society and Economy, 34*(4), 549–579.
Schein, E. H. (1986). *Organisation culture and leadership*. Jossey-Bass.
Schein, E. H. (2009). *The corporate culture survival guide* (New and Revised ed.). Jossey-Bass: A Wiley Imprint.
Schein, E. H. (2010). *Organizational culture and leadership* (4th ed.). Jossey-Bass.
Schein, E. H., & Schein, P. (2017). *Organizational culture and leadership* (5th ed.). Wiley.

Searcy, C. (2016). Measuring enterprise sustainability. *Business Strategy and the Environment, 25*(2), 120–133.

Shams, S. M. R., Vrontis, D., Weber, Y., Tsoukatos, E., & Galati, A. (2020). Stakeholder engagement for a sustainable development of business models. In S. M. R. Shams, D. Vrontis, Y. Weber, E. Tsoukatos, & A. Galati (Eds.), *Stakeholder engagement and sustainability* (pp. 1–13). Routledge.

Sharma, A., & Kearins, K. (2011). Interorganizational collaboration for regional sustainability: What happens when organizational representatives come together? *The Journal of Applied Behavioral Science, 47*(2), 168–203.

Shrivastava, P. (2018). Business not-as-usual to achieve SDGs under climate change. In J. R. McIntyre, S. Ivanaj, & V. Ivanaj (Eds.), *CSR and climate change implications for multinational enterprises* (pp. 21–36). Edward Elgar Publishing.

Silva, S., Nuzum, A.-K., & Schaltegger, S. (2019). Stakeholder expectations on sustainability performance measurement and assessment. A systematic literature review. *Journal of Cleaner Production, 217*, 204–215.

Slawinski, N., Pinkse, J., Busch, T., & Banerjee, S. B. (2017). The role of short-termism and uncertainty avoidance in organizational inaction on climate change: A multi-level framework. *Business & Society, 56*(2), 253–282.

Smircich, L. (1983). Concepts of culture and organizational analysis. *Administrative Science Quarterly, 28*(3), 339–358.

Sroufe, R. (2017, September). Integration and organizational change towards sustainability. *Journal of Cleaner Production, 162*, 315–329.

Starik, M., Stubbs, W., & Benn, S. (2016). Synthesising environmental and socio-economic sustainability models: A multi-level approach for advancing integrated sustainability research and practice. *Australasian Journal of Environmental Management, 23*(4), 402–425.

Steffen, W., Richardson, K., Rockström, J., Cornell, S. E., Fetzer, I., Bennett, E. M., Biggs, R., Carpenter, S. R., de Vries, W., de Wit, C. A., Folke, C., Dieter, G., Heinke, J., Mace, G. M., Persson, L. M., Ramanathan, V., Reyers, B., & Sörlin, S. (2015). Planetary boundaries: Guiding human development on a changing planet. *Science, 347*(6223), 736–748.

Stiglitz, J. (2016). *The great divide: Unequal societies and what we can do about them*. Penguin.

Stoughton, A. M., & Ludema, J. (2012). The driving forces of sustainability. *Journal of Organizational Change Management, 25*(4), 501–517.

Stubbs, W. (2017). Characterising B Corps as a sustainable business model: An exploratory study of B Corps in Australia. *Journal of Cleaner Production, 144*, 299–312.

Stubbs, W., & Cocklin, C. (2008). Conceptualizing a sustainability business model. *Organization Environment, 21*(2), 103–127.

Sull, D., Turconi, S., & Sull, C. (2020). When it comes to culture, does your company walk the talk? *MITS Loan Management Review, 61*(4), 1–11.

Svensson, G., Ferro, C., Høgevold, N., Padin, C., Carlos Sosa Varela, J., & Sarstedt, M. (2018). Framing the triple bottom line approach: Direct and mediation effects between economic, social and environmental elements. *Journal of Cleaner Production, 197,* 972–991.

Teece, D. J. (2010). Business models, business strategy and innovation. *Long Range Planning, 43*(2), 172–194.

Tung, A., Baird, K., & Schoch, H. (2014). The relationship between organisational factors and the effectiveness of environmental management. *Journal of Environmental Management, 144,* 186–196.

United Nations. (2020). *The sustainable development goals report 2020* (pp. 1–68). United Nations. https://unstats.un.org/sdgs/report/2020/The-Sustainable-Development-Goals-Report-2020.pdf

Van Bommel, K., Henkemans, M. B., Brinkhorst, T., & Meurs, M. (2020). A review of sustainable business models: Past accomplishments and future promises. *Journal of Sustainability Research, 2*(3), 1–25.

Vandenberghe, C., & Peiro, J. M. (1999). Organizational and individual values: Their main and combined effects on work attitudes and perceptions. *European Journal of Work and Organizational Psychology, 8*(4), 569–581.

von Weizsacker, E. U., & Wijkman, A. (2017). *Come on! Capitalism short-termism, population and the destruction of the planet. A report to the Club of Rome.* Springer Nature.

Walls, J. L., & Berrone, P. (2017). The power of one to make a difference: How informal and formal CEO power affect environmental sustainability. *Journal of Business Ethics, 145*(2), 293–308.

Ward, B., Bufalari V., Tulay, M., Murphy, S. E., Joshi, R., & Cohn Martin, N. (2020). *COVID-19 and inequality: A test of corporate purpose.* KKS Advisors.

Warrick, D. D. (2017). What leaders need to know about organizational culture. *Business Horizons, 60*(3), 395–404.

Welford, R. (1997). *Hijacking environmentalism: Corporate responses to sustainable development.* Earthscan.

Winn, M. I., & Pogutz, S. (2013). Business, ecosystems, and biodiversity: New horizons for management research. *Organization and Environment, 26*(2), 203–229.

Woodruff, R. B. (1997). Customer value: The next source for competitive advantage. *Journal of the Academy of Marketing Science, 25*(2), 139–153.

World Meteorological Organization. (2019a). *WMO greenhouse gas bulletin* (15th ed., Vol. 2019a, pp. 1–8). World Meteorological Organization.

World Meteorological Organization. (2019b). *WMO statement on the state of the global climate in 2018* (pp. 1–39). World Meteorological Organization.

World Wide Fund for Nature. (2018). *Living planet report 2018: Aiming higher*. World Wide Fund for Nature

World Wide Fund for Nature. (2020). Living planet report 2020: Bending the curve of biodiversity loss. In R. Almond (Ed.), *Living planet report* (pp. 1–145). World Wide Fund for Nature. Zoological Society of London. https://f.hubspotusercontent20.net/hubfs/4783129/LPR/PDFs/ENGLISH-FULL.pdf

Wright, C., & Nyberg, D. (2017). An inconvenient truth: How organizations translate climate change into business as usual. *Academy of Management Journal, 60*(5), 1633–1661.

Xie, X., & Zhu, Q. (2020). Exploring an innovative pivot: How green training can spur corporate sustainability performance. *Business Strategy and the Environment, 29*(6), 2432–2449.

Zibarras, L. D., & Coan, P. (2015). HRM practices used to promote pro-environmental behavior: A UK survey. *The International Journal of Human Resource Management, 26*(16), 2121–2142.

CHAPTER 11

The Customer Value Concept: How Best to Define and Create Customer Value?

Angelina Zubac

INTRODUCTION

Two of the most important concepts in strategic management and management are the concepts of *value creation* and *value appropriation*.[1] This is because they explain in highly processual terms how organisations are able to adapt and evolve by gaining access to and deploying resources[2] and, in turn, how they contribute to economic development and growth (Zubac, 2018; Zubac et al., 2012). When an organisation successfully invests in, configures and uses resources to create new sources of profit

---

[1] Value appropriation is also known as value capture.

[2] In this paper, resources are both the assets and capabilities that are used and developed at an organisation to achieve its strategic objectives.

A. Zubac (✉)
University of Queensland, Brisbane, QLD, Australia
e-mail: a.zubac@business.uq.edu.au; angelina.zubac@aim.com.au; az@strategylink.com.au

value has been created.[3] When an organisation successfully invests in, combines and uses resources to sustain a competitive advantage and build wealth value has been appropriated. A balance between these two organisation-wide processes must be achieved because organisations must be able to fund their activities and operate efficiently to be economically sustainable (Moran & Ghoshal, 1999).

Remarkably, despite value creation's criticality, managers and researchers have in the past tended to focus on value appropriation and downplay the importance of value creation. There has also been a corresponding tendency to underrate the importance of *customer value creation*. This has largely been attributed to the fact that organisational performance can be impacted by a range of factors. For instance, when a competitor realises an organisation is earning above average profits (supernormal profits) within a particular market, they will normally try to capture a (larger) share of that market. Likewise, employees are likely to ask for a higher salary if they believe the organisation is earning above average profits (Blyler & Coff, 2003; Coff, 1999; Porter, 1980, 1985, 1991; Slater & Narver, 1994, 1995a, 1995b). It is only in recent times that managers and researchers alike have concluded value creation is just as important to concentrate on as value appropriation. The same can be said for customer value creation, which is perplexing as most organisations depend on their customers for their survival (Priem, 2007).

However, customer value has been defined many ways over the last decades. This has meant that it can be very difficult to understand how customer value creation problems are best tackled. The reality is that some definitions of customer value are much more suited to solving some customer value creation-related dilemmas and conundrums than others (Ramirez, 1999; Woodruff, 1997).

With this in mind, this chapter explains three of the most popular categories for defining customer value, that is, customer value is (1) the amount customers are willing to pay, (2) an equity position customers perceive they have in an organisation and (3) an inherently multidimensional concept. The objective is to clarify the circumstances under which the different approaches for defining customer value are most useful. Thus, in the next section, the three categories of definitions are discussed,

---

[3] Value can be created for the organisation by successfully creating value for customers but it could also be created other ways, such as by developing a part of the business that is later sold or investing in another company's shares in anticipation of earning dividends.

including their pros and cons. In the section that follows, a multidimensional approach is confirmed as the most versatile. In support of this argument, Woodruff's (1997) multidimensional definition of customer value is described. In addition, two frameworks are development. They explicate the ways in which Woodruff's highly regarded definition can be used to build a boundary-spanning, customer value learning, co-creation and co-delivery (platform-based) system as an active participant within an institutionally complex ecosystem. Such a system should enable an organisation to more readily create customer value over its lifetime.

The Different Categories of Customer Value Definitions

This section explains the three categories of definitions, including their pros and cons. The theories that motivated the development of the definitions that emerged over time are also discussed, including why it is now commonly accepted that organisations are more likely to create performance-enhancing levels of customer value if they are customer-centric or services-oriented as opposed to "goods" or production oriented (Delgado-Guzmán et al., 2019; Priem et al., 2013; Ramírez, 1999; Vargo & Lusch, 2004, 2008, 2010, 2016). "Services" using a services-dominant logic are not "the residual aspect of a good". They are the "application of specialized competences (knowledge and skills) through the deeds, processes, and performance for the benefit of another entity or the entity itself" (Vargo & Lusch, 2004: 2). This shift in thinking was necessary because organisations operate in markets that are far more competitive (D'Aveni et al., 2010), connected and interdependent (Jacobides, 2019; Jacobides et al., 2018), and institutionally complex (Peng et al., 2009) than they were in the past.

Customers' Willingness to Pay More Than the Cost to Produce: The Pros and Cons

In the 1980s when positioning theory (industrial organisation logic) dominated management and marketing thinking, customer value was mostly defined in much the same way, that is, as the amount customers are willing to pay (Delgado-Guzmán et al., 2019; Desarbo et al., 2001; Zubac et al., 2010). For instance, Porter (1980, 1985, 1991) argued customer value is the benefit customers receive when they pay for a product and/or service. When a customer is willing to pay it is because they believe the products and/services on offer represent a more compelling value proposition than the products and/or services of competitors. Gale (1994) also defined customer value in relative price and quality terms. The idea of a trade-off is very heavily implied here too. Customers are more likely to become a party to an exchange and transact with the organisation if they perceive that the sacrifice (payment for the product and/or service) is worth it (Carricano, 2014; Grönroos, 1997; Zeithaml, 1988). These ideas are consistent with classical economics which assumes the equilibrium price is the price at which suppliers will supply enough to meet customers' demands at that price (Bowman & Ambrosini, 2000; Priem, 2007).

One of the advantages of approaching customer value creation from a positioning or as an outcome of supply meeting demand at a certain price is that it becomes easier for managers to make operational, tactical of even strategic decisions designed to make the organisation more competitive. For instance, after analysing the organisation using activity-based cost analysis techniques, the organisation's value chain can be reconfigured to implement a generic cost leadership strategy (Porter, 1980, 1985, 1991). This argument is predicated on the idea that industries have value chains where suppliers and customers sit on opposite ends of the chain, and organisations in the middle. If the focal organisation adds value to the inputs (raw materials, etc.) provided by suppliers at a price that customers are willing to pay, the organisation should do well (Normann & Ramírez, 2000).

Likewise, when customer value is approached as the price customers are willing to pay, it should be easier for managers to make pricing decisions. The problem is that there are all kinds of information asymmetries that can confront an organisation's decision-makers. These can make finding the right price to charge customers more trial and error than about getting it right the first time. For instance, it may not always be obvious that customers are willing to pay a higher price because they perceive the organisation's products and/or services to be higher quality. Of course, if it does eventually become apparent customers are happy to pay a higher price, it will be in the organisation's best interests to not disappoint customers in future by decreasing product and/or service quality (Nagle, 1984, 1993).

There may also be situations when it is necessary to cut prices to stay competitive or solvent. The problem is that excessive price cutting could give some customers the impression the product and/or service was overpriced in the first place. Thus, the decision to cut prices may turn out to be a poor one in the longer-run. Customers may become unwilling to pay anything other than the lower price, making it difficult for the organisation to cover its costs. Some of these problems can be avoided by investing in advertising and by finding ways to track how customers' perception of the ideal price tends to fluctuate. These activities can be very costly. In most cases, the best course of action is to find ways to compete on non-price terms—by offering something to customers that is particularly distinctive. However, learning about customers' specific requirements to avoid investing in product and/or service characteristics customers do not want also incurs costs. No matter the pricing strategy adopted, it can be a challenge to apportion costs to different segments of customers (Holden & Nagle, 1998; Nagle, 1993). As prospect theory has shown, it can also be very difficult to describe a given value proposition in a way that does not lead to customers negatively assessing and valuing what is on offer (Smith & Nagle, 1995).

Comparing the most widely used pricing strategies to each other, a *cost-add* or (cost-driven) strategy is the easiest because once the costs of production are determined it is just a matter of deciding what percentage over and above these costs should be added to determine a final price. The problem with this technique is that it is difficult to understand whether customers did not buy for non-price reasons. However, in the case of a *value-based* pricing strategy, one must first recognise what exactly customers value and whether the organisation can profitably deliver on that value. This is very difficult to do if the organisation is resource constrained or its people do not have the requisite training or commitment to be appropriately customer-oriented. Of course, it is not in the customer's best interest either to tell suppliers they are willing to pay more (Smith & Nagle, 1994). A *profit-based* pricing strategy is the most complicated of all the pricing strategies to implement. Profit-based pricing involves finding ways to improve the profit contribution for each product and/or service sold by understanding customers' price sensitivities and all of the (fixed and variable) costs associated with delivering value via each unit to be sold to different segments of customers. This includes the costs associated with communicating that value to them. When the contribution margin for each unit is positive, the organisation earns profits (Smith & Nagle, 2002: 25). The problem with this technique is that customers may end up be divided into two groups—those who are associated with the incurring of high fixed costs and those who are not. Many market development opportunities may be lost as a result of a bias in favour of one group of customers emerging over time.

The problem may not be about choice of pricing strategy at all. Research demonstrates that regardless of whether an organisation is a price-taker or price-maker, it tends to be easier for managers to use the cost-add method of pricing. Indeed, this is the case for the majority of organisations where cost-add is used by default. Fortunately, cost-add is only occasionally "the essence" of the pricing technique; customers' values were still important to consider at many organisations (Amaral & Guerreiro, 2019: 1851). When managers understand the benefits value-based pricing can generate, they tend to price in a manner that is consistent with best practice. These managers have an uncanny ability to identify when customers will become price sensitive or indifferent to a change in price. The problem is that many managers are unable to understand the value-price link (Hinterhuber et al., 2021; Liozu, 2017; Liozu et al., 2012).

In summary, when customer value is approached as the amount customers are willing to pay, it is easier to formulate and implement tactical or strategic value chain and pricing decisions. This is a good thing. But easier is not the same as saying it is easy. Even satisfied and loyal customers will defect if they believe other organisations can better satisfy their needs; approaching customer value in purely trade-off terms could lead to an organisation underperforming in the longer-run (Jones & Sasser, 1995).

Some Sort of Equity Position: Pros and Cons

Clearly, there are very good reasons why customer value should be approached very strongly from the customers' view, that is, as an equity position customers perceive they have in an organisation through its products and/or services. As the literature suggests, this is because customers are the ultimate arbiters of value. Unless they believe their needs are being treated seriously, it can be very difficult for an organisation to successfully build a loyal customers base (Slater & Narver, 1994; Zeithaml, 1988: 14), including a satisfied customer base with high lifetime value (Lemon et al., 2001; Rust et al., 2004; Zeithaml et al., 2001). When an organisation consults with customers to understand their expectations, they can effectively deliver on them (Kroll et al., 1999; Parasuraman et al., 1988), and be responsive to their changing needs (Flint et al., 2002).

Logically, a nuanced understanding of customers' values is difficult to obtain without first investing in a relationship designed to attract or lock in customers. Some sort of interaction, whether fleeting or sustained, must first occur for customers to become emotionally or practically tied to the organisation. It is then incumbent on the organisation to translate what they learn through the customer relationship into something customers view as valuable. When the market environment is competitive and customers are not spoilt for choice, taking the time to build strong relationships with customers can make all the difference (Slater & Narver, 1994, 1995a, 1995b; Spanos & Lioukas, 2001; Srivastava et al., 2001). "The relationship approach puts customer processes, or rather the internal value-generating processes of customers, not products at the center (sic) of marketing" (Grönroos, 2004: 102).

In the new millennium, organisations must engage with customers constructively to do well (Richardson & Thompson, 2019). Successful organisations "do not just add value, they reinvent it ..... the value-creating system itself, within which different economic actors – suppliers, business partners, allies, customers – work together to co-produce value. Their key strategic task is the reconfiguration of roles and relationships among the constellation of actors in order to mobilize the creation of value in new forms and by new players. And their underlying strategic goal is to create an ever-improving fit between competences and customers" (Normann & Ramírez, 2000: 65–66). Thus, customers are no longer "consumers" who destroy value. They are partners and need to be treated as such even if the relationship the organisation has with the customer is mostly one-way (Jacobides, 2019; Ramírez, 1999). Managers must think in both relational and resource-based terms while at the same time focusing on what needs to be added to the product and/or service by way of an underlying solution or technology: "To be able to manage the value creation in a relational context the firm has to focus on the resources – personnel technologies, knowledge and information, customers' time and the customer itself – as well as on the competencies of the firm to acquire and manage these resources" (Grönroos, 1997: 417).

Many authors have argued that the task of interacting with customers can be simplified if the sole objective is to learn about their value-in use requirements. This is because value-in-use is purported to be customers' main concern (Bowman & Ambrosini, 2000; Priem, 2007). Value-in-use analysis allows managers to identify how customers want to use or be provided with the organisation's products and/or services, as well as understand changes in their value-in-use requirements over time. It also allows managers and marketers to determine if the organisation's products and/services are perceived to be competitively priced based on the value-added. Another benefit of value-in-use analysis is that it can be used to pinpoint the "transformation processes" that are required to create value for customers and invest in resources as is appropriate (Bowman & Ambrosini, 2000: 3). However, the problem with a value-in-use approach is that customers may value the relationship they have with the organisation much more than what is ultimately able to be delivered in an in-use situation. Likewise, the organisation may end up underinvesting in other relationships, such as the relationship it has with important supply partners or complementors (Grönroos, 2012: 1531).

In theory, value-in-use analysis can be used to better understand if the money customers pay because their in-use requirements were better met by the organisation ends up being captured by the organisation or by other parties instead. That is, using value-in-use principles, it is possible to separate out that level of new value created for customers in use situations from that part eventually captured by the organisation. In other words, one should be able to differentiate between "innovation that establishes or increases the consumer's valuation of the benefits of consumption (i.e. use value)" and that part which constitutes an exchange of value or what customers ultimately paid: "from the consumer's viewpoint, value creation involves increasing use value or decreasing exchange value, each of which can increase consumer surplus". The problem is it may not be so easy in practice to effectively monitor and address the different ways competitors, suppliers or even its customers can lay claim to the value which would normally accrue to the organisation (Priem, 2007: 220). It is not easy to understand why the value created through customers does not get captured by the organisation. Individuals, organisations and society may moderate or interject to some extent in this value creation-capture process (Lepak et al., 2007).

Similarly, organisations can only successfully approach customer value from an equity position view by understanding and defining for decision-making purposes the organisation's customer value creation architecture. A customer value creation architecture is the extent to which "the value offering and customer equity (the firm viewpoint), and customer value and brand equity (the customer viewpoint)" is balanced. Stated differently, when an organisation's builds a customer base which represents high lifetime value because customers are willing to pay a premium and prefer the organisation's products and/or services, the organisation is said to have brand equity. The resource-investments that may be required to strike a balance and build a brand that creates appropriable value (value able to be captured by the organisation) may be substantial. Investments in an organisation's innovation, marketing and production processes are required at the very least (Ngo & O'Cass, 2010: 496). The problem is that even if it is possible to be meticulous and eventually define the customer creation architecture accurately, customers' needs are always changing. A value-in-use approach has its limits in this way too.

A Multidimensional Concept: Pros and Cons

As the preceding discussion confirmed, customers do not just want a certain level of quality and functionality in return for a good price and their loyalty; customers want all their current and future needs addressed. They will not settle for anything less if they think a competitor has a better value proposition on offer. This is profoundly reflected in the more recent literature on customer value, which argues customers want their needs met along multiple dimensions. However, in this literature, there are many definitions of customer value that could be described as multidimensional (Delgado-Guzmán et al., 2019; DeSarbo et al., 2010; Khalifa, 2004; Kelly et al., 2017; Ramirez, 1999; Richardson & Thompson, 2019). Readers should examine this literature if keen to learn more about it.

To cut to the chase, of all the multidimensional definitions available to use to base customer-related decisions on, Woodruff's (1997) highly respected definition of customer value is arguably the most versatile of all the definitions available. This definition can be used in a variety of ways when making weighty resource-based, customer value creation decisions, including when attempting to build profitable customer relationships (Zubac et al., 2010). Woodruff (1997: 142) defines customer value as "*a customer's perceived preference for and evaluation of those product attributes, attribute performances, and consequences arising from use that facilitate (or block) achieving the customer's goals and purposes in use situations*". This definition of customer value allows managers to learn about customers' (1) desired product attributes and attribute performances, (2) desired consequences in use situations and (3) goals and purposes. For instance, if someone was selling wheat in Asia, the first dimension might involve understanding how to price the wheat suitably for these customers and the quality of wheat required. The second dimension might involve understanding if the wheat can be used to make flour and then noodles which turns a certain colour when cooked. The third dimension might involve understanding that some Asian manufacturers plan to offer bread products in future. The benefit of understanding each of these dimensions is that managers can then determine post-delivery if the organisation has successfully delivered on each of these value dimensions, that is, whether customers have achieved a certain level of (4) attribute-based satisfaction, (5) consequence-based satisfaction and (6) goal-based satisfaction.

In short, Woodruff's definition can be used to learn about customers by establishing some sort of customer learning system. This idea is depicted in Fig. 11.1, which combines in a rudimentary fashion two frameworks developed by Woodruff in his very influential 1997 paper: Woodruff's *Customer Value Hierarchy* and *Translating Customer Value Learning into Action* frameworks. Together these frameworks allow

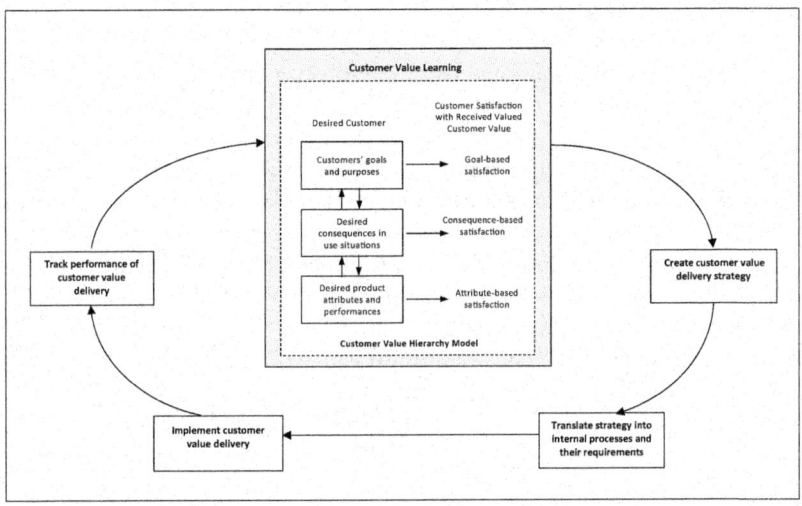

Fig. 11.1 Actioning customer value learning (*Source* Adapted from Woodruff [1997])

managers to develop a deconstructed view of customers' values and make resource-investment decisions accordingly. This includes improve on customer value delivery by applying continual quality control principles. The first Woodruff framework is reflected in the large square in the middle of Fig. 11.1. As can be observed by starting from the bottom of the hierarchy, it is very important to understand the attributes and attribute performances customers are looking for when making the decision to purchase. Moving up the hierarchy, the focus shifts to understanding what it is customers want to achieve—their value-in-use requirements. Finally, moving up to the top of the hierarchy, it should be clear that it is also very important to understand customers' goals and purposes post-purchase. To the right of the hierarchy, it can be observed that if one understands these three dimensions, it should be possible to understand the extent to which customers have been satisfied along each of these dimensions, as indicated to the right of the individual squares.

Critically, as the arrows moving up and then down the customer value hierarchy framework shows, as customers gain more appreciation of the goals and purposes they could achieve with the product and/or service, they may require different value-in-use outcomes, which in turn leads to their attribute and attribute performance requirements changing. The degree to which they can be satisfied post-purchase may also change as a result. For instance, building on the wheat example, if it is discovered the noodles that are being manufactured with the purchased wheat are not turning the "right" colour when cooked, the organisation's technologists might investigate whether there is a better wheat protein mix to offer these customers, ensuring a better value-in-use outcome. More to the point, if it is subsequently learned some customers are keen to start manufacturing bread to sell across Asia, it might be prudent to begin offering customers training in best practice bread manufacturing methods. All such findings are likely to have very real organisational resource-investment implications. This too is depicted in Fig. 11.1. As the boxes and arrows going in a clockwise direction show, it should be possible to translate customer value learning into customer value delivery objectives. The strategy articulates the resource-investments that are necessary at the organisation, including how best to monitor delivery performance.

In summary, Woodruff's (1997) definition has power because of its capacity to be used to develop a powerful customer learning system but also to develop, implement and measure the performance of the organisation's customer value strategy and make timely adjustments when required.

WOODRUFF'S (1997) DEFINITION AND THE CONTEMPORARY ORGANISATION: TWO FRAMEWORKS

However, the question is can Woodruff's multidimensional definition of customer value be used to understand the resource-investments that must be made at an organisation, including how to build a superior, dynamic capability base? By the same token, can it be used to be as customer centric and outward looking as it is now necessary to be to ensure an organisation can cope with the pressures placed upon it by the external environment, which is now more complex than it was than ever before? Also, can it be used to achieve high levels of strategic alignment within and across an organisation and intra-organisationally or to address stakeholders needs? The answer is a resounding yes.

Understanding Customer Value and Investing in Resources to Create and Deliver Customer Value

Resource-based theory research has demonstrated time and time again that organisations achieve sustainable or temporary competitive advantages because some of their resources are exceptional (D'Aveni et al., 2010). Though still important to invest in resources to be operationally efficient (Powell, 2017; Winter, 2003), organisations are more likely to be high performing if they develop and actively use certain dynamic capabilities (Helfat et al., 2007). By the same token, organisations are more likely to be high performing if they possess dynamic capabilities which enable the organisation to sensitively address its customers' needs (Srivastava et al., 2001; Woodruff, 1997). Like all dynamic capabilities, such capabilities must be developed and reconfigured regularly to ensure the organisation can compete effectively and be consistently high performing (Sirmon et al., 2011).

As the management and management literatures have revealed, most of these dynamic capabilities can be easily described (Eisenhardt & Martin, 2000). Many of them will be associated with the marketing function (Landroguez et al., 2011; Srivastava et al., 2001). However, it should be kept in mind that "customer value is created by core capabilities throughout the entire organization". This means customer value could be created by any part or by anyone at the organisation. When an organisation has a market-oriented culture, it is responsive to customers' changing needs. Neither is it overly customer-led (Slater & Narver, 1994: 24). If an organisation becomes overly customer-led, it loses the ability to roll out products and/or services that address customers' latent or future needs. Sometimes customers are simply unable to predict or articulate what they might want in future (Slater & Narver, 1999).

With all of this in mind, Woodruff's (1997) multidimensional definition of customer value was used to study how high performing accounting and software engineering organisations as compared to low performing accounting and software engineering organisations learned, created and delivered customer value through their products and/or services (Zubac, 2009). As demonstrated in Table 11.1, which summarises the study's main findings, the dynamic (strategic) capabilities that were especially important to possess and lever across the three dimensions Woodruff argues are key were identified. These customer value creating capabilities could be divided into three categories of dynamic capabilities: dynamic managerial, dynamic technical and dynamic marketing capabilities. As Table 11.1 reveals, the accounting and software engineering organisations that took part in the study had a number of capabilities in common. For instance, strategic analysis and planning capabilities were considered to be important managerial capabilities. However, there were stark differences in the technical capabilities required to deliver value to customers when delivering on customers' value-in use requirements.

Though Table 11.1 is instructive, it is also clear methods must be developed that provide even more guidance about how high performing organisations achieve their customer value creation objectives. This is over and above the general guidance provided by combining two of Woodruff (1997) frameworks, as depicted in Fig. 11.1. Indeed, there are potentially many (sub)processes and cognitions that may need to be combined to enable an organisation to remain relevant over time.

Teece's (2007: 1319) framework for explicating dynamic capabilities arguably provides this guidance. In Teece's framework, dynamic capabilities are conceived as "distinct skills, processes, procedures, organizational structures, decision rules, and disciplines". These enable the whole organisation in three ways: by making it possible to (1) sense and understand opportunities and threats, (2) seize opportunities and mitigate threats and

Table 11.1 Comparing accounting and software engineering firms

	Dynamic (strategic) managerial capabilities		Dynamic (strategic) technical capabilities		Dynamic (strategic) marketing capabilities	
	Accounting	Software engineering	Accounting	Software engineering	Accounting	Software engineering
Customers' goals and purposes After the received product and/or service was paid for and used	Strategic analysis and planning Market decisions/agility Organisational/team change	Strategic analysis and planning Market decisions/agility Customer future needs forecasting			Customer learning Customer problem learning	Customer learning Customer problem learning
Customers desired in use consequences While the product and/or service is being used/delivered	Strategic analysis and planning Organisational design Cross-functional team formation and development Complex problem solving for customers People management Performance measurement	Strategic analysis and planning	Standard template and methods development, especially for accounting, and consulting projects Tender submissions	Business/outsource partner relationship development Requirements and exceptions reassessment for quality control Technical assessment policies Code templates and methodologies Tender submissions	CRM management CRM data analysis	CRM management CRM data analysis

	Dynamic (strategic) managerial capabilities		Dynamic (strategic) technical capabilities		Dynamic (strategic) marketing capabilities	
	Accounting	Software engineering	Accounting	Software engineering	Accounting	Software engineering
Product and service attributes At point when the decision to purchase is being made	Strategic analysis and planning Resource management	Business case analysis Project business case approval process	Market trends analysis Regulatory change analysis	Region-specific product development Business requirements collection and management Software development and release Product/service pricing Regulatory change analysis R&D/commercialisation	Focused customer learning Product/service bundling Brand/product positioning Customer communications Customer/client acquisition	Customer engagement Product/service bundling Brand/product positioning Customer acquisition strategy development and execution

Source Adapted from Zubac (2009)

(3) reconfigure or transform the organisation to achieve the organisation's strategic and operational goals. These ideas are depicted in Fig. 11.2. As one can see by comparing "A" to "B" and "C" of the diagram, it should be possible to identify and map the managerial, technical and marketing dynamic capabilities that are or will be important to invest in and develop to create and deliver customer value multidimensionally. These can be further categorised in sensing, seizing and reconfiguring/transforming terms in line with Teece's arguments. These capabilities could be made up of a great many organisation-wide (sub)processes and cognitions. Maps could be developed to understand how these dynamic capabilities are developed and used, and by whom.

Furthermore, in line with how Wernefelt (1984: 171) established in the early days of resource-based theory that resources and the activities of a value chain are "two sides of the same coin", it should also be possible to map how different strategic activities enable customer value to be created and delivered. These can include those activities that are normally associated with the traditional value chain (Porter, 1980, 1985), value chains that explain knowledge-based or heavily networked organisations (Stabell & Fjeldstad, 1998), and those that explain how knowledge and technology can be levered by partnering and establishing strategic communities (Kodama, 2009). This is depicted in the section labelled "D" in Fig. 11.2, albeit in a highly stylised manner.

Being Customer Centric and Applying Service-Dominant Logic

These resource-based ideas are consistent with co-creation logic, defined as "an interactive process of resource integration involving a broad set of actors for the benefit of all" (Chih et al., 2019: 602). Critically, they are also consistent with service-dominant logic. Service-dominant logic ideas have been enthusiastically and widely embraced by both the management and research communities. According to this logic, though the "good" may still be important, customer value is created through services. Services in this conceptualisation are not "the residual aspects of a good", which was how they were traditionally described. Services are the "application of specialized competences (knowledge and skills) through the deeds, processes, and performance for the benefit of another entity or the entity itself". Though the traditional approach to defining services may have some relevance at times, this expanded definition makes it possible to better appreciate how organisations must function along vertical and

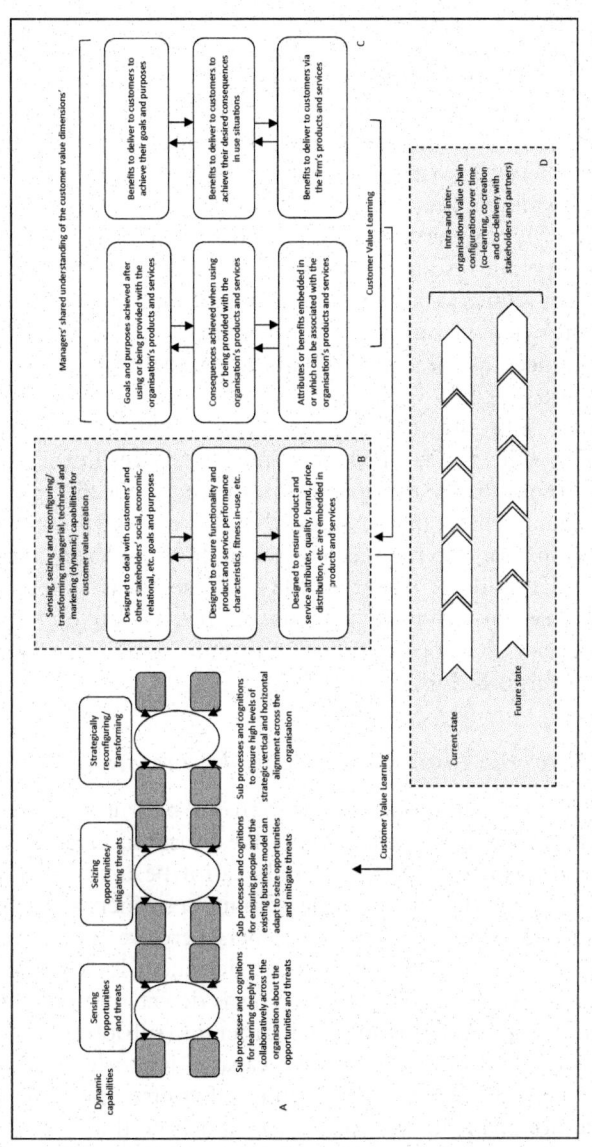

Fig. 11.2 Building customer value (dynamic) capabilities to transform the organisation into a customer value delivery powerhouse

horizontal lines to create and deliver customer value. It also reflects the role organisations play within the economy and society, including the role they play within a particular market-based ecosystem. In the ecosystems of today, success is tied to how well the organisation is able to interact with many parties, including its customers, partners, stakeholders, etc. Service-dominant logic allows one to understand how these interactions stimulate creativity and the ability to create new forms of (shared) customer value that has ecosystem-wide implications. By the same token, consistent with resource-based view theory, service-dominant logic helps all the players to understand the operant resources that need to be developed to create and deliver customer value, including new forms of customer value: "A service-centered (sic) view identifies operant resources, especially higher-order, core competences, as the key to obtaining competitive advantage" (Vargo & Lusch, 2004: 2, 12).

Knowledge and skills are operant resources within the service-dominant paradigm while goods—products and/or services in the traditional sense, are transmitters of operant resources. Indeed, operant resources may be hierarchical in the sense that some standalone while others are composites or interconnected through the players within the network (Madhavaram & Hunt, 2008). These ideas reflect the fact that "science has moved from a focus on mechanics to one on dynamics, evolutionary development, and the emergence of complex adaptive systems" (Vargo & Lusch, 2004: 15).

Value Networks: Institutionally Complex Ecosystems

With these ideas in mind, it should be clear that Woodruff's customer value definition and ideas about customer value learning, creation and delivery is as relevant as it ever was. Not only can it be used to understand customer value approached as (1) the amount customers are willing to pay and (2) an equity position that customers perceive they have in an organisation, it can be used to apply service-dominant logic to better address customers' multidimensional needs. This is depicted in Fig. 11.2. This diagram demonstrates the way in which different (sub)processes and cognitions can be used to develop dynamic capabilities to learn about, co-create and deliver customer value over time. Of course, the challenge if applying service-dominant logic is to understand how the underlying capability base is held together, especially when the organisation is cooperating with customers, its partners and other stakeholders to learn, create and deliver customer value. This too is depicted in Fig. 11.2. However, it is more powerfully depicted in Fig. 11.3.

As Fig. 11.3 illustrates, it is possible to understand how to work with customers, partners and stakeholders in combination to create customer value multidimensionally. As can be observed, the organisation could just work with customers but within the service-dominant paradigm it is expected the organisation will simultaneously find ways to work with customers and partners. The same applies when stakeholders must be included in the customer value learning, creation and delivery process within the given ecosystem. The diagram also shows that a range of (sub)processes and cognitions can be assembled and turned into operant resources[4] or, in more resource-based terms, dynamic capabilities. These may be developed and utilised within an organisation only. However, it is quite possible some dynamic capabilities may end up being shared between the various partners.

These ideas are consistent with Kelly et al.'s (2017: 13) arguments that in more complex environments customer value creation may resemble the rings of an onion. In the centre, sits economic value, and in the next outer rings there is perceived value, relational value and in the final outer layer, experiential value. Importantly, "experiential value refers to the sense of value a customer gets from the whole experience of dealing with a supplier ...... A more sophisticated way of thinking about experiential value extends the idea of relationship to a concern with the well-being of the whole network and system of business, customer and societal interactions". From this perspective, Woodruff's definition of customer value is especially pertinent. Again, this is because not only can it be used when customer value is approached as (1) the amount customers are willing to pay, and (2) an equity position that customers perceive they have in an organisation, it can be used to describe customer value learning, creation and delivery within a complex environment using service-dominant logic. For instance, since pricing is more complicated a task than it ever was, the definition can be used to understand how customers assess price along multiple value dimensions, and very strong relative and relational terms (Ingenbleek, 2014).

---

[4] In this paper, consistent with the literature, operant resources are those that are customer value related and able to be linked to a competitive advantage or value creation at the organisational level.

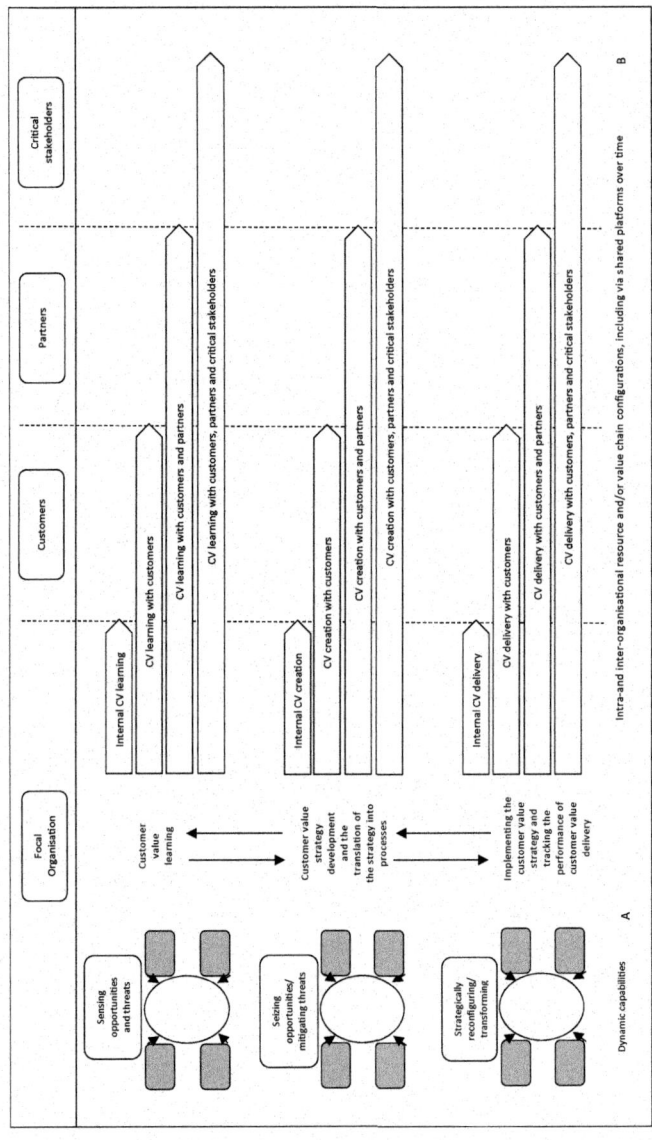

Fig. 11.3 Learning about, and creating and delivering customer value within an institutionally complex ecosystem

The reality is that in a hypercompetitive world, where industries are converging because of technological change, the demand side of value creation cannot be ignored. Neither is it wise to ignore how blurred organisational boundaries have become (Priem et al., 2013). Likewise, it would also be foolhardy to discount the importance of the organisation's role within its ecosystem. According to Jacobides et al. (2018: 2255), ecosystems are more than just a network, which may include markets, alliances and supply chains; they are "interacting organizations (sic), enabled by modularity, not hierarchically managed, bound together by the nonredeployability of their collective investment". Though they are rule-based, it is rare for the players to enter into formal agreements with the ecosystem in mind. It is the interdependence between the players that binds them. Customer value is created within an ecosystem because complementors with unique and generic complementary value offerings are attracted to the ecosystem to compete but also cooperate within it.

Like any other system, all ecosystems have a life-cycle and may morph into something entirely new. Many start out as a supply chain. As more players become involved in the customer value delivery process and complementariness of some offerings create value for customers, the dyadic relationships between the organisation and customer, organisation and supply partner, and so forth becomes less critical. It is the network interactions that are key. They are the means by which the co-learning, co-creation and co-delivery efforts of all the parties become possible (Letaifa, 2014). Indeed, it is increasingly necessary to think of supply chains in ecosystem terms. Getting the "good" through the supply chain is still important but not as important as finding ways to benefit from the different ways value is created at each point and pooled along the supply chain by different parties (Lusch et al., 2010). Thus, supply chains are much less customer-driven and much more customer centric now compared to the last decades (Liu & Deitz, 2011; Martinelli & Tunisini, 2019). So much is about the system now. Organisations are more likely to succeed when the systemic nature of customer value is taken into account when learning, creating and delivering customer value. This is likely to involve finding ways to establish and utilise interconnected platforms that enable the free-flow of knowledge within an ecosystem. When managers adopt an ecosystem mindset, they can more effectively develop such dynamic capabilities, differentiating the organisation by the way in which its network position can be levered (Pynnönen et al., 2011: 57).

In addition, though organisations may be connected informally by the complementariness of their product and/or service offering, becoming interdependent as a result, this will be within a given institutional context. Indeed, it has been argued that institutions must be considered as the third leg of strategy. If positioning theory and resource-based theory explain high performance by linking success to the level of power an organisation can exert within its industry and the distinctiveness of the organisation's resource base, respectively, institutional considerations are important because they explain isomorphic change. More precisely, they explain how by becoming similar to a competitor an organisation can improve its performance or gain a competitive advantage by increasing its legitimacy (Peng et al., 2009). Cognisant of these facts, Vargo and Lusch (2016: 17) have expanded their service-dominant thesis to reflect the presence of informal and formal institutions within an ecosystem:

> The emerging narrative of S-D logic is a dynamic one ..... it is a narrative of cooperation and coordination in ecosystems, as well as the reconciliation of conflict between them. Institutions are instrumental in these cooperation and coordination activities by providing the building blocks (Ostrom 2005) for increasingly complex and interrelated resource-integration and service-exchange activities in nested and overlapping ecosystems organized around shared purposes.

Conclusion

In summary, Woodruff's (1997) customer value definition has power in a number of ways. This is because in addition to making it possible to understand customer value in product and/or service attribute and value-in-use terms, that is, as (1) the amount customers are willing to pay, and (2) an equity position that customers perceive they have in an organisation, it can be used to develop a customer learning system and apply service-dominant logic to create customer value multidimensionally. In other words, not only can this definition be used to understand and deliver on customers' attribute and attribute performances, and value-in-use requirements, it can be used to understand customers' higher-level goals and purposes. The latter is especially useful for understanding how customers' values are changing or have changed. Most importantly, it can be used to understand how to build the dynamic capabilities that must be developed to more competently learn about, create and deliver customer value. This includes the dynamic capabilities used solely within the organisation but also which are shared and used across its boundaries. When the organisation is operating within an ecosystem where many parties are interconnected, such dynamic capabilities are likely to be realised as a platform.

For all these reasons, if one is to choose between the three different approaches for defining customer value discussed in this chapter, a multi-dimensional approach is recommended. Woodruff's multidimensional definition has various strengths: it is versatile and can be used at all stages of the organisation's life and when partnering on a grand scale. It is also a means by which it is possible to differentiate the organisation when it must compete within an institutionally complex ecosystem environment but also achieve legitimacy within that environment.

REFERENCES

Amaral, J. V., & Guerreiro, R. (2019). Factors explaining a cost-based pricing essence. *Journal of Business & Industrial Marketing, 34*(8), 1850–1865.

Blyler, M., & Coff, R. W. (2003). Dynamic capabilities, social capital, and rent appropriation: Ties that split pies. *Strategic Management Journal, 24*(7), 677–686.

Bowman, C., & Ambrosini, V. (2000). Value creation versus value capture: Towards a coherent definition of value in strategy. *British Journal of Management, 11*(1), 1–15.

Carricano, M. (2014). Pricing myopia: Do leading companies capture the full value of their pricing strategies? *Management Decision, 52*(1), 159–178.

Chih, Y., Zwikael, O., & Restubog, S. L. (2019). Enhancing value co-creation in professional service projects: The roles of professionals, clients and their effective interactions. *International Journal of Project Management, 37*(5), 599–615.

Coff, R. W. (1999). When competitive advantage doesn't lead to performance: The resource-based view and stakeholder bargaining power. *Organization Science, 10*(2), 119–133.

D'Aveni, R. A., Battista, G., & Smith, K. G. (2010). The age of temporary advantage. *Strategic Management Journal, 31*(13), 1371–1385.

Delgado-Guzmán, J. A., Molina-Quintana, B., & Quintana-León, M. B. (2019). Theoretical aspects of creating customer value. In J. Gil-Fafuente, D. Marino, & F. C. Morabito (Eds.), *Economy, business and uncertainty: New ideas for a Euro-Mediterranean industrial policy* (pp. 327–339). Springer Nature.

DeSarbo, W. S., Jedidi, K., & Sinha, I. (2001). Customer value analysis in a heterogenous market. *Strategic Management Journal*, 22(9), 845–857.
DeSarbo, W. S., Ebbes, P., Fong, D. K. H., & Snow, C. C. (2010). Revisiting customer value analysis in a heterogenous market. *Journal of Modelling in Management*, 5(1): 8–24.
Eisenhardt, K. M., & Martin, J. A. (2000). Dynamic capabilities: What are they? *Strategic Management Journal*, 21(10–11), 1105–1121.
Flint, D. J., Woodruff, R. B., & Gardial, S. F. (2002). Exploring the phenomenon of customers' desired value change in a business-to-business context. *Journal of Marketing*, 66(4), 102–117.
Gale, B. T. (1994). *Managing customer value: Creating quality and service that customers can see*. The Free Press.
Grönroos, C. (1997). Value-driven relational marketing: From products to resources and competencies. *Journal of Marketing Management*, 13(5), 407–419.
Grönroos, C. (2004). The relationship marketing process: Communication, interaction, dialogue, value. *The Journal of Business & Industrial Marketing*, 19(2), 99–113.
Grönroos, C. (2012). Conceptualising value co-creation: A journey to the 1970s and back to the future. *Journal of Marketing Management*, 28(13–14), 1520–1534.
Helfat, C. E., Finkelstein, S., Mitchell, W., Peteraf, M., Singh, H., Teece, D., & Winter, S. G. (2007). *Dynamic capabilities: Understanding strategic change in organizations*. Blackwell.
Hinterhuber, A., Snelgrove, T. C., & Stensson, B.-I. (2021). Value first, then price: The new paradigm of B2B buying and selling. *Journal of Revenue and Pricing Management*, 20, 403–409.
Holden, R. K., & Nagle, T. T. (1998). Kamikaze pricing: When penetration strategies run amok, marketers can find themselves in a dive-bomb of no return. *Marketing Management*, 30, 140–147.
Ingenbleek, P. T. M. (2014). The theoretical foundations of value-informed pricing in the service-dominant logic of marketing. *Management Decision*, 52(1), 33–53.
Jacobides, M. G. (2019, September–October). In the ecosystem economy, what's your strategy? *Harvard Business Review*, 129–137.
Jacobides, M. G., Cennamo, C., & Gawer, A. (2018). Towards a theory of ecosystems. *Strategic Management Journal*, 39(8), 2255–2276.
Jones, T. O., & Sasser, W. E. (1995, November–December). Why satisfied customers defect. *Harvard Business Review*, 88–100.
Kelly, S., Johnston, P., & Danheiser, S. (2017). *Value-ology*. Palgrave Macmillan.
Khalifa, A. S. (2004). Customer value: A review of recent literature and an integrative configuration. *Management Decision*, 42(5), 645–666.

Kodama, M. (2009). Boundaries innovation and knowledge integration in the Japanese Firm. *Long Range Planning, 42*(4), 463–494.

Kroll, M., Wright, P., & Heiens, R. A. (1999). The contribution of product quality to competitive advantage: Impacts on systematic variance and unexplained variance in returns. *Strategic Management Journal, 20*(4), 375–384.

Landroguez, S. M., Castro, C. B., & Cepeda-Carrión, G. (2011). Creating dynamic capabilities to increase customer value. *Management Decision, 49*(7), 1141–1159.

Lemon, K. N., Rust, R. T., & Zeithaml, V. A. (2001). What drives customer equity. *Marketing Management, 10*(1), 20–25.

Lepak, D. P., Smith, K. G., & Taylor, M. S. (2007). Value creation and value capture: A multilevel perspective. *Academy of Management Review, 32*(1), 180–194.

Letaifa, S. B. (2014). The uneasy transition from supply chains to ecosystems. *Management Decision, 52*(2), 278–295.

Liozu, S. M. (2017). Value-based pricing special issue: Editorial. *Journal of Revenue and Pricing Management, 11*(1), 1–3.

Liozu, S. M., Hinterhuber, A., Boland, R., & Perelli, S. (2012). The conceptualization of value-based pricing in industrial firms. *Journal of Revenue and Pricing Management, 11*(1), 12–34.

Liu, G., & Deitz, G. D. (2011). Linking supply chain management with mass customization capability. *International Journal of Physical Distribution & Logistics Management, 41*(7), 668–683.

Lusch, R. F., Vargo, S., & Tanniru, M. (2010). Service, value networks and learning. *Journal of the Academy of Marketing Science, 38*, 19–31.

Madhavaram, S. R., & Hunt, S. D. (2008). The service-dominant logic and a hierarchy of operant resources: Developing masterful operant resources and implications for marketing strategy. *Journal of the Academy of Marketing Science, 36*(1), 67–82.

Martinelli, E. M., & Tunisini, A. (2019). Customer integration into supply chains: Literature review and research propositions. *Journal of Business & Industrial Marketing, 34*(1), 24–38.

Moran, P., & Ghoshal, S. (1999). Markets, firms, and the process of economic development. *Academy of Management Review, 24*, 390–412.

Nagle, T. T. (1984). Economic foundations for pricing. *The Journal of Business, 57*(1), S3–S26.

Nagle, T. T. (1993). Managing price competition. *Marketing Management, 2*(1), 36–45.

Ngo, L. V., & O'Cass, A. (2010). Value creation architecture and engineering: A business model encompassing the firm-customer dyad. *European Business Review, 22*(5), 496–514.

Normann, R., & Ramírez, R. (2000, July–August). From value chain to value constellation: Designing interactive strategy. *Harvard Business Review*, 65–77.
Parasuraman, A., Zeithaml, V. A., & Berry, L. L. (1988). SERVQUAL: A multiple-item scale for measuring consumer perceptions of service quality. *Journal of Retailing*, 64(1), 12–40.
Peng, M. W., Sun, S. L., Pinkham, B., & Chen, H. (2009). The institution-based view as a third leg for a strategy tripod. *Academy of Management Perspectives*, 23(3), 63–81.
Porter, M. E. (1980). *Competitive strategy: Techniques for analyzing industries and competitors*. Free Press.
Porter, M. E. (1985). *Competitive advantage: Creating and sustaining superior performance*. Free Press.
Porter, M. E. (1991). Towards a dynamic theory of strategy. *Strategic Management Journal*, 12(S2), 95–117.
Powell, T. C. (2017). Strategy as diligence: Putting behavioral strategy into practice. *California Management Review*, 59(3), 162–190.
Priem, R. L. (2007). A consumer perspective on value creation. *Academy of Management Review*, 32(1), 219–235.
Priem, R. L., Butler, J., & Li, S. (2013). Toward reimagining strategy research: Retrospection and prospection on the 2011 AMR decade award article. *Academy of Management Review*, 38(4), 471–489.
Pynnönen, M., Ritala, P., & Hallikas, J. (2011). The new meaning of customer value: A systemic perspective. *Journal of Business Strategy*, 32(1), 51–57.
Ramirez, R. (1999). Value co-production: Intellectual origins and implications for practice and research. *Strategic Management Journal*, 20(1), 49–65.
Richardson, N., & Thompson, M. C. (2019). A new positioning framework for organizational value: Juxtaposing organizational value positions with customer centricity. *Strategic Change*, 28(2), 123–132.
Rust, R. T., Lemon, K. N., & Zeithaml, V. A. (2004, January). Return on marketing: Using customer equity to focus marketing strategy. *Journal of Marketing*, 68, 109–127.
Sirmon, D. G., Hitt, M. A., Ireland, R. D., & Gilbert, B. A. (2011). Resource orchestration to create competitive advantage: Breadth, depth, and life cycle effects. *Journal of Management*, 37(5), 1390–1412.
Slater, S. F., & Narver, J. C. (1994). Market orientation, customer value, and superior performance. *Business Horizons*, 37(2), 22–28.
Slater, S. F., & Narver, J. C. (1995a). Marketing orientation and the learning organization. *Journal of Marketing*, 59(3), 63–74.
Slater, S. F., & Narver, J. C. (1995b). Market-oriented is more than being customer-led. *Strategic Management Journal*, 20(12), 1165–1168.
Smith, G. E., & Nagle, T. T. (1994). Financial analysis for profit-driven pricing. *Sloan Management Review*, 35(3), 71–84.

Smith, G. E., & Nagle, T. T. (1995). Frames of references and buyers' perception of price and value. *California Management Review,* 38(1), 98–116.
Smith, G. E., & Nagle, T. T. (2002, Winter). How much are customers willing to pay? *Marketing Research,* 20–25.
Spanos, Y. E., & Lioukas, S. (2001). An examination into the causal logic of rent generation: Contrasting Porter's competitive strategy framework and the resource-based perspective. *Strategic Management Journal,* 22(10), 907–934.
Srivastava, R. K., Fahey, L., & Christensen, H. K. (2001). The resource-based view and marketing: The role of market-based assets in gaining competitive advantage. *Journal of Management,* 27(6), 777–802.
Stabell, C. B., & Fjeldstad, Ø. D. (1998). Configuring value for competitive advantage: On chains, shops, and networks. *Strategic Management Journal,* 19(5), 413–437.
Teece, D. J. (2007). Explicating dynamic capabilities: The nature and micro-foundations of (sustainable) enterprise performance. *Strategic Management Journal,* 28(13), 1319–1350.
Vargo, S. L., & Lusch, R. F. (2004). Evolving to a new dominant logic for marketing. *Journal of Marketing,* 68(1), 1–17.
Vargo, S. L., & Lusch, R. F. (2008). Service-dominant logic: Continuing the evolution. *Journal of the Academy of Marketing Science,* 36, 1–10.
Vargo, S. L., & Lusch, R. F. (2010). From repeat patronage to value co-creation in service ecosystems: A transcending conceptualization of relationship. *Journal of Business Marketing Management,* 4, 169–179.
Vargo, S. L., & Lusch, R. F. (2016). Institutions and axioms: An extension and update of service-dominant logic. *Journal of the Academy of Marketing Science,* 44, 5–23.
Wernefelt, B. (1984). A resource-based view of the firm. *Strategic Management Journal,* 5(2), 171–180.
Winter, S. G. (2003). Understanding dynamic capabilities. *Strategic Management Journal,* 24(10), 991–995.
Woodruff, R. B. (1997). Customer value: The next source for competitive advantage. *Journal of the Academy of Management Science,* 25(2), 139–153.
Zeithaml, V. A. (1988). Consumer perceptions of price, quality, and value: A means-end model and synthesis of evidence. *Journal of Marketing,* 52(3), 2–22.
Zeithaml, V. A., Rust, R. T., & Lemon, K. N. (2001). The customer pyramid: Creating and serving profitable customers. *California Management Review,* 43(4), 117–142.
Zubac, A. (2009). *Investing in resources to create customer value: The strategic, organisational & performance implications.* Digital Thesis Publications. https://digital.library.adelaide.edu.au/

Zubac, A. (2018). Capitalism as discourse: How can strategic management scholars contribute new insights and refocus debate? *Journal of Management & Organization, 24*(2), 189–208.

Zubac, A., Hubbard, G., & Johnson, L. W. (2010). The RBV and value creation: A managerial perspective. *European Business Review, 22*(5), 515–538.

Zubac, A., Hubbard, G., & Johnson, L. W. (2012). Extending resource-based logic: Applying the resource-investment concept to the firm from a payments perspective. *Journal of Management, 38*(6), 1867–1891.

CHAPTER 12

Strategic Processes and Mechanisms of Value Creation and Value Capture: Some Insights from Business Organisations in Poland

Wojciech Dyduch

INTRODUCTION

One of the main tasks of contemporary strategic management is to create value. Scholars and management practitioners seek to identify the sources of value creation in order to lever the processes and mechanisms that increase firm performance and lead to competitive advantage in the long run.

The concepts of value creation and value capture (VCVC) have gained much attention in the management literature in recent times (Call & Ployhart, 2021; Niesten & Stefan, 2019). It can concern creating value for customers or for organisations. The marketing perspective focuses on a maximum amount a customer is willing to pay to obtain the desired good (Mahajan, 2020). The organisational perspective concentrates on

---

W. Dyduch (✉)
University of Economics in Katowice, Katowice, Poland
e-mail: dyduch@ue.katowice.pl

© The Author(s), under exclusive license to Springer Nature Singapore Pte Ltd. 2022
A. Zubac et al. (eds.), *Effective Implementation of Transformation Strategies*, https://doi.org/10.1007/978-981-19-2336-4_12

identifying the sources of revenues as well as maximising value for the owner, managers and other stakeholders involved in the strategy realisation (Burkert, 2013). Particularly, from the resource-based perspective, value creation is understood as the result of successfully bargaining in the competitive environment for economic gain (Chatain & Zemsky, 2011; Skilton, 2014) or the outcome of orchestrating the resources necessary to exploit opportunities, develop innovations and create more value (Teece, 2018). These perspectives are interconnected. More insights and perspectives about the sources of customer value can be found in the wider management literature, including the relational view, supply chain perspective or in the stakeholder orientation literature. All of these areas in the management literature, associate effectively implemented strategies with value creation (Davidow, 2018) and consequently seek to identify the specific processes that enable strategies to be successfully implemented (cf. Zubac et al., 2021).

In spite of sound theoretical foundations, still little is known about the specific strategic mechanisms that are selected and utilised by organisations to create value, protect the value that was created from erosion and capture even more value over time. The question remains, which particular processes and mechanisms of VCVC are key and lead to high firm performance. Few publications have tackled this problem in the rich context of Central and Eastern Europe, seventeen years after European Union (EU) accession. This is despite the growing opportunity-base in the economies of Central and Eastern Europe.

The aim of this chapter is threefold. First, some theoretical insights of value creation and capture are presented, with the attention focused on resource-based theory, competitive positioning theory and stakeholder orientation theory as these perspectives dominate the scholarly discussion in strategic management field. The reasoning of this study is embedded in the following sequence: (a) value is created when organisations offer goods that customers are willing to pay for, (b) in order to offer attractive in-use value, organisations need to be innovative, (c) to develop innovations, organisations need to invest in valuable resources, secure a proper position in the competitive environment, as well as skillfully develop relations with key stakeholders. Second, the results of research carried out at 316 organisations in Poland in 2019 are presented. The research identified the specific VCVC processes and mechanisms that impact firm performance. Third, through the use of factor analysis, a conceptual model is derived that could have implications for managerial practice, namely identifying the business lifecycle, orchestrating resources, developing stakeholder synergy and dividing the created value accordingly in order to create even more value.

This study adds to the strategic management theory by identifying the key variables describing value creation and capture, as well as demonstrating their impact on organisational performance. Thus, it contributes to VCVC research as it identifies some of the most important processes and mechanisms used by entrepreneurial organisations in Poland to VCVC.

VALUE CREATION AND VALUE CAPTURE—SOME THEORETICAL INSIGHTS

From the customer perspective, value is defined as the maximum amount an individual is willing to pay to procure a good or to avoid something undesirable, or as the perceived worthiness of the product or service by the potential user (Pitelis, 2009; Porter & Kramer, 2011). The concept of use value is associated with the product's or service's design, performance attributes, such as ease of use or its innovativeness, which leads to the consumer's willingness to pay for it (Prahalad & Ramaswamy, 2004). The customer and organisation perspectives are therefore highly interconnected, as the ability to develop innovative products and services with high in-use value is contingent on the unique resources and knowledge sharing capabilities that the organisation is able to access and utilise. Likewise, the organisation is more likely to be high performing if it is stakeholder oriented and it possesses effective inter-organisational relationship building capabilities—capabilities that allow the organisation to have a significant social impact on its supply chain and B2B activities (Siemieniako et al., 2021).

Thus, when an organisation earns economic rents by providing innovative products and services with high in-use attributes, value is created. Naturally, this leads one to think about how the strategy reflects resource-based logic (Fischer, 2011). Some scholars posit, that a sufficient condition for companies to be innovative is the ability to generate or discover new ideas (Bilton & Cummings, 2010) and turn them into innovative products or services that meet end user needs (Cooper, 2011). However, creative ideas themselves do not create value—only innovations commercialised and tested in market conditions can be the source of value creation. It can be assumed, however, that the majority of value translated into a unique product or service occurs at the idea generation or discovery process stage (Bilton & Cummings, 2010). Therefore, to be strategic, it is crucial for managers to support the initial stages of value creation, such as investing in organisational creativity, innovativeness and entrepreneurship, as all of these stages in the chain can create value and lead to improved performance (Davidow, 2018).

If the organisation is able to exploit its full strategic potential, it can become even more innovative and deliberate in how it approaches value creation (Horth & Vehar, 2014). This outcome can be achieved by: (a) developing the creative strategy that embraces innovation, (b) focusing on strategic leadership, (c) communicating challenging strategic issues throughout the organisation, (d) creating highly diverse teams, (e) providing organisational members with access to creative methods and experiences, (f) designing and building systems that nurture innovation, and (g) investing in ideas that do not at first seem to be a strategic fit by spanning boundaries and breaking down barriers for innovation. Thus, it is worth ensuring the organisation can exploit its strategic potential. This is the starting point for nurturing innovation and stimulating value creation.

It is important to invest in the resources that can strengthen the organisation's capacity for value creation (Mahoney & Qian, 2013). It is also important to strengthen the following strategic resource-investment processes by focusing on (a) value growth (the processes used to increase existing value continuously), (b) new value creation (preparing and commercialising new products, services and technologies) and (c) value co-creation (creating value together with organisations and end users through continuous interaction and idea exchange) (Vargo & Lusch, 2004).

Contemporary organisations create value by combining resources they possess or control with resources owned or controlled by customers, suppliers and end users (Kyprianou, 2018). Involving customers in value creation as vital stakeholders makes it possible to co-create value, which in turn makes it easier for managers to identify consumers' needs and preferences more effectively and to increase the overall amount of value that is created for various stakeholders (Tantalo & Priem, 2014). This was not possible using the classical perspective (Amit & Han, 2017).

Often, strategically important resources needed for value co-creation are beyond or not in an organisation's control (Brown et al., 2001). This makes the assessment of their potential to contribute to value creation uncertain. Eventually, the decision may be made to create an innovation ecosystem that the organisation and other organisations may participate in VCVC to enable the co-creation of value inter-organisationally (Dattee et al., 2018). There are many challenges associated with co-creating value through an innovation ecosystem, as demonstrated by the experience of organisations within software ecosystems, video game platforms, credit card payments, etc. In these systems, it was difficult to define who contributed the most to the value that was created. Similarly, value can be easily captured by complementors, who can start their own ecosystem. To avoid such unwanted value capture, key players of the ecosystem need to set the rules (Dattee et al., 2018), or experiment with the business models (Kyprianou, 2018). They also need to influence the strategies that are developed by organisations within the ecosystem and monitor their own strategies, updating them as necessary to ensure that the emerging value proposition will enable the firm to capture some of the created value (Dattee et al., 2018).

The potential outcome of introducing innovations can influence the perceived value by the stakeholders (Willumsen et al., 2019). Thus, it is worth analysing how the created value will be perceived by stakeholders, while developing mechanisms that allow value capture, protecting as much value as possible, and to "share the pie" with other groups of the task environment, actors and stakeholders accordingly.

Even though value created by organisations is important for stakeholders, their expectations, and perceptions as to the value created may differ (Oliveira & De Muylder, 2012). Since value creation and value capture require taking into account stakeholders' needs, the co-relations between stakeholders should be analysed during the strategy formulation and implementation process. It will not be possible to create more value otherwise (Priem et al., 2019). Superficial analyses can lead to compromises and capturing less value that was created through the synergies created through the inter-organisational relationship (Tantalo & Priem, 2014).

In order to create value in the long run, organisations not only can carry out regular analyses to identify value creating activities and strategic points of control, but also support strategic thinking in order to capture value. The logic of value creation and value capture comprises: (a) discovering value (what intended value will be created), (b) designing value (how value will be created), (c) delivering value (how value will be obtained) and (d) retaining or capturing value (Piboonrungroj et al., 2017).

Organisations need to focus not just on value creation but on value protection, value capture and the development of appropriation mechanisms, i.e. strategically viable ways of protecting and capturing more value (Ritala, & Tidström, 2014). As to the latter, some organisations are able to capture more value than others, even though they do not create as much value. It is not enough to possess or control unique resources. It is also necessary to develop organisational capabilities that allow the organisation to exploit the value capture opportunities that appear (Barney & Arikan, 2005). Because the value co-created with stakeholders may have a synergetic effect, it becomes challenging to ensure an appropriate share of that value and that an appropriate level of value is captured. It is important to invest in the development of such value capture mechanisms as a result (Tondolo & Bitencourt, 2014).

The strategy-making process is an important mediating mechanism for explaining long-term value creation. For example, it has been found that implementing less risky strategy-making, adopting mechanisms of strategic actions that mitigate risks as well as greater autonomy in decision-making contribute to value creation in the long term (Jeong & Harrison, 2017).

The necessary condition for retaining the value created is the organisation's ability to protect the created value and to capture even more value through stakeholder synergy (Coff, 2010). This ability may depend on the bargaining power, negotiating position, and the level of competition in the task environment; some appropriation mechanisms are required allowing various stakeholders to adapt to potential costs, the level of risk and revenues (Sridharan & Simatupang, 2013).

In order to retain the majority of value, the company can secure its revenues through various so-called appropriation mechanisms, e.g. trade secrets, standards, dominant position in certain product categories, brand, reputation, time to market. Securing value does not mean protecting it against all stakeholders but developing the relational ability to cooperate and "divide the pie" in a just manner.

In innovative ecosystems capturing value requires the ability to identify control points, i.e. the critical places, where most of the value is created (Dattee et al., 2018). Since these control points depend on the innovative ecosystem vision, resources available, and how strategies are implemented, they are not static; thus, capturing value becomes a continuous, dynamic and recurrent process (Pagani, 2013), with dynamic control of drifting and sliding positions of value creation (Dattee et al., 2018: 486). In order to make the control points less volatile, organisations need to strategically navigate the process of value creation in order to capture most of it.

Value-creation leadership capabilities can be helpful in identifying the control points (Kollenscher et al., 2018). These are the combination of purposeful processes focused on directing the organisation and enhancing organisational value by ensuring transformational leadership across levels, that is, at the micro level (interpersonal influence), strategic leadership at the macro level (shaping the vision and strategy), and architectural leadership at the meso perspective (shaping structures) to create a unified model of corporate leadership. The value-creation leadership achieved reflects shareholder value maximisation goals, where the business objective is to increase the value of organisation for its shareholders, measured as a discounted cash flow.

Value creation impacts firm performance. If performance is treated as a multi-dimensional construct, encompassing both the long-term competition-related customer or shareholder perspective and the short-term operational profits, then the value created can be seen as a portion of the operational financial result occurring to relevant stakeholder groups, resulting from the adopted strategic perspective (Jeong & Harrison, 2017).

It is possible for organisations to create value in the short term, for instance, by implementing a cost-leadership strategy in most of the value chain activities (Subrahmanyam, 2019), by financial manoeuvring (Kollenscher et al., 2018: 29) or by adopting focused, customer-oriented and well-timed marketing and sales strategies (Terho et al., 2015). However, in the long run value creating processes must be developed to ensure a vertically and horizontally aligned strategy; and special attention must be paid to cutting costs wherever practicable and, thus, help increase value. In other words, all outdated physical production logic needs to be eliminated (Davidow, 2018).

Table 12.1 is a summary of the theoretical insights presented above. Apart from the leading perspectives in strategic management discussed above (resource-based view, competitive positioning and stakeholder theories) other views, such as real options reasoning, transactional costs, intellectual property rights, project management, marketing management, value-based management and business model design are presented.

Table 12.1 Value creation and value capture: selected theoretical perspectives

Theoretical perspective	Value creation and value capture (VCVC)
Resources (Resource-based view) (Amit & Han, 2017; Barney, 1991; Brown et al., 2001)	Value and economic rents are created through possessing or controlling and using valuable, rare and unique resources, including complementary resources needed to commercialise innovations. Strategic investments in above-average resources with low mobility and competitor accessibility strengthen value creation and value capture. Rare and valuable resources can generate economic rents. However, they need to be supported by the organisation's capabilities to appropriate value and to divide the value among stakeholders. Value capture is not frictionless because the contracts that link value chains are incomplete
Dynamic capabilities (Resource-based view) (Teece, 2016)	Value is created through the organisation's ability to adapt to changed market conditions. These can be hostile, complex but also benign environmental conditions. The ability to quickly obtain, combine, shift and transform resources to exploit opportunities that appear in the environment is the source of value creation. Organisations that develop opportunity-identifying capabilities in the long run are seldom able to react quickly. They must become good at shifting resources in order to take up emerging opportunities
Competitive environment perspective (Competitive positioning theory) (Tondolo & Bitencourt, 2014)	Value is created in various places along the organisation's value chain or inter-organisationally across a sector. Effective value creation and capture happens through strategic investments in activities that translate into value while reducing the support for activities that are unlikely to contribute to value creation

(continued)

Table 12.1 (continued)

Theoretical perspective	Value creation and value capture (VCVC)
Value chain (Competitive positioning theory) (Piboonrungroj et al., 2017)	Value creation and capture depend on the company position in the competitive environment, its relations with deliverers, buyers, competitors; the bargaining powers of different parties, rent appropriation rules, the ability to understand stakeholder expectations and their perception of value
Stakeholder orientation (Sridharan & Simatupang, 2013)	Value is created through effective stakeholder synergy, which requires developing a stakeholder orientation within the organisation's strategy. Taking into account stakeholders' expectations leads to the ability to effectively create coalitions, ecosystems or market rules, and secure resources that are otherwise inaccessible for commercialising innovations
Real options reasoning (McGrath, 1997; Miller & Folta, 2002)	Value is created through investments that enhance managerial flexibility and which are oriented towards strategic activity, including strategies that can be modified as new information about the external environment becomes available. Applying, options value logic, strategic decisions are different from typical investment decisions; they can create value for the option holders over time. Value is captured through the ability to identify the optimal timing for realising a given option
Relational view (Dyer & Singh, 1998; Henkel & Hoffmann, 2019)	Value is created through a cooperation or coopetition strategy. Relational rent is the outcome of organisation's functioning in the network, which allows organisations to access other stakeholders' resources. Complementary resources, ability to collaborate and stakeholder synergy can be the source of competitive advantage. The captured value depends on the bargaining and negotiating structure of the network actors

(continued)

Table 12.1 (continued)

Theoretical perspective	Value creation and value capture (VCVC)
Transactional costs perspective (Zajac & Olsen, 1993)	The strategic task of every organisation is to create value. Strategies and management systems need to reconcile the paradox that exists between cost reduction and value creation stemming from the strategic choices made
Property rights perspective (Mahoney & Qian, 2013)	Undefined or imprecisely defined property rights have a negative impact on value creation. Value protection mechanisms and proper legal arrangements strengthen the organisation's capacity to transfer knowledge and its value creating potential while reducing the value capture risk
Project management perspective (Willumsen et al., 2019)	In project management, value is what is achieved over the break-even point, that is, between the value created for customers and the profit for the organisation. Value is an outcome of the project, including input factors such as the product design and functionality usability, special features, value perception, market value, costs
Corporate social responsibility (Porter & Kramer, 2011)	The value created is an economic and/or social benefit, derived by managing costs, competing effectively and sustainably earning profits. Value creation is understood to be the result of a common effort. The organisational benefits by ensuring its activities create social and environmental benefits. This perspective assumes that privatising profits and socialising costs is suboptimal and not an effective way to divide the value that is captured
Firm performance (Jeong & Harrison, 2017)	Value reflects the organisation's performance. Organisational performance reflects the economic value that stakeholders (customers, competitors) derive over the medium-term. Value creation translates into firm performance

(continued)

Table 12.1 (continued)

Theoretical perspective	Value creation and value capture (VCVC)
Marketing management (Mahajan, 2020; Terho et al., 2015)	Value is the difference between the willingness to pay (the highest amount of money that the end user is willing to pay for a product or service) and opportunity cost (the lowest price the deliverer can sell the product). Marketing actions that are positively received by customers lead to a willingness to pay. The willingness to pay stems for the perception the product is innovative. This is the result of the organisation possessing relational and value co-creation capabilities
Value-based management (Burkert, 2013)	Value-based management promotes the maximisation of value for stakeholders. The management team activities are assessed and confronted with desired results. Value management systems allows them to reconcile organisation's goals with stakeholders' expectations
Business model perspective (Amit & Zott, 2012)	The central point of a business model is to create value for customers and for the organisation through exploiting entrepreneurial opportunities and through identifying the sources of revenues

Understanding value creation in traditional terms only as a willingness to pay for desired features is limiting. This reflects the customer (marketing) perspective only. Since organisations function in dynamic environments, develop relations with stakeholders, and compete, other perspectives come into play. It is necessary to approach strategy utilising the strategic perspective while embracing the logics inherent in the resource-based, competitive positioning and stakeholder orientation theories. What is more, it is observed that in inefficient, imperfect or failing markets, organisations are high performing if they reflect the economic perspectives (transaction costs, value-based management, real options logic). This allows them to better develop strategy and create more value (Mahoney & Qian, 2013).

Value Creation and Value Capture Processes and Mechanisms—Empirical Research Results

Research Methodology

Based on the literature review, a survey instrument was developed as a first step. Conclusions from the contemporary research on value creation and capture were used to prepare statements that described hypothetical situations in organisations. The respondents' task was to think of their organisation's actual situation in regard to its strategy, innovativeness, relations with stakeholders, and the sources of value creation and appropriation (processes and mechanisms). These statements were required to be assessed on a 7-grade Likert scale. Since the organisational phenomena in question is difficult to assess objectively, managers were encouraged to assess the statements based on their perceptions and experience. The assessment of the scale, thus, reflects their predominant tendencies and or general attitudes. The structure of the questionnaire is presented in Table 12.2.

The questionnaire was presented to respondents in 316 randomly chosen organisations in Poland using the PAPI (Pen-and-Paper Interview) method. Poland was chosen as it is a fast-developing post-accession economy that creates a rich context for studying value creation and value capture processes and mechanisms in organisations. This is because Poland is an EU member since 2004, it is a country where opportunity-based entrepreneurship has dominated necessity-based entrepreneurship since 2014, it has experienced dynamic GDP growth and low unemployment levels in the last years. Thus, Polish companies are likely to use interesting VCVC processes and mechanisms.

The sample consisted of companies operating in production (26.6%, 84 firms), trade (25.6%, 81 firms) and services (47.8%, 151 firms). The sample included organisations that were small, including 200 small (63.3%), 80 medium (25.3%) and 36 small (11.4%) enterprises. Micro-firms were not researched. One company was represented by one respondent. Overall, 132 CEOs, 22 directors, 93 managers, 69 strategic and sales analysts were surveyed. The respondents declared that they had significant experience in preparing and commercialising new products (142), are at least experts (29), know the area (96), or are involved in new product development (49). As far as stakeholder relations were

Table 12.2 The questionnaire structure

Survey section	Theoretical perspective	No. of statements	Statement example
Strategic potential for value creation	Resource-based theory	16	'We have above-average infrastructure, valuable resources and possibilities to shift them quickly in order to exploit opportunities that emerge'
Value-creating processes	Resource-based theory	22	'Value in our organisation is created based on rare, valuable and unique resources'
Competitive environment	Competitive positioning theory Stakeholder orientation	11	'Our competitors offering similar products or services take a significant part of our market share'
Value capture	Competitive positioning theory Stakeholder orientation	32	'In the last three years we filed for more patents than our main competitor'
Value creation strategies	Resource-based theory Competitive positioning theory Stakeholder orientation	15	'We are first in the branch to introduce innovations, thus benefiting from time-to-market and first-mover rent'
Organisational performance	Resource-based theory	9	'Average return on sales in the last three years in relation to our main competitors can be assessed as... (1–7)'

concerned, 72 respondents declared they were experts, 163 had a significant experience, 49 know the area and 32 have something to do with stakeholder relations.

The obtained data was analysed with statistical methods. First, the assessments of the questionnaire statements were compared to identify VCVC activities that managers undertake most frequently, as well as to demonstrating the processes and mechanisms that were assessed as lowest. Second, due to a lot of questionnaire statements, factor analysis was used to reduce the number of activities and to identify the twelve crucial ones. Third, ordered logistic regression was used to analyse the impact of VCVC processes and mechanisms onto organisational performance.

Assessing VCVC Processes and Mechanisms

The assessments of the questionnaire statements are presented in summary form. That is, to demonstrate a more accurate picture, the assessments from all 316 managers were summed up and compared. The numbers fall in the range between 316 (if all respondents answered 1) and 2212 (if all respondents answered 7).

The results suggest that few organisations prepare and commercialise break-through technologies, unique products or services. The managers at the researched companies identified that value is created by possessing adequate competencies, employees and a proper organisational design (1650) rather than creativity, idea generation and developing innovations (1543). The lowest assessment (1274) was attributed to possessing or developing high technologies and break-through innovations that require complementary resources hard to obtain in the market. As a result, possessing complementary resources for launching new technologies (1430) and implementing investment-intensive technologies (1394) was found to be relatively low. Even though the majority of companies did not declare introducing break-through technologies as a source of value creation, still they indicated that introducing innovations in general defines their market position (1528).

The overall conclusion that can be drawn is that the main source of value creation at the researched organisations is creating value for customers (1647) and offering attractive products the customers are willing to pay for (1650). The managers at 203 organisations also indicated that value creation is normally understood to be the result of creating value for customers by increasing the in-use value of products and services, as well as generating profits from this increase. However, only 15 indicated that increases in value are realised through break-through innovations or unique technologies. The majority of managers indicated that their organisations prefer to invest in incremental innovations, imitate other firms and exploit existing ideas (1683) rather than generating new ideas (1420) as a strategic choice. Relational, marketing or financial capabilities were indicated to be of most importance (1675). However, the researched companies are in general able to indicate which activities in the value chain create value (1624), and they possess or control necessary resources to strategically invest in these activities, for example, they are aware that quality products and marketing are the sources of value creation, so they invest in high-quality materials and spend money on developing marketing strategies (1595).

Organisations declare that they dispose of core competences (1616), strategically invest in unique resources (1621) and benefit from various resources that create value (1616). They create value by increasing in-use value perceived by customers (1701), possessing marketing capabilities (1685), managerial, logistics or financial resources (1624), and by offering products in appropriate markets (1660). When new opportunities appear, the companies are ready to reduce costs and shift resources to exploit them and create more value (1626). They can also retain value by selling cash cows they once invested in (1621).

As far as the competitive environment is concerned, the researched organisations indicated that the existence of many competitors who can observe and imitate some unique solutions is seen by them as the biggest threat (1596). At the same time, the managers who participated in the study indicated that they do not think that their value is captured by competitors (1330). They also took the expectations of the task environment actors into consideration (1595) and sought to divide the value created among actors involved in value co-creation accordingly (1559). Managers posit that their organisations offer products and services similar to those of the competition (1706), but at the same time they do not think that competitors offer similar products (1460). The bargaining power of distributors, buyers or contractors is not seen as a threat that could reduce value (1362), which proves that cooperation with buyers and distributors is perceived to be good (1428), although the companies in the study tended to prefer to do as much as possible within their own internal network and were disinclined to share knowledge with companies they cooperate with (1575). The threat of capturing value by employees (1330) or competition (1339) was assessed as low.

Value capture in the researched organisations was understood as protecting the knowledge about what customers are willing to pay

(1665). The researched organisations protected the value created (1632), had developed appropriation mechanisms (1499), protected their intellectual property (1472), and creative ideas (1441). The managers taking part in the study were convinced that the cooperation between functional units leads to synergy (1528). Possessing patents (1220), value capture through patents (1189), and preventing imitation (1190) was assessed as relatively low. The managers at the organisations of the study indicated that they did not file many patent applications (1084). Other appropriation mechanisms were assessed as higher, but they were not major factors. This included time to market (1268), intellectual property rights (1308), knowledge about appropriation procedures (1441). Nonetheless, the analyses presented here demonstrate that, overall, organisations capture value through some appropriation mechanisms.

Empirical Variables Describing VCVC Processes and Mechanisms

The literature review identified a number of VCVC processes and mechanisms present in organisations, as well as variables that describe these processes and mechanisms. To further narrow down the picture of value creation and capture, and to identify the key variables that describe the process, factor analysis was carried out as a next step with the intention to reduce the questionnaire items to the most significant constructs. The Varimax rotation identified six factors labelled as: (a) strategic potential, (b) resource-based value creation, (c) value capture through changes in market share, (d) value capture through interactions with the task environment, (e) legal mechanisms of value capture and (f) appropriation of rents. The Promax rotation identified similar factors, labelled as (a) strategic potential, (b) resource-based value creation, (c) value capture through interactions with stakeholders (d) value capture through interactions with the task environment, (e) legal mechanisms of value capture, (f) patents and intellectual property rights, (g) value creation for customers, (h) appropriation rents. Promax rotation thus identified three additional factors (patents & intellectual property rights, interactions with stakeholders, value creation for customers. Based on these two rotations, in order to generate more universal categories, the additional Oblimin rotation with Kaiser normalisation was carried out, where the five factors that appeared in both Varimax and Promax rotations were given as granted. The Oblimin rotation identified twelve components, that is, the appropriate questionnaire statements can be labelled as: (x_1)

strategic potential, leadership and managerial abilities, (x_2) value creation for the organisation, (x_3) value creation for customers, (x_4) controlling resources necessary for value creation, (x_5) shortages in resources for break-through innovations, (x_6) stakeholder relations, (x_7) observing and imitating competitors, (x_8) losing value, (x_9) exploiting entrepreneurial opportunities, (x_{10}) patents and other appropriation mechanisms (x_{11}) human resources for value creation, (x_{12}) strategic control for value capture. Obviously, only these factors were chosen that correspond to at least two questionnaire statements and take the value of at least 0.5.

The Impact of Value Creation and Value Capture on Organisational Performance

In order to analyse which identified factors have the highest influence on firm performance, eight ordered logistic regression models were generated, all of them statistically significant. Table 12.3 presents how value creation and value capture variables (VCVC) influence various measures of firm performance. The influence is reflected in the odds ratios.

In the case of the ordered logistic models, the regression coefficient direction (negative or positive) matters. The positive value means that the probability of performance increases will be higher in organisations that adopt a given value creation or capture mechanism, contrary to these firms that do not. In turn, the negative coefficient value indicates that the probability of decreasing firm performance will be higher in the organisations that adopt a given mechanism (described by the independent variable). What matters, are the odds ratios (presented in Table 12.3) demonstrating the level of a given probability. When regression coefficients are negative, odds ratios take values below 1; when positive, odds ratios are higher than 1.

The researched organisations have a higher chance of increasing sales when they implement a suitable value creation strategy supported by leadership and managerial capabilities (43.3% higher probability compared to firms that do not), observe competitors' solutions (28.4%) and protect the value through patents (24%). Increasing market share is 74.4% more probable in case of organisations that develop relations with stakeholders and 33% more probable among these that observe competitors' solutions. The larger the company, the lower the probability of a market share increase when developing relations with stakeholders and observing competitors. Sustaining the return on sales is 61% more probable among companies

Table 12.3 The influence of VCVC variables on firm performance

Independent variables	Model 1 (Sales increase)	Model 2 (Increase in market share)	Model 3 (Return on sales)	Model 4 (Net profit)	Model 5 (Customer loyalty)	Model 6 (Organisation growth)	Model 7 (Ability to launch innovations)	Model 8 (Sustaining cash flow)
(x_1) Strategic potential, leadership and managerial capabilities	1.433**	1.297	1.332*	1.367*	1.234	1.544*	1.492**	1.367*
(x_2) Creating value for organisation	0.948	1.138	0.977	0.889	0.804	0.932	1.090	1.051
(x_3) Creating value for customers	0.925	1.001	0.944	0.926	0.869	0.803	0.841	0.832
(x_4) Resources under control for value creation	1.218	1.260	1.299	1.494*	1.483***	1.410**	1.126	1.250
(x_5) Shortages in resources necessary for break-through innovations	1.022	1.061	1.006	1.022	0.886	0.911	1.036	1.187*
(x_6) Stakeholder relations	1.173	1.744***	1.610**	1.092	1.616***	1.076	1.255	1.277

Independent variables	Model 1 (Sales increase)	Model 2 (Increase in market share)	Model 3 (Return on sales)	Model 4 (Net profit)	Model 5 (Customer loyalty)	Model 6 (Organisation growth)	Model 7 (Ability to launch innovations)	Model 8 (Sustaining cash flow)
(x7) Observing and imitating competitors	1.284**	1.330**	1.274**	1.231*	1.176	1.339*	1.344*	1.166
(x8) Losing value	0.955	0.895	0.857	0.864	0.841	0.780*	0.835	0.808
(x9) Exploiting entrepreneurial opportunities	1.145	0.951	0.999	0.994	1.245*	1.016	1.017	1.010
(x10) Patents and other appropriation mechanisms	1.240**	1.149	1.263	1.281**	1.139	1.352***	1.174*	1.179**
(x11) Human resources for value creation	0.786	0.875	0.792	0.955	1.149	1.035	0.979	1.091
(x12) Strategic control for value capture	1.204	1.247	1.125	0.981	1.203	1.061	1.109	1.183
Log-likelihood	−414.178	−406.317	−405.583	−431.807	−443.633	−413.066	−439.107	−417.220
LR chi²	76.22	118.42	98.10	82.25	103.50	110.52	103.55	107.86
Prob > chi²	0.000	0.000	0.000	0.000	0.000	0.000	0.000	0.000
Pseudo R²	0.084	0.127	0.107	0.087	0.104	0.118	0.105	0.114

*** $p \leq 0.01$; ** $p \leq 0.05$; * $p \leq 0.1$

that develop relations with stakeholders, observe competitors (27.4%) and use patents to protect the value created (26.3%). The larger the company, the more difficult it is to increase the return on sales.

Companies that implement a suitable value creation strategy supported with leadership and managerial competences have a 36.7% higher chance of increasing net profit. Profit generation is also influenced by controlling resources for value creation (49.4%), observing competitors (23.1%) and protecting value by patents (28.1%). On the other hand, sustaining customer loyalty is influenced by controlling the resources necessary for value creation (48.3), developing relations with stakeholders (61.6%) and exploiting entrepreneurial opportunities (24.5%). Sustaining customer loyalty is more difficult by up to 70% in larger firms than in smaller ones. The probability of keeping the organisation's growth at the current pace is higher by 54.4% when companies have a proper value creation strategy, leadership and managerial competencies while higher by 41% when firms control resources necessary for value creation and 78% higher in firms that observe and imitate competitors.

The probability of introducing innovations based on creative ideas is 49.2% higher in organisations that implement a proper value creation strategy supported by leadership and managerial competencies; 34.4% higher in organisations that observe competitors' solutions and 17.4% higher in organisations protecting value by patents. The organisations that introduced a suitable value creation strategy supported by leadership and managerial competencies have a 36.7% higher probability of sustaining cash flow. Firms that did not possess the necessary capabilities and technologies to prepare innovations have 18.7% greater chances of losing cash flow.

Summary

The aim of this chapter was to demonstrate selected theoretical perspectives on value creation and value capture, to assess the VCVC processes and mechanisms at organisations in Poland, and to identify empirically key variables of value creation and capture that influence performance. The obtained results lead to three following conclusions.

First, value creation among the researched organisations is largely understood as increasing the use value for customers and generating sales profits (cf. Mahajan, 2020; Terho et al., 2015). Creating value based on break-through innovations and technologies is present in few organisations. The key elements of the value creation strategy are: controlling key resources, proper functional competencies, as well as developing relations with stakeholders (Siemieniako et al., 2021; Tondolo & Bitencourt, 2014).

Second, as far as value capture is concerned, the researched organisations tend to use legal mechanisms of value capture (Coff, 2010). Patents seem to be the key mechanism of value protection. However, few of the organisations filed patent applications. Despite this, possessing patents positively impacted firm performance. The threat of capturing value from others largely boils down to the presence of many competitors in a given sector, where scope exists to observe and imitate (Bilton & Cummings, 2010). Organisations seem to operate effectively in the competitive environment when it is conducive to coopetition and when taking stakeholders' expectations into consideration while preparing the value creation strategy. When this is the case, they sought to divide the value in a just manner among stakeholders involved in its creation (cf. Priem et al., 2019).

Third, companies that implement a proper value creating strategy supported by leadership and managerial competencies, control resources necessary to prepare innovations (Amit & Han, 2017), observe competitors' moves, develop relations with stakeholders, are aware of the control points in the supply chain where value can be created and protected (Piboonrungroj et al., 2017) are more likely to be high performing.

Summing up, the researched organisations create value for customers by increasing in-use value of the existing product portfolio. The research, however, confirmed that managers in Poland can manoeuvre their organisations to more skillfully operate in the competitive environment and protect the value that is created through various appropriation (or value capture) mechanisms. It is also evident that some value creating processes and mechanisms are more likely to influence firm performance than others. The most prominent of these are illustrated in Fig. 12.1.

The contribution of this study is threefold. First, it adds to the theoretical literature on value creation and capture by demonstrating the most significant processes and mechanisms of value creation and value capture in the post-accession economy in a country where opportunity-based entrepreneurship is widespread.

Second, the research demonstrates that value creation and value capture processes and mechanisms influence various dimensions of firm

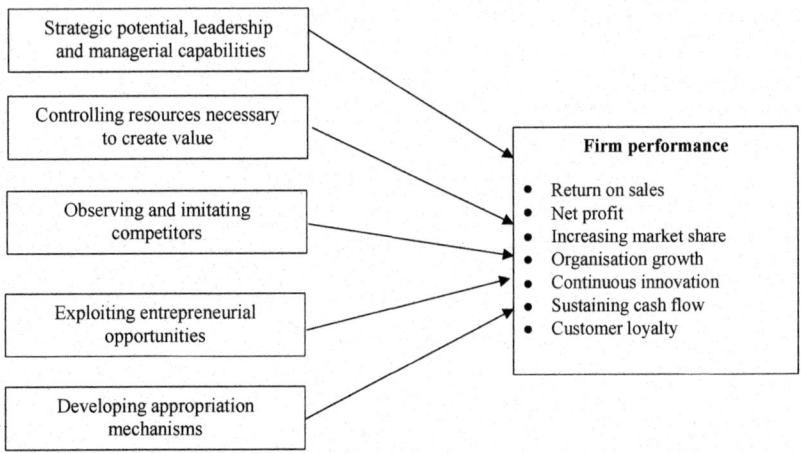

Fig. 12.1 Strategic processes and mechanisms of value creation and capture influencing organisational performance

performance, such as return on sales, net profit, cash flow, customer loyalty and organisation growth.

Third, with relatively little empirical research carried out into value creation in Central and Eastern Europe before the COVID-19 pandemic, it can be expected that the economic impact of this lengthening crisis will require further research in this area. Nonetheless, this chapter contributes to value creation and capture studies by identifying the most important mechanisms and processes of value creating strategies and their impact on firm performance.

Several categories of practical implications are crucial with regard to organisation's actions to create and capture value (Fig. 12.2). First, managers need to identify the phase of the business lifecycle their organisation is in at the present time. If it is in the development phase, accompanied by a healthy bottom line, it is worth investing in preparing and commercialising innovations that will become the source of future value creation. Concentrating on increasing the in-use value for customers of existing products may only produce short-lived benefits. Second, it is important to aim at possessing or controlling critical (rare, valuable and sometimes complementary resources) necessary to develop innovations. Third, it is important to identify activities along the value and supply

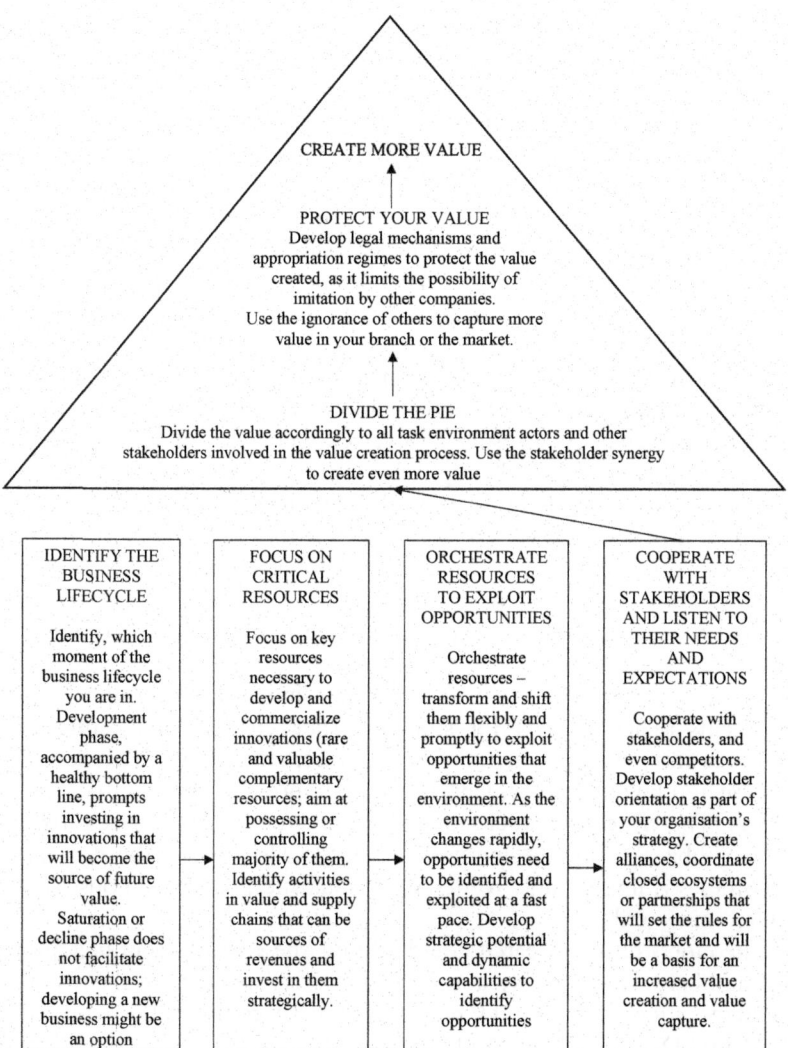

Fig. 12.2 The value creation and capture pillars

chains that are a source of value and to invest in them strategically. Fourth, it is advisable to cooperate with stakeholders, or even competitors because of the potential benefits associated with doing so. Creating alliances, operating in closed ecosystems or partnerships that set the rules for the market can lead to increased value creation. At the same time, organisations need to ensure "the pie"; is divided in a manner that is agreeable to all the parties. All stakeholders involved in the process of value creation should get their part of the final value. Finally, legal measures and the so-called appropriation regimes (strategy-related value protection mechanisms) are needed to capture the value created, as this limits the threat of imitation by other parties.

Naturally, this study has some limitations: sample limitations, research instrument limitations and context limitations. First, the sample was randomly selected. As a result, an overrepresentation of service companies can be noticed, which might have influenced the final outcomes. The researched organisations were also of various size and age, which also creates possibilities for varying interpretations of the research results.

The survey design based on literature conclusions and further selection of measurements used in the questionnaire also may be a limitation. To address this issue, future research could use known operationalisations, and tested scales.

The research context creates yet another limitation. Although Poland represents a rich context for studying value creation and capture, as it is a country with opportunity-based entrepreneurship, dynamic GDP growth and low unemployment, it is not a representative country for the region. Therefore, the conclusions from this study will not necessarily be generalisable. Finally, the method of selection for testing the first three hypotheses is limited only to descriptive statistics, which demonstrates a limitation as well.

Therefore, future research could address these issues identified above in a number of ways. Firstly, a more longitudinal approach to the research could be adopted. It would be interesting to compare the data from the COVID-19 pandemic and see how the structure and composition of value creation processes have changed in the organisations studied. It would also be useful to carry out similar research to examine the VCVC processes after the coronavirus crisis. For future research, a revised version of the questionnaire could be used, and more precise measures of VCVC could be implemented. It could also be useful to carry out a comparative analysis in other CEE countries. Overall, this study represents an attempt to develop new knowledge and a better understanding of the processes and mechanisms that lead to VCVC and improved organisational performance.

Acknowledgements I kindly acknowledge the financial support in carrying out the research from the National Science Centre in Poland (grant no 2015/17/B/HS4/00935).

REFERENCES

Amit, R., & Han, X. (2017). Value creation through novel resource configurations in a digitally enabled world. *Strategic Entrepreneurship Journal, 11*(3), 228–242.
Amit, R. & Zott, Ch. (2012). Creating value through business model innovation. *MIT Sloan Management Review, 53*, 41–49.
Barney, J. B. (1991). Firm resources and sustained competitive advantage. *Journal of Management, 17*, 99–120. https://doi.org/10.1177/014920639 101700108
Barney, J. B., & Arikan, A. M. (2005). The resource-based view. In M. A. Hitt, R. E. Freeman, & J. S. Harrison (Eds.), *The Blackwell handbook of strategic management*. Blackwell. https://doi.org/10.1111/b.9780631218616.2006. 00006.x
Bilton, C., & Cummings, S. (2010). *Creative strategy. Reconnecting business and innovation*. Wiley.
Brown, T. E., Davidsson, P., & Wiklund, J. (2001). An operationalization of Stevenson's conceptualization of entrepreneurship as opportunity-based firm behavior. *Strategic Management Journal, 22*, 953–968. https://doi.org/10. 1002/smj.190
Burkert, M. (2013). Differences in the sophistication of value-based management—The role of top executives. *Management Accounting Research, 24*(1), 3–22.
Call, M. L., & Ployhart, R. E. (2021). A theory of firm value capture from employee job performance: A multidisciplinary perspective. *Academy of Management Review, 46*, 572–590. https://doi.org/10.5465/amr.2018. 0103
Chatain, O., & Zemsky, P. (2011). Value creation and value capture with frictions. *Strategic Management Journal, 32*, 1206–1231. https://doi.org/10. 1002/smj.939
Coff, R. W. (2010). The coevolution of rent appropriation and capability development. *Strategic Management Journal, 31*, 711–733.

Cooper, R. G. (2011). *Winning at new products*. Basic Books.
Dattee, B., Alexy, O., & Autio, E. (2018). Maneuvering in poor visibility: How firms play the ecosystem game when uncertainty is high. *Academy of Management Journal, 61*(2), 466–498. https://doi.org/10.5465/amj.2015.0869
Davidow, M. (2018). Value creation and efficiency: Incompatible or inseparable? *Journal of Creating Value, 4*(1), 123–131. https://doi.org/10.1177/2394964318768904
Dyer, J., & Singh, H. (1998). The relational view: Cooperative strategy and sources of interorganizational competitive advantage. *The Academy of Management Review, 23*(4), 660–679.
Fischer, T. (2011). *Managing value capture*. Gabler Verlag-Springer.
Henkel, J., & Hoffmann, A. (2019). Value capture in hierarchically organized value chains. *Journal of Economics & Management Strategy, 2019*(28), 260–279. https://doi.org/10.1111/jems.12278
Horth D. M., & Vehar, J. (2014). *Becoming a leader who fosters innovation (white paper)* (pp. 2–25). Center for Creative Leadership.
Jeong, S.-H., & Harrison, D. A. (2017). Glass breaking, strategy making, and value creating: Meta-analytic outcomes of women as CEOs and TMT members. *Academy of Management Journal, 60*(4), 1219–1252. https://doi.org/10.5465/amj.2014.0716
Kollenscher, E., Popper, M., & Ronen, B. (2018). Value-creating organizational leadership. *Journal of Management & Organization, 24*(1), 19–39. https://doi.org/10.1017/jmo.2016.33
Kyprianou, Ch. (2018). Creating value from the outside in or the inside out: how nascent intermediaries build peer-to-peer marketplaces. *Academy of Management Discoveries 4*(3), 336–370. https://doi.org/10.5465/amd.2017.0081
Mahajan, G. (2020). What is customer value and how can you create it? *Journal of Creating Value, 6*(1), 119–121. https://doi.org/10.1177/2394964320903557
Mahoney, J. T., & Qian, L. (2013). Market frictions as building blocks of an organizational economics approach to strategic management. *Strategic Management Journal, 34*(9), 1019–1041.
McGrath, R. (1997). A real options logic for initiating technology positioning investments. *The Academy of Management Review, 22*(4), 974–996. https://doi.org/10.2307/259251
Miller, K. D., & Folta, T. B. (2002). Option value and entry timing. *Strategic Management Journal, 23*, 655–665.

Niesten, E., & Stefan, I. (2019). Embracing the paradox of interorganizational value co-creation–value capture: A literature review towards paradox resolution. *International Journal of Management Reviews, 21,* 231–255. https://doi.org/10.1111/ijmr.12196

Oliveira, W. A., & De Muylder, C. F. (2012). Value creation from organizational project management: A case study in a government agency. *JISTEM—Journal of Information Systems and Technology Management, 9*(3), 497–514. https://doi.org/10.4301/S1807-17752012000300004

Pagani, M. (2013). Digital business strategy and value creation: Framing the dynamic cycle of control points. *Management Information Systems Quarterly, 37,* 617–632.

Piboonrungroj, P., Williams, S., & Simatupang, T. (2017). The emergence of value chain thinking. *International Journal of Value Chain Management, 8,* 40. https://doi.org/10.1504/IJVCM.2017.10003558

Pitelis, C. N. (2009). The co-evolution of organizational value capture, value creation and sustainable advantage. *Organization Studies, 30*(10), 1115–1139.

Porter, M. E., & Kramer, M. R. (2011). Creating shared value. *Harvard Business Review, 89*(1), 2–17.

Prahalad, C. K., & Ramaswamy, V. (2004). *The future of competition: Co-creating unique value with customers.* Harvard Business School Press.

Priem, R. L., Krause, R., Tantalo, C., & McFadyen, A. (2019). Promoting long-term shareholder value by "competing" for essential stakeholders: A new, multi-sided market logic for top managers. *Academy of Management Perspectives.* https://doi.org/10.5465/amp.2018.0048

Ritala, P., & Tidström, A. (2014). Untangling the value-creation and value-appropriation elements of coopetition strategy: A longitudinal analysis on the firm and relational levels. *Scandinavian Journal of Management, 30*(4), 498–515. https://doi.org/10.1016/j.scaman.2014.05.002

Siemieniako, D., Kubacki, K., & Mitręga, M. (2021). Inter-organisational relationships for social impact: A systematic literature review. *Journal of Business Research, Elsevier, 132*(C), 453–469.

Skilton, P. F. (2014). Value creation, value capture, and supply chain structure: Understanding resource-based advantage in a project-based industry. *Journal of Supply Chain Management, 50,* 74–93. https://doi.org/10.1111/jscm.12053

Sridharan, R., & Simatupang, T. M. (2013). Power and trust in supply chain collaboration. *International Journal of Value Chain Management, 7*(1), 76–96.

Subrahmanyam, S. (2019). Carrefour's competitive strategy—Cost leadership and differentiation: A case study. *Pacific Business Review International, 11*(8), 137–145.

Tantalo, C., & Priem, R. L. (2014). Value creation through stakeholder synergy. *Strategic Management Journal, 37*(2), 314–329.

Teece, D. J. (2016). Dynamic capabilities and entrepreneurial management in large organizations: Toward a theory of the (entrepreneurial) firm. *European Economic Review, 86*, 202–216. ISSN 0014-2921. https://doi.org/10.1016/j.euroecorev.2015.11.006

Teece, D. J. (2018). Business models and dynamic capabilities. *Long Range Planning, 51*, 40–49, https://doi.org/10.1016/j.lrp.2017.06.007

Terho, H., Eggert, A., Haas, A., & Ulaga, W. (2015). How sales strategy translates into performance: The role of salesperson customer orientation and value-based selling. *Industrial Marketing Management, 45.* https://doi.org/10.1016/j.indmarman.2015.02.017

Tondolo, V. A. G., & Bitencourt, C. C. (2014). Understanding dynamic capabilities from its antecedents, processes and outcomes. *Brazilian Business Review, 11*(5), 122–144. https://doi.org/10.15728/bbr.2014.11.5.6

Vargo, S. L., & Lusch, R. F. (2004). Evolving to a new dominant logic for marketing. *Journal of Marketing, 68*(1), 1–17.

Willumsen, P., Oehmen, J., Stingl, V., & Geraldi, J. (2019). Value creation through project risk management. *International Journal of Project Management, 37*(5), 731–749. https://doi.org/10.1016/j.ijproman.2019.01.007

Zajac, E., & Olsen, C. (1993). From transaction cost to transactional value analysis: Implications for the study of inter-organizational strategies. *Journal of Management Studies, 30*, 131–145.

Zubac, A., Dasborough, M., Hughes, K., Jiang, Z., Kirkpatrick, S., Martinsons, M. G., Tucker, D., & Zwikael, O. (2021). The strategy and change interface: Understanding "enabling" processes and cognitions. *Management Decision, 59*(3), 481–505. https://doi.org/10.1108/MD-03-2021-083

PART IV

The Resource Strategy

CHAPTER 13

Introduction: The Resource Strategy

Angelina Zubac, Danielle Tucker, Ofer Zwikael, Kate Hughes, and Shelley Kirkpatrick

The three chapters in this section make it abundantly clear that the resource strategy is especially important to get right for two special reasons. First, the resource strategy explicates how the organisation's financial, customer value creation and non-market strategies are to be

A. Zubac (✉)
University of Queensland, Brisbane, QLD, Australia
e-mail: a.zubac@business.uq.edu.au; Angelina.zubac@aim.com.au; az@strategylink.com.au

D. Tucker
University of Essex, Colchester, Essex, UK
e-mail: dtucker@essex.ac.uk

O. Zwikael
Australian National University, Canberra, ACT, Australia
e-mail: ofer.zwikael@anu.edu.au

K. Hughes
Technological University Dublin, Dublin, Ireland
e-mail: kate.hughes@hughes-scm.com

© The Author(s), under exclusive license to Springer Nature Singapore Pte Ltd. 2022
A. Zubac et al. (eds.), *Effective Implementation of Transformation Strategies*, https://doi.org/10.1007/978-981-19-2336-4_13

implemented using the resources (tangible and intangible assets and capabilities) at the organisation's disposal. Second, it enables the process of organisation (coordination) in itself, including the way in which the organisation will implement its specific strategies while ensuring its day-to-day operations. As will be elaborated upon below, Chapter 14 by Maris Martinsons is especially pertinent since it examines five contingent change-leadership related elements that can be associated with a successful change outcome. Chapter 15 by Stephen Abrahams, on the other hand, explains how a structured approach to project management and investments in resources accordingly enables an organisation to be responsive to change. Finally, Chapter 16 by Danielle Tucker and Stella Lind explains how essential it is to invest in the trust transfer process when integrating two family businesses post-merger or post-acquisition.

Thus, as depicted in Fig. 13.1, all three chapters provide insight into how the resource strategy enables an organisation to more purposively use its resource base, that is, rationalise the (sub)processes and cognitions it currently possesses to develop operationally and strategically distinct dynamic capabilities. The objective is to ensure the organisation can be responsive to change emanating from the external and internal institutional environments. As 'A' in Fig. 13.2 illustrates, strategic projects are necessary to refine how the organisation implements its strategies through its day-to-day operations and through its project function. These reflect the organisation's current implementation, financial, customer value creation and non-market strategies at any one time. The areas labelled 'B' and 'C' in Fig. 13.2 illustrate that, as the organisation matures and is able to deal with far more complexity within its external and internal environments, it needs to develop very distinct and fit-for-purpose capabilities. In most cases, these are likely to be realised as a platform in some way. This is because platforms can be used to achieve greater levels of vertical and horizontally alignment, including by providing resources that can be shared intra- and inter-organisationally.

The first chapter in this section by Maris Martinsons, *Communicating and shaping strategic change: A CLASS framework*, examines strategic change when the strategy being implemented 'builds on' or 'breaks with'

S. Kirkpatrick
The MITRE Corporation, McLean, VA, USA
e-mail: skirkpatrick@mitre.org

13 INTRODUCTION: THE RESOURCE STRATEGY

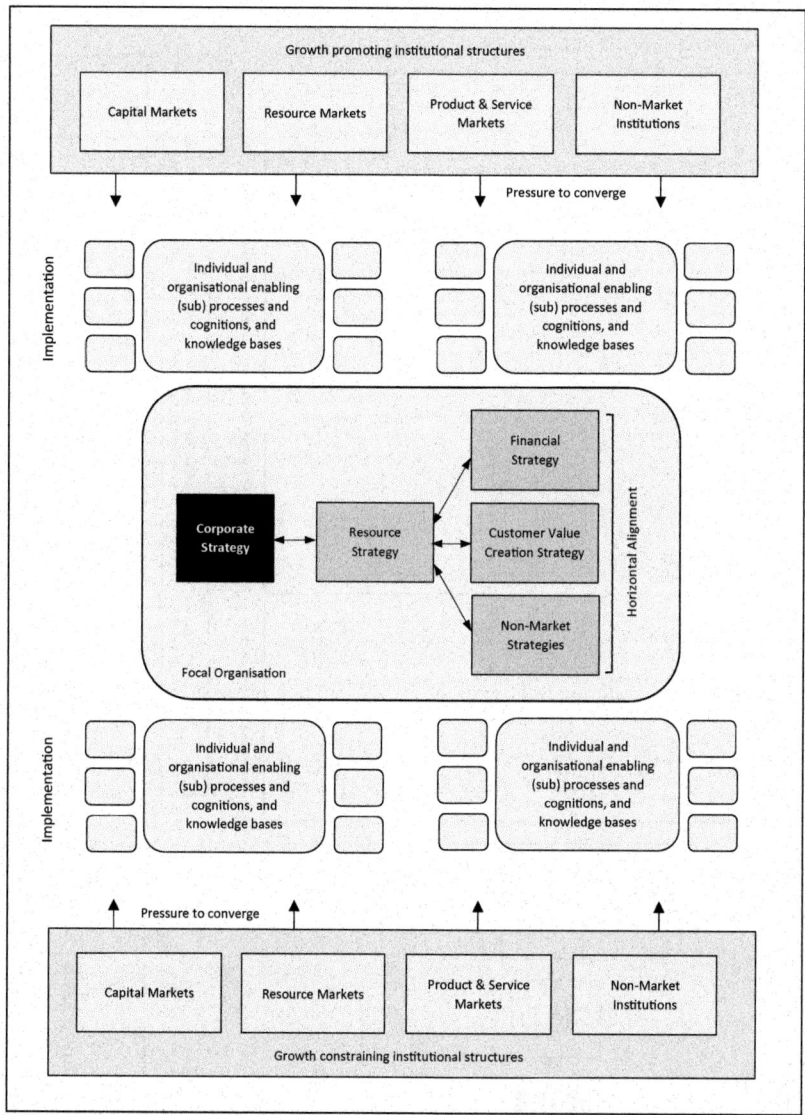

Fig. 13.1 Implementing strategy and organisational change: A resource strategy focus

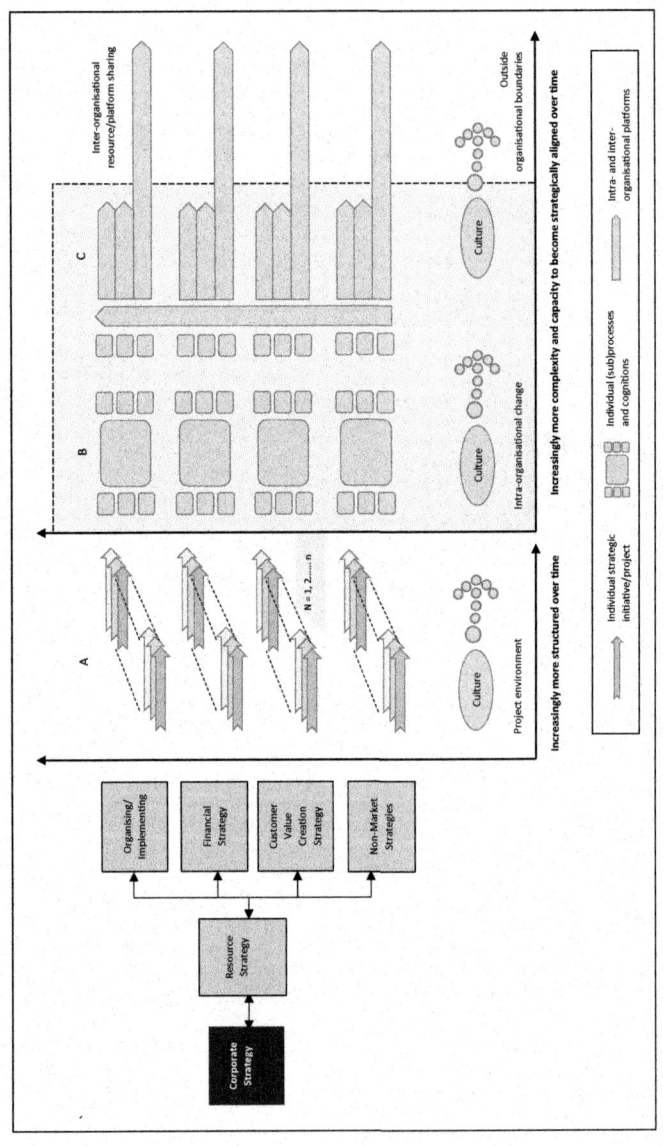

Fig. 13.2 Building a strategically aligned organisation and positive culture

the past. As Martinsons explains, five contingent variables need to be understood and managed to achieve a successful change outcome with stakeholders irrespective of the breadth and depth of the change. When the contemplated change is radical and large-scale, the change was more likely to be successful if an external hire was appointed. Internal leader hires were more appropriate when the contemplated change is large-scale but not radical. The way in which the change was communicated and the symbolism used by leaders within either context depended on how stakeholders were likely to respond to change given its level of radicalness. Put another way, organisations are more likely to achieve successful organisational change outcomes if they invest in leaders who can develop communication processes that are symbolically and, therefore, cognitively appropriate given the change context and stakeholders' likely response. To this end, a framework is developed in the chapter that can be used to understand the specific resource investments in people and communications that may be necessary when a programme of change is being contemplated. Referred to as *The Class Framework*, it explicates the five elements of large-scale strategic change: the radicalness of the change, the leaders managing the change, how change is articulated, the symbolism used to describe the change, and stakeholders' likely response (CLASS).

The second chapter in this section by Stephen Abrahams, *A structured approach to project management as a strategic enabling priority*, uses five case examples to demonstrate why it is so important to implement a strategy's various projects using a structured project management approach. Critically, by explaining each capability set within the widely utilised Project Management Framework (PMF) in best practice terms, Abrahams explains that organisations can use the project management function to achieve high levels of strategic alignment across the organisation while further developing the dynamic capability base of the organisation in both project and non-project areas. This means managers can use the project function to practicably implement a strategy while being sensitive to new opportunities and their risks, and how the strategy is likely to change over time. The five cases demonstrate how the investment in project methods can enable the organisation well into the future no matter what its strategic priorities.

The third chapter in this section by Danielle Tucker and Stella Lind, *Family firms and mergers and acquisitions: The importance of transfer of trust*, considers the trust transfer process that necessarily must occur at family businesses integrating their resources and cultures post-acquisition or post-merger. The authors found that the process occurs in stages. Depending on the extent to which trust is evident and the extent to which the psychological contract previously in place at each of the organisations needs consolidation or repair to be able to integrate the business, it should be possible to join two family businesses successfully. In summary, trust can be transferred when the family businesses coming together have similar values, the new owner is as invested in building strong employee relationships as was the exiting owner, and the psychological contract confirmed or established for the next phase of the family business is fitting. In short, the culture that is subsequently developed at the new family entity post-acquisition or post-merger matters.

In the final analysis, despite addressing very different resource-based issues, the three chapters underscore how advantageous an effectively formulated and implemented resource strategy can be. They also draw attention to the fact that it is no easy task to understand how to invest in the organisation's resource base for the future. There are many challenges associated with ensuring the organisation can remain operationally effective while implementing its strategy; the reality is few strategies end up being implemented in full.

Whether intended or not, strategies are always adjusted. As new opportunities or threats become obvious, the way the organisation invests in and uses its resource base will change. Figure 13.3 illustrates the likely dynamics as the organisation matures or when its managers adapt how they implement their resource-investment decisions. Organisations are constantly challenged when rationalising their (sub)processes and cognitions to implement their financial, customer value creation and non-market strategies; they also must continually ensure an effective implementation process. Key change management and project implementation processes need to be put in place, as well as be appropriately utilised and developed over time.

Without a doubt, the people side of the implementation process is just as important as the non-people side of the resource-investment process in this regard. The (sub)processes and the cognitions associated with motivating and driving people become dynamic capabilities when they allow the sensing, seizing and reconfiguring/transforming activities to purposively occur across the organisation and/or inter-organisationally, including when integrating two organisations post-acquisition or merger. They also help to determine the type of culture that develops at the organisation.

13 INTRODUCTION: THE RESOURCE STRATEGY 325

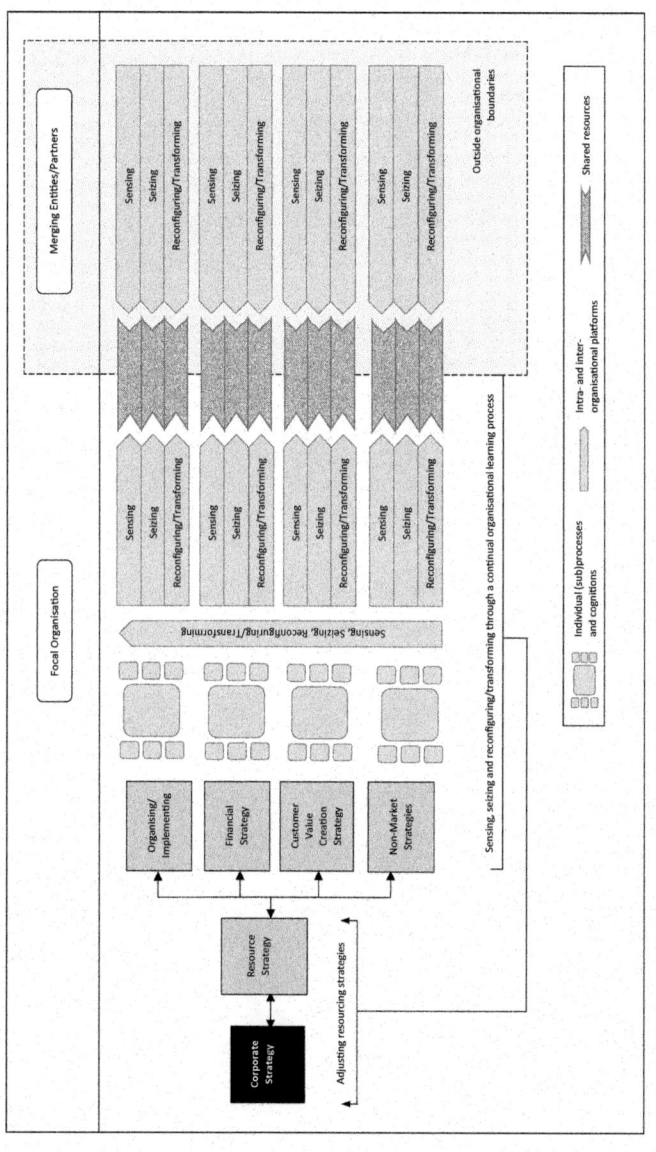

Fig. 13.3 Implementing/Continually refining a horizontally aligned and cooperation-based resourcing strategy

CHAPTER 14

Communicating and Shaping Strategic Change: A CLASS Framework

Maris G. Martinsons

INTRODUCTION

Organisations are dynamic and evolving entities that tend to change continually (Graetz & Smith, 2010; Morgan, 1997; Nonaka, 1994; Sanchez & Heene, 1997). Even with these gradual and incremental changes, there are times when an organisation requires a much more substantial change. From the management literature (Henricks et al., 2020; Oreg & Berson, 2019) it is clear that such a strategic organisational change is difficult to achieve without effective leadership and effective communication. This naturally prompts at least two questions: (1) what makes an effective leader? and (2) how can such a change be communicated effectively?

A substantial and large-scale organisational change will, almost by definition, affect many different people with differing and often conflicting

---

M. G. Martinsons (✉)
Department of Management, City University of Hong Kong, Kowloon, Hong Kong, China
e-mail: maris.martinsons@cityu.edu.hk

© The Author(s), under exclusive license to Springer Nature Singapore Pte Ltd. 2022
A. Zubac et al. (eds.), *Effective Implementation of Transformation Strategies*, https://doi.org/10.1007/978-981-19-2336-4_14

priorities. The success of such a strategic change will thus depend on (1) how well it is planned and designed; (2) how well it is described and explained to the stakeholders; (3) how the stakeholders receive and interpret the descriptions and explanations; (4) what the implementation is expected to involve; (5) how it is expected to affect these different stakeholders; (6) what the implement actually involves; and (7) how it actually affects different stakeholders.

This process is made more complicated because these elements are almost invariably contingent on whether the strategic change is deemed to be mostly additive (about *building on the past*) or substitutive (about *breaking with the past*). Related to the choice of building on or breaking with the past is the issue of who should lead the change. From both my personal experience and the research evidence (Gill, 1995; Graetz, 2000), it is clear that a key success factor for a strategic organisational change is having a leader with sufficient authority and responsibility. The appointment decision is essentially a choice of whether the primary change leader should be appointed internally or hired from outside the organisation.

Based on the existing literature and the extensive research and consulting experience of the author, it is suggested that an internally-appointed leader is more likely to have a formal plan with thematic language to communicate the change (Gilley, 2005; Kanter et al., 1992; Miles, 1997). The aim is to share the mindset and metaphorical language of the top management team with the stakeholders who will contribute to and/or be affected by the change (Martinsons et al., 2019; Morgan, 1997; Oswick et al., 1997).

Conversely, it is suggested that external hires will be more likely to articulate a bold yet less formal vision with much of the symbolism emerging from the reactions of stakeholders. Regardless of the leadership and communication choices, the perceptions of people involved with and affected by the strategic change must be understood and acknowledged. It is especially important to make sense of what the organisation means to different stakeholders and their assorted degrees of support and resistance for a given change (Appelbaum et al., 1998; Auster et al., 2005).

With all of these issues in mind, the author has developed a framework that addresses 5 key elements of strategic organisational change: the **Change** itself, the **Leaders** of the change, **Articulation** of the change, the **Symbolism** of the change and the response of **Stakeholders** to the change (**CLASS**). The CLASS framework has proved to be useful in guiding the planning, communication and implementation of many strategic organisational change initiatives. It is also being used as the foundation for an ambitious academic research project.

The application of this framework has been used by organisational leaders to classify the type of organisational change that they plan to implement. The framework can be used at different stages of the communications process/implementation process. The communication of this classification to stakeholders *before* any change is undertaken will increase their understanding of what is happening in the organisation. This in turn should help to reduce their levels of both uncertainty and anxiety. If different deductive and/or inductive processes of strategic change are used at different stages by different leaders, then key information about the latest development can also be communicated *during* the change. The mode and media for such communication will depend on the nature of the organisation, the change and its leaders.

The Phenomenon

A strategic change is a significant movement of an organisation away from its existing state towards a more desirable future state. This is consistent with the definition of Zubac (2016). The aim of changing "the strategy" may be to develop or sustain a competitive advantage or simply to improve key dimensions of performance, such as profits, customer satisfaction and employee engagement.

A strategic change does not usually just happen. It requires some preparation and planning (Kanter et al., 1992). Such a change is difficult to achieve without effective leadership and effective communication (Zubac et al., 2021). Thus, it is critical to appoint a leader (or leadership team) with courage and commitment to the change. The leader must have the ability to clearly and convincingly communicate what will happen and why as the strategic change is initiated, planned, implemented and completed (Katzenbach, 1996). Thus, before the strategic change is initiated, at least two key questions must be answered: who can provide this leadership? How can they communicate the intended change effectively?

The first question involves issues of personal characteristics and organisational fit. However, a choice must also be made between an internal appointment and an external hire. Meanwhile, the communication of a strategic change by the leadership and management of an organisation will be more systematic and effective if it is underpinned by a solid framework. A specific framework to classify and communicate the key elements of a strategic change has been developed and refined by the author of this chapter. He has already found it to be helpful for smoothly initiating and successfully completing many strategic changes in a wide variety of organisations operating in different countries and cultures.

THE DEVELOPER

After graduating with degrees in engineering and business administration, I started my professional career at a large and global consulting firm that has undertaken thousands of strategic management engagements throughout the world. There I was involved at first in systematically and comprehensively analysing the strengths, weaknesses, opportunities and threats of organisational clients. Based on systematic analysis, our consulting teams then commonly planned and often helped to implement large-scale changes in the client organisation that aimed to improve key performance indicators.

My decades of management consulting experience now include dozens of strategic changes in a wide assortment of contexts (Hempel & Martinsons, 2009; Martinsons et al., 2009). I have served organisational clients of many sizes competing across an assortment of industries that have operated in various institutional and cultural environments across six continents.

While personally transitioning from the fast-paced and keenly competitive world of consulting to the more deliberate and reflective world of academia, I completed a PhD degree with a dissertation that examined how organisational leaders collected, organised and processed assorted information to reduce environmental uncertainty, make better decisions, and more clearly communicate their intentions. My research concluded that the information came primarily from sources external to the organisation and yet almost invariably informed key decisions about organisational change, including—whether or not to undertake it? What would be the goals and specific objectives of a change initiative? Who would lead the change initiative? What organisational elements or content would change? What process would be used to plan, communicate, implement and evaluate the change?

For more than three decades, I have been researching, teaching and consulting on topics and issues under the broad umbrella of strategic management and organisational change. Much of my professional work has been underpinned by the fundamental principles of action research

(Davison et al., 2004, 2012, 2021). I have applied this theory-driven method for not only academic research projects but also adapted it for a wide variety of strategic consulting engagements (Davison & Martinsons, 2007).

The consistent general aim of my university-based research projects has echoed my management consulting engagements: to improve the performance of organisations and their leaders. As a result of the lessons that have been learned from these projects, I have inductively developed a framework to provide guidance for the leaders and agents of organisations who are enacting strategic change.

This chapter identifies and describes the CLASS framework that I have developed and refined over time for classifying, communicating and controlling strategic change.

The Framework

I have used the CLASS acronym to identify this framework because it includes the following five elements:

1) The fundamental nature of the strategic organisational **Change;**
2) The **Leader** of the strategic organisational change;
3) The **Articulation** of the strategic change in terms of a plan and/or vision;
4) The **Symbolism** that is used to communicate the strategic change; and
5) The **Stakeholders' response** to the strategic change, which needs to be managed in order to achieve success.

Table 14.1 provides a concise summary of alternatives for each of the five elements.

The sub-sections that follow describe each of the five elements in greater detail. They also specify a set of propositions that were developed inductively from strategic consulting engagements, action research activities and extensive deliberations. These propositions are codified in order to guide the strategic change management activities of organisational leaders. They are also the basis for an ambitious research project that ultimately aims to examine 100 strategic organisational changes.

Table 14.1   CLASS Framework

Strategic CHANGE	Additive Enhance or Augment, 'build on the past'	Substitutive Replace or Reinvent, 'break with past'
Change LEADER(S)	INTERNAL Appointment	EXTERNAL Hire
ARTICULATION of the Change	FORMAL Plan	INFORMAL Vision
SYMBOLISM *Vocabulary and Metaphors*	DEDUCTIVE Shaped by the formal discourse of the change leader(s)	INDUCTIVE Extracted from the informal discourse of different stakeholders
STAKEHOLDERS' RESPONSE *Support and/or Resistance*	SUPPORT General acceptance of the strategic change and the narrative of its leader(s). This support should be nurtured and guided	RESISTANCE Widespread opposition to the strategic change. Emergence of a rogue narrative. This resistance needs to be understood and managed

The Fundamental Nature of the Strategic CHANGE: Additive or Substitutive?

This framework is most directly relevant to changes that have a consequential impact on the overall long-term performance of the organisation. The ability of the organisation to survive and/or thrive often depends on the outcome of these change efforts. These types of changes almost invariably require leadership from the very top of the organisation and will significantly impact a wide range of stakeholders.

Large-scale organisational changes can be classified in a number of ways. The scope of change may be general, spanning the entire organisation, or more limited, with a focus on specific strategic or even mission-critical parts of the organisation. Meanwhile, the pace of change may be rapid and radical or slower and gradual. The degree of change is expected to be major if it genuinely is a "strategic change". However, the nature of such a strategic change can take on different modes based on **addition** and/or **substitution** (Albert, 1992; Martinsons, 1993).

An **additive** mode of strategic change enhances or augments the existing organisation by adding specific elements. It can be accommodated within the existing culture and commonly occurs as an incremental process. For example, a traditional newspaper may decide to also distribute its news content digitally. This may involve developing a website, sending e-news alerts to mobile phones, and creating podcasts and video clips as different information technologies emerge over time. The employees of the existing organisation, who include content generators (journalists, photographers and editors) and newspaper production staff, would be augmented by information technology specialists and assorted support personnel.

Figure 14.1 illustrates the communication flows that may be associated with an additive strategic change

A **substitutive** mode of strategic change replaces or reinvents the old organisation by substituting specific existing elements with new ones. We

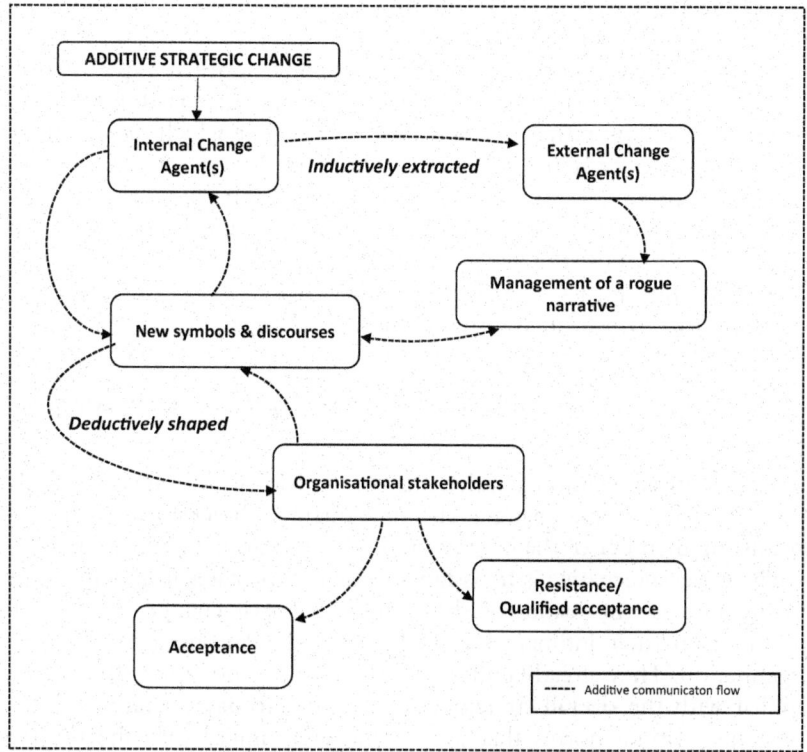

Fig. 14.1 The CLASS framework for an additive change

can define such a substitutive organisational change as one that represents a revision of its fundamental purpose or mission of the organisation or a change in its strategy. Existing products and processes may be discarded and substituted by new ones. Based on the McKinsey 7S model (Waterman et al., 1980), the existing structure and systems may be radically revised. Even a substantial fraction of the existing workforce may be replaced or given very different roles and responsibilities. For example, a traditional newspaper may decide to make a substitutive strategic change in order to become a strictly digital news provider. It will stop procuring paper and ink, abandon its physical printing and distribution processes, and lay off or redeploy the employees involved with the procurement, production and physical distribution processes.

Figure 14.2 illustrates the communication flows that may be associated with a substitutive strategic change.

The research evidence is consistent with my personal experience in that it is generally easier to make an additive change that builds on an existing foundation rather than a substitutive change which must entirely or largely replace or reinvent key elements of the organisation. Related to this, my propositions to guide change leaders and managers are:

P1: Additive forms of strategic change will be more common than substitutive forms of strategic change.

P2: Additive forms of strategic change will be, on average, more successful than substitutive forms of strategic change.

The Strategic Change LEADER: Internal Appointment or External Hire?

Another critical decision is selecting the individual or individuals who will lead the strategic change. The fundamental choices are to appoint an existing member of the organisation or to hire someone from outside.

The easier alternative is to assign an existing manager from within the organisation as the leader of the change. Internal change leaders will benefit from their intimate knowledge of and relationships within the organisation. They already understand the mission and vision while being familiar with the overall strategy as well as day-to-day operations. They share the cultural norms that prevail and are familiar with the historic quirks that distinguish the organisation from others. Furthermore, if the strategic change involves sensitive information, it is preferable to have an internal leader who has a long-term commitment to the organisation.

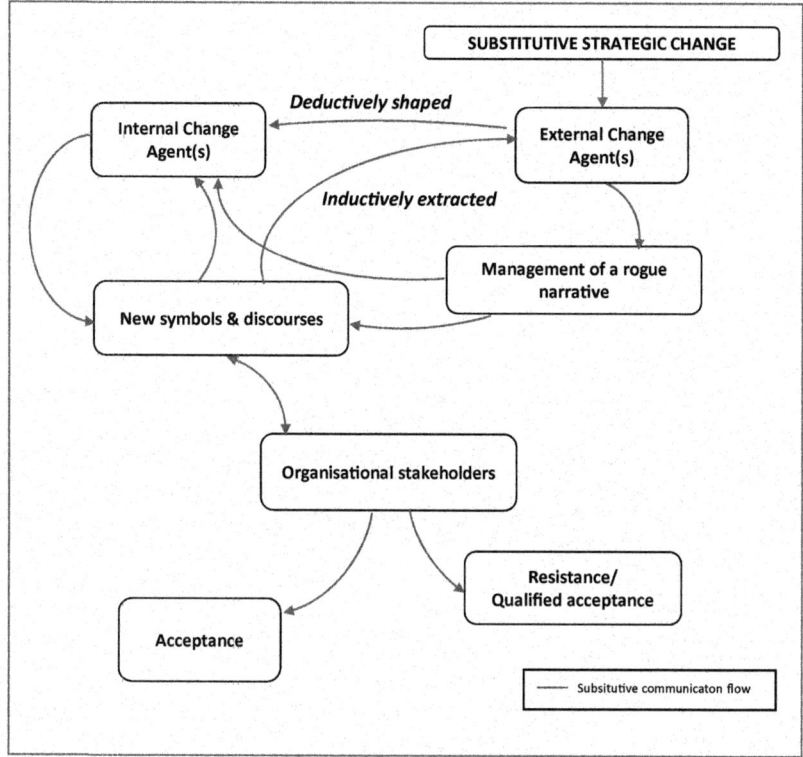

Fig. 14.2 The CLASS framework for a substitutive change

When Steve Ballmer was retiring as the chief executive of Microsoft, the corporation had experienced decades of success with its two core products, Windows and Office. The historical focus of the organisation on microcomputer software was evident from its concise name. However, the board of directors and senior executives of Microsoft recognised that the golden age of the personal computer had come and gone. There was an urgent need to change the strategic focus of the company from desktop microcomputing to mobile and cloud computing. A strategic change was essential. Nevertheless, the board decided to promote an insider, Satya Nadella, rather than hire someone from outside to be the next chief executive. Nadella was given the responsibility of leading the transformation that would shape the future of Microsoft.

Given the Microsoft example, we may ask: why consider an external hire? Such a choice implies that existing management was perceived to be ineffective or viewed as too rigid and unadaptable to enact the strategic change. The externally hired leader will bring a fresh pair of eyes and ears as well as distinctive expertise and/or experience.

The decision to hire someone from outside the organisation to lead the change has at least two significant short-term drawbacks. First, we can expect a higher degree of organisational instability as the new hire climbs a learning curve, acquiring organisation-specific knowledge and developing personal relationships. Second, the morale and motivation of some employees can be expected to decline because they were not considered qualified to lead the change.

Prior research suggests that the performance of external hires is comparatively inferior to that of internal appointees (Bidwell, 2011). However, there is a high variance in the findings that leads to competing theories (Georgakakis & Ruigrok, 2017). The wide range of outcomes, from almost total success to almost complete failure, by outsiders can be explained by competing hypotheses (Helfat & Bailey, 2005). Their experience in previous organisations may enhance their performance. Lessons learned from previous failures as well as successes in the past are likely to be helpful. Undoubtedly, those who are members of the leadership team in the best-run companies (Peters & Waterman, 1982) are often recruited to improve the performance of less successful firms by undertaking some type of strategic change.

However, no two organisations are the same. Thus, these external appointees typically face a steep learning curve related to nuances of their new organisation. They may also face negative sentiment among employees, who resent the appointment of an outsider rather than one of their own. These are among the factors that commonly undermine their performance (Strang & Macy, 2001).

It is useful to consider factors related to the external hire when forecasting their performance. For example, we may ask: why was the most recent organisational leader not asked to lead the strategic change. Was that leader terminated involuntarily (fired with cause or simply dismissed)? Did the leader retire or leave voluntarily under some other circumstances? Did the past organisational leader simply step aside, perhaps recognising that they lacked the capabilities to successfully lead the strategic change?

Both the depth and breadth of experience of external hires should be considered. To be specific, it is relevant to know the number of years and the number of different contexts, such as different countries and industries, in which they have worked, and the number of different organisations that have employed the individual.

Longer and more successful tenures in other organisations are likely to enhance the personal reputation and legitimacy of an individual. Meanwhile, experience with strategic changes in different contexts should be helpful to prepare the leader for the unplanned complications that are almost inevitable. A common complication in a private enterprise involves the role of directors. Boards of directors tend to not only authorise or approve a proposed strategic change, but also to exert influence on it at different stages (Golden & Zajac, 2001). My experience suggests that an individual who is given the responsibility to lead a strategic change should also ask for and receive the scope of authority needed to implement it completely. This includes adequate decision rights and resources.

The relationship between the type of strategic change and the source of leadership is also worth considering. One theory suggests that an internally-appointed leader with extensive organisational experience will be more appropriate if the aim is to enhance or augment what already exists (Daum, 1975). An additive change that builds on the past will benefit from a leader who is intimately familiar with that past. For example, Microsoft has not completely abandoned its microcomputer software products. It has added Azure, a cloud computing service, and Surface, a tablet computer device, while also extending existing product lines such as Windows and Office.

My experience suggests that internally-appointed change leaders are often able to leverage a strong organisation-specific knowledge base. This enables them to move quickly and enact an intended strategic change. If the time to complete the strategic change is limited, due to either a radical change in the environment or an organisation that is close to death, then it would be foolhardy to recruit, select and orient an external appointee. Only a courageous and quick decision to transform an organisation by someone who knows its strengths and weaknesses can save it.

Based on surveys that I have conducted at the diagnosis stage in more than two dozen strategic change projects, internal appointees tend to face lower levels of resistance from stakeholders. Thus, the implementation of the strategic change led by such a leader will proceed more smoothly.

However, existing organisations can reach a plateau with their internal leadership (Graeff, 1983; Martinsons, 1993). Under such circumstances, an external hire is essential to enhance or augment key elements of the existing organisation. For example, the South China Morning Post newspaper in 2016 appointed a young and tech-savvy chief executive, Gary Liu. Liu had previously worked at Google, American Online and Spotify. He was given the specific responsibility for transforming the highly respected newspaper, which was founded back in 1903, into a multi-media news provider. The intention was to leverage and build on the existing reputation and news gathering capabilities of the South China Morning Post. Nevertheless, the organisation and its capabilities had to be fundamentally reinvented to prioritise digital rather than physical content and distribution channels.

If the primary aim is to reinvent the existing organisation or replace its key elements, then an external leader may be the right person to lead that type of substitutive strategic change. They can bring big and bold new ideas into the organisation. For example, PayPal was established as a cryptography company and subsequently became a service provider for personal digital assistant (PDA) devices. Only after years of trial and error did new leadership transform PayPal into an online payment service provider.

Meanwhile, the transformation of Apple after Steve Jobs was rehired is legendary. Jobs co-founded Apple with Steve Wozniak in 1976. Two decades later the company that they had established was struggling. It was producing and trying to sell everything from digital cameras and portable CD players to appliances that could enhance television viewing. After rejoining Apple as its chief executive in 1997, Steve Jobs discarded the company's mass market orientation and adopted a clear focus strategy. It outsourced its manufacturing and targeted a narrow range of products at two specific market segments: professional designers like architects and primary schools in wealthier neighbourhoods. The introduction of computer-based learning tools in the latter segment nurtured a generation of very young users whose loyalty to Apple would have very long-term benefits. This strategic change helped to ensure that Apple as a business organisation would survive. Under the leadership of Jobs the company then capitalised on successive waves of "the next big thing": digital music with the iPod and iTunes, smart capabilities added to mobile phones with the iPhone, and tablet computers with the iPad.

More generally, external candidates should be hired to lead the strategic change if and only if they are significantly superior to the internal candidates. There is no doubt that the brilliance of Steve Jobs was unmatched by anyone at Apple when he was rehired. However, Netflix already had a visionary chief executive, Reed Hastings, when it initiated a strategic change from a company merely renting digital video discs to become a producer and provider of streamed entertainment. There was no reason for Netflix to bring in an outsider. Many organisations have talented members who are willing and able to step up when a strategic change is needed.

Following from experience and the logic above, my propositions to guide practice are:

P3: Strategic changes led by internal appointees will be more common than those led by external hires.

P4: Strategic changes led by internal appointees will be, on average, more successful than those led by external hires.

ARTICULATION of the Strategic Change: Formal Plan or Informal Vision?

Management theorists generally advocate the development of a strategic plan to guide the future of an organisation (Hayes, 1986; Martinsons, 1993; Mintzberg, 1998). It typically consists of components such as a mission statement, a vision statement, long-term goals and objectives, a description of and timetable for major actions and activities, and details about how often the actions and activities will be reviewed and updated.

A strategic change that involves a large commitment of resources may also be based on a formal plan. That planning document would commonly identify (1) where the organisation currently is (situational analysis) and (2) what (coordinated) actions and activities it needs to take to reach a desired destination in future. The emphasis is on the current state, the journey and the final state (Lewin, 1947; Martinsons, 1993).

The plan for a strategic change may be directional, with a limited amount of information, or detailed, with a lot of specific information (Ansoff, 1991; Mintzberg, 1991). The latter type of plan would likely include details about the amount and allocation of resources along with the specific roles and responsibilities of different departments or individuals.

Participation in the development of such a strategic change plan will depend on the culture of the organisation and the allocation of decision rights within it (Noda & Bower, 1996; Posch & Garaus, 2020). Some organisational stakeholders are likely to contribute significantly to the initial development of the plan while others may be asked to review the plan and offer ideas or comments to revise or refine it. The stakeholders who are invited to contribute to the development and review of the plan will depend on the culture of the organisation (Burgelman, 1983; Hassard & Sharifi, 1989; Johnson, 1992; Martinsons et al., 2009).

My experience suggests that there is a vast difference among organisations regarding the amount to which different stakeholder perspectives are considered in the planning, design and implementation of a strategic change. For example, I personally participated in the development of a strategic change plan at both a management consulting firm and a research university although I was not a member of the top management team. At the university, a half dozen of us spent three months on a part-time basis analysing the current situation and identifying key environmental opportunities. Another six weeks were spent drafting a skeletal plan. Teams that included domain experts were then formed to create detailed plans for five strategic change priorities, including student learning and career development, faculty recruitment and retention and globalisation. The creation of these five priority plans over a four month period was followed by four more months of consultations with stakeholders and review by them. The total time from initiation to approval took nearly a year and a half. Conversely, as an external consultant, I have served several clients where "the big boss" finalised and communicated a major change within a few days without involving anyone else in the organisation.

The end results of these assorted processes are also likely to be highly variable. They can range from a formal planning document that has resulted from many months of time and effort to a brief and superficial outline of an intended change that has been crafted in a few hours.

Strategic change can be treated as a systematic process that requires detailed planning and participation from a representative cross-section of stakeholders. Alternatively, it can be viewed as a general intention and as something that should concern only a few people at the top of the organisational hierarchy. Meanwhile, implementation is often considered to be more or less unproblematic in that it follows naturally from the planning activities. Strategic management consulting and research has been largely based on a linear model of diagnosis, formulation and implementation (Chaffee, 1985). The assumption is that the strategies and the tangible changes that a specific organisation requires can be planned in a rational and systematic manner (Schoemaker, 1993).

Despite this assumption, the leaders of some organisations will not develop a formal plan. This may reflect the personality of the leaders as well as the cultures of the organisation and/or the society where it operates. Moving from North America to Greater China, I was personally surprised by the comparative simplicity and informality of strategic planning. The big bosses at the top of a hierarchy in a Chinese family business tend to keep their ideas to themselves. Due to concerns about losing discretionary power and "losing face" if their grand plans fail, Chinese leaders tend to codify and share far less information than their North American counterparts.

Quinn (1980) suggests that those who are "managing strategic change in large organisations should not—and do not—follow highly formalized textbook approaches in long-range planning, goal generation, and strategy formulation." Instead, he contends that they "artfully blend formal analysis, behavioral techniques, and power politics to bring about cohesive, step-by-step movement toward ends which initially are broadly conceived, but which are then constantly refined and reshaped as new information appears". Quinn describes this integrating methodology as "logical incrementalism".

Some strategic changes will emerge with little or no formal analysis. They will be based on an informal vision of a desirable or superior state of/for the organisation. The fundamental aim is to survive during a particularly difficult period of time and/or to achieve a better future. My experience suggests that, in the absence of a formal plan, strong leadership is essential to shape the organisational journey.

Charismatic leaders are able to achieve extensive followership and reduce resistance through their personal characteristics and communicated ideas (Conger & Kanungo, 1987; Tucker, 1968). Leaders who are widely perceived to be charismatic and intellectually stimulating can, like falling dominoes, cascade their transformational inclinations downwards in the organisational hierarchy (Bass et al., 1987).

Steve Jobs generated strong support for the transformation of Apple by effectively communicating the essence of his intended strategic change shortly after he returned to the company that he co-founded. His charismatic personality renewed a sense of optimism among the stakeholders of Apple even before his leadership team developed a detailed plan for implementing the strategic change. However, there are very few if any organisational leaders who can match the stage management and storytelling skills of Steve Jobs (Sharma & Grant, 2011).

Following from personal experience and the logic above, my propositions to guide practice are:

P5: Strategic changes based on formal plans will be more common than those based on informal visions.

P6: Strategic changes based on formal plans will be, on average, more smoothly implemented than those based on informal visions.

SYMBOLISM for the Strategic Change: Deductive or Inductive?

When faced with a strategic change, personal perceptions of the organisation will be challenged and likely exposed to reconstruction. If the leaders are to truly manage the communications of a strategic change, then they must sense what the organisation means to different stakeholders as well as the processes by which those meanings may be changed (Gioia & Chittipeddi, 1991; Martinsons et al., 2019; Oswick et al., 1997; Schnackenberg et al., 2019).

A formal document or the vision of a leader may include specific symbolism that communicates key aspects of the strategic change. Top-down phrases and symbols like "going on a journey" or "creating a finely-tuned machine" can help those involved with or affected by the change to make sense of it. From the leadership perspective, the aim of top-down communication is to reduce the risk of confusion and anxiety about the change. The management literature clearly concludes that frequent and honest communication reduces the uncertainty and anxiety of those impacted by an organisational change. This in turn can be expected to reduce their resistance because they have a clearer understanding of what that change will involve.

Storytelling that includes analogies and metaphors can be helpful to give and make sense of how an organisation will move towards new strategies, structures and systems (Boje, 1991). Strategic plans and announcements may include conceptual and generative language based on themes such as: taking a journey, turning a small cat into a large lion, becoming more like a finely-tuned machine or relocating to a better place.

The cognition of the organisation and its leaders—how they interpret its environment—is likely to influence how a strategic change is framed. An organisational change can be represented as a positive development, for example, to take advantage of an opportunity like cloud computing was for Microsoft. Alternatively, it can be framed as an initiative to avoid a negative outcome. For example, the dominant company of film photography, Kodak, faced a dire future as digital photography became dominant. Its leaders acknowledged that a strategic change was urgently needed to preclude an organisational failure such as the bankruptcy or liquidation.

The framing of the intervention as expanding gains or avoiding losses should be supported by observable evidence. This evidence will ideally be in the form of quantitative data from sources such as financial accounts or market research. Alternatively, it can be from a scenario analysis that reveals the emergence of attractive technologies or shifts in demographic profiles. For a framing to be convincing, it must be based on more than a highly subjective interpretation or personal perception.

The communication of an intended change can also benefit from the appropriate use of metaphorical language (Martinsons et al., 2019; Palmer & Dunford, 2000). Famous examples of leaders using metaphors to communicate strategic change include Lou Gerstner and Steve Elop. Gerstner was a former McKinsey and Company consultant who was hired by IBM in the early 1990s, when it was struggling to survive. He viewed IBM as a big elephant that figuratively lacked the agility to dance. Gerstner framed the upcoming transformation of the technology conglomerate as a positive development. He envisioned IBM becoming more agile and dramatically improving several dimensions of its business performance.

Meanwhile, in February 2011 the incoming chief executive of Nokia, Stephen Elop, issued a memo to his staff warning that they were "standing on a burning platform". He saw Nokia's business as an oil rig that was on fire. Elop figuratively forced Nokia and its workers to jump into the North Sea. Since clinging to a "burning platform" would mean certain death, the memo clearly communicated that the former Microsoft executive was planning radical action to avoid a certain disaster. The strategic change had a high probability of failure, but Elop envisioned it as the only hope to revive the business fortunes of Nokia.

Analogies, which communicate the likeness between two entities, are more effective for additive changes. For example, "our life is like a race". In contrast, metaphors, such as "our future will be a difficult but ultimately worthwhile journey" are more appropriate for substitutive changes (Cornelissen et al., 2011). Meanwhile, relational analogies and metaphors are generally more effective to support strategic changes, as opposed to analogies or metaphors that simply highlight common attributes.

If the communication of the strategic change by its leaders is insufficient or ineffective, then other stakeholders may inductively develop their own language and symbolism. Bottom-up (grassroots) vocabulary and symbols are commonly the result of poor planning or inadequate interaction between change leaders and other stakeholders.

The rise of social media introduces new ways in which stakeholders can communicate and receive feedback on their words and actions. Social media messages can be generated and spread quickly in large volumes with a format that encourages almost instantaneous feedback. For example, the availability of the "like", "love", "sad" and angry options in Facebook enable massive positive or negative reactions in a matter of minutes or even seconds. Under such circumstances, the leaders of a strategic change would lose control of the messaging to partly unknown (and unknowable) and heterogeneous sources. Managing and especially counteracting rogue narratives through social media is becoming increasingly important for organisational leaders.

A strategic change will be viewed differently by different stakeholders. One of the most important responsibilities of a change leader is to shape or at least guide these views. If a change is unsuccessful, the subsequent analysis may highlight factors such as leadership errors, organisational dysfunctions and inadequate resources such as insufficient time, too few staff or not enough funding. Even then, stronger leaders can use specific phrases and symbols to shape the conversation and maintain confidence about the future of the organisation.

Following from personal experience and the logic above, my propositions to guide practice are:

P7: Strategic changes shaped by top-down phrases and symbols will be more common than those based on inductive symbolism.

P8: Strategic changes based on top-down phrases and symbols will result in higher levels of perceived organisational success than those based on inductive symbolism.

STAKEHOLDERS' RESPONSE to the Strategic Change: Support or Resistance?

Ultimately, the success of a strategic change depends on whether or not it is accepted by stakeholders. Since such a change, by definition, has a large scale that spans a broad scope of activities. It will aim to significantly improve the overall performance of the organisation. Otherwise, all the time and effort will not be worthwhile. In the coronavirus era, the survival of the whole organisation is often at stake.

The planned change will almost inevitably involve and/or affect many different stakeholders. They are likely to have different perceptions of the strategic change. Many factors can shape the degree of support for or resistance to a specific strategic change. Resistance can be due to negative self-interest (less power, influence and/or rewards), a high degree of comfort with the status quo, a lack of trust in those in authority (and specifically the change leaders), misunderstanding of key change elements or simply rigidity/inflexibility.

Conversely, support and even advocacy for a strategic change may be based on positive self-interest (greater power, influence and rewards), dissatisfaction with the status quo, a high level of trust in the change leaders or simply a tolerance for uncertainty and/or a more adventurous spirit.

An additive change that builds on the past can be expected to face less resistance than a strategic change that breaks with the past. It is more comforting to keep something that already exists instead of starting with a completely clean slate. Entrenched elements of the organisation may be difficult to dismantle and reinvent or replace completely.

Meanwhile, a leader who is familiar with those involved with or affected by the strategic change is likely to face preconceived perceptions. These may be positive if the leader is respected or negative if otherwise. A leader coming from outside the organisation will usually face fewer preconceptions. Thus, an external hire may be better able to shape both the conversation associated with the change and the attitudes towards the change.

Those affected by a significant change will experience different emotions over time. An adaptation of psychological research (Kübler-Ross, 1969) suggests that humans will go through a sequence of stages when faced with change: denial and anger, bargaining, depression, revising, deserting and eventually acceptance (Ashkanasy & Dorris, 2017). Thus, the reaction to a strategic change over time, that is during the duration of the process, can be expected to vary. However, it is noted that the early emotional stages of denial and anger as well as bargaining and depression are more likely to result in resistance to a strategic change than support for it.

The degree of support for or resistance to a strategic change is expected to depend on many factors. These include the recent performance and current condition of the organisation, the characteristics of its culture, and the way that different people learn about the change. There will be less uncertainty, anxiety and resistance if key information is communicated formally. Conversely, the grapevine or other forms of gossip will fill information gaps if the communications of the change leadership are inadequate. The result is likely to be highly distorted or even completely wrong information. This has been identified as one of the "silent killers" for the implementation of strategic change (Beer & Eisenstat, 2000). This highlights the importance of preventing rogue narratives so that they do not have to be managed and/or counteracted at a later stage.

The success of the strategic change is more generally contingent on how effectively the response of stakeholders is managed. Even if the organisational initiative is generally supported, the change leader still needs to manage how people interpret what they need to do to support it. Conversely, if a substantial amount of resistance is encountered, there will be a need to manage this resistance through tangible actions.

Among the most important responsibilities of a change leader is to reduce this resistance and increase support for the strategy that has been planned or envisioned. Actions such as clear and consistent communication throughout the process, employee involvement and engagement, facilitation/support to help individuals adapt, and negotiation with influential stakeholders can eliminate or reduce resistance to change (Kotter & Schlesinger, 1989).

The leaders of a strategic change have a responsibility to not only inform stakeholders about it, but also to make them comfortable with what will happen. At a minimum, it is recommended that several key questions are answered: why are we making the change? What are the expected benefits of the change? What will change? When will we start the change and how long is it expected to take? How will we change? (e.g. all at once or at different times in different parts of the organisation)? Who will be involved in the change? And what are their roles and responsibilities?

An effective leader will be able to reduce resistance to a strategic change using the management tools at his/her disposal and, ideally, generate substantial support for it. The examples of Steve Jobs returning to the helm of Apple and Lou Gerstner transforming IBM are illustrative. Frequent communications throughout the strategic change process that convey a clear and consistent message will undoubtedly be helpful to achieve this.

Following from personal experience and the logic above, two more propositions to guide practice are provided.

P9: Strategic changes will initially face more resistance than support from stakeholders.

P10: Strategic changes with lower overall levels of resistance and higher overall levels of support will in retrospect be evaluated as being more successful.

APPLICATION OF THE FRAMEWORK

The CLASS framework has been developed and refined over time to classify or categorise dozens of strategic changes in the past. The specific framework presented here is applicable to a wide range of large-scale changes that those in authority may consider or an organisation is already undergoing. Such a classification or categorisation has proven to be useful for communicating the specifics of the large-scale organisational change that is planned or envisioned. It is also helpful for two critical management activities—the initial planning or envisioning of the strategic change, and subsequently its control as it is being implemented.

The CLASS framework is now being applied in an ambitious research project that plans to ultimately examine a total of 100 strategic changes. The application of this framework is expected to be helpful for both discovering the frequency of different phenomena and the effectiveness of different approaches across the 100 different initiatives (Table 14.2).

More generally, those who are in charge of, involved with or affected by a strategic change will benefit if they have a better understanding of what will happen or is happening already. The CLASS framework is useful to communicate this understanding and thus reduce the vicious cycle of uncertainty, anxiety and resistance.

Strategic organisational change is nevertheless a complex and often messy process. It is important to recognise that the framework provides guidance but does not prescribe an either-or choice with any of the five elements. For example, a strategic change may include both additive and substitutive aspects. An ambitious change may simultaneously enhance and reinvent an organisation. Figure 14.3 illustrates the types of flows that may be associated when the additive and substitutive modes of strategic changes occur simultaneously and independently. Meanwhile, Fig. 14.4 depicts the flows that may occur when the aforementioned modes are simultaneous and more closely integrated.

Table 14.2 Summary of Propositions to Guide Strategic Change Based on the CLASS Framework

P1: Additive forms of strategic change will be more common than substitutive forms of strategic change
P2: Additive forms of strategic change will be, on average, more successful than substitutive forms of strategic change
P3: Strategic changes led by internal appointees will be more common than those led by external hires
P4: Strategic changes led by internal appointees will be, on average, more successful than those led by external hires
P5: Strategic changes based on formal plans will be more common than those based on informal visions
P6: Strategic changes based on formal plans will be, on average, more smoothly implemented than those based on informal visions
P7: Strategic changes shaped by top-down phrases and symbols will be more common than those based on inductive symbolism
P8: Strategic changes based on top-down phrases and symbols will result in higher levels of perceived organisational success than those based on inductive symbolism
P9: Strategic changes will initially face more resistance than support from stakeholders
P10: Strategic changes with lower overall levels of resistance and higher overall levels of support will in retrospect be evaluated as being more successful

IMPLICATIONS AND CONCLUSION

Leo Tolstoy (1900) wrote that "Everyone thinks of changing the world, but no one thinks of changing himself". Simply put, change efforts often falter because individuals overlook the need to make fundamental changes in themselves. Tolstoy's dictum is a useful starting point for a strategic change leader.

After working for decades to improve the performance of organisations, I am convinced that systematic frameworks and effective communication are very beneficial. This particular framework will help the leaders of large-scale organisational changes to adopt a more systematic, more comprehensive and ultimately more successful approach.

The CLASS framework that I have developed has been intentionally kept fairly simple. My experience is that this makes it easy to explain and use. I believe that it can be applied to classify, communicate and control virtually any type of strategic change. Its application has already proven to be effective in making change leadership more deliberate, thoughtful, and reflective.

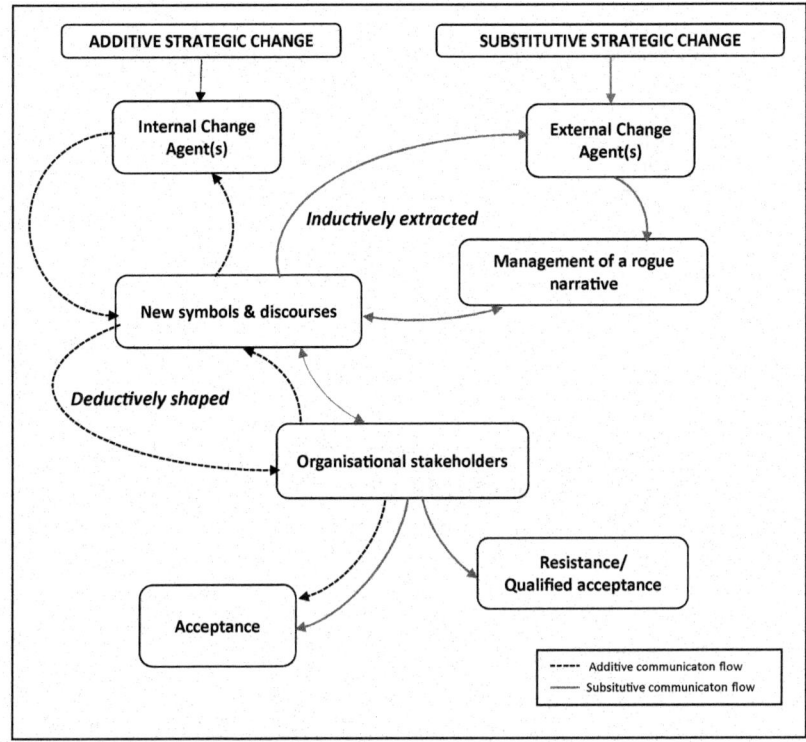

Fig. 14.3 The CLASS framework for interdependent strategic changes

Large-scale organisational changes commonly aim to significantly improve key dimensions of performance. These major changes are inherently complex, resource-intensive, disruptive, and hence risky. Many of them fail. The ultimate aim of sharing the CLASS framework is to improve our understanding and communication of strategic changes so that in future they are more likely to be completed successfully.

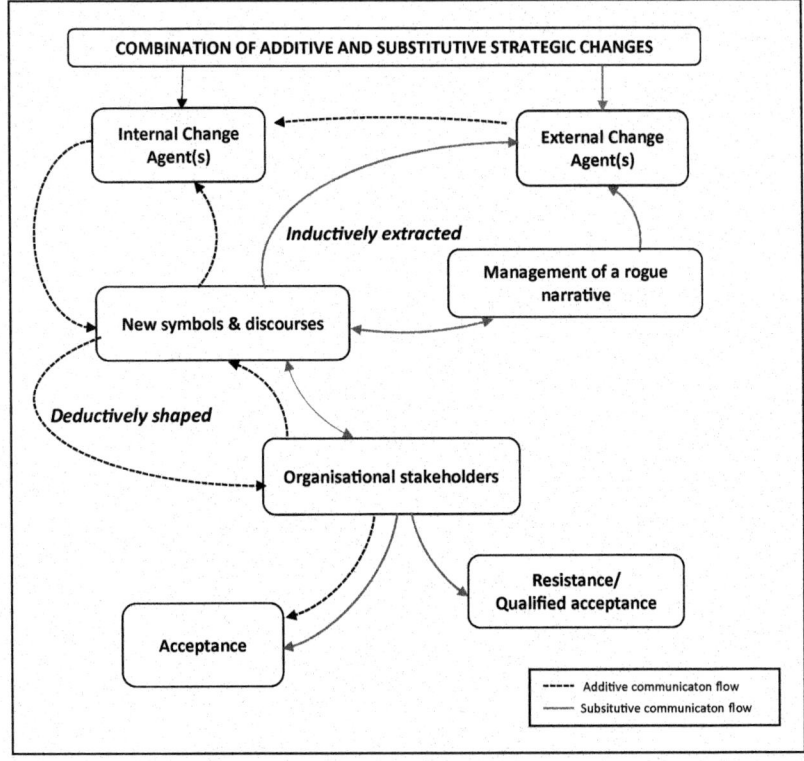

Fig. 14.4 The CLASS framework for an integrated strategic change

Acknowledgements Dozens of organisations on six continents have invited the author to help them diagnose, plan, design, implement and evaluate a wide range of strategic-level changes. In addition, the author has led and/or been involved with a series of specific action research projects that have been funded in whole or in part by the University Grants Council/Committee in Hong Kong. These strategy consulting engagements and action research projects are the foundation on which the the CLASS framework and the associated insights shared here have been built.

The author is most grateful to **Angelina Zubac** for developing the diagrams that are included in this chapter.

He also wishes to acknowledge several anonymous reviewers who provided constructive criticism and helpful suggestions on earlier versions of this manuscript.

REFERENCES

Albert, S. (1992). The algebra of change. *Research in Organizational Behavior,* 14, 179–229.
Ansoff, I. (1991). Critique of Henry Mintzberg's "The design school: Reconsidering the basic premises of strategic management." *Strategic Management Journal,* 12, 449–461.
Appelbaum, S. H., St-Pierre, N., & Glavas, W. (1998). Strategic organizational change: The role of leadership, learning, motivation and productivity. *Management Decision,* 36(5), 289–301.
Ashkanasy, N., & Dorris, A. D. (2017). Emotions in the workplace. *Annual Review of Organizational Psychology and Organizational Behavior,* 4, 67–90.
Auster, E., Wylie, K., & Valente, M. (2005). Strategic organizational change. Pagrave Macmillan.
Bass, B. M., Waldman, D. A., Avolio, B. J., & Bebb, M. (1987). Transformational leadership and the falling dominoes effect. *Group & Organization Management,* 12(1), 73–87.
Beer, M., & Eisenstat, R. A. (2000). The silent killers of strategy implementation and learning. Sloan Management Review, Summer issue, 29–40.
Bidwell, M. (2011). Paying more to get less: The effects of external hiring versus internal mobility. *Administrative Science Quarterly,* 56(3), 369–407.
Boje, D. M. (1991). Consulting and change in the storytelling organization. *Journal of Organizational Change Management,* 4(3), 7–17.
Burgelman, R. A. (1983). A model of the interaction of strategic behavior, corporate context, and the concept of strategy. *Academy of Management Review,* 8(1), 61–70.
Chaffee, E. E. (1985). Three models of strategy. *Academy of Management Review,* 10(1), 89–98.
Conger, J. A., & Kanungo, R. N. (1987). Toward a behavioral theory of charismatic leadership in organizational settings. *Academy of Management Review,* 12, 637–647.
Cornelissen, J. P., Holt, R., & Zundel, M. (2011). The role of analogy and metaphor in the framing and legitimization of strategic change. *Organization Studies,* 32, 1701–1716.
Daum, J. (1975). Internal promotion—A psychological asset or debit? A Study of the Effects of Leader Origin, *Organizational Behavior and Human Performance,* 13(3), 404–413.
Davison, R., & Martinsons, M. G. (2007). Action research and consulting: Hellish partnership or heavenly marriage? In N. Kock (Ed.), Information systems action research: An applied view of emerging concepts and methods, Integrated Series in Information Systems, 13. Springer.
Davison, R., Martinsons, M. G., & Kock, N. (2004). Principles of canonical action research. *Information Systems Journal,* 14, 65–86.

Davison, R. M., Martinsons, M. G., & Ou, C. X. J. (2012). The roles of theory in canonical action research. *MIS Quarterly, 36,* 763–786.
Davison, R. M., Martinsons, M. G., & Malaurent, J. (2021, forthcoming). Improving action research by integrating methods. Journal of the Association of Information Systems.
Georgakakis, D., & Ruigrok, W. (2017). CEO succession origin and firm performance: A multilevel study. *Journal of Management Studies, 54*(1), 58–87.
Gill, R. (1995). Change management–or change leadership? *Journal of Change Management, 3*(4), 307–318.
Gilley, A. M. (2005). *The manager as change leader.* Greenwood Publishing.
Gioia, D. A., & Chittipeddi, K. (1991). Sensemaking and sensegiving in strategic change initiation. *Strategic Management Journal, 12,* 433–448.
Golden, B. R., & Zajac, E. J. (2001). When will boards influence strategy? Inclination × power = strategic change. *Strategic Management Journal, 22,* 1087–1111.
Graeff, C. L. (1983). The situational leadership theory: A critical view. *Academy of Management Review, 8,* 285–291.
Graetz, F. (2000). Strategic change leadership. *Management Decision, 38*(8), 550–564.
Graetz, F., & Smith, A. C. T. (2010). Managing organizational change: A philosophies of change approach. *Journal of Change Management, 10*(2), 134–154.
Hayes, R. H. (1986). Strategic planning - forward in reverse. *Harvard Business Review, 63*(6), 82–90.
Hassard, J., & Sharifi, S. (1989). Corporate culture and strategic change. *Journal of General Management, 15*(2), 4–19.
Helfat, C. E., & Bailey, E. E. (2005). External succession and disruptive change: Heirs-apparent, forced turnover and firm performance. *Strategic Organization, 3*(1), 47–83.
Hempel, P. S., & Martinsons, M. G. (2009). Developing international organizational change theory using cases from China. *Human Relations, 62*(4), 459–499.
Henricks, M. D., Young, M., & Kehoe, E. J. (2020). Attitudes toward change and transformational leadership: A longitudinal study. *Journal of Change Management, 20*(3), 202–219.
Johnson, G. (1992). Managing strategic change—Strategy, culture and action. *Long Range Planning, 25*(1), 28–36.
Kanter, R. M., Stein, B. A., & Jick, T. D. (1992). *The challenge of organizational change.* The Free Press.
Katzenbach, J. R. (1996). Real change leaders: How you can create growth and high performance at your company. *McKinsey Quarterly, 1,* 148–162.

Kotter, J. P., & Schlesinger, L. A. (1989). Choosing strategies for change. In D. Asch & C. Bowman (Eds.), *Readings in Strategic Management* (pp. 294–306). Palgrave.
Kübler-Ross, E. (1969). *On death and dying*. Macmillan.
Lewin, K. (1947). Frontiers in group dynamics: Concept, method and reality in social science: Social equilibria and social change. *Human Relations, 1*, 5–41.
Martinsons, M. G. (1993). Strategic innovation: A lifeboat for planning in turbulent waters. *Management Decision, 31*(8), 4–11.
Martinsons, M. G., Davison, R., Boswood, T., & Mitchell, R. (2019). Communicating organizational development: Metaphors in strategic plans, (U.S.) Academy of Management Best Paper Proceedings.
Martinsons, M. G., Davison, R. M., & Martinsons, V. (2009). How culture influences IT-enabled organizational change and information systems. *Communications of the ACM, 52*(4), 118–123.
Miles, R. H. (1997). *Leading corporate transformation: A blueprint for business renewal*. Jossey-Bass Publishers.
Mintzberg, H. (1998). *Strategy safari: A guided tour through the wilds of strategic management*. Free Press.
Mintzberg, H. (1991). Learning 1, planning 0: Reply to Igor Ansoff. *Strategic Management Journal, 12*, 463–466.
Morgan, G. (1997). *Imaginization: New mindsets for seeing, organizing and managing*. Berrett-Koehler Publisher.
Noda, T., & Bower, J. L. (1996). Strategy making as iterated processes of resource allocation. *Strategic Management Journal, 17*(S1), 159–192.
Nonaka, I. (1994). A dynamic theory of organizational knowledge creation. *Organizational Science, 5*(1), 14–37.
Oreg, S., & Berson, Y. (2019). Leaders' impact on organizational change: Bridging theoretical and methodological chasms. *Academy of Management Annals, 13*, 272–307.
Oswick, C., Keenoy, T., & Grant, D. (1997). Managerial discourses: Words speak louder than actions? *Journal of Applied Management Studies, 6*(1), 5–12.
Palmer, I., & Dunford, G. (2000). Conflicting uses of metaphors: Reconceptualizing their use in the field of organizational change. *Academy of Management Review, 21*, 691–717.
Peters, T. J., & Waterman, R. H. (1982). *In search of excellence: Lessons from America's best-run companies*. Harper & Row.
Posch, A., & Garaus, C. (2020). Boon or curse? *A Contingent View on the Relationship between Strategic Planning and Organizational Ambidexterity, Long Range Planning, 53*(6), 101–119.
Quinn, J. B. (1980). *Strategies for change: Logical incrementalism*. Irwin.
Sanchez, R., & Heene, A. (1997). Managing for an uncertain future. *International Studies of Management & Organization, 27*(2), 21–42.

Schnackenberg, A. K., Bundy, J., Coen, C. A., & Westphal, J. D. (2019). Capitalizing on categories of social construction: A review and integration of organizational research on symbolic management strategies. *Academy of Management Annals, 13*(2), 375–413.

Schoemaker, P. J. (1993). Strategic decisions in organizations: Rational and behavioural views. *Journal of Management Studies, 30,* 107–129.

Sharma, A., & Grant, D. (2011). Narrative, drama and charismatic leadership: The case of Apple's Steve Jobs. *Leadership, 7*(1), 3–26.

Strang, D., & Macy, M. W. (2001). In search of excellence: Fads, success stories, and adaptive emulation. *American Journal of Sociology, 107*(1), 147–182.

Tolstoy, L. (1900). Three methods of reform in Pamphlets, translated from the Russian by Aylmer Maude, 29.

Tucker, R. C. (1968). Theory of charismatic leadership. *Daedalus, 97*(3), 731–756.

Waterman, R., Peters, T., & Phillips, J. (1980). Structure is not organization. *Business Horizons, 23*(3), 14–26.

Zubac, A. (2016). Strategy implementation as a dynamic capability: Going beyond the organizational change interface. In C. A. Schreisheim, & L. L. Neider (Ed.), Current Research and Theory in Transforming Organisations, 105–137.

Zubac, A., Dasborough, M., Hughes, K., Jiang, Z., Kirkpatrick, S., Martinsons, M. G., Tucker, D., & Zwikael, O. (2021). The strategy and change interface: Understanding "enabling" processes and cognitions. *Management Decision, 59*(3), 481–505.

CHAPTER 15

A Structured Approach to Project Management as a Strategic Enabling Priority

Stephen Abrahams

INTRODUCTION

There is much evidence to show that the use of a structured approach to project management within organisations will significantly enhance ability to successfully implement strategy, improve customer satisfaction and enhance reputation. For example, the Project Management Institute's 2020 Pulse of the Profession® (2020: 5) survey revealed that organisations that are highly mature in their project management capabilities *met their goals* 77% of the time compared with 56% for low maturity organisations and *suffered project failure* 11% of the time compared with 21%.

Yet for many organisations, the approach to project management is often ad-hoc or inconsistently applied. Strategic goals are seldom cascaded in practical ways through successive levels of leadership to guide project decision-making. With the exception of some large corporations,

---

S. Abrahams (✉)
Swinburne University of Technology, Hawthorn, Australia
e-mail: sabrahams@swin.edu.au; stephen@progenuity.com.au

© The Author(s), under exclusive license to Springer Nature Singapore Pte Ltd. 2022
A. Zubac et al. (eds.), *Effective Implementation of Transformation Strategies*, https://doi.org/10.1007/978-981-19-2336-4_15

while strategic goals exist, the measurement and review process is generally superficial in nature and provides limited assurance that projects align to strategy. Outcomes and benefits are usually "talked-up" at the proposal stage, yet once the project is approved, attention shifts to the creation of deliverables and the focus on realising sustainable benefits is often lost. Business units typically conduct siloed rather than collaborative development of their project list, leading to unclear priorities and duplication of effort. Stakeholders routinely complain that they are not involved in projects at the right time. Teams are often overstretched in their capacity to deliver on projects because resource forecasts are not effectively balanced between business-as-usual (BAU) and project work. Political behaviour is common as managers compete for the same resources, and both project outcomes and staff morale suffer as results fall short of client and organisational expectations. This situation is illustrated in Figure 15.1, below.

For over twenty years, Bridges (Speculand, 2020: 3) have been conducting research into the effectiveness of strategy implementation. During this time, they have consistently found that leaders habitually *underestimate the challenges of implementing strategy*, while employees struggle to understand the right actions for implementation. Poor communication, lack of discipline and regular reviews in implementation are significant factors in why strategy fails in implementation. In

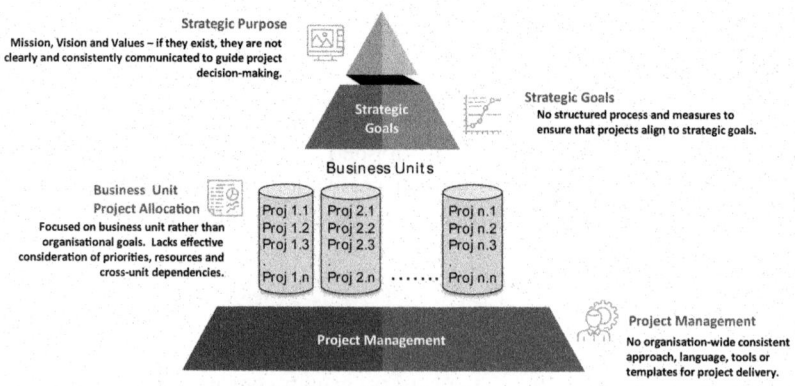

Fig. 15.1 A Typically Siloed and Ad-Hoc Approach to Project Management (*Source* Author's own creation)

the 2020 survey, approximately one out of two strategy implementations are still failing. Only one out of five leaders appraises the implementation at least once a month, and only 28% of organisations have an effective measurement system in place for tracking strategy implementation. Bridges summarise the leadership opportunities for effective strategy implementation in four words: Discipline, Communications, Measures and Reviews. One of the most effective methods of realising these four elements of leadership opportunity for strategy implementation is through the development and adoption of a structured approach to project management.

Purpose

The purpose of this chapter is to show how a clearly defined, widely deployed and continuously improved project management framework (PMF) can bring consistent structure, increased productivity and greater levels of project success. The chapter is structured to show how each of the layers in the PMF work together to effectively enable strategic implementation and organisational change management.

Research Methodology

The findings in this chapter have been developed from the design and implementation of project management frameworks, attaining quality certification in project delivery processes, training facilitation and coaching in portfolio, programme and project management in corporate, government and not-for-profit organisations over more than 25 years. The chapter will draw on case studies from work conducted with five organisations: the Australian Centre for the Moving Image (ACMI); Hassell Studio, an international architecture and design practice; the Victorian Agency for Health Information (VAHI) for the development and implementation of their respective project management frameworks; MLC School in Sydney, a private girls' school, for the development and implementation planning of their strategic plan; and Timberlink, a private timber manufacturing and wholesaling company, for the development and implementation of their innovation management framework.

Using a Project Management Framework to Create Strategic Alignment

The progressive development and disciplined application of a structured PMF provides a critical enabling capability that supports the successful achievement of strategic goals and outcomes. A PMF is defined here as the set of processes, roles and responsibilities, tools and systems that are used to guide project ideas from inception to realisation. The effective adoption of a PMF can provide a comprehensive and transparent set of organisational enabling processes (Zubac et al., 2021: 486) towards the implementation of strategic goals. What is more, through the inclusive and collaborative engagement of executives, leaders and teams and successive levels of the organisation, it has the additional benefit of facilitating a structured approach to organisational and individual change management.

With reference to Figure 15.2, strategic implementation begins with a clear *strategic purpose* that underpins the direction, actions and behaviours in the organisation. *Strategic goals,* when clearly communicated and cascaded through successive levels of leadership and management, provide meaningful guidance and focus on each level of the organisation. *Portfolio Management* is used to optimise the selection of project priorities and dependencies to achieve organisation-wide goals. *Programme Management* then examines the resourcing and coordination required across the organisation to deliver the portfolio. *Project Management* provides

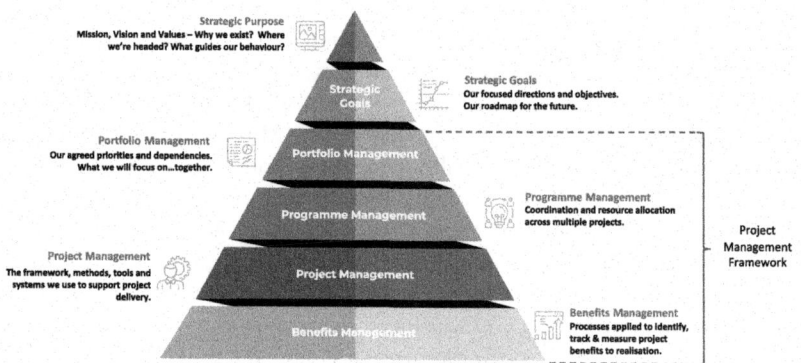

Fig. 15.2 Strategic Alignment and Enablement Pyramid (*Source* Author's own creation)

a consistent set of life cycle based processes, tools and templates used to deliver the outputs of each project. Finally, the discipline of *Benefits Management* helps to ensure that the projects benefits promised in the business case are realised and sustained beyond the end of the project. What follows in the remainder of this chapter is a presentation of each of these elements together with approaches that can be taken for effective implementation.

ENGAGING WITH THE STRATEGIC PURPOSE AND GOALS

The strategic purpose of an organisation, that is, the mission, vision and values, sits at the top of this strategic alignment and enablement pyramid. Strategic alignment is supported when project participants have the elements of their organisation's strategic purpose in mind, to provide focus and guide decisions within the framework and the projects flowing from it. The strategic purpose is commonly set by the executive and approved by the Board. The values tend to be more meaningful in guiding behaviour when staff at all levels are consulted during the formulation of the strategic purpose. Consultative development of the strategic purpose can be considered to be the first in a series of organisational enabling processes (Zubac et al., 2021: 486) towards the implementation of strategic goals.

While strategic goals may provide direction for the organisation of *what* needs to be achieved, they are often communicated in such high-level language, that it can be difficult for successive levels of management and their teams, to cascade these goals into practical steps for achievement. The creation of a strategic "*roadmap*" as shown in Figure 15.3, is a second organisational enabling process (Zubac et al., 2021: 486) towards the implementation of strategic goals. A road-mapping workshop was used with the MLC School to engage the cross-functional leaders of the executive team in working together to create an integrated multi-year timeline of practical enabling steps that would achieve their strategic goals and collective vision. The roadmap was then used with the Council as part of the approval process. Once the strategic plan was approved, road-mapping was used as a visual planning technique to engage staff at all levels of the school to identify smaller projects and initiatives that would form the building blocks for the implementation of larger projects and programmes. Six teams totalling approximately fifty members of staff developed the implementation roadmaps for each of the strategic pillars.

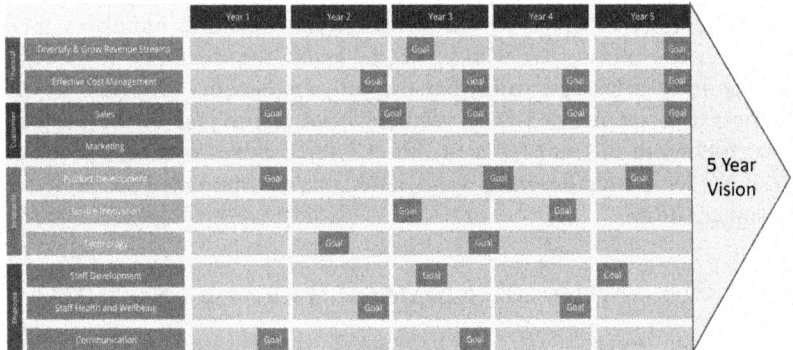

Fig. 15.3 Strategic goals roadmap against business themes (*Source* Author's own creation)

In this way, the strategic road-mapping (sub)process helped to improve understanding between those who developed the strategy and managers required to implement it (Zubac et al., 2021: 486). Such an inclusive approach helped in the development of practical steps for achievement, but also provided significant support for organisational change management, as leaders and their teams at all levels took ownership of the roadmap.

The roadmap has been periodically adjusted in response to emerging changes in both strategic and operational environments. For example, at the beginning of 2020, the adoption of online learning was scheduled for 2023 in the strategic roadmap. Once the COVID-19 pandemic forced the community into lockdown, the online learning objective was made a top priority and was introduced within a matter of weeks. Other elements of the roadmap were adjusted to accommodate this change.

Portfolio Management

Once the strategic purpose and roadmap have been developed, Project Portfolio Management (PPM) is the first layer of the organisation's PMF. Alexander (2019: 1) describes PPM as "*a strategic alignment process by which an organisation's projects are evaluated to identify the purpose, fit, and benefits as they relate to company goals*". In practical leadership terms, PPM can be used to facilitate consensus between business unit leaders from across an organisation for the priority of programmes and projects required to achieve the common vision. While there are many candidate programmes and projects that *could* be undertaken, there are only finite resources and funds and a finite capacity for change in a given period. PPM enables different stakeholder perspectives to be heard about candidate programmes and projects, so gaps in knowledge about planning information can be identified, thus reducing the likelihood of decision-making bias. Successful PPM is characterised by the application of an agreed process and "rules" for transparent and rational decision-making for reaching consensus about priorities. PPM is therefore, the third organisational enabling process (Zubac et al., 2021: 486) towards the implementation of strategic goals.

Portfolio Decision Making Steps

PPM is typically performed by the senior executive group. In its simplest form, the executives meet to agree the priority and dependencies between their top 5-10 programmes and projects in the coming year. This can be extended to include a much larger number of projects and programmes, broader evaluation criteria including competitive positioning, risk, costs, benefits and resourcing requirements. Typical steps in a portfolio management decision-making cycle are illustrated in Figure 15.4 below.

Project Portfolio Matrix

One way of facilitating PPM is through the use of a project portfolio matrix as shown in Figure 15.5 below. In this example, candidate projects are assessed in terms of:

- *Strategic Priority Alignment*—Their relative contribution to each of the strategic goals or themes.
- *Risk of Not Proceeding*—Changing compliance requirements may dictate that a project or programme must proceed, even though it may otherwise have a relatively low contribution to strategic goals.
- *Risk of Proceeding*—This may include consideration of a range of risks including technical complexity, stakeholder and change management, skill and resource availability.
- *Costs*—Direct and indirect.

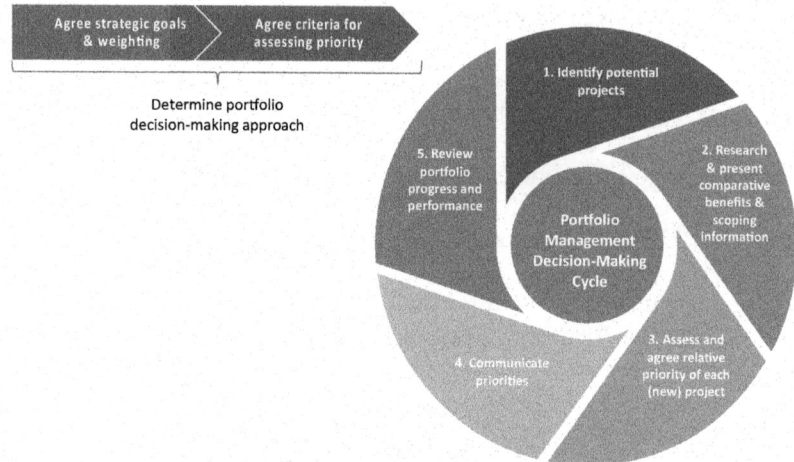

Fig. 15.4 Portfolio Management Decision Making Cycle (*Source* Author's own creation)

- *Duration*—Longer duration projects may need to be broken into sub-projects or phases.
- *Resources*—Provides an indication of the skills and resource commitment required over the duration to achieve the required outcomes.
- *Other factors*—Such as risk during implementation and project to project dependencies.

In practice, this matrix is used by members of a senior executive (cross-functional) team to identify their respective top strategies or projects for the next, say, five-year period (column(a)). Then as a group, to work together in making an assessment of the relative influence (see legend from 0–5) or contribution each strategy or project will make towards the achievement of weighted corporate goals and objectives (column(b)). This is then followed in turn, with an assessment of the risk, cost, duration and resources (columns (c) to (f). Then a final collective assessment is made on the priority rank of each project. While there may be more projects on the list than the organisation has the capacity to perform during the period, this matrix provides a necessary first step in reaching collective agreement across the executive of organisational priorities.

(a) Proposed strategies or projects	(b) Strategic Priority Alignment						(c) Risk of Not Proceeding			(d) Sizing - Cost				(e) Sizing - Time	(f) Sizing - Resources									(g) Priority Rank
	2025 Corporate Goals						Consequences			Direct Costs (Consultants, Capital)			Indirect Cost	Time	Resourcing									RANK
Proposed strategies or projects	Financial	Customer	Innovation	Staff	Communication	Strategic Alignment Weighted Scores	Compliance requirement, Service Continuity to client, Market share loss or Safety	Likelihood	Overall Risk of Not Proceeding = Highest Level Risk * Likelihood (out of 25)	Estimated Project Cost $K - Best Case	Estimated Project Cost $K - Likely	Estimated Project Cost $K - Worst Case	Total Indirect Costs (Internal staff = Total Resource FTE x duration) in resource	Duration (months)	Total FTE by Resource Category	Marketing	Finance	Sales	Engineering	Purchasing & Logistics	Training	Legal, Risk and	IT	
Strategic Priorities Weightings -->	20%	20%	20%	20%	20%																			
CRM System	4	5	4	2	4	19.00	1	5	5.00	$300	$400	$500	49.20	12.0	4.10	0.50	0.50	0.10	0.25	0.50	2.00	0.00	0.00	
Customer Experience Culture Program	4	5	4	5	4	22.00	0	0	0.00	$0	$0	$0	0.00	0.0	0.00	0.00	0.00	0.00	0.00	0.00	0.00	0.00	0.00	
Innovation Management Framework	5	4	5	3	3	20.00	0	0	0.00	$0	$0	$0	0.00	0.0	0.00	0.00	0.00	0.00	0.00	0.00	0.00	0.00	0.00	
Employee Development Program	3	4	4	5	3	19.00	0	0	0.00	$0	$0	$0	0.00	0.0	0.00	0.00	0.00	0.00	0.00	0.00	0.00	0.00	0.00	
	0	0	0	0	0	0.00	0	0	0.00	$0	$0	$0	0.00	0.0	0.00	0.00	0.00	0.00	0.00	0.00	0.00	0.00	0.00	
	16	18	17	15	14																			

Legend:	
0	No perceived influence (e.g. <1%)
1	Very minor influence on objective.(<5%)
2	Minor influence on objective. (5-15%)
3	Significant influence (15-39%)
4	Major influence (40-75%)
5	Critical influence (76-99%)

Fig. 15.5 Example Project Portfolio Matrix for determining project and Programme Priorities (*Source* Author's own creation)

At both ACMI and MLC School, the PPM process and matrix described above, enabled senior executives to work together across functions to reach consensus about the priority and sequence that the integrated set of projects would contribute to strategic goals. When facilitated in an open and transparent way, this helped to build trust in executive decision-making processes and subsequently reduced infighting over resources at the programme and project management levels. Pearson et al., (2020: 7) report that executive support has been one of the top three factors of project success for over twenty-five years. As such, effective PPM is a crucial organisational enabling process towards the implementation of strategic goals and supporting change management at the executive level.

Pipeline Approach—Go/No-Go Assessment

In commercial consulting organisations, while the above approach is used for internal projects, for potential client-facing revenue generating projects a staged "Go/No-Go" assessment is typically conducted to determine the level of project risk, attractiveness and competitive advantage before proceeding to bid for the opportunity. Such a process is usually completed by a partner or principal and then verified by at least two others to assist in reducing decision-making bias and supports the business development pipeline.

Stage 1—Identify—Typical questions for identifying opportunities include:

1. Have we spoken to the client about the opportunity before now?
2. Is the client financially sound?
3. Is the budget likely to be adequate for the scope?
4. Is the project consistent with our strategic vision?
5. Is the opportunity free of significant risk?

Stage 2—Assess and Commit—Typical questions before committing to opportunities include:

1. Is the client willing and able to invest in delivering the project?
2. Is the project aligned to our capabilities?
3. Is the project of strategic importance?

4. Is the project scope clearly defined?
5. Does the client prioritise quality over cost?
6. Is the project timeframe adequate for effective delivery?
7. Do we have the appropriate expertise and resources to deliver the project?
8. Do we have prior involvement with or specific knowledge of this project?
9. Do we have specific competitive advantage or influence?
10. Overall chance of success?

Updating the Strategic Roadmap

Once project priorities have been agreed, the strategic roadmap is then be updated to include key enabling programmes, projects and their respective dependencies as agreed during the PPM process. The updated strategic roadmap is illustrated in Fig. 15.6 below. It is important at this level of planning that portfolio managers also identify the strategic resource requirements. That is, those new skills, competencies and capacity that will be required to meet the identified strategic goals and enabling programmes and projects.

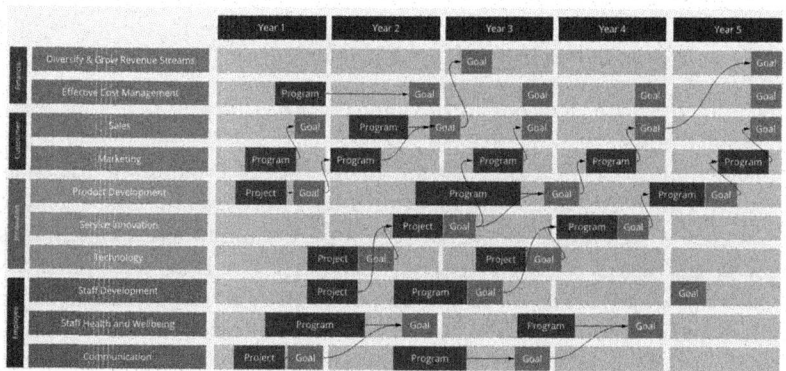

Fig. 15.6 Strategic roadmap showing goals, key enabling programmes, projects and dependencies (*Source* Author's own creation)

Benefits of Portfolio Management

The benefits of effective PPM as an organisational enabling process towards the implementation of strategic goals and supporting change management include:

- Improved transparency and consensus in organisational decision-making at the executive level through a cross-functional collaborative process.
- Improved clarity by successive levels of leadership and employees of the goals and direction of the organisation. Employees can see where their contribution makes a difference as part of the bigger picture, leading to greater levels of engagement and motivation towards the achievement of strategic success.
- Reduced risk through early detection and peer validation.
- Clear understanding of organisational priorities and dependencies.
- Reduced stress and improved morale as staff can engage with a clear, yet achievable set of priorities.
- Improved visibility by senior leaders in tracking progress of the strategic plan and its implementation at a high level.
- Ability to adapt more easily and in a controlled way to changing circumstances and new projects.

PROGRAMME MANAGEMENT

Once priorities are determined through the PPM process, the fourth set of organisational enabling processes (Zubac et al., 2021: 486) towards the implementation of strategic goals are at the level of Programme Management, the next layer of the organisation's PMF. Programme Management represents a significant challenge for most organisations. Programmes typically consist of related projects in the portfolio. Even with priorities decided through PPM, many organisations struggle to get the balance right between enough resources and too many projects or programmes. Programme management is the discipline that involves integrated planning and management between the components of work within the portfolio including resource, governance, risk, stakeholder and communications management. The programme management function is typically performed by dedicated programme managers, a project management office (PMO) or programme management team representing the different business units of the organisation.

One of the key challenges at the programme level is the effective identification, forecasting, sourcing and deployment of resources. Strasser (2021) identifies the importance of tactical resource planning and the challenges of coordinating the medium-term resourcing requirements of project teams for project managers versus the operational demands for the same resources by their line managers. Many organisations have significant difficulty in predicting the future workload and skill requirements of their portfolios and programmes, then balancing this with BAU or operational workloads. This challenge is illustrated in Fig. 15.7 below. Common complaints from supporting business units and teams at ACMI were that *"they didn't identify the need for our involvement until just before our people were required"* and *"if only they involved us earlier in the scoping and processes, we could have addressed these issues much earlier, before they became much more difficult and costly to fix"*.

Organisations that do perform resource management effectively, tend to have the following five elements in common:

1. Early identification and involvement of key resource-contributing stakeholders in the scoping and planning processes.

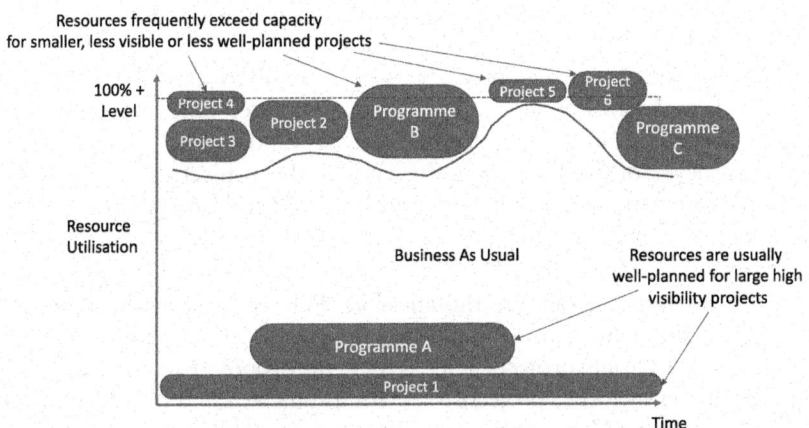

Fig. 15.7 Portfolio, Programme, Project Resource Planning Challenge (*Source* Author's own creation)

2. A holistic view of the resourcing required for the entire project portfolio. This view is made visible to all key stakeholders.
3. Resource (functional) managers are responsible (and accountable) for regular and ongoing project skills forecasting and planning.
4. Detailed organisation-wide skill forecasting for all projects and high-level resource forecasts for BAU activities.
5. Regular (e.g. monthly) project time tracking, reviews and updates against forecasts.
6. Regular (e.g. quarterly) portfolio and programme reviews to adjust portfolio and programme priorities with changing circumstances and risks.

Hassell, for example, has most of these elements in place, and time is set aside at least monthly, for collaborative reflection, planning, review and adjustment of the portfolio and the associated resource plan within and between studios on a national and international basis. Some organisations hold a reserve of resources for unforeseen projects that occur due to changing external influences. That doesn't mean keeping a "slush fund" to make up for inefficiencies or poor planning. It means that there will always be challenges and opportunities that occur that weren't anticipated and maintaining a reserve will allow for an effective and timely response. For commercial organisations, the holding of resource reserves is carefully balanced with the backlog of future work. This is illustrated in Fig. 15.8, below.

Each project is usually predicated on a business case where benefits significantly outweigh the costs. Unless resource time and effort are being tracked, it becomes very difficult to validate the business case with any level of confidence at the end of the project. Two levels of resource forecasting are often used—*project-based* and *functional* resource management.

- *Project-Based Resource Management* Full time equivalent (FTE) forecasts of utilisation by individual resource or skill type are estimated for each project. This allows the proposed commitment of resources to future projects to be communicated and made visible to their respective line managers. An example of this type of resource planning developed with ACMI is shown in Fig. 15.9 below.

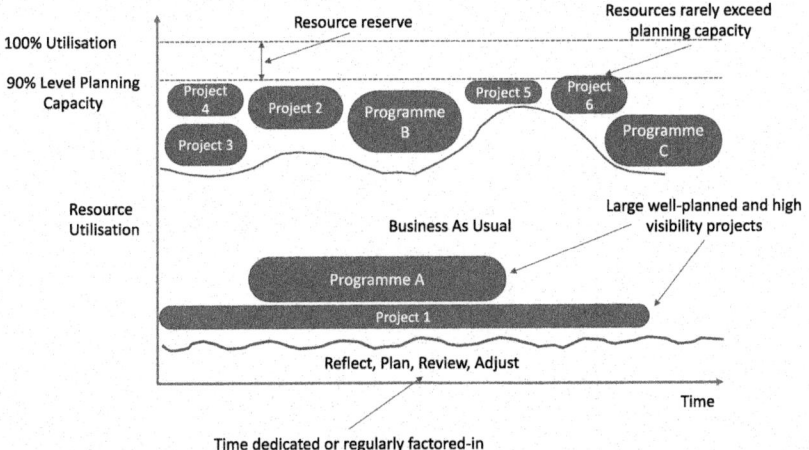

Fig. 15.8 Effective portfolio, programme and project resource management (*Source* Author's own creation)

- *Functional Resource Management* Line or functional unit managers are focused on the control and allocation of their team members to perform the operational work of their business unit. For this to work effectively alongside project resourcing, line managers require visibility and an understanding of potential future projects and the impact this will have on the availability of their resources and completion of operational work. An example of functional resource management is illustrated in Fig. 15.10 below.

Effective Programme Management

Effective programme management for enabling strategy and change management includes:

- Improved resource forecasting leads to more effective, efficient and transparent identification and resource allocation.
- Improved visibility and communication about operational work and project demands leading to improved collaboration and information sharing across the organisation.

Exhibitions & Touring	Role	FY 2020-2021												FY 2021-2022			
		Jul	Aug	Sep	Oct	Nov	Dec	Jan	Feb	Mar	Apr	May	Jun	Jul	Aug	Sep	Oct	Nov	Dec	Jan
Exhibition A																				
	Exhibitions Project Coordinator	90%	100%	100%	100%	100%	100%	61%	80%	95%	100%	100%	0%	0%	0%	0%	0%	0%	0%	0%
	Exhibition AV Technical	105%	100%	100%	100%	100%	100%	100%	100%	100%	75%	30%	0%	0%	0%	0%	0%	0%	0%	0%
	Assistant Registrar	100%	100%	100%	100%	100%	100%	100%	100%	100%	100%	100%	100%	0%	0%	0%	0%	0%	0%	0%
Exhibition B																				
	Senior Exhibitions Project Coordinator	0%	0%	0%	0%	0%	0%	0%	85%	85%	90%	80%	75%	40%	25%	25%	25%	0%	0%	0%
	Exhibitions Project Coordinator	0%	0%	0%	0%	0%	0%	0%	0%	80%	90%	90%	90%	90%	80%	60%	40%	0%	0%	0%
	Exhibition AV Technical	0%	0%	0%	0%	0%	0%	0%	0%	80%	100%	80%	80%	80%	0%	0%	0%	0%	0%	0%
	Exhibition AV Technical (Touring)	0%	0%	0%	0%	0%	0%	0%	0%	85%	90%	100%	100%	100%	100%	60%	20%	0%	0%	0%
	Assistant Registrar	0%	0%	0%	0%	0%	0%	0%	60%	100%	100%	100%	100%	100%	100%	60%	20%	0%	0%	0%
	Exhibition Preparator	0%	0%	0%	0%	0%	0%	0%	0%	90%	100%	100%	100%	0%	0%	0%	0%	0%	0%	0%

Fig. 15.9 Project-based resource management (not real figures) (*Source* Author's own creation)

Role	Resource	FY 2020-2021												FY 2021-2022			
		Jul	Aug	Sep	Oct	Nov	Dec	Jan	Feb	Mar	Apr	May	Jun	Jul	Aug	Sep	Oct	Nov	Dec	Jan

Melbourne

Exhibitions and Touring

Registrar

Role	Jul	Aug	Sep	Oct	Nov	Dec	Jan	Feb	Mar	Apr	May	Jun	Jul	Aug	Sep	Oct	Nov	Dec	Jan
Registrar (Renewal)	90%	100%	100%	100%	100%	100%	61%	80%	35%	100%			0%	0%	0%	0%	0%	0%	0%
Assistant Registrar	165%	100%	100%	100%	100%	100%	100%	100%	100%	75%	30%		0%	0%	0%	0%	0%	0%	0%
Assistant Registrar (Touring)	100%	100%	100%	100%	100%	100%	100%	100%	100%	100%	100%		0%	0%	0%	0%	0%	0%	0%
Assistant Registrar (Renewal)	100%	100%	100%	100%	100%	100%	100%	100%	100%	100%			0%	0%	0%	0%	0%	0%	0%

Head of Touring

Role	Jul	Aug	Sep	Oct	Nov	Dec	Jan	Feb	Mar	Apr	May	Jun	Jul	Aug	Sep	Oct	Nov	Dec	Jan
Senior Coordinator, Touring Exhibitions	100%	100%	100%	100%	100%	100%	100%	100%	100%	100%			0%	0%	0%	0%	0%	0%	0%
Coordinator, Touring Exhibitions	100%	100%	100%	100%	100%	100%	100%	100%	100%	100%	100%	100%	0%	100%	0%	0%	0%	0%	0%
Junior Designer, Touring	100%	100%	100%	100%	100%	100%	100%	90%	95%	0%	0%	0%	0%	0%
	100%	100%	100%	100%	100%	100%	100%	100%	100%	100%			0%	0%	0%	0%	0%	0%	0%

Exhibitions Manager

Role	Jul	Aug	Sep	Oct	Nov	Dec	Jan	Feb	Mar	Apr	May	Jun	Jul	Aug	Sep	Oct	Nov	Dec	Jan
Exhibitions Project Coordinator	100%	80%	80%	75%	100%	100%	100%	100%	80%				0%	0%	0%	0%	0%	0%	0%
Senior Exhibitions Project Coordinator	100%	100%	100%	100%	100%	100%	85%	85%	75%				0%	0%	0%	0%	0%	0%	0%
Temporary Exhibitions Project Manager	100%	100%	100%	100%	40%	30%	20%	20%	20%	100%			0%	0%	0%	0%	0%	0%	0%
Exhibition Preparator	100%	100%	100%	50%	100%	95%	95%	95%	95%	50%	50%	50%	50%	50%	50%	0%	0%	0%	0%

Fig. 15.10 Functional resource management (not real figures) (*Source* Author's own creation)

- Increased agility with the ability to respond more rapidly and effectively to changing strategic priorities.
- Reduced managerial and employee stress and improved morale.
- Improved identification and management of risks and knowledge gaps that exist between or across related projects and programmes.
- Enhanced identification and engagement of common stakeholders, supported by improved communication planning and monitoring.

PROJECT MANAGEMENT

The effective structuring of Project Management in organisations usually takes the form of three elements:

- *Project Governance and Reporting Structure:* Provides the structure, roles and responsibilities for how projects are to be governed and reporting is managed from initiation to completion.
- *Project Life Cycle and Guidelines:* Provides the detailed advice and guidance on typical project phases, activities, sizing criteria, approval and reporting flows.
- *Project Tools and Templates:* A selection of tools and templates that recommends format and content of project management forms, documents and systems required for scoping, planning, approval and monitoring.

It is these three elements that collectively make up the fifth set of organisational enabling processes (Zubac et al., 2021: 486) towards the implementation of strategic goals.

Governance and Reporting Structure

The governance and reporting structure is the management framework within which portfolio, programme and project decisions are made and how progress is monitored and reported. It provides a logical decision-making structure and oversight function that is aligned with the organisation's governance model and that encompasses the project life cycle. The governance framework provides the project manager and team with structure, processes, decision-making models and tools for managing the project, while supporting and controlling the project for successful delivery.

Project Sponsors and Steering Committees are accountable for the governance of individual projects and their respective benefits and outcomes. Their mandate includes ensuring that alignment is established and maintained throughout the project between project goals and organisational objectives. The project team under the leadership of the Project Manager is responsible for delivering a project and its respective outputs. All projects have a project sponsor and a project manager as a minimum requirement. An example of a portfolio, programme and project governance structure is shown in Fig. 15.11.

A clearly defined set of responsibilities for each of the roles in the governance structure, improves clarity and consistency of decision-making. This in turn, improves efficiency and effectiveness in project

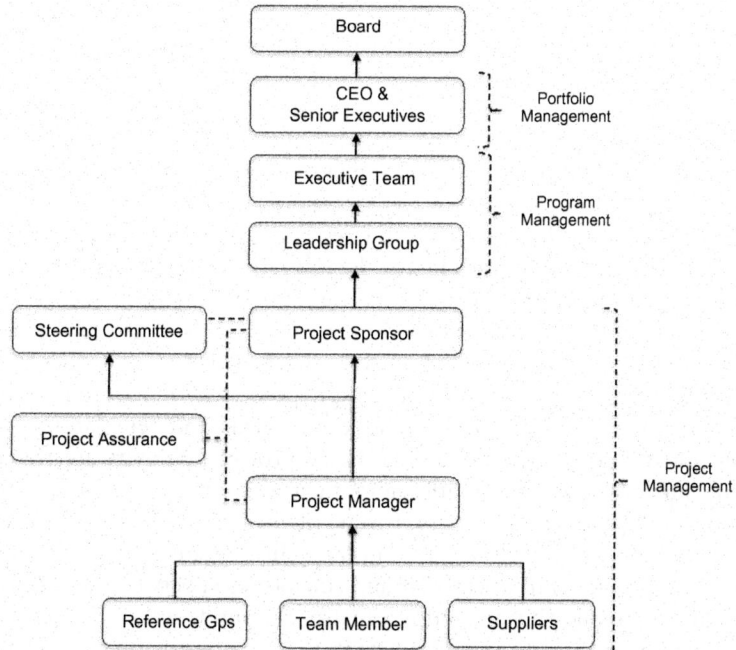

Fig. 15.11 Example Organisational Project Governance Structure (*Source* Author's own creation)

approval and delivery processes, thus, reducing the cost and time required for project delivery and simultaneously increasing the return on investment.

Governance structures tend to be most effective where there are:

1. Clearly defined levels of authority and approval processes for different "sizes" of projects.
2. Clearly defined portfolio, programme and project governance roles and responsibilities for each role.
3. Single point of accountability for sponsorship of projects.
4. Consistent and regular reporting and review from the highest levels of the organisation for adherence to the governance structure and processes.

Life Cycle Guidelines

The Project Life Cycle is the sequence of phases and associated activities used to produce project deliverables and outcomes. Life Cycle terminology and even the number of phases will differ from one organisation to the next, and in some cases from one department to the next. An example of an organisational project life cycle phases and activities is illustrated in Figure 15.12 below.

Documented project life cycle phases and activities help to provide structure and increase consistency in the ongoing development and application of project management knowledge. For example, in the case of Hassell Studio, their professional practices library is a globally shared online knowledge management system. Each activity is supported by knowledge resources that include design processes, activity definitions and workflows, policies, guides, checklists, forms and templates, references, glossaries, tools and systems. Once project managers are trained in the life cycle phase activities and their supporting resources, they commonly report significant improvement in their team's productivity and professionalism in project delivery. This "shared language" also supports enhanced interoperability and collaboration between studios and disciplines across both state and international boundaries.

Perhaps one of the most important tools for successful delivery of benefits *and* support for change management has been the introduction during the initiate phase of a stakeholder impact assessment checklist.

Project Phases

Initiate	Plan	Deliver	Close
Project idea or opportunity identified	Develop work breakdown & schedule	Project startup	Close finances
Project sizing & impact assessment	Determine resourcing & budget	Deliverable development & refinement	File records & artefacts
Assess strategic alignment & portfolio priority	Develop risk, quality & procurement plans	Control variations & monitor risks	Evaluate project
Assign sponsor & approve for investigation	Develop change management plan	Prepare organisation for change and handover	Capture lessons learned
Schedule in program plan	Confirm governance & reporting	Track and report progress	Celebrate wins
Prepare scope document &/or business case	Finalise project plan	Deliverable Review & Acceptance	Controlled adjustment of deliverables
Approve scope &/or business case	Approve project plan/s	Approve deliverables & handover	Approve closure

Fig. 15.12 Example Project Life Cycle Phases and Activities (*Source* Author's own creation)

This helps to ensure that the requirements, scope and risks are clearly defined from the start. It also supports effective change management by analysing and engaging stakeholders to understand the impact of the project on them and then develop consultative and collaborative strategies to support the achievement of outcomes of mutual benefit. An example of a stakeholder impact assessment checklist is shown in Fig. 15.13 below.

Project Sizing and Approvals

The nature of project management is that one "*size*" does not fit all projects. Project sizing is used to assist in determining the level of management and governance associated with each project, thus streamlining approvals and governance requirements for lower risk projects. Factors considered in assessing the size of a project may include:

Stakeholder / Impact	Y/N	Stakeholder / Impact	Y/N	Stakeholder / Impact	Y/N
Core Business		**Member Communications**		**Policy and Quality**	
Policies, processes or procedures		Member billing, maintenance & management		Policies and procedures	
Business practices, data or file storage		Method or approach to member liaison		Data and statistics	
Audit operations		Inform, consult or engage members		Legislation and jurisdiction	
		Process changes that affect members		Keywords	
Finance		**Communications**		External reporting	
Purchases/resources > approved budget		Comms strategy for staff		ICT	
Complaint classification, escalation, or reclass.		Comms with external stakeholders		IT systems	
Member billing, maintenance & management		May attract media attention		Intranet or desktop applications	
Reporting, analytics or KPI's		Legislation		Telecommunications systems	
Commercial arrangements in contracts		Content on website or intranet		ICT infrastructure & office equipment	
Company Secretary		**Legal Counsel**		Building and accommodation changes	
Board/Council to approve or be consulted		Jurisdictional or constitutional implications		Security or disaster recovery	
Insurance – WorkCover, indemnity, building		Policies and procedures		Internal/external hosting arrangements	
Accommodation & building changes		Legal arrangements in contracts		Contracts involving an IT component	
Strategic and business planning		Major changes to employment arrangements			
Risk management		High level dealings with Members			
Environmental management		Board/Council to approve or be consulted			
Human Resources		**Admin Team**			
Training – new or updates		Filing, mail and emails			
OH&S – effect on the way people work		Staff location movement			
Job design, description, conditions		Accommodation changes			
Career paths or promotion		Building maintenance and furniture			
Performance review, career paths, promotions		Stationery supplies			
People management policy & procedures		Staff amenities			
Staff attraction or retention		Visitors			

Fig. 15.13 Stakeholder Impact Assessment Checklist (*Source* Author's own creation)

- Total cost,
- Team size,
- Project duration,
- Staff hours,
- Internal or public facing,
- Technical complexity,
- Requirements uncertainty,
- Reputational risk,
- Level of skills and experience in delivering projects of this type.

As size increases, the level of detail required to develop the scope, business case and plan the project also increases. This increasing detail is also accompanied by the requirements for higher levels of approval authority and reporting, progressing from manager to executive, senior executive, CEO and then Board levels. Figure 15.14 provides an example of a project approval and reporting flow similar to that developed for VAHI and ACMI. This *"sized"* approach to project management reduces the

15 A STRUCTURED APPROACH TO PROJECT MANAGEMENT ... 377

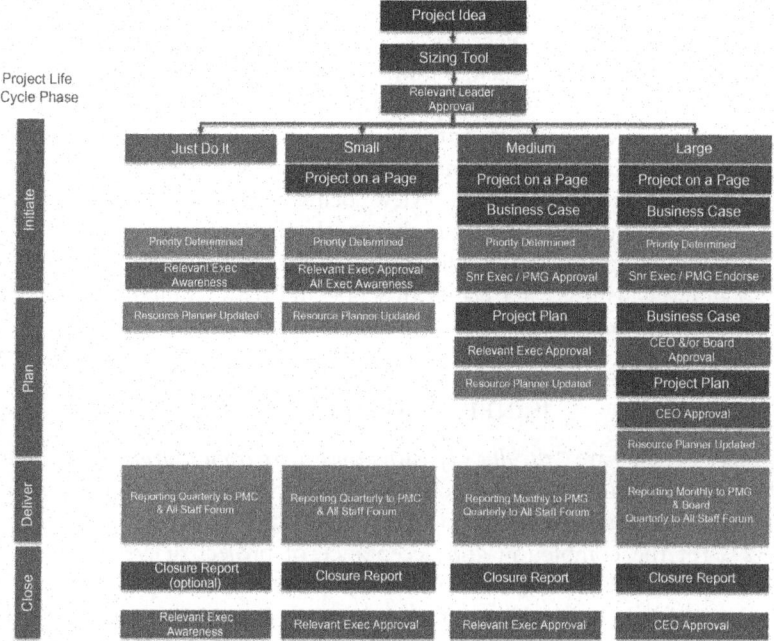

Fig. 15.14 Project Approval and Reporting Flows by Project Size (*Source* Author's own creation)

level of governance for projects of lower risk, thus streamlining approval processes and empowering managers to proceed with project delivery.

Effective Structured Project Management

An effective structured project management for enabling strategy and change management includes:

- Enabling staff to more easily develop self-confidence in their project delivery skills by providing a clear understanding of their roles and responsibilities at each phase.
- Providing a mechanism for effectively tracking progress so that project performance can be measured and value demonstrated to partners and stakeholders.

- Promote clear accountability through well-defined portfolio, programme and project governance roles.
- Supports effective collaboration and interoperability through consistent and shared project management language and process.
- Initiatives can progress with commensurate levels of effort required for approval, management and reporting. Greater levels of investigation, evaluation and review being reserved for projects and programmes representing higher levels of organisational risk.
- Early sizing and stakeholder impact assessment provides managers at all levels with greater clarity of scope and risks required for effective decision-making to approve, manage and govern projects.

BENEFITS MANAGEMENT

Project benefits are *"the flows of value that arise from a project"*. Further, the ability of an organisation to realise project benefits is strongly associated with successful organisational performance (Chih & Zwikael, 2015: 352). Yet the completion and acceptance of project deliverables alone, does not ensure the realisation of project benefits. For project benefits to be realised, it is important that benefits management planning be conducted throughout the project life cycle and extended into operations. The Project Management Institute (PMI, 2016: 2) defines Benefits Realisation Management as the *"set of processes and practices for identifying benefits and aligning them with formal strategy, ensuring benefits are realised as project implementation progresses and finishes, and that the benefits are sustainable—and sustained—after project implementation is complete"*. Benefits management makes up the sixth set of organisational enabling processes (Zubac et al., 2021: 486) towards the implementation of strategic goals. So how can we define and measure benefits?

Benefits Definition and Measurement

One of the challenges facing organisations is to link benefits to strategic outcomes and then to determine appropriate success indicators that can be readily measured. A benefits management framework (BMF) provides a structured approach for clearly identifying the benefits for each of the required strategic objectives. Then for each benefit, a range of key performance indicators are identified to measure changes in benefit levels being experienced by the target customer or business group over time. An

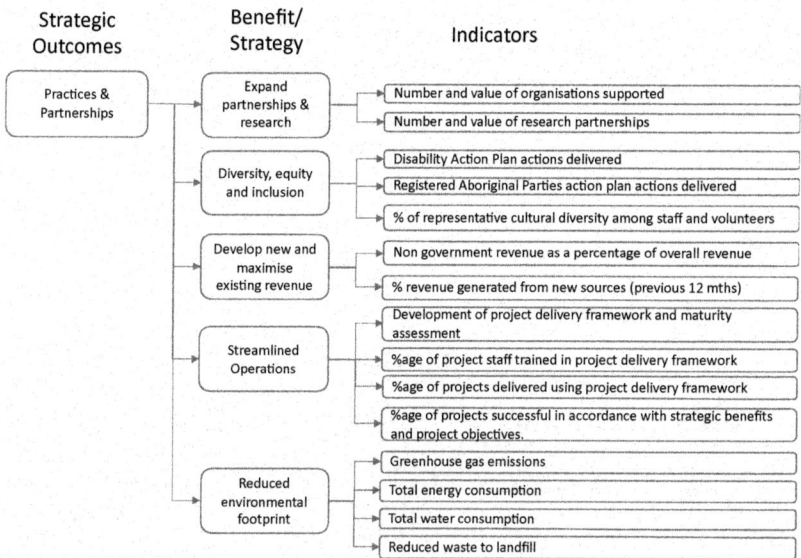

Fig. 15.15 Example of indicators as measures of benefits that deliver strategic outcomes (*Source* Author's own creation)

approach similar to that illustrated in Fig. 15.15 was adopted by ACMI as a method for linking strategic outcomes to project outputs and measures of performance.

Realising Benefits

Identifying target benefits and key performance indicators (KPI's) is one thing, achieving them through effective implementation and then sustaining them in the long run is yet another. Projects typically conclude with the acceptance and handover of outputs such as a new system, product, facility or event. Yet the achievement of the outcomes may require significant ongoing work to enable the project benefits to be realised and sustained. Zwikael and Smyrk (2019: 275) explain that the target outcomes of projects may not be realised as the outputs are made available in an operational and not a project environment. Such environments may lack the dedicated structure and resources afforded to project delivery. The solution they suggest (Zwikael & Smyrk, 2019: 275) is

Project Phases					
Initiate	Plan	Deliver	Realise & Sustain Benefits		Close
Project idea or opportunity identified	Develop work breakdown & schedule	Project startup	Communicate benefits & sustain plan to broader stakeholders		Close finances
Project sizing & impact assessment	Determine resourcing & budget	Deliverable development & refinement	Monitor operations		File records & artefacts
Assess strategic alignment & portfolio priority	Develop risk, quality & procurement plans	Control variations & monitor risks	Assess & report benefits against roadmap & targets		Evaluate project
Assign sponsor & approve for investigation	Develop change management plan	Prepare organisation for change and handover	Regular review of operations & benefits/disbenefits		Capture & share lessons learned
Schedule in program plan	Confirm governance & reporting	Track and report progress	Conduct controlled continuous improvement		Celebrate wins
Prepare scope document &/or business case	Finalise project plan	Deliverable Review & Acceptance	Capture & share lessons learned		Controlled adjustment of deliverables
Identify benefits realise & sustain approaches/baseline	Develop benefits realise & sustain roadmap & plan	Establish benefits realise & sustain governance & capability	Develop business cases to respond to significant operational issues		Confirm and communicate benefits achieved to key stakeholders
Approve scope &/or business case	Approve project plan/s	Approve deliverables & handover	Approve reports & new business cases		Approve closure

Fig. 15.16 Example project life cycle adjusted for benefits realisation and sustainment activities (*Source* Author's own creation)

to take an early portion of the operational environment and treat it as another phase of the project. At ACMI, we achieved this by including a new phase in the project life cycle called the sustain phase, similar to that shown in Fig. 15.16. Once an exhibition has been delivered, it then needs to be sustained for months and in some cases years. Indicators are monitored during the sustain phase and processes of regular review and continuous improvement are used to maximise the achievement of benefits for the investment made.

Summary of Benefits of Structured Benefits Realisation Management

The advantages of structured benefits realisation management for enabling strategy include:

- A clear definition of benefits and their associated KPI's provides a focus for project activities that links directly to strategic outcomes.

- Early and effective benefits planning throughout the project life cycle.
- Regular communication, monitoring, reporting and review towards realising and sustaining project benefits and outcomes.

ESTABLISHING AN EFFECTIVE PROJECT MANAGEMENT FRAMEWORK

One of the challenges in establishing an effective PMF is demonstrating to executive management and senior leadership that the value a PMF will deliver is worth the investment and resources required. The following is a list of some of the questions posed by managers at case study organisations when challenging the introduction of a structured PMF approach include:

- *Question:* "*Won't a structured approach reduce our ability to respond quickly to new opportunities as they arise?*"
  Response: An effective and structured PMF provides for a broader and more integrated understanding of the opportunities that will optimise the achievement of strategic goals. As new opportunities emerge, they can be easily and effectively assessed against existing priorities and the availability of resources determined. This allows for a rapid response without compromising the delivery of existing projects or business operations.
- *Question:* "*Our resources are already overloaded with the existing programs. The idea of keeping some resources in reserve is a luxury that we just can't afford.*"
  Response: By starting at the portfolio level, we can work together to determine those programmes and projects that will deliver the greatest benefit...our highest priorities. At the programme level, we can then work together to determine what capacity we have across the organisation to deliver those projects. From that capacity we create a whole of organisation programme plan. A reserve of resources can be allocated to non-time critical projects. As new and emerging priorities arise, the reserve can be redeployed onto those activities.
- *Question:* "*Couldn't we use the additional effort required for structured portfolio, programme and project management to deliver more projects?*"

Response: Without structured PMF priorities are often unclear, duplication of project effort occurs, collaboration suffers, resources are overstretched and project success levels are reduced. The effort required for effective PPP Management tends to be far less than the effort required to address these problems.

- *Question: "Won't such an approach restrict my department's ability to act independently."*

Response: Seldom are any projects delivered independently of other departments, from whom resources and subject matter expertise are usually required. A structured PMF, will enable you to have clear visibility and control of those projects that can be delivered independently, and work more collaboratively with other departments on interdependent projects to achieve greater cross-functional outcomes and benefits.

So what steps are used to establish an effective PMF in organisations? Unfortunately, there does not appear to be a magic formula, however the following steps, not necessarily in this order, are part of more successful PMF implementations:

1. *Recognition*—that unstructured or inconsistently applied approaches to portfolio, programme and project management significantly undermine the effective achievement of strategic goals and objectives. To assist with this, questions were put to the executive and broader leadership teams at ACMI to help uncover current problems with unclear priorities, a lack of transparency in project selection, overstretched resources, ineffective stakeholder engagement and reduced success in delivering outcomes. This has helped to galvanise support for the widespread adoption and application of the PMF.
2. *Leadership*—that organisational leadership reaches agreement on the adoption of a PMF and provides full support for its implementation. This should come from the highest levels of the executive and requires strong and unwavering commitment. A staged approach may be used where the organisation gradually builds competence and trust in a new way of project selection, programming and delivery. At ACMI, the CEO and executive team participated in workshops to design the framework and how it would be implemented.

3. *Vision*—that a vision for PMF together with measurable benefits and objectives is communicated throughout the organisation. This could take the form of a roadmap to be developed over two or more years. At ACMI, the leadership group were asked to describe their ideas of what effective project management would look like. This was used to help shape the vision for effective project delivery.
4. *PMF Project*—that a PMF project and team with clear roles and responsibilities be created, funded and resourced to develop and implement the framework. Like a project that is unplanned, if left to grow organically, few benefits will be achieved. At ACMI, a dedicated team was formed, with representation and champions across all business units.
5. *Train and Coach*—managers and staff at all levels are given training and coaching in their PMF roles and responsibilities to support the required changes and to build confidence in the framework to achieve the greatest possible benefits. The CEO and executive at ACMI joined with the broader leadership team to participate in the training to support the rollout of the framework and address questions about its implementation.
6. *Prototype and refine*—that portfolio, programme and project management processes, tools and templates be prototyped, piloted and progressively refined to meet the many and varied needs of the organisation. At ACMI, pilot projects have been identified to enable staff at all levels to develop competence and confidence in the use of the PMF.
7. *Digitise and automate*—as the framework is developed, processes are digitised and automated to reduce administrative overhead and streamline effective decision-making. The ACMI information technology team have developed and implemented online tools and forms to support project delivery.
8. *Evaluate and review*—the implementation is evaluated and reviewed regularly against proposed benefits to identify further opportunities for improvement. ACMI's PMF steering committee meets regularly to review the state of implementation progress, change management aspects and determine next steps. With a greater focus on benefits, projects become less about a *"mechanical"* production line process of delivery and more a creative process of continuous improvement and innovation.

Further Research

Of further consideration are the disbenefits. That is, the unintended or negative consequences and impact of projects on other organisations, stakeholders and the environment. For example, the development of plastics as a packaging material and for containing liquids has significantly reduced the cost and ease of packaging—a significant benefit. However, one of the unintended impacts is that a large amount of plastic ends up in waterways and oceans, on beaches and in the creatures that inhabit those environments. Unfortunately, few organisations look at the end-of-life disposal and recycling of their products. Further research could include the activities required during the project life cycle to deal effectively with whole-of-life disbenefits by including an end-of-life phase into the project life cycle. A sustainable or circular economy framework could be established that allows organisations and their projects to be certified to a given level of compliance. In this way, organisations may not only be rewarded for the benefits achieved from their projects, but also incentivised to consider the full life cycle of their outputs such that whole-of-life disbenefits are minimised.

CONCLUSION

Extant the literature tells us that leaders habitually underestimate the challenges of implementing strategy. Poor communication, lack of discipline and regular reviews in implementation are significant factors in why strategy fails during implementation. Evidence suggests that a structured approach to project management will significantly enhance organisational ability to successfully implement strategy. This chapter has discussed how six processes can be most effective in enabling effective strategy implementation and change management. Adapting the model presented by (Zubac et al., 2021: 487), the revised diagram with the six enabling processes for strategy implementation and change management is shown in Figure 15.17. These distinct processes represent the dynamic capabilities that must be developed, utilised and refined by the organisation to allow the implementation of its strategies in an aligned manner while being receptive to change, as necessary, when opportunities arise and the risk profile of the organisation suggest as much.

Consultative development of the strategic purpose improves strategic alignment and engagement at all levels of the organisation. *Strategic*

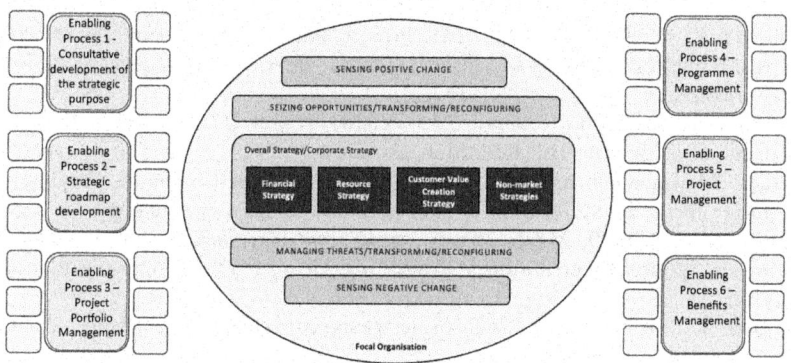

Fig. 15.17 Enabling Processes for Strategic Outcomes and Change Management (*Source* Adapted from the Model presented by Zubac et al., 2021: 487)

roadmap development engages cross-functional leaders in consensus building activities and provides staff at all levels with clear communication of the organisational vision. *Portfolio Management* improves transparency in organisational decision-making, improves goal clarity and provides a clear understanding of organisational priorities and dependencies. *Programme management* improves resource forecasting and allocation for both operational and project work, thereby increasing the ability to respond more rapidly and effectively to changing strategic priorities. Structured *project management* enables staff to more easily develop self-confidence in their project delivery skills, while supporting collaboration and early sizing and stakeholder impact assessment. *Benefits management* enables the early and effective planning for the realisation and sustainment of benefits during and beyond the project life cycle. Finally, eight steps were suggested for the effective implementation of a PMF in organisations.

References

Alexander, M. (2019, April). "What is project portfolio management? Aligning projects to business goals," in CIO Australia, https://www.cio.com/art icle/3388686/what-is-project-portfolio-management-aligning-projects-to-business-goals.html

Chih, Y.-Y., & Zwikael, O. (2015). Project benefit management: A conceptual framework of target benefit formulation. *International Journal of Project Management, 33*(2015), 352–362.

Pearson, N., Larson, E., & Gray, C. F. (2020). *Project Management in Practice* (2nd ed.). McGraw-Hill Education (Australia).

Project Management Institute. (2020, May). Ahead of the curve: Forging a future focused culture. *Pulse of the Profession® 2020*, www.pmi.org

Speculand, R. (2020, May). *20-year results from surveying strategy implementation*, White Paper, Bridges Consulting Group, www.bridgesconsultancy.com

Strasser, J. (2021, May). www.theprojectgroup.com/blog/en/challenges-of-tactical-resource-planning/

Zubac, A., Dasborough, M., Hughes,K., Jiang, Z., Kirkpatrick, S., Martinsons, M., Tucker, D., & Zwikael, O. (2021). The strategy and change interface: understanding "enabling" processes and cognitions. In *Management Decision, 59*(3), Emerald Insight at https://www.emerald.com/insight/publication/issn/0025-1747/vol/59/iss/3

Zwikael, O., & Smyrk, J. (2019). Project management—A benefit realisation approach. *Springer, Switzerland*,. https://doi.org/10.1007/978-3-030-03174-9

CHAPTER 16

Family Firms and Mergers and Acquisitions: The Importance of Transfer of Trust

Danielle Tucker and *Stella Lind*

INTRODUCTION

In this chapter, we examine family firms, why they merge with each other and why trust during family firm merger is especially important. Organisational strategy in family firms is embedded in the identity and values of the family ownership, and organisational change presents key challenges, heightened by emotional and personal dependence between owners and employees. Here, we focus on these interpersonal relationships based on social exchange expectations (Young-Ybarra & Wiersema, 1999). Specifically, we draw from theory on psychological safety (Vandekerkhof, et al., 2018) and psychological contracts (Rousseau, 1995) to

---

D. Tucker
University of Essex, Colchester, UK
e-mail: dtucker@essex.ac.uk

S. Lind (✉)
KPMG AG Wirtschaftsprüfungsgesellschaft, The Squaire, Frankfurt, Germany
e-mail: stellalind@kpmg.com

© The Author(s), under exclusive license to Springer Nature Singapore Pte Ltd. 2022
A. Zubac et al. (eds.), *Effective Implementation of Transformation Strategies*, https://doi.org/10.1007/978-981-19-2336-4_16

understand how the dynamics of these relationships shape family firm mergers and acquisitions (M&As).

Most organisations labelled family firms are what are known as **owner-managed** family firms, where a specific owner (family) acts as a figurehead(s), is actively involved in the business and is well-known by the workforce. Family firms are traditionally perceived as stable, long-lasting and characterised with a **long-term-orientation** and **responsibility** towards their employees (Lee, 2006). It is argued that family firms embody **high trust environments** (Gomez-Mejia, 2011).

However, these firms also face challenges which are intensified by their family ties; for example, struggling to find the right successor. Reasons for this are varied, including not having enough offspring, talent assessment issues or family rivalry has led to conflict. Mergers between family businesses or an acquisition of another family business create another layer of uncertainty for the employees in the business.

If they do not find a successor in their own family, they may seek acquisition from another organisation to maintain their business (Ahlers et al., 2017). In this chapter, we argue that the perceived complexity and associated uncertainty for employees can be reduced by placing trust at the centre of family firm M&As.

Our examination of the M&A processes in family firms through a trust perspective has led to the development of a framework. The framework focuses on the experience of employees to understand how to effectively manage the trust transfer from the old to new family firm and make the integration a success. It provides family firms with recommendations for successful management of the family firm acquisition process.

MERGERS AND ACQUISITIONS IN FAMILY FIRMS

Family firms are a multifaceted and heterogeneous group of organisations. Nevertheless, one can derive some common elements. The family firm business model is usually viewed positively across the world due to the importance of non-financial goals for family firms (known as **socioemotional wealth**) that produces an incentive for them to demonstrate trustworthy behaviour (Hauswald, 2013).

Family firms have a strong collective identity (Sundaramurthy, 2008) and family values (Chirico & Salvato, 2008; Chirico et al., 2011; Siebke, 2015) that serve as guiding principles to define acceptable norms of behaviour and relationships among family members. These family values derive from family members' similar upbringing (Carlock & Ward, 2010); therefore, there is strong consistency in the way that owner family members typically make decisions, and behave (Siebke, 2015).

Family firms are often depicted as commitment-intensive organisations (Chirico el al., 2011) because of the family members' devotion and emotional attachment to the enterprise (Gómez-Mejía et al., 2007). So, for family firm owners, the family firm is an embodiment of the family's pride and identity that should ideally be maintained for the next generation (Zellweger et al., 2010). Therefore, family firms tend to be less driven by immediate financial results and can be prepared to sacrifice short-term gains for the achievement of longer-term goals, and create trust through their commitment to keeping business viable for future generations (Carlock & Ward, 2010; Graves & Thomas, 2008). Family firms tend to show emotional commitment to the firm's survival (Chirico & Salvato, 2008; Chirico et al., 2011), especially those still located in the town or region where they were founded; they are also unlikely to risk what they have built over generations by becoming overstretched or diversifying from their roots (Kenyon-Rouvinez, 2001). Family firms tend to avoid change and are more risk averse (De Vries & Carlock, 2010). Change needs to be actively managed in family firms but is usually driven by one family member director (De Vries et Carlock, 2010). One reason for their high willingness to trust is that family firms are regarded as responsible, long-term oriented employers (Lee, 2006). This is also the reason why family firm employees are less likely to leave the organisation.

When they cannot find the right successor or when the firm's traditional sector faces structural change or disruption (Kachaner et al., 2012), family firm owners may consider an acquisition in order to ensure the firm's long-term survival and protect its socioemotional wealth (Gomez-Meija et al., 2007). A stewardship-based exit strategy (Hernandez, 2012) is a strategy developed out of an "ongoing sense of obligation or duty to others" (p. 174), and generally provides for business continuity and care of the firm, and the employees (DeTienne & Chirico, 2013). This may involve family firm owners making personal financial sacrifices in order to further the long-term vision and to protect the long-term welfare of other stakeholders (Miller et al., 2008). If family firm owners have to choose a partner for a merger, financial aspects are less important than the values and trust in the new owner. Family firm owners prefer to sell to somebody unlikely to intervene in the corporate processes and culture of the firm they developed (Gómez-Mejía et al., 2007), which may be another family firm with similar values.

One example case that we followed in our research was a German family firm that bought its direct competitor, an Italian family firm. The Italian owner had to sell the company as no blood relative was willing to take the firm into its sixth generation. The old owner described the process of finding an acquisition partner. *"We had rejected many offers until we have found the right one. We were very picky"*. The main reason he chose the German acquiring case company is that they also belonged to a catholic family with similar values: *"We just trusted this family firm to have the right value set. I immediately knew that our people are in safe hands here"*.

Regardless of value matching, selling the firm to another owner is a "leap of faith" for family firm owners. A merger or acquisition is a dynamic process of change involving the organisation and its employees in various phases. Therefore, the old, as well as the new, owner is crucial in steering the merger process. A lengthy process of structural integration of the participating organisations puts organisational trust to the test.

Organisational Trust and Family Firms

Since establishing that organisational trust is important in family firms M&As, trust scholars have identified that two key dimensions are common in most definitions of trust: (i) **positive expectations of another party** and (ii) **a willingness to be vulnerable** (Dietz & Den Hartog, 2006). Positive expectations generally refer to perceptions or beliefs about the trustees' intention. If the trustor is willing to trust, they become vulnerable to the trustee who may abuse the trust placed in them. Therefore, trust is associated with insecurity, risk and a low level of **control** (Nienaber et al., 2015).

Organisational trust refers to the trusting assessment of organisational members towards the organisation as a whole (Bhide & Stevenson, 1992; Dulac et al., 2008). Throughout our research we see that trust is a mosaic of different levels and dimensions of trust, including the organisation as an entity and also that trusting a new organisation is a complex process where a lot of shifts and transfers of power and position are going on. Considering the specific constellation in family firms, organisational trust in the leadership/the owner and organisational trust in the whole organisation can overlap—the family owners represent the organisation, their values are the organisation's values, and trust in them is trust in the organisation.

Organisational trust is described as one of the secrets of highly successful businesses (Stahl & Sitkin, 2005). Employees' trust in the organisation can be especially valuable in family firms as a component of the socioemotional wealth typical of family firms (Gomez-Mejia et al., 2011). Since strong family bonds are based on trust, it is not surprising that family firms are perceived as having more trustworthy policies and practices compared to their non-family counterparts. This could be demonstrated by research conducted among consumers which shows that they associate trust with family firms when compared to non-family firms (Orth & Green, 2009). However, a reliance on trust in family firms, can also lead to weak decision-making due to blind faith or laxity should trust be abused.

Family firms tend to behave consistently according to a set of principles, including honesty, fair treatment and promise fulfilment (Azizi et al., 2017). Therefore, employees in family firms often display a high degree of trust in their organisation and its leadership. In our research, we learned that, even in times when their relationship with the firm is challenged, employees in family firms feel less vulnerable because they perceive the risk to be low and their jobs safer. Family firm employees have more positive expectations about their employer (e.g. Carlock & Ward, 2010). Therefore, for family firms, how a transfer of ownership is handled will have consequences for the transfer of employee trust to new owners and the merged organisation.

Drawing on the general M&A literature, we find that in times of change, there is a high level of vulnerability and uncertainty (Nienaber et al., 2015). Especially in the context of M&A, the perspective of **vulnerability** and **uncertainty** is of particular importance as perceived vulnerability is the result of loss of control experienced when things change. Perceived control rests upon complex and ambiguous situational factors. During significant periods of organisational change, employees often find it difficult to determine whether they can expect the organisation to act with integrity, competence and benevolence in a new reality. This seems to be especially true for M&A processes that are characterised by organisational identity ambiguity. Scholars argue that organisational trust is likely to be weaker after a merger than it was before (Stahl & Sitkin, 2005). Some M&A literature argues that trust can be permanently breached in this context (e.g. cf. Shleifer & Summers, 1988). An event such as the announcement of an acquisition can cause circumstances that long-term employees relied upon to suddenly change, e.g., their contract or their career expectations (Stahl & Sitkin, 2010) and this may cause them to lose trust in the organisation.

Is this the same in family firms? For family firms, the significant change of M&A appears contrary to their usual risk averse nature. They are not used to transformational change and the uncertainty of this process may feel foreign and especially uncertain. In the case where a family firm is acquiring another family firm, the issue of trust is especially a concern for the smaller merger partner (the firm which is being acquired—being most vulnerable in the transaction), although the degree of trust involved in the M&A process may be important to both sides in the transaction. The company being acquired must place trust in a new owner family but, also, the acquiring firm employees must adjust their relationship—switching from rivalry to partnership.

Trust takes years to build, seconds to break and forever to repair. "The greater the uncertainty and vulnerability, the more trust is needed and the harder it is to retain or develop" (Sørensen et al., 2011: 406). For family firms embarking on M&A, it is important that trust is not broken beyond repair.

Identifying the warning signs of loss of trust may be more difficult for family firms. Organisational change literature, primarily based on non-family firm transitions, identifies the most common indicator of a loss of trust as a high rate of turnover. However, due to the typical long tenure rate in family firms, it is more likely that the employees use alternative strategies for dealing with their loss of trust: They may become less committed or less engaged, for example.

In summary, the process of trust during Family Firm (FF) M&A is different from "non-family" firms as it takes place in a heightened emotional and ambiguous trust environment. We argue that employees in family firms find it easier to accept a situation of vulnerability in times of uncertainty, if they trust the leadership and/or the owner, yet their experience of uncertainty may be heightened because they are not sure if the current leadership structure will be maintained and their role within the business will remain largely the same—the stakes are high.

FRAMEWORK

Based on our research studying seven family firms involved in family firm M&A processes, we developed a framework for understanding organisational trust processes during family firm M&As. The framework provides family firm practitioners with recommendations for successfully managing the acquisition process of another family firm by presenting three different stages of trust development—questioning trust, observing trust and regaining trust. It shows how trust can be transferred from one family firm to another (see Fig. 16.1).

At the first stage, an event such as the M&A announcement will heighten the vulnerability of family firm employees and there is a potential for a loss of trust (Steinmeier & Jöns, 2011; Stahl & Sitkin, 2010) when long-term employees realise that the firm which they have developed a trust relationship with may suddenly change (Stahl & Sitkin, 2010). **Questioning trust** is the first stage. Here, it is important to note the difference between a (potentially temporary) loss of trust and a (more irreversible) breach of trust (Robinson, 1996). We found that where existing trust in the family firm was high, the announcement of a

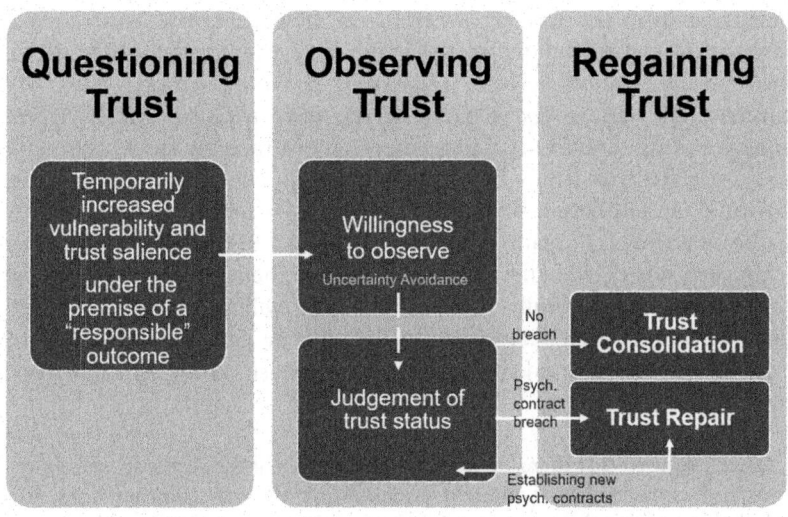

Fig. 16.1 A framework for family firm M&A trust transfer processes (*Source* Author's own creation)

family firm merger can cause a loss of trust, but this does not necessarily lead to a trust breach under the premise of a **"responsible" outcome**. A responsible outcome means that basic conditions such as job security are not perceived to be damaged. A trust breach can be understood in reference to the psychological contract (Rousseau, 1995): The level of uncertainty and the vulnerability experienced by organisational members during change leads to a processing of trust-relevant information by the employees. This, in turn, leads to an increased salience of the trust relationship, as trust becomes more relevant for the employees in this situation. Based on this information processing, organisational members reassess their trust in management and in the organisation (Bordia et al., 2004; Lines et al., 2005). If this assessment comes to the conclusion that the negative expectations of the employees are, indeed, realised and the employees feel harmed, organisational trust can no longer be considered justified. As a result, it may be withdrawn. Some researchers argue that this is particularly the case when the psychological contract between employees and the organisation is not fulfilled.

The next stage we refer to as the **stage of observing trust**. If the employees do not detect an initial trust breach, their reaction shows that there is a **willingness to observe** whether they can potentially transfer their trust from the former owner to the new company. This stage of observation may be unique to the family firm M&A process because of the high assimilation between ownership and organisational trust. We consider this stage to be a pause in the trust transfer process, where employees take time to make judgements about the new family firm. Our study revealed that family firm employees enjoy working in a high trust environment and have a strong desire to transfer their high level of trust to the new owner/organisation. They want to believe that the former owner will not decide anything that is not in their interest. During this observation period, family firm members are willing to tolerate uncertainty for a time. One employee explains that he gave the new company a chance after he realised that both family firms stand for the same good values:

> Since I realised that there are no major differences in the corporate cultures of both organisations, I thought I should give the new company a try. I quietly observed the new owner's behaviour in the first 100 days.

This observation may be very intense and will focus on evaluating whether the behaviour of the new owners is representative of the values upon which their previous trust was based. In family firms, these values relate to job security and caring about the employees' well-being.

This increased salience of the trust relationship (all trust information becomes particularly noticeable or important) and based on this information processing, organisational members reassess their trust in management and in the organisation. They especially observe fairness and information and communication processes.

Uncertainty is an unpleasant state which, eventually, needs to be resolved (cf. Baker & Carson, 2011). Therefore, after some time, employees need to decide on the outcome of their **judgement of the trust status**. This is in line with research from Bordia et al. (2004) and Lines et al. (2005), who say that the level of uncertainty leads to a processing of trust-relevant information.

The third stage we refer to as the **regaining trust** stage. Depending on the outcome of the observation, it comes to a breach of the psychological contract or not. This means that trust may need to be repaired or consolidated. We distinguish between **trust repair** and **trust consolidation** in the aftermath of family firm M&As because it makes a difference to the amount of effort needed:

If there is a positive outcome of the judgement of the trust status, there is no breach of the psychological contract. After the period of observation, the focus is on consolidating trust. This is achieved by continuing with the actions undertaken in the observation period—while the scrutiny will be less, it is important that the organisation remains consistent with the values demonstrated during this period. In this case, employees are not so sceptical; they can focus on new ventures and the future. The psychological contracts are still valid.

A perceived breach of the psychological contract can be the result of an unfavourable judgement of the trust status. This means that there are more advanced trust repair strategies necessary. The organisation will need to take action in order to repair trust. In one of our case studies, the owner of another firm overpromised the acquisition's success. In reality, it emerged that the transaction put the merged firm into a challenging financial situation. Withholding important information and not addressing negative news was considered a breach of trust by employees. The owner explained that after this mistake, it took a very long time until he regained his employees' trust.

After a difficult start, it was hard to win back trust. It took a lot of effort and patience. I wish I had been aware about the pitfalls earlier. This would have saved us a lot of time and trouble.

The feedback loop from trust repair to judgement of trust status shows that it requires more actions but could help in establishing new psychological contracts. This means, that there is an ongoing process. A psychological contract breach is not permanent and irreparable but with effort a regaining of trust is possible.

We argue that this model can be applied to all M&As but with family firms, the trust consolidation and repair process will involve very specific family-related issues. In the next section, we will explore key influencing factors specific to family firms on each stage of the trust process.

Factors which Influence Trust

In this section, we look more deeply at the influencing factors on organisational trust in the integration process of family firms that are indicated in our framework. These factors are also shown in Table 16.1. As discussed, the level of trust can vary, depending on the organisation's actions as trust develops in a process.

Influencing Factors of Questioning Trust

After the M&A announcement, employees' vulnerability is heightened. Redundancies in the midst of M&A are common, but much less so in the case of long-term oriented family firms. **Job security** is an important condition for trust. The typically high level of trust in family firms (e.g. De Vries & Carlock, 2010) acts as a barrier to speculation that job losses may occur when organisations merge. The premise is that the firm would not agree to an acquisition which would be likely to result in a negative outcome for the employees because the family firm owner takes their responsibility for employees seriously and would not jeopardise that.

Even when admitting that they were disappointed by this decision, one interviewed employee still believed that the former owner did also care about their well-being, e.g. a responsible outcome:

> Knowing the former owner for such a long time, I knew that he made sure that we all do not end up on the street, but that he sold to someone who has good intentions to keep all jobs and to even further develop this

Table 16.1 Examples of specific actions for trust at family firms during the M&A/integration process

Influencing factor	Questioning Trust	Observing Trust	Trust Consolidation More intense actions	Trust Repair
Communication	Justification of the M&A decision, also from the old owner Sensemaking of joint firm's business case Communicating the firm's values	Trust-sensitive communication should especially focus on fairness in the integration, small gestures and signals can make a difference in the process Deliberate vision for the joint family firms	Constant trust-sensitive communication of trustworthiness	Communication that focuses on the company's values, the justification of the M&A decision, and the sensemaking of joint firm's business case
Organisational Support	Offering organisational support	Role models for change that live the company's values	Active and ongoing support from role models for change, e.g., through specific support programmes	

(continued)

company. I fully understood his justification of the business case. At the end, he did not have any other choice - he ran out of ideas how to further develop this business and the younger generation did not want to take over.

Communication is an important influencing factor of organisational trust that plays a crucial role in all of the different stages of the integration process. During the announcement of the M&A decision, communication of the former owner's **justification of the M&A decision** will be the focus of the employees' interest. Explaining to the employees, the rationale of the acquisition and emphasising the choice of acquiring a family firm with similar values when announcing the acquisition, can soothe employee's anxiety about the uncertainty of change. In our study, one former owner describes how he and his father made a very personal

Table 16.1 (continued)

Influencing factor	Questioning Trust	Observing Trust	Trust Consolidation More intense actions	Trust Repair
Employee Involvement	-	-	Employees have active roles in the project teams to design the new joint organisation	Trustful/positive encounters with their new colleagues, e.g., in project teams that are led by role models that function as multipliers
Leadership	Showing integrity between former and new owner	Develop a sense of identification with the new owner, who actively lives the company's values	Active demonstration of trustworthiness by the new owner	Strongly demonstrating the company's vision by the new owner and showing personal drive during integration and actively focusing on the sceptics

and emotional speech. He admitted to his employees that he did not feel capable of fighting competitors without a strong investor in the background but reassured them of his certainty that he had found the right partner with this family firm and its owner. Communication which acknowledges the collective identity that is typical for family firms will be particularly effective (Sundaramurthy, 2008). One employee shared how he felt relieved after the announcement of who the buyer was:

> Already in the first communication, the similarities between both companies were highlighted. Also, I appreciated that the owner family presented themselves as an honourable, traditional, as well as very successful company.

In contrast, in one firm in our study, the former owner did not explain his reasons for the sale but left immediately. One employee explains how this lack of communication impacted the opportunity to build a trusting relationship with the new owner:

> We still feel abandoned by the former owner. Directly after the announcement, he already took off. It was hard to have a relaxed relationship with the new owner afterwards.

In summary, explaining to employees the logic behind the acquisition very carefully and emphasising the advantages of being acquired by a respectable family firm when announcing the acquisition can prevent a loss of trust.

Influencing Factors of Observing Trust
In the observing trust period, employees observe the new organisation to decide whether they can transfer their trust from the former owner to the new company.

Communication remains important at this stage also. However, in contrast to the questioning phase, scrutiny is on communication from the new owner family. Demonstrating trustworthiness can start with small gestures. For instance, in the aforementioned German/Italian acquisition, the new owner made a public announcement, where he emphasised the values, he and his family represent in their long firm history. He also emphasised his competence and the success of the German firm. There were behavioural similarities between the former and the new owner—they both spoke openly and candidly with their employees:

> They were not sweet-talking. They just said how it is and that we need to cut costs. I respect them for their open and honest communication of even bad news.

It was important for the new organisation to communicate and demonstrate **fairness** in the critical observation period. The concept of organisational fairness describes how an employee judges the behaviour of the organisation based on the decisions, processes and actions of other employees and leaders (Greenberg, 1986). The support for fairness as a pre-condition for trust is strong (Steinmeier & Jöns, 2011).

Fairness may also be judged in terms of the consistency between one's words and one's actions. In one of our case studies, the new owner promised employees compensation for the extra hours they worked for the integration project but failed to implement this before employees complained. The owner explained that this was a mistake and he simply forgot but acknowledges that he failed to earn the employees' trust in this early stage, and it took a very long time until he regained them.

> Forgetting to compensate the extra work as a gesture of recognition led to a loss of trust. Especially at the start of our new relationship, paying attention to details is crucial. This was then regarded as very unfair.

Also, at this stage, it is critical to ensure that workforce members are given time to develop trust in one another and that they are supported in doing so. Giving the employees the right **organisational support** during the integration process—specifically emotional support—was very important to the employees to feel they are cared for, therefore, demonstrating benevolence (a key aspect of trustworthiness). Moreover, the HR director claimed that organisational trust after an acquisition comes with management presence only:

> Being present, holding their hands and being there for all kinds of questions is especially important at the beginning of the integration process. From my experience, this helps to avoid subsequent problems.

Having key figures in the organisation acting as **role models for change** provides direction and leadership during the integration process. We found that some of the best role models are the owners themselves that directly encounter the new employees. The advantage of this is that it allows owners to be observed. It can be tempting for owners to hold back from engaging with employees for fear of making a mistake or their actions being misinterpreted but, in fact, their visibility and involvement is important. One owner, who bought another family firm, describes his manifold role during the difficult times of the integration as follows:

> My role was to be the motivator and to lead the way. I knew that I was constantly the centre of everybody's attention.

Our research also shows that employees very closely observe the representatives of the new family firm. They are trying to consider whether to develop a sense of identification with the new owner (Cheney & Tompkins, 1987).

Influencing Factors of Regaining Trust

Regaining trust is, of course, not easy and is a slow process. In family firm M&As, as a result of the observation period described above, a need to regain trust will follow an unsuccessful start to the integration process and there may be a need to undo interpretation by employees as well as demonstrating future trustworthiness—the starting point is not a "blank slate". Our research identified the following factors which will help to regain trust and to (re-)establish psychological contracts with the newly merged family firm (see also Table 16.1).

In the trust repair and trust consolidation state, things are not done completely different, but things are done in a different intensity. Repairing trust after a psychological contract breach requires more actions. Concretely, this means that more time and effort to establish new psychological contracts is needed.

Involving employees in the integration helps employees to regain trust in the organisation. An effective way to counteract the negative effects of M&As on employees is by involving them in the process of actively shaping the new company. Employees describe that actively working on integration projects can be motivating for those involved—turning those who are affected into active participants. Being able to shape the change process means that employees are more likely to feel in control of the process and invest in it. Long-serving employees often generate a sense of ownership and want to be involved in important company decisions. Consequently, it is important to consider their experience and concerns when building project teams to design the new joint organisation. By actively working together, the "they" of the companies can quickly turn into "we". One of the employees described that once the employees regained their trust in the new owner and that trust was consolidated, it also diffused into trust in the organisation more generally after a while:

> After a difficult start in the new company for us folks of the old company, I was assigned to a project during which I was able to work closely with the new owner. I was very critical and observed his behaviour with great alertness. But he was really engaged in supporting everybody. In fact, he was actually a good role model to work with and showed me great care. During this project, I started to trust him and finally started to think that this whole acquisition was not too bad at the end.

New owners and significant other senior managers are representatives of the new firm. This means that regaining trust centres on the trustworthiness of key individuals. Our research cases illustrate that especially **the actions and behaviours of the owner as leader** were essential for trust-rebuilding processes. The owner family often acts as a role model in family firms (Siebke, 2015), for example, if the owner has a strong vision and personal drive during integration, as in the above example. Our research showed that when employees trust the new owner, there is potential to start to trust the newly merged firm. This means that the owner is the one who really helps to regain trust. We argue that, in the context of family firms, it is the owner who matters most as he/she stands as a symbol for the whole organisation. One can see that there is an overlap between the family firm owner(s) and the whole organisation as the owner stands for his company.

Thanks to **trustful/positive encounters with their new colleagues**, the employees of the acquired company get to know the acquiring company and feel welcomed. For example, a joint summer party in one organisation was described as a turning point in trust relationships. Getting to know the other side allowed employees to resolve their uncertainties.

This means that for regaining trust, it is critical to ensure that new workforces are given enough time to regain trust by trustful/positive encounters with new colleagues, through role models and, especially, the owner as role model and by involving groups from the combining entities into integration projects. This helps them to establish a trustful relationship with the new owner.

RECOMMENDATIONS AND CONCLUSIONS

Many family firms tend to underestimate the issue of trust when acquiring firms; we argue that trust needs to be systematically managed during the integration process. Family firms have both unique opportunities and specific challenges in ensuring the transfer of trust from one organisation to another. Our framework places organisational trust at the centre of the M&A process and provides useful lessons for firms interested in sustaining trust during organisational change. It particularly builds on the inherent strengths of the high trust environment of family firms. Here are some more concrete ideas and practical takeaways for a smooth trust transfer:

- **Similar values matter.** Seeking an acquiring/merging partner that shares similar values is a way to create an opportunity to maintain or restore employees' trust in the organisation. Moreover, communicating this value congruence to employees is an essential part of the process to make the integration process as smooth as possible.
- **Capitalise on the owner-owner relationship.** A good owner-owner relationship can help to better transfer the trust to the newly integrated firm's owner. If the former owner is considered a credible role model for employees, it can be helpful to actively involve them in all communication matters. They can help to reassure employees that their views have been taken with the best of intentions.
- **Know that actions and behaviours are being closely observed.** The integration process is very delicate as the new family firm owner is under intense observation during this time. Each interaction will be reviewed against adherence with the psychological contract. The openness of all parties involved becomes a matter of importance. In particular, the behaviour of the new integrated firm's owner and their management team will never be observed as carefully as at the beginning of the integration process. This means trust-sensitive communication is essential. Employees particularly pay attention to fairness, and small gestures and signals can make a difference.

For family firms, trust transfer from the old to the new owner is, indeed, possible. The new organisation needs to actively demonstrate their trustworthiness. Where action is needed to regain trust, our empirical findings offer a starting point for organisations and a direction for future research.

REFERENCES

Ahlers, O., Hack, A., Madison, K., Wright, M., & Kellermanns, F. W. (2017). Is it all about money? Affective commitment and the difference between family and non-family sellers in buyouts. *British Journal of Management, 28*(2), 159–179.

Azizi, M., Bidgoli, M. S., & Bidgoli, A. S. (2017). Trust in family businesses: A more comprehensive empirical review. *Cogent Business & Management, 4*(1), 1–17.

Baker, D. S., & Carson, K. D. (2011). The two faces of uncertainty avoidance: Attachment and adaptation. *Journal of Behavioral and Applied Management, 12*(2), 128.

Bhide, A., & Stevenson, H. (1992). Trust, uncertainty, and profit. *The Journal of Socio-Economics, 21*(3), 191–208.

Bordia, P., Hunt, E., Paulsen, N., Tourish, D., & DiFonzo, N. (2004). Uncertainty during organizational change: Is it all about control? *European Journal of Work and Organizational Psychology, 13*(3), 345–365.

Carlock, R. S., & Ward, J. L. (2010). Making the parallel family and business planning process work. In *When Family Businesses Are Best* (pp. 28–49). Palgrave Macmillan.

Cheney, G., & Tompkins, P. K. (1987). Coming to terms with organizational identification and commitment. *Communication Studies, 38*(1), 1–15.

Chirico, F., & Salvato, C. (2008). Knowledge integration and dynamic organizational adaptation in family firms. *Family Business Review, 21*(2), 169–181.

Chirico, F., Sirmon, D. G., Sciascia, S., & Mazzola, P. (2011). Resource orchestration in family firms: Investigating how entrepreneurial orientation, generational involvement, and participative strategy affect performance. *Strategic Entrepreneurship Journal, 5*(4), 307–326.

DeTienne, D. R., & Chirico, F. (2013). Exit strategies in family firms: How socioemotional wealth drives the threshold of performance. *Entrepreneurship Theory and Practice, 37*(6), 1297–1318.

De Vries, M. F. K., & Carlock, R. S. (2010). *Family business on the couch: A psychological perspective*. John Wiley & Sons.

Dietz, G., & Den Hartog, D. N. (2006). Measuring trust inside organisations. *Personnel Review, 35*(5), 557–588.

Dulac, T., Coyle-Shapiro, J. A., Henderson, D. J., & Wayne, S. J. (2008). Not all responses to breach are the same: The interconnection of social exchange and psychological contract processes in organizations. *Academy of Management Journal, 51*(6), 1079–1098.

Gomez-Mejia, L. R., Cruz, C., Berrone, P., & De Castro, J. (2011). The bind that ties: socioemotional wealth preservation in family firms. *Academy of Management Annals, 5*(1), 653–707.

Gómez-Mejía, L. R., Haynes, K. T., Núñez-Nickel, M., Jacobson, K. J., & Moyano-Fuentes, J. (2007). Socioemotional wealth and business risks in family-controlled firms: Evidence from Spanish olive oil mills. *Administrative Science Quarterly, 52*(1), 106–137.

Graves, C., & Thomas, J. (2008). Determinants of the internationalization pathways of family firms: An examination of family influence. *Family Business Review, 21*(2), 151–167.

Greenberg, J. (1986). Determinants of perceived fairness of performance evaluations. *Journal of Applied Psychology, 71*(2), 340.

Hauswald, H. (2013). *Stakeholder trust in family businesses*. Springer Science & Business Media.
Hernandez, M. (2012). Toward an understanding of the psychology of stewardship. *Academy of Management Review, 37*(2), 172–193.
Kachaner, N., Stalk, G., & Bloch, A. (2012). What you can learn from family business. *Harvard Business Review, 90*(11), 102–106.
Kenyon-Rouvinez, D. (2001). Patterns in serial business families: Theory building through global case study research. *Family Business Review, 14*(3), 175–191.
Lee, J. (2006). Family firm performance: Further evidence. *Family Business Review, 19*(2), 103–114.
Lines, R., Selart, M., Espedal, B., & Johansen, S. T. (2005). The production of trust during organizational change. *Journal of Change Management, 5*(2), 221–245.
Miller, Breton-Miller, L., & Scholnick, B. (2008). Stewardship vs. stagnation: An empirical comparison of small family and non-family businesses. *Journal of Management Studies, 45*(1), 51–78.
Nienaber, A.-M., Hofeditz, M., & Romeike, P. D. (2015). Vulnerability and trust in leader-follower relationships. *Personnel Review, 44*(4), 567–591.
Orth, U. R., & Green, M. T. (2009). Consumer loyalty to family versus non-family business: The roles of store image, trust and satisfaction. *Journal of Retailing and Consumer Services, 16*(4), 248–259.
Robinson, S. L. (1996). Trust and breach of the psychological contract. *Administrative Science Quarterly*, 574–599.
Rousseau, D. M. (1995). *Psychological contracts in organizations: Understanding written and unwritten agreements*. SAGE Publications.
Siebke, V. (2015). Family values at the heart of the family firm (Dissertation), WHU – Otto Beisheim School of Management Vallendar.
Shleifer, A., & Summers, L. H. (1988). Breach of trust in hostile takeovers. *Corporate takeovers: Causes and consequences* (pp. 33–68). University of Chicago Press.
Sørensen, O. H., Hasle, P., & Pejtersen, J. H. (2011). Trust relations in management of change. *Scandinavian Journal of Management, 27*(4), 405–417.
Stahl, G. K., & Sitkin, S. B. (2005). Trust in mergers and acquisitions. In G. K. Stahl, & M. Mendenhall (Eds.), *Mergers and acquisitions: Managing culture and human resources* (pp. 82–108). Stanford Business Press.
Stahl, G. K., & Sitkin, S. B. (2010). Trust dynamics in acquisitions: The role of relationship history, interfirm distance, and acquirer's integration approach. In *Advances in Mergers and Acquisitions*. Emerald Group Publishing Limited.
Steinmeier, S., & Jöns, I. (2011). Vertrauen im Fusionsprozess: Einflussfaktoren und Auswirkungen. *Wirtschaftspsychologie, 2*, 62–74.

Sundaramurthy, C. (2008). Sustaining trust within family businesses. *Family Business Review*, *21*(1), 89–102.

Vandekerkhof, P., Steijvers, T., Hendriks, W., & Voordeckers, W. (2018). Socioemotional wealth separation and decision-making quality in family firm TMTs: The moderating role of psychological safety. *Journal of Management Studies*, *55*(4), 648–676.

Young-Ybarra, C., & Wiersema, M. (1999). Strategic flexibility in information technology alliances: The influence of transaction cost economics and social exchange theory. *Organization Science*, *10*(4), 439–459.

Zellweger, T., Eddleston, K., & Kellermanns, F. W. (2010). Exploring the concept of familiness: Introducing family firm identity. *Journal of Family Business Strategy*, *1*(1), 54–63.

PART V

Non-Market Strategies

CHAPTER 17

Introduction: Non-market Strategies

Angelina Zubac, Danielle Tucker, Ofer Zwikael, Kate Hughes, and Shelley Kirkpatrick

It would be easy to assume that non-market strategies are only necessary for organisations operating primarily in the non-market environment. However, this would be wrong. All organisations are impacted by the non-market environment to some extent. The non-market and market environments are subject to continual institutional change too. Much of this change depends on individual stakeholders' objectives. These may be

A. Zubac (✉)
University of Queensland, Brisbane, QLD, Australia
e-mail: a.zubac@business.uq.edu.au; azubac@bigpond.net.au; az@strategylink.com.au

D. Tucker
University of Essex, Colchester, Essex, UK
e-mail: dtucker@essex.ac.uk

O. Zwikael
Australian National University, Canberra, ACT, Australia
e-mail: ofer.zwikael@anu.edu.au

K. Hughes
Technological University Dublin, Dublin, Ireland

© The Author(s), under exclusive license to Springer Nature Singapore Pte Ltd. 2022
A. Zubac et al. (eds.), *Effective Implementation of Transformation Strategies*, https://doi.org/10.1007/978-981-19-2336-4_17

of a personal nature or something that the stakeholder wants to achieve on behalf of an institution. Therefore, organisations with integrated non-market and market strategies are likely to be higher performing than those without integrated strategies. The two chapters in this section come to the same conclusion, albeit in very different ways. David Rosenbaum and Elizabeth More's study of the roll-out of the National Disability Insurance Scheme (NDIS) in Australia found organisations that more readily adapted to a demand-driven services model from a supply-driven services model tended to be more successful. Angelina Zubac, on the other hand, reviews the extant institutions and stakeholder literatures to demonstrate the importance of formulating and implementing aligned non-market and market strategies over time.

As depicted in Fig. 17.1, in line with the idea that the corporate strategy is an amalgam of its non-market strategies and three essential market strategies, both chapters explain how a carefully researched and considered non-market strategy can enable an organisation. As one can see by examining Fig. 17.1 and as the chapters explain, organisations need to develop non-market strategies that allow them to respond to a range of institutional pressures emanating from both the non-market and market institutional environments. This is because the market-based institutional environment influences the evolution of the non-market institutional environment, and the non-market institutional environment influences the evolution of the markets within the institutional environment. The non-market strategy must explicate which (sub)processes and cognitions can be used to develop integrated non-market and market strategies. Integrated non-market and market strategies allow the organisation to achieve specific cultural or ethical objectives and/or compete effectively. Ideally, these (sub)processes and cognitions are combined to build sensing, seizing and reconfiguring dynamic capabilities. Dynamic capabilities allow the organisation to better adapt to changes in the external environment as they arise.

---

e-mail: kate.hughes@hughes-scm.com

S. Kirkpatrick
The MITRE Corporation, McLean, VA, USA
e-mail: skirkpatrick@mitre.org

17 INTRODUCTION: NON-MARKET STRATEGIES 411

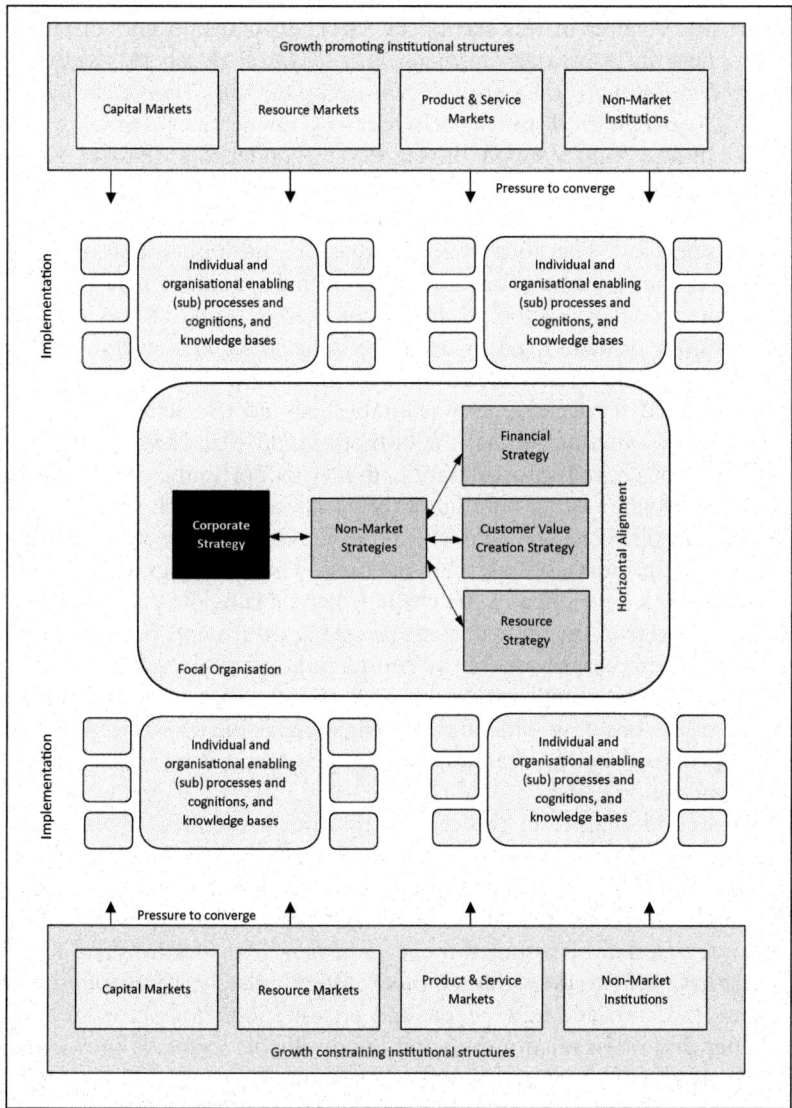

Fig. 17.1 Implementing strategy and organisational change: a non-market strategies focus

The first chapter in this section by David Rosenbaum and Elizabeth More, *Towards a Strategic Management Framework for the Nonprofit Sector: The Roll-out of Australia's National Disability Insurance Scheme (NDIS)*, is an empirical study which examines how service provider organisations moved from a supply-driven services model to a demand-driven services model. The chapter provides insight into the ways in which organisations use their people and resources to balance non-market and market priorities. The authors found that, in the input phase of their transformation, organisations tended to be more successful if a service leadership model was adopted and a commercial mindset was encouraged without dismantling the culture of trust built in the past. In the process phase, changes tended not to be resisted if the appropriateness of an intended service change was established and effectively communicated. In the outcome phase, the authors found that change could be consolidated across the organisation if new opportunities are pursued transparently while being mindful of their risks, and if employees believed they could still focus on their clients' well-being despite the organisation becoming more commercially oriented. These findings are reflected in a framework developed in the chapter that explains the processual and recursive aspects of the three phases for moving from a non-profit business model to a commercial model. By considering stakeholders' perspectives pre-, mid- and post-implementation, in particular, their concern that the essence of the business—uncompromising compassionate services—could be compromised by the changes, the change process is more likely to be a constructive process.

The second chapter in this section by Angelina Zubac, *When Everything Matters: Non-Market Strategies, Institutions and Stakeholders' Interests*, reviews the extant institutions and stakeholder literatures. The chapter demonstrates that non-market and market strategies cannot be easily integrated if it is assumed the management of institutions and stakeholders have little to do with each other. More precisely, it was found that institutions determine how people and organisations interact to develop exchange and other relationships and build valuable forms of knowledge. It was also found that stakeholders determine how institutions evolve over time. A recursive relationship exists between institutions and stakeholders that needs to be understood when developing and implementing a strategy. These ideas are illustrated and summarised in Fig. 17.2 which is an abridged version of a framework developed in the Zubac paper. As shown in the left side of Fig. 17.2 in 'A', the corporate strategy informs

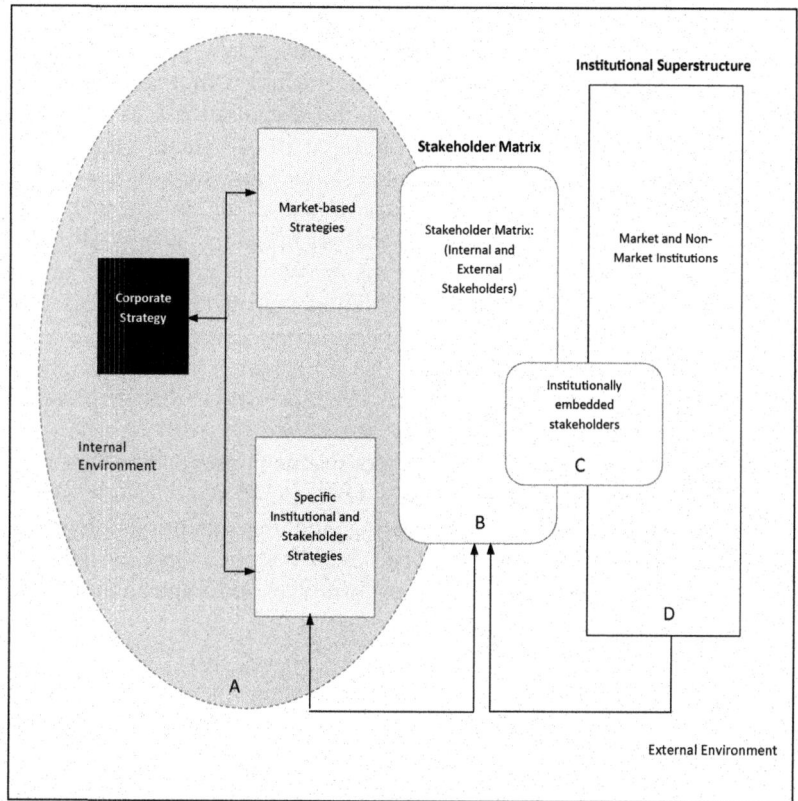

Fig. 17.2 Integrating market and non-market strategies

the development the organisation's non-market and market strategies. The non-market and market strategies developed at the organisation informs the development of the corporate strategy over time. If this is done well, that is, the various non-economic and economic strategies inform each other in an integrated manner, the institutional environment will have been addressed effectively, including the specific non-economic and economic institutions able to impact the organisation significantly.

The drivers for achieving such a successful outcome are clarified in Fig. 17.2 by the inclusion of 'B', 'C' and 'D'. Taken together, these parts of the diagram demonstrate the importance of considering the interests and needs of internal and external stakeholders at all stages of the strategy process. This is indicated by the inclusion of the stakeholder matrix, labelled 'B', which includes all the organisation's internal and external stakeholders. However, as indicated in 'C' some internal and external organisational stakeholders may have some sort of association with, be embedded within, or be socially defined by an external institution of (potential) importance to the organisation. This is allowing for the fact that some institutions may be organisations and markets are a form of institution. These stakeholders help to define the specific institutions within the institutional superstructure (society, the economy, etc.) that need to be addressed by the organisation through its non-market and market strategies, that is, via its various stakeholder-and institution-specific strategies.

The two chapters in this section complement each other in a way that most readers will find clarifying. One uses a real-life example to demonstrate the benefits of formulating and implementing integrated non-market and market strategies. The other develops a theoretical framework that can be used by managers to formulate and implement aligned non-market and market strategies.

CHAPTER 18

Towards a Strategic Change Management Framework for the Nonprofit Sector: The Roll-Out of Australia's National Disability Insurance Scheme (NDIS)

David Rosenbaum and Elizabeth More

INTRODUCTION

In this chapter, we consider the link between strategy and transformational change from the viewpoint of nonprofit organisations implementing the Australian National Disability Insurance Scheme ("NDIS"). There is a two-fold focus in this research. On the one hand, it has been suggested that change management in the nonprofit sector has historically

---

D. Rosenbaum (✉)
King's Own Institute, Sydney, NSW, Australia

E. More
Study Group, Sydney, NSW, Australia
e-mail: EMore@studygroup.com

© The Author(s), under exclusive license to Springer Nature Singapore Pte Ltd. 2022
A. Zubac et al. (eds.), *Effective Implementation of Transformation Strategies*, https://doi.org/10.1007/978-981-19-2336-4_18

had little research focus (Rosenbaum et al., 2017).[1] On the other hand,[2] the implementation of the NDIS represents a generational shift in the provision of services to people with a disability. The historic supply-driven model has changed to a demand-driven model where the Australian Government has recognised the substantial challenges for both the service user as well as the service provider (Andrews, 2018). These challenges are compounded by the strategic issues these organisations face, both from an implementation and a sustainability perspective, as both provider and client navigate their way through a complex set of application rules that, to this day, continue to evolve and morph as market realities become more apparent. As many in the sector have suggested, there is a visual image that has evolved throughout this period of ongoing implementation, of an aeroplane being assembled as it is taking off from the runway. There are both challenges as well as opportunities for service providers in this environment, and the strategic responses of those in the sector will potentially determine the degree of success or otherwise of the entire NDIS.

The correlation between strategy design and implementation, as well as the management of transformational change, becomes apparent as these nonprofit organisations deal with a myriad of challenges and do so in a confined environment where competitive market forces are at play. The NDIS is based on revenue generation from the provision of NDIS services, with the structure of the revenue being limited by government determined pricing constraints which leave these nonprofit organisations three choices to achieve long-term financial sustainability. These include incorporating in their business models the ability to source additional revenue from within the NDIS framework by expanding into other areas of service delivery which they may have felt were previously outside their core service skills in their earlier incarnations; develop revenue streams from the provision of other non-NDIS services such as those associated with social enterprise activities; and/or focusing on the efficiency with which NDIS-related services are delivered and, thereby, concentrating on overall cost reductions across their organisations, resulting in increased

---

[1] These 460,000 + participants require wide-ranging supports which are reflected by the levels of disability they each have.

[2] An NDIS Plan outlines the goals, aspirations and supports that an NDIS registered participant requires. It is a written document and is unique to each registered NDIS participant who has completed the assessment process.

gross margins at the service delivery-end of their activities. Many have accelerated fundraising and philanthropic activities.

The strategic implications for nonprofit service providers in dealing with both NDIS implementation and long-term sustainability of their organisations in this fast-moving and developing environment are many. These include devising appropriate marketing and business development processes and collateral that will be required to strengthen their ability to involve themselves in a highly competitive market, which is now characterised by the "opening" of the disability services support market to commercial service providers, as well as the competition that is now evident between nonprofit service providers. Additionally, moving from historical block funding of service provision to unit funding, challenges the financial management skills of the sector, necessitating upskilling as well as financial system enhancements. Finally, the ability to attract and retain appropriately skilled staff across all areas of service provision continues to challenge service delivery in the context of increasing demand, low levels of remuneration, differing work expectations and increased competition for limited resources. All this within the context of upholding the nonprofit (for purpose) organisation missions in the sector.

In this chapter, we consider the application of the NDIS Implementation Framework ("NDISIF"), constructed from our research findings, as a means of addressing the dual challenges of strategically moving from a supply-driven to a demand-driven approach to the delivery of disability services in the nonprofit sector, as well as the operationalisation of transformational change within mission and values-based organisations. Our findings reference a framework as distinct from a model. The former identifies how implementation works, based on the detailed analysis of the interviews from participating organisations at a given point in time, while the latter represents a cognitive mapping of procedural steps in a process that links with specific goals (Egan, 1985). In doing so, we have identified a range of strategic success factors that support the NDISIF, and that may apply to a broader range of nonprofit disability service providers. In this manner, a framework acts as a guide, as distinct from a model that provides a prescriptive approach. Applied in this manner, the NDISIF supports organisations planning for, and undertaking implementation of the NDIS, as well as those wishing to improve their current implementation strategies and processes.

The framework needs to be considered in the context of the broader issues that impact successful implementation of the NDIS, which have been related to the Australian Disability system more broadly. Issues of poor industry planning; the state of inter and intra government service structures; challenging workforce issues; questionable pricing structures, as well as service access equity are examples of these (Gilchrist et al., 2019). The problematic constraints that this place on the implementation of, and the ongoing management of the NDIS, must be addressed at both the strategic and operational levels by individual service providers in the absence of broader social policy reforms.

REVIEW OF PREVAILING LITERATURE

Existing literature is diverse, given the areas identified as relevant to this current research. In terms of the management of change, previous research undertaken by Rosenbaum et al. (2017) provided deep insights into wide-ranging issues associated with change management specifically in the Australian nonprofit sector.

While that research identified four principle activities that should be considered as part of any change management approach within the nonprofit sector, it also highlighted the need for extended studies given the limited historic research in this sector, recognising that much of the prevailing research into change management originated from the commercial sector. The development and implementation of organisational strategy, with regards to the level of transformational change required to prepare for and to implement the NDIS in nonprofit organisations, reflects the comparative complexities associated with organisational needs (Gray & Wilkinson, 2016), as well as the sequencing attributes related to behavioural change outcomes and the timing associated with staff engagement in building the vision (Noble et al., 2017). The need to change mindsets and consequent strategy, structures and processes wrought by the NDIS's radical reform, was paramount in all the organisations involved, pointing to ongoing strategic refinements undertaken in parallel with implementation.

Unique nonprofit sector attributes were identified in existing research (Rosenbaum et al., 2017), suggesting that different approaches to the management of organisational change warranted focused research. This was further supported by the extensive literature review undertaken by Rosenbaum et al. (2018) which sought to contextualise ongoing approaches to change management within historic origins (Lewin, 1946). In doing so, the review of the relevant change management literature identified key application categorisations, namely considering change as a project (Beckhard & Harris, 1987; Bullock & Batten, 1985; Kotter, 1996; Taffinder, 1998); seeing change as a response to resistance (Carnall, 2007; Kübler-Ross, 1969; Senge, 1990); and considering change as an interpretive process (Bridges, 1991; Warner et al., 1992; Dunphy et al., 2007; Nadler & Tushman, 1997). These considerations were further analysed in an earlier pilot research study (Rosenbaum & More, 2021) involving two nonprofit disability service providers.

Leadership in the context of change represents a further focus with regards this current research, as does the identification and application of existing leadership models and the development of nuanced approaches to leadership in this sector. The Interactional Framework, underpinning a range of leadership considerations, highlights the important relationship between leaders, followers and the situational context within which leaders' function (Beer, 1999; Huy, 2001; Kotter, 2005). Emanating from this approach are issues of adaptive leadership (DeRue, 2011), complexity leadership (Lichtenstein et al., 2006; Uhl-Bien et al., 2007) and learning agility (De Meuse et al., 2010).

Leadership responses to the emotionality of transformational change among change recipients, further represents a key research focus, especially in the context of recent literature reviews which have failed to clearly identify the specific roles of leaders in instigating change and how such change evolves in organisational settings (Oreg & Berson, 2016). This further focuses attention on how leaders deal with individual change recipient's emotions as part of a change process. Over the last decade or so, there has been a growing awareness among researchers of the need to deal with the perceptions of individuals within change programmes, and recognising that a focus on the organisation must be balanced with an appropriate focus on the individual (Bamford & Forrester, 2003; Becker, 2007; Shin et al., 2012). While much of such research has been centred on analysis associated with levels of resistance to change and issues that either compound or support such resistance, emphasis has now also been applied in research associated with perceptions of individuals experiencing change (Isett et al., 2013; Lines et al., 2005). The leadership implications of this change in focus manifests in the leadership attributes and behaviours required in managing organisational change.

Cultural characteristics necessary for successful organisational change support further research. The existence of predominant and sub-cultures both facilitate change and simultaneously give rise to resisting change

(Baker, 2007). This necessitates understanding the nature and impact of the predominant culture, while identifying the source and relative impact of the key sub-cultures, as well as the extent to which these inhibit and enhance change outcomes. The critical lens of analysing and understanding organisational cultural characteristics, in terms of artefacts, espoused beliefs and values, as well as many underlying assumptions (Burke, 2013), is pivotal to understanding aspects of organisational readiness for change (Cameron & Green, 2009). This is very relevant in the context of generational change, such as the NDIS, where organisations face substantial challenges in developing and implementing new models for service delivery and design, and where client relationships move from a supply-driven model to a demand-driven model.

METHODOLOGY APPLIED TO THIS RESEARCH

Given the focus of understanding how nonprofit disability service providers have implemented the NDIS, a qualitative analysis methodology was identified as the appropriate method for pursuing this aim. As has been historically identified, qualitative analysis focuses on the extraction of themes and patterns of relationships that enable researchers to better understand the phenomenon under study (Nechully & Pokhriyal, 2019), herein as change management in nonprofit disability service organisations.

Two interposed qualitative methods have been deployed in this research, namely Grounded Theory and Framework Analysis. In terms of Grounded Theory, the ingredients of symbolic interactionism have underpinned its development, focused on understanding and interpreting patterns of human behaviour (Chenitz & Swanson, 1986). It is these patterns that are being studied and provide the foundations for the inductive approach to the development of theory. The coding process involved in this method enables the researcher to develop the analysis of the interview data to the point of naturally identifying the linkages between raw data and core variables, deemed necessary to this theory development (Boychuk Duchscher & Morgan, 2004).

In terms of Framework Analysis, the application of analysing interview transcripts to undertake thematic analysis across many individual cases and in the context of retaining the contextual connections at the interviewee level (Gale et al., 2013), further strengthens the overall qualitative framework within which we, as qualitative researchers, can develop inductive theory. One of the distinctive features of Framework Analysis is the creation of thematic matrices and locating interviewees within it (Kiernan & Hill, 2018). This enables linkages to be identified between themes and participants.

The interaction between Grounded Theory and Frame Work Analysis enables the former to identify the behavioural variables that influence the implementation of the NDIS among these service providers, whereas Frame Work Analysis supports the development of the NDIS Implementation Framework ("NDISIF") in response to these behavioural variables.

Interviews were conducted in seven nonprofit organisations across Australia. These organisations were of varying sizes, ranging from turnover of less than AUD500K through to turnover of greater than AUD50M. In total, 46 interviews were conducted with staff from across these organisations, from front-line service delivery staff through to board members. The focus of these interviews was aimed on understanding the personal perceptions and feelings of the employees, how these were dealt with by the organisation, and how these impacted on the processes and outcomes of the NDIS implementation processes.

These interviews, some of which were undertaken face-to-face, while others were undertaken via teleconference links, were all audio recorded as a basis for developing detailed transcripts. They were approached on a semi-structured and open-ended basis so as to ensure maximum engagement with the interview participants. Additionally, this approach provided the basis for thick rich descriptions of the interviews to support theory development (Birks & Mills, 2011).

Our NDIS Implementation Framework was based on the analysis of 600+ pages of interview transcripts, highlighting those elements of a transformational change that were required in order to underpin successful implementation of the NDIS in nonprofit service providers.

Research Findings

Detailed Findings

Reference has been made in this chapter to an NDISIF, developed as an aid for nonprofit disability service providers to successfully implement the NDIS. As suggested, these implementations are not being undertaken within a static environment that allows for either the internal or external environment to be effectively frozen, enabling implementation to be undertaken irrespective of what is happening in these environments. Rather, these implementations are being undertaken *in parallel* with the realities of ongoing business activities, including most recently during a pandemic. These realities therefore necessitate flexibility, adaptability and innovation on the part of organisational employees, organisation-wide leadership and strategically focused and organisationally sensitive Boards.

Figure 18.1 identifies the higher-level attributes of the NDISIF which are considered in more detail in this chapter and in the context of the detailed iterative processes identified further in Fig. 18.3

The NDISIF has been framed around three core development phases, being the inputs that effectively prepare the organisation for the changes being undertaken, the processes that specifically address the implementation, and finally the outcomes of the implementation that define the manner in which the nonprofit disability service provider consolidates its achievements during the implementation and supports the organisation moving forward during the post-implementation activities. The phases identified in Fig. 18.1 each contain a range of parameters that need to be considered as part of the overall NDISIF, as further explained in the following sections.

1. *Inputs Phase*

The Input Phase is both customer and organisation driven, especially when you consider the NDIS shifts the focus from a supply-driven approach to a demand-driven approach, albeit the market

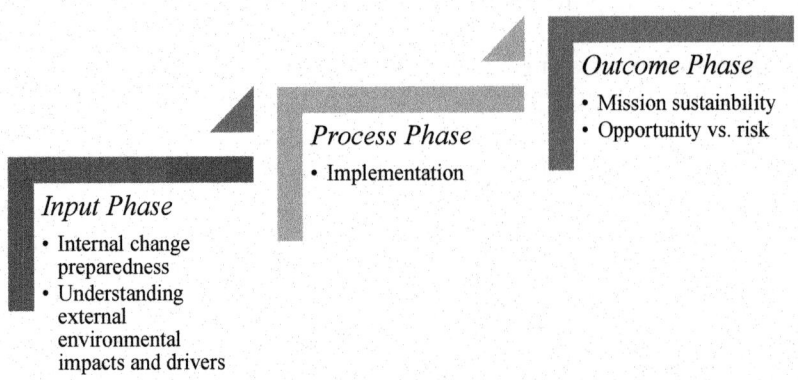

Fig. 18.1 NDIS implementation framework—the high-level context

being defined in a somewhat limited manner due to the laws of supply and demand being partially curtailed by the central government Agency, the National Disability Insurance Agency ("NDIA"), laying restrictions on maximum price settings by providers.

An overarching feature of the Input Phase is the preparedness factors necessary to ensure the organisation is ready to implement change. This entails three key components that affect the internal organisational settings, namely, leadership, culture and change management.

- *Leadership*

    Our research has identified Servant Leadership, where servanthood is the essence of leadership, as being the most relevant leadership style for nonprofit disability service organisation leaders implementing the NDIS as discussed below. This is valid irrespective of the stage at which these organisations are along the implementation continuum. An important factor to consider is the criticality of recognising the implementations exist along a continuum, as government agencies charged with overseeing the system continue to refine the NDIS from the perspective of customer and provider experiences, as well as by changing Federal Government funding realities.

    While Servant Leadership has a rich depth of academic analysis from its origins (Greenleaf, 1977) through to the present (Hernández-Perlines & Araya-Castillo, 2020), operational clarification as to its precise characteristics have often been ill-defined. More recent research has provided a conceptual model of Servant Leadership and its identified characteristics, which are said to include empowerment, humility, authenticity, interpersonal acceptance, providing direction and stewardship (Van Dierendonck, 2011). The predominant focus is outwards rather than inwards, suggesting effective leadership focuses on what leaders can do for their followers, as distinct to what leaders can do for themselves.

    The NDISIF recognises that effective leadership is not about the leader per se, but rather about followers, and the ability for leaders to enable followers to fully realise their own potential (Frei & Morriss, 2020). It therefore becomes imperative for leaders, during all stages of the NDIS implementation, to see themselves as enablers, where innovation is the product of such an enabling environment. This recognises that in unstable circumstances, of which the NDIS is a good example, innovative solutions to service delivery challenges will guide strategy and organisational success. Such an approach suggests a bottom-up strategic management model that is far more effective in these environments where innovation is a necessary ingredient in driving strategic change (Levesque, 2020). The focus in the NDISIF should, therefore, be leadership that is visionary, supportive and participative (Oreg & Berson, 2016).

- *Culture*

This research suggests that the required organisational culture necessary for success in implementing and maintaining the NDIS, must be recognised by employees as one that is supportive, inclusive, empowering and accountable. This is underpinned by strong levels of trust within workplace relationships at all levels (Page et al., 2019).

Evidence suggests that the cultural attributes, which may be fundamental to successful NDIS implementation and beyond, require the careful resolution of internal conflict between the purpose mindset of service provision, based on mission, with the pragmatic reality of commercialism. The NDIS has shifted the focus from a supply-driven model to a demand-driven model, where service users ensure that service providers are far more responsive to market demands. This, in part, necessitates a degree of cultural adaptability among existing staff who will be well versed in the pre-NDIS environment which was predicated on a supply-driven business model of service provision being determined largely by service providers (Corritore et al., 2020).

There is also an issue of organisational sub-cultures, often with professional stereotypes, directly relating to the operational and strategic silos that have historically tended to exist within many disability service organisations. This may have an impact on the way change is managed across the organisation (Locke & Guglielmino, 2006), suggesting that perhaps change is developed and focused at two levels—one being organisation-wide and the other being departmental or team-level. Historically, within a number of disability service organisations, different service areas have traditionally developed and provided services that specialise in their own areas of expertise, for example, in areas of community-based programmes, respite, recreation, to name a few. As these have developed, they have tended to do so within internal organisational silos.

Evidence from our research also supports the view that there are those within these organisations who are optimistic and supportive of the changes and those who are more hesitant and concerned about how the changes will be undertaken and unfold. This necessitates a leadership response that encompasses both mindsets. Viewing this from the perspective of positive and negative forces that impact on the change (Rosenbaum et al., 2018), it becomes a matter of ensuring those who are the optimists are constantly engaged and supported so they remain focused and on board. The less optimistic need to be well managed, shown the positives for them and the organisation in the change, supported and trained throughout the process of implementation and beyond.

What has become apparent within these service provider organisations is that their cultures of helping and compassion, very much grounded in the past, continue to prevail, despite being outmoded and ill-suited to the task of implementing the NDIS (Lilius et al., 2008). Unfortunately, it is clear, however, that such an approach has come at a cost to both employees and the sector itself. So, the strategic challenge is one of rebuilding culture and ensuring sustainability, one that goes beyond purely financial and organisational sustainability, to consider personnel sustainability at the service delivery-end of the spectrum. The balance that now needs to be derived is one that enables the achievement of financial sustainability in this new demand-driven system, within the context of maintaining the ongoing focus on organisational mission within programme design and delivery.

Finally, a further challenge to culture exists where physical locations of the organisations are dispersed (Memon & Kinder, 2017). A predominant head-office approach seems to become evident, especially in the nexus between city and regions. The challenge here, therefore, is to overcome this head-office syndrome to ensure communication is effective across the entire organisation, irrespective of physical location and/or distance from head office, so as to further reinforce this balance between commerciality and compassion.

- *Change*

This research has concluded that a delicate balance needs to be identified between the perceived need for a clearly defined procedural approach to change on the one hand, and a fully adaptable and perhaps less defined process on the other. Both leadership and cultural characteristics, as discussed earlier, influence the effectiveness of change, where adaptability is a necessary ingredient.

Such a balance can be overcome through developing a broad strategic change guide which would be fully adaptable at the organisational level, accounting for the variability of the planning phase, the execution phase and end phase. Our research suggests that Lewin's approach may prove beneficial (Lewin, 1946), but only with all elements of Lewin's model applied, rather than the more often publicised three-step model which actually was a shortened descriptor of his work (Rosenbaum et al., 2018). A more accurate description of Lewin's model of change appears in Fig. 18.2.

Viewed in this manner, the elements of Force Field Analysis, Group Dynamics and reflective processes, when combined with the key elements of unfreezing, moving and refreezing, provide the flexibility that NDIS-related change necessitates.

The foundational elements of Lewin's approach are broad enough to capture a wide range of organisation-specific change actions. Unfreezing effectively ensures that the organisation is change-ready and enables change leaders to address visioning, resistance, technical preparedness and initial training to fill identified skills gaps and emotional response strategies necessary to support staff. Moving enables change leaders to consolidate these previous elements and apply them further as the organisation works through the change processes, ensuring training is further developed and targeted, staff are emotionally supported, systems and processes are designed and implemented in consultation with staff, communications are focused

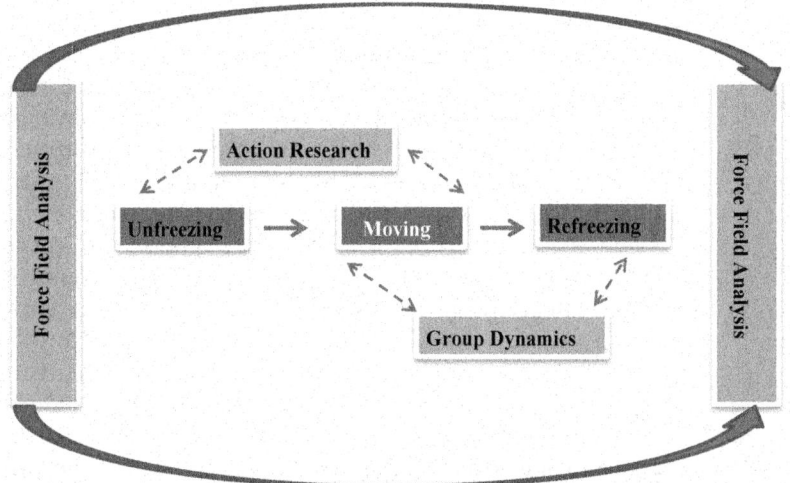

Reproduced from Rosenbaum et al. (2018)

Fig. 18.2 A more accurate depiction of Lewin's 3-step model of change (Reproduced from Rosenbaum et al. (2018))

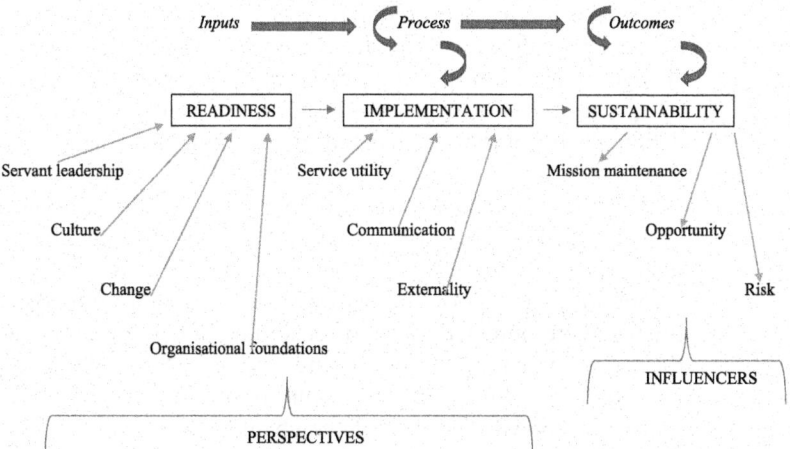

Fig. 18.3 NDIS implementation framework

and meaningful, and organisational flexibility enables staff to develop innovative responses to the change challenges. Refreezing gives further impetus to the post-implementation stage, where confidence in the changes becomes obvious, staff develop affinity with the new systems and processes, and feel a sense of optimism about the future, plus consolidating strategic opportunities while appreciating and working through the risks. Force Field Analysis supports this entire change process (Baulcomb, 2003) throughout all elements of the cycle. Reflective processes in a change management environment (Mcardle & Reason, 2008) support the flexibility of trialling different approaches at key stages and ensuring that an iterative approach can be applied and, therefore, refined as momentum is achieved. Finally, Group Dynamics enables key positioning to take place throughout the organisation to support both the change process and the refreezing aspect of the change (Lucas & Kline, 2008).

As we identify, the change process must be aligned with the organisation's overall strategy. One of the key aspects to this is understanding the relevant stakeholders, and the extent to which they are to be considered. This lays the foundations for effectively "unfreezing" the status quo to enable the reasons for change to be best understood by all involved, while facilitating the process of moving forward. Reflective processes assist in defining what must be changed and scoping the changes as they form.

A critical aspect appears to be the levels of interaction required outside the organisation and carefully developing the intra-organisational networks identified as necessary throughout this process. This means encouraging and identifying these interactions and becoming adept at applying them, grounded in understanding and developing "outside the box" style thinking and application. This further reinforces the "moving" aspect of the change and provides a base for reaching change sustainability as part of the "refreezing", enabling the ongoing change flexibility considered inevitable within a continually modified system. It, however, introduces an element of chaos to the change at all stages of the process, something which can only be addressed by strengthening employee resilience and encouraging, as well as supporting, innovation throughout all levels of the organisation.

Understanding the workload repercussions on those impacted by the change becomes critical during this organisational change process (Hauck et al., 2008). What must be considered and addressed, as part of the refreezing stage, is that workloads have shifted away from front-line service delivery staff to more done with individual clients from an administrative perspective. In part, this is informed by the application of Lewin's Force Field Analysis, used to identify the initial and ongoing forces that both drive and impede the change process. The operational and strategic aims are to address those impeding forces, whist ensuring the driving forces remain active and built upon throughout the change.

- *Organisational Foundations*

Our research points to a broad range of necessary organisational aspects which must either be present before the NDIS implementation or put in place during and following the implementation to improve outcomes. If not present, then these will be regarded as restricting forces that may impede the progress of effective change.

There is a connection between the necessity to review the organisational structure required to adapt to the changing external environment, and the manner in which, and the structure of, training, where design, content and delivery is paramount, and where capabilities and skills gaps are clearly identified for ongoing development (Wilkinson et al., 2019). Given what is clearly known about the NDIS, from an operational perspective as well as the requirements associated with its demand-driven business model, organisational structure reviews appear to have been a necessary process, especially during the planning phases of the implementation (Waddell et al., 2019). An important element in executing organisational design activities is to consider the manner in which these are communicated, as well as the degree to which staff are consulted and supported in both the design and the roll-out of these structural changes (Harney et al., 2018). Key to this is trust in leadership, where staff recognises that such organisational changes are being undertaken for reasons of maximising employee engagement as well as improving client service outcomes.

The issue of organisational structure may become more relevant from a situational perspective, meaning that, dependent on the stage of implementation, diverse structures may work differently. So, the issue may be more of one where, rather than considering flat versus hierarchical, perhaps flexibility in organisational design must be dealt with as a pre-change issue, understanding how this may look and how this may operate. In order to consider this, there must be a clear understanding of how well the organisation is functioning pre-implementation, suggesting that existing organisational problems need to be addressed before implementing the NDIS, and not seeing it addressing and fixing pre-NDIS issues. In fact, the latter perspective may well compound such organisational design problems.

A further element for consideration in this area is defining the specific nature of the strategic and operational roles of the human resource function within the organisation (El-Dirani et al., 2019). Evidence in the current research questions the roles that HR played in the strategic planning, implementation and post-implementation phases of the NDIS roll-outs. Specifically, people interaction skills, where there was a specific need to provide varying levels of emotional support, deal with professional expectations, and strategically responding to the earlier mentioned skills gaps, as changes were necessarily identified and implemented, may require a special focus (sometimes missing) throughout these processes.

A further issue for consideration was the apparent presence of what we have referred to as "head office syndrome" (Bouquet et al., 2016). If the evidence suggests that internal communications are often ineffectual because they inadvertently lead to feelings of exclusion and/or that top management do not appreciate front-line service delivery challenges, processes should be put in place to ensure only appropriately sensitive communications are used.

2. Process Phase

- **Service Utility**

    Our research has identified the need for NFP disability service providers to better, and more clearly, define the appropriateness of the services they provide to key stakeholders in a redefined and contested marketplace.

    Existing conceptions of service have been challenged by the need to become more commercially adept and focused, thereby impacting strategic programme design as well as service delivery, which need to incorporate a business and marketing orientation, more understanding of programme costs, strategic use of social media, and understanding the "business" of effectively promoting and selling welfare services. Success in NDIS implementations, when viewed through such a commercial lens, appears to be aided by the generation of optimism (Tan & Tiong, 2005) through identification of opportunities, as distinct from the ongoing and sometimes relentless highlighting of sector threats and weaknesses.

    Service utility at this level is best understood as how advocacy-related activities need to be reconsidered and redefined in the light of the funding structures within the NDIS. Further compounding this required cultural shift, in both attitude and action, has been the move from industry advocacy to client advocacy. This potentially changes employees' perceptions of themselves and how they fit into this sector, necessitating a change to employees' mindsets with regards defining service delivery, especially in terms of advocating for their client (Hoefer, 2019).

    There is a general view that the concept of advocacy (Kimberlin, 2010) has now changed from being one of advocating within the sector, to advocating for individual disability service recipients' packages, so that they can get the services they need. This change of focus is directly correlated with more limited funding pathways under the NDIS (Andrews, 2020). Bringing advocacy down to this level, where it directly affects the individual looking for funding, may extend the concept for service providers and especially individuals, moving from the certainty of block funding to that of competition and negotiation.

This further impacts the relationship between what the organisation values and how such values will be upheld, challenging some organisations and their employees seeking to balance their personal service values with the commercial imperatives now required. This is supported by historical research indicating a correlation between levels of voluntary staff turnover and congruence between personal and organisational culture (Chapman & Mayers, 2013).

At its simplest, the new considerations of service utility are characterised by service provision that needs to be paid for—changing from the pre-NDIS emotional approach to the largely post NDIS transactional approach. Under these new arrangements, underpinning programme design and service delivery, are the transactional realities that must now define organisational success. The consequences are developing programmes and services that are simultaneously value for money for service users, as well as financially sustainable for the organisation.

- *Internal Communications*

Our research has identified that effectiveness of internal communications is a strong determinant of success in NDIS implementation among nonprofit service providers. Key elements of the communications framework include strong top-down but coordinated communication pathways; consistency regarding the change messaging; communication that underpins a strong understanding of the role that customer choice plays in both programme design and service delivery; recognising the need to minimise the deleterious impacts of organisational silos in the delivery of integrated services; and the effective use of wide-ranging brainstorming sessions, involving extensive cross-sections of the organisation in order to consistently address implementation challenges, proactively and reactively.

Associated with these considerations, is the nature and style of the language of change as used in all the communications across the organisation, focusing attention on limiting the jargon often used in the process. Additionally, the careful structure and use of language that resonates with those experiencing change, often tends to normalise the process. This helps avoid over-emphasising any negative aspects that some may see requiring special attention, while recognising that changed processes in both programme design and service delivery will be a necessary and naturally evolving process.

A further internal communications element is the organisational ability to encourage, absorb and positively react to bottom-up communications. This ability must also be overt and recognised as an organisational strength as it impacts the processes of change, organisational culture, as well as a range of emotional responses by those experiencing change.

Additionally, communications must be authentic and sincere, and not interpreted as a "tick-box" approach in an overall change strategy. Communication effectiveness resides in both emotional connection and meaning among those involved, otherwise insincerity will be identified and requisite connection and understanding, would disappear. There is an element of trust in this communications interplay and, if trust is absent, or appears to be absent, then change outcomes may not be maximised (Frei & Morriss, 2020), as distrust and/or cynicism sets in, undermining the full impact of Servant Leadership.

Communications media require an additional focus (Burt & Taylor, 2000) from the perspective of purpose and usage, ranging from the social content, which recognises the role of story-telling and sense-making (Rosenbaum et al., 2019) through to the informational component, which responds to wide-raging NDIS-related technical matters. This also recognises that, given the age diversity within NFP disability service providers, no one individual or predominant communications media addresses all requirements.

- *Externality*

An obvious reliance on both the efficiency and effectiveness of the external Agency, the NDIA, which oversees the roll-out of the NDIS, played an integral part in a wide range of issues that challenged the ability of nonprofit service providers to deliver the NDIS into their organisations. Evidence from our research indicated that there was an initial lack of trust in the external Agency with regard to the consistency and quality of communications originating from it. The poor communications in the earlier stages of the implementation caused a substantial degree of frustration, caused in part, by the frequent changes of Agency staff. This resulted in inconsistent Agency messaging which service providers felt was threatening high-quality outcomes for their clients. Different approaches were identified at the interviewed organisations that attempted to counter such shortcomings. These approaches tended to take a proactive stance in how they strategically structured their communications with the Agency, relying on persistent telephone and email follow up communications with appropriate Agency staff, whenever these could be achieved. This led, on occasion, to timely identification of Agency staff movements that service providers could then flag as possible risks to ongoing communications.

While improvements had been noted during this research, with organisational staff initially rating the quality of interactions with the Agency at 3 out 10, this had improved to around 7 out of 10, after some extended period of time, with increased direct contacts and improved accountability at the Agency. Many interviewees however, felt that these communication issues should have been dealt with at the very early stages of the NDIS roll-out, as interaction problems should have been anticipated given the size of the sector, the number of organisations involved, and the comparative limited resources of the Agency at the time. Issues of inappropriate modes of communication between the Agency and people with a disability, further negatively impacted the ability for these organisations to deliver effective and efficient outcomes for their clients. As late as 2019, the issue of challenging communications remained a focus of criticism (Andrews, 2019), where the Parliamentary Joint Standing Committee on the NDIS indicated that, "*However, evidence received during the inquiry suggests that a number of communication issues persist, and that more needs to be done to improve access and facilitate greater understanding for NDIS participants, providers and other stakeholders*" (Pg. 49).

Shortcomings with how external networks, used for both advocacy-related matters and for strategic purposes, were sent communications, were also identified as problematic. This was of concern as the use of networks appeared to strengthen the advocacy position as well as reinforcing the ongoing importance of sector advocacy to staff in a post NDIS environment, noting the issues identified earlier with regards the shifting focus from sector advocacy to individual client advocacy. These networks also supported both staff and organisations in the challenges faced during implementations. The development and maintenance of such external sector networks were regarded as a necessary step in both supporting staff through change, while also supporting participating organisations in achieving their strategic objectives.

3. *Outcome Phase*

- *Opportunity and Risk*

  Successful implementations of the NDIS reflect the recognition of and prioritisation of opportunities associated with the new market model. In other words, when there is a fit between the services a disability organisation provides and the industry position to which it aspires, the potential for it to achieve greater levels of strategic alignment across all areas of the business, to meet the demands of a changing market over time, will be much enhanced. While the NDIS means shifting the focus of client expectations in accordance with a demand-driven business model, this represents both a risk to the service provider organisation, as well as an opportunity. The former relates to organisations not responding to the new demands, while the opportunities relate to those organisations that can respond and strategise accordingly.

  Our research identified an important linkage between the success of the implementations, with the ability for organisations to identify, focus and exploit the opportunities potentially available, both during and following the change processes, as distinct from a more restricted conservative or risk averse approach focused on what problems may lie ahead. Such a proactive, business-oriented approach challenges many nonprofit service providers, at all levels of their organisations, to adapt from the perspective of capitalising on opportunities, while recognising and evaluating risks, within a risk-reward framework.

The investment in infrastructure, as an example, reflected this risk and opportunity aspect of the changes associated with the NDIS implementation. The risk related to early adoption, while the opportunity was regarded as giving the organisation ample time to prepare and remain, therefore, ahead of the overall process, both from a staff and a client servicing perspective, reflecting a commitment to preparation and planning that staff appreciated but also felt challenged by, especially with regards the implementation. This approach recognised the challenges associated with the use of new systems, increasing organisational capacity and enabling future opportunities to be identified and developed (Benjamin, 2008).

If risk and opportunity are viewed as two sides of the one evaluative process, and one which is well communicated to all staff, this may form a powerful element in them embracing the changes, as the opportunities resulting from risk-reward assessments may enable a more expansive service capability to their clients, which represents a fundamental focus in their daily roles and responsibilities.

Understanding the NDIS from the viewpoint of opportunities rather than challenges pivots the mindset around the future rather than the past. Instilling this within relevant staff becomes a training and staff development challenge as in some cases it goes to the heart of staff capabilities as well as prevailing organisational culture.

- *Mission Maintenance*

Our research suggests that the maintenance of the organisational mission, in the face of substantial NDIS market change, must be a central focus of all organisational efforts in order to ensure ongoing staff acceptance and successful transitioning (Rosenbaum et al., 2017). The drive towards, and potentially the need for, a commercial or part-commercial strategic focus, must not challenge the concerns that many front-line service delivery staff have for the well-being of their clients (Dawson & Daniel, 2010).

The strength of the values commitment among staff in such nonprofits as disability service providers, must be maintained and leveraged, in order to ensure high levels of service provision, especially when faced with the competitive pressures from within the sector, from both other nonprofit service providers and commercial for-profit operators. The assumption that financial priorities are consistent across commercial and nonprofit organisations alike, may not readily be understood as still being in keeping with their mission focus (Hall, 2017).

Connections by staff to organisational mission and values that preceded the NDIS-related transformations, play a pivotal role in staff perceptions of the change. Therefore, it is important that staff can continue to identify within the transformation the pre- and post-organisational characteristics and attributes that originally may have attracted them to the organisation, especially with regard to services focused on client well-being. Accordingly, collective continuity of organisational identity becomes important, both during the transitioning as well as in the post-transitioning period (Venus et al., 2019).

NDIS Implementation Framework

Our research, detailed earlier, has identified the NDIS Implementation Framework ("NDISIF") that builds on the observations made in the course of analysing the numerous interviews which resulted in the 600 + pages of interview transcripts, and in the context of the extensive literature review that both supported and drove the research.

We have differentiated a framework from a model, where the latter is aimed at providing a procedural stepped approach to describe how a process may function from the beginning point to an end point, as well as being somewhat standardised across many differing circumstances. We recognise that there exist wide-ranging characteristics that differentiate nonprofit service providers from each other, as well as different nonprofit service providers being at different stages of their NDIS implementation. Accordingly, we have opted to develop a framework that reflects the realities of variabilities and focuses on considerations as distinct to prescriptiveness. Consequently, we recognise the following variables that currently exist to varying degrees across all nonprofit disability service organisations:

1. Organisational size,
2. Status of current NDIS implementation,

3. Lack of clarity regarding organisational issues that may either remain outstanding and to be addressed or have not yet been identified,
4. Possible failure of earlier attempts at NDIS implementation,
5. Changed organisation or market circumstances that may require a rethink as to a historic NDIS implementation approach or,
6. Expansion strategies that may require a reconsideration of challenges associated with historic approaches to NDIS implementation.

The Implementation Framework depicted in Fig. 18.3 recognises the "Perspectives" discussed in previous sections and sees these as being the identified elements of the Framework that organisations implementing the NDIS must consider throughout the "Readiness" and "Implementation" phases. The "Influencers", also discussed earlier, remain the cornerstone of their own unique organisational characteristics. These underpin their "Sustainability" and effectively drive them forward during the post-implementation processes, as they seek to maintain their overarching mission, embed Opportunity maximisation, while considering and mitigating Risk. This Framework is embedded within an iterative process rather than a pure linear process, recognising the practicalities of change as identified in this chapter.

IMPLICATIONS FOR THEORY AND PRACTICE

How Do These Findings Inform the Theory of Planned and Strategic Organisational Change Management for This Sector?

Fundamentally, this topic area is generally under researched and the available research on the NDIS has not really tackled the actual change management approaches and practices. Nor, indeed, has there been adequate collaboration of partnering with the NFP organisations as we have done, endeavouring to provide a richer analysis of benefit to the providers, clients, the agencies and governments involved (Rosenbaum & More, 2021).

In providing an implementation framework rather than a model, with its phases across leadership, culture and change management, we have incorporated a broad flexibility that can encompass key variables in the sector allowing for the fluidity of change management necessitated by a VUCAD environment (Volatility; Uncertainty; Complexity; Ambiguity; Delayed Feedback).

What Do These Findings Mean for Nonprofit Disability Service Provider Organisations?

Important challenges facing nonprofit managers and leaders are outcomes of radical change embodied in the NDIS implementation. Demands from the NDIS can often be challenging to manage, including constant changes since the NDIA commenced, especially pricing arrangements and client supports. Additionally, governments now expect more efficiency and effectiveness in relationships with nonprofits and with stakeholders (including customer satisfaction) involved in the NDIS arena.

Unsurprisingly, some of the effects on organisational behaviour of having to rely upon a large range of funding sources, including most heavily, government funding with some private donations and philanthropy, are increasingly challenging, especially that of uncertainty. With the introduction of the NDIS, the sector faced increased competition both from other nonprofits and for-profits in the marketplace. In recent times, COVID 19 has also had an impact on donor support, although this was volatile and increasingly competitive with the growth of nonprofits generally, even before the pandemic.

For many, organisational financial sustainability is fundamentally a key motivator in adopting the NDIS. Therefore, for some of the organisations we studied, the NDIS was adopted rapidly, often without apparent detailed strategy, in order to remain sustainable and continue servicing their mission, their client base, and the broader community in which they exist. NDIS is growing to be a substantial portion for revenue for many nonprofits but the issue of how financially sustainable they are for many remains, ever watchful of price changes and the like, and considering the possible need to further diversify funding sources, especially with the COVID 19 impact, but even previously, the threat of financial vulnerability remains.

Success in implementing the NDIS points to achieving government aims and objectives efficiently, and positive political recognition; from a consumer perspective success means fulfilling the needs of customers (and their families and supporters) in terms of the packages; and from an organisation's perspective, success resides in remaining and growing more viable and sustainable, able to fulfil organisational mission, and maintain and grow productive government relationships that ensure ongoing resources.

From a strategic perspective, recent research has explored sustainability perceptions across five key aspects—people, business model, operations, strategy and culture (Ceptureanu et al., 2018), where emphasis has been placed on the need for entrepreneurship, an outcomes focus, innovative practices, professionalisation of staff and volunteers, and a market orientation to be adopted by the sector. The need to retain and uphold a nonprofit's social mission may also conflict with such changes or, at least, make it more difficult.

Research in the Australian context (Zhai et al., 2017) found that nonprofits were vulnerable largely because of increasing delivery costs; a higher administration burden in relation to programme expenses; challenges to fulfilling an organisation's mission; problems with Boards; threats from the external environment; and ongoing financial challenges and constraints.

We also found challenges from:

- Ongoing emotional and psychological stress on staff in a challenging recruitment environment,
- Needing to upgrade organisational systems and processes, including across funding arrangements, with data collection needing constant attention, to gauge true costs of services that cannot be easily understood, especially with growing demands for superior quality in servicing clients,
- Growing pressure to consider collaborations, mergers and acquisitions,
- Rising talent wars in competition for staff, including financial dimensions of this
- A need to ensure the appropriate business models are employed,
- Dealing with technology changes, with the potential of digital health, and the requisite appropriate training and personnel needs, including adopting those for extending the reach of NFP providers given the flexibility of the NDIS in terms of service location,
- Problems emanating from organisations being reactive rather than strategic in taking up the NDIS without analysing effectively current offerings and how the NDIS fits into these, and what may need to change to gain the full benefit for both clients and organisations,
- Facing the need to build appropriate strategic lenses through which to develop and refine strategic plans, including the potential for

external consultancies to assist (size and costs affecting strategic decision making),
- Dealing with the increasing complexities of risk management; and, fundamentally,
- Upholding mission while reframing cultural dimensions in terms of expectations, practices and mindsets.

What Do These Findings Mean for Nonprofit Disability Service Provider Leaders and Managers?

A key issue for NFP leaders and managers is to accept and deal effectively with these challenges of change (Akingbola et al., 2019):

The nature of the environment of organizations especially nonprofits is not just change, it is constant change. Nonprofit organizations are arguably in a perpetual state of change. For example, they must constantly scan, analyse, and adapt to the changing needs of clients, the community, funders, the government, and other stakeholders. As the first step, non-profit organizations and their stakeholders must understand what organizational change is all about. (pg. 2)

Leadership, governance and NFP Boards are challenging, including the Board-Executive relationship in the NDIS environment. One useful guide is provided by the Australian Institute of Company Directors (Butler, 2019) in terms of considering and adhering to ten NFP Governance principles across: organisation purpose and strategy; board roles and responsibilities; board composition; board effectiveness; organisational risk management; organisational performance; board accountability and transparency; meaningful stakeholder engagement; clarity of behavioural expectations, conduct and compliance; having a culture supporting the organisation's purpose and strategy. The most successful of the organisations we interviewed in this research adhered to these principles.

Moreover, their leadership and managers ensured the organisation adopted more business-like perspectives and practices in a more market orientation of public service, while maintaining social purpose and roles. They were also effective in managing government relations and regulatory requirements. Fundamentally, their approach was mired in adopting learning organisation principles and practices to enhance the capacity and pragmatics for change strategy and management.

The challenges facing the sector suggest consideration of some new and/or enhanced perspectives on NFP leadership and management:

- Use of the Implementation Framework to enable adaptable organisation design and processes.
- A bottom-up strategic management approach, balancing a planned design and process with flexibility requisite in a challenging environment.
- Cultural competence focused on trust, effective support, building resilience, empowering and accountable.
- Increased systems integration and avoidance of silos in service delivery.
- Future orientation—dealing with both optimists and pessimists, enhancing a focus on opportunities.
- Changing mindsets—mission and commercial sustainability.
- Effective authentic change communication—media use and messaging content and style for diverse audiences, internal and external.
- Regulatory and legal frameworks becoming more demanding.
- Technology and systems training required with changing structures and financial demands.
- Leadership styles affecting staff commitments—Servant Leadership emerging as the most relevant overseeing change fluidity.
- Social entrepreneurship and innovation.
- Increased marketing and advancement.
- Advocacy both internal and external.
- Diversity and inclusion in the workplace.
- Risk management, including consideration of changes to risk appetite.
- Cybersecurity considerations crucial along with data analytics.
- Increased and more complex stakeholder engagement—clients, families, supporters, government, media.
- Partnerships with other nonprofits becoming more important.
- Reputation management being crucial, given increased client choice and government demands.

Skilled, qualified, committed human resources are central to successful implementation of the NDIS and so issues around attracting rewarding, performance managing and developing such resources are critical. However, the issue of the role of Human Resources managers or departments was not as clear as one might have hoped in our research findings.

Leadership demands in a challenging NDIS environment fundamentally require attention on productivity, satisfaction, accountability, survival and growth—all to best meet the organisation's mission.

What Do These Findings Mean for Government Agencies Dealing with Nonprofit Organisations?

The NFP organisational structure is essential to the key strategies of the health sector, especially since the introduction of the NDIS and its transformational change in the disability sector. It makes a significant contribution to society in providing its services to vulnerable parts of our society. Capacity issues become a salient consideration (Ahmed, 2017) *"The institutional significance lies in the non-profit sector's capacity to retain its distinctive characteristics and promote important services through collaboration, while the practical significance lies in making collaboration a basis for overcoming the constraints of resources and expertise of different sectors"* (Pg. 25).

The essential characteristics of this sector are focused on achieving social objectives and their missions, grounded in social goals. They are distinct from, but interdependent with the state in terms of funding and regulation. Nonprofits can play supplementary and complementary roles with government and also have a collaborative relationship with the public sector in terms of efficiency, effectiveness, expertise and closer proximity with stakeholders. Sometimes they are in adversarial relationships and also with for-profit business organisations (Ahmed, 2017).

Certainly, as our research demonstrates, demands from the NDIS can often be challenging to manage, including constant changes since the NDIA commenced, including pricing arrangements and client supports. Agencies need to recognise this and endeavour to minimise constant change and prioritise consistency and stability where possible. This goes hand in hand with a better understanding of and approach to key stakeholders involved, especially in terms of inter-organisational communication—improved and timely information flows, availability, dedicated communication links, appropriate modes of communication and ways of helping organisations better balance their mission maintenance and commercial imperatives. As in our Implementation Framework and variables involved, grounding interaction in the realisation that there is no one size fits all approach would be helpful.

Furthermore, from a change and success angle, environmental variables grounded in government relationships at state and federal levels, necessarily impact on internal variables, including strategy and sustainability (Ceptureanu et al., 2018). The need for effective government and nonprofit collaboration is crucial in the NDIS arena, in a time of growing complexity. The need for such collaboration has been supported through a move from public administration, to public management, to public governance within the theory of deliverology (Brock, 2020), the changes often seeing such collaboration allowing nonprofits more access to and influence on policy processes. There is need for both control and collaboration in governance aspects of this relationship.

Importantly, it has been suggested regarding effective nonprofit—government collaboration (Yan et al., 2018), nonprofits can play pivotal roles as enablers in service provision and capacity building; as coordinators in bridging the gap between the two sectors, and mediating in internal and external areas of politics; and as facilitators in initiating social change through effective partnering with government, building and sustaining networks, advocating in public policy processes, leading and innovating to solve health challenges.

Conclusion

This chapter has identified how nonprofit disability service providers have implemented Australia's innovative NDIS and assessed their successes and challenges. Using the results and analysis of the 46 interviews with application of a qualitative research method, we developed an Implementation Framework to help both current and future nonprofit disability service providers in implementing successful transformational change. That Framework delineated findings in terms of three phases of change—input, process and outcomes, and highlighted leadership and organisational cultural aspects critical in this system change from the previous supply-driven to a demand-driven disability services system.

This research and its findings may assist CEOs and nonprofit Boards how best to improve their NDIS organisation implementation to achieve the best outcomes for government, clients and their families, for the organisations themselves in surviving, growing and better meeting their missions, and for the broader community and society in general. It may also provide a basis for further research in the roll-out of the NDIS, including that of the change perspective. Roll-out was to be completed by 2020 but currently just over 250,000 have received packages, though, for many, it will be the first time they receive the disability support they need. Users and service providers continue to face challenges regarding the NDIS implementation, including the latest interview scheduling processes, and these challenges, while providing the impetus and focus for this research, have not been eliminated.

In terms of limitations, there is a need to involve more organisations across the country, including being cognisant of the many variables that make for differences in implementation mentioned earlier. And more involvement with the Agencies and governments involved would provide a richer basis for the research, including evaluating how the NDIS implementation itself has impacted policy development, processes and practices. Indeed, future research in this sector could follow up the rest of the NDIS roll-out and assess the changes and further lessons and, hopefully, improvements for key stakeholders in the later process. Increased research into such processes from an Implementation Science perspective may also be useful. That could include the under research of nonprofit HR and Boards in the change process.

References

Ahmed, S. (2017). *Effective non-profit management: Context, concepts, and competencies*. Routledge.

Akingbola, K., Rogers, S. E., & Baluch, A. (2019). *Change management in nonprofit organizations: Theory and practice*. Springer.

Andrews, K. (2018). *Market readiness for provision of services under the NDIS by joint standing committee on the NDIS*. Commonwealth of Australia.

Andrews, K. (2019). *NDIS planning interim report by joint standing committee on the NDIS*. Commonwealth of Australia.

Andrews, K. (2020). *Report into supported independent living by joint standing committee on the NDIS*. Commonwealth of Australia.

Baker, D. (2007). *Strategic management in public sector organisations* (First ed.). Chandos Publishing (Oxford) Limited.

Bamford, D. R., & Forrester, P. L. (2003). Managing planned and emergent change within an operations management environment. *International Journal of Operations & Production Management, 23*(5), 546–564.

Baulcomb, J. S. (2003). Management of change through force field analysis. *Journal of Nursing Management, 11*(4), 275–280.

Becker, K. L. (2007). Impact of personal style on change experience.

Beckhard, R., & Harris, R. T. (1987). *Organizational transitions: Managing complex change.*

Beer, M. (1999). Developing organizational fitness: towards a theory and practice of organizational alignment. Paper presented at the *14th Annual Conference of the Society of Industrial and Organizational Psychology*, Atlanta, GA.

Benjamin, L. M. (2008). Bearing more risk for results: Performance accountability and nonprofit relational work. *Administration & Society, 39*(8), 959–983.

Birks, M., & Mills, J. (2011). *Grounded theory—A practical guide* (1st ed.). Sage Publications.

Bouquet, C., Birkinshaw, J., & Barsoux, J.-L. (2016). Fighting the "headquarters knows best syndrome". *MIT Sloan Management Review, 57*(2), 59.

Boychuk Duchscher, J. E., & Morgan, D. (2004). Grounded theory: Reflections on the emergence vs. forcing debate. *Journal of advanced nursing, 48*(6), 605–612.

Bridges, W. (1991). *Managing transitions.* Perseus.

Brock, K. L. (2020). Government and non-profit collaboration in times of deliverology, policy innovation laboratories and hubs, and new public governance. *VOLUNTAS: International Journal of Voluntary and Nonprofit Organizations, 31*(2), 257–270.

Bullock, R. J., & Batten, D. (1985). It's just a phase we're going through: A review and synthesis of OD phase analysis. *Group & Organization Studies, 10*(4), 383–412.

Burke, W. W. (2013). *Organization change: Theory and practice*: Sage Publications.

Burke, W. W., & Litwin, G. H. (1992). A causal model of organizational performance and change. *Journal of Management, 18*(3), 523–545.

Burt, E., & Taylor, J. A. (2000). Information and communication technologies: Reshaping voluntary organizations? *Nonprofit Management and Leadership, 11*(2), 131–143.

Butler, P. (2019). New guidance. *Company Director, 35*(2), 56.

Cameron, E., & Green, M. (2009). *Making sense of change management* (2nd ed.). KoganPage.

Carnall, C. A. (2007). *Managing change in organizations.* Pearson Education.

Ceptureanu, S. I., Ceptureanu, E. G., Bogdan, V. L., & Radulescu, V. (2018). Sustainability perceptions in Romanian non-profit organizations: An exploratory study using success factor analysis. *Sustainability, 10*(2), 294.

Chapman, D. S., & Mayers, D. (2013). Predicting voluntary turnover with culture, employee values and their congruence. *Paper presented at the Academy of Management Proceedings.*

Chenitz, W. C., & Swanson, J. M. (1986). *From practice to grounded theory: Qualitative research in nursing.* Addison Wesley Publishing Company.

Corritore, M., Goldberg, A., & Srivastava, S. (2020). The new analytics of culture. *Harvard Business Review* (January–February), 77–83.
Dawson, P., & Daniel, L. (2010). Understanding social innovation: A provisional framework. *International Journal of Technology Management, 51*(1), 9–21.
De Meuse, K. P., Dai, G., & Hallenbeck, G. S. (2010). Learning agility: A construct whose time has come. *Consulting Psychology Journal: Practice and Research, 62*(2), 119.
DeRue, D. S. (2011). Adaptive leadership theory: Leading and following as a complex adaptive process. *Research in Organizational Behavior, 31,* 125–150.
Dunphy, D., Griffiths, A., & Benn, S. (2007). *Organizational change for corporate sustainability* (2nd ed.). Routledge.
Egan, G. (1985). *Change agent skills in helping and human services settings* (1st ed.). Brooks/Cole Publishing Company.
El-Dirani, A., Houssein, M. M., & Hejase, H. J. (2019). An exploratory study of the role of human resources management in the process of change. *Open Journal of Business and Management, 8*(1), 156–174.
Frei, F., & Morriss, A. (2020). Begin with trust The first step to becoming a genuinely empowering leader. *Harvard Business Review, 98*(3), 112–121.
Gale, N. K., Heath, G., Cameron, E., Rashid, S., & Redwood, S. (2013). Using the framework method for the analysis of qualitative data in multi-disciplinary health research. *Journal of Medical Research, 13*(1), 117.
Gilchrist, D. J., Knight, P. A., Edmonds, C. A., & Emery, T. J. (2019). *Six years and counting: The NDIS and the Australian Disability Services System—A white paper, a report of not-for-profits*. Retrieved from Crawley, Australia.
Gray, K., & Wilkinson, J. (2016). Managing organizational change. In J. Edmond (Ed.), *Human factors in the chemical and process industries: Making it work in practice*. Elsevier.
Greenleaf, R. K. (1977). *Servant leadership: A journey Into the nature of legitimate power and greatness*. Paulist Press.
Hall, M. (2017). Do business practices help or hinder the management of non-profits? *Third Sector Review, 23*(2), 5.
Harney, B., Fu, N., & Freeney, Y. (2018). Balancing tensions: Buffering the impact of organisational restructuring and downsizing on employee well-being. *Human Resource Management Journal, 28*(2), 235–254.
Hauck, E. L., Snyder, L. A., & Cox-Fuenzalida, L.-E. (2008). Workload variability and social support: Effects on stress and performance. *Current Psychology, 27*(2), 112.
Hernández-Perlines, F., & Araya-Castillo, L. A. (2020). Servant leadership, innovative capacity and performance in third sector entities. *Frontiers in Psychology, 11,* 290.
Hoefer, R. (2019). *Advocacy practice for social justice*. Oxford University Press.

Huy, Q. N. (2001). In praise of middle managers. *Harvard Business Review*, 79(8), 72–79, 160.
Isett, K. R., Glied, S. A., Sparer, M. S., & Brown, L. D. (2013). When change becomes transformation: A case study of change management in medicaid offices in New York City. *Public Management Review*, 15(1), 1–17.
Kiernan, M. D., & Hill, M. (2018). Framework analysis: A whole paradigm approach. *Qualitative Research Journal*, 18(3), 248–261.
Kimberlin, S. E. (2010). Advocacy by nonprofits: Roles and practices of core advocacy organizations and direct service agencies. *Journal of Policy Practice*, 9(3–4), 164–182.
Kotter, J. P. (1996). *Leading change*. Harvard Business Press.
Kotter, J. P. (2005, 2005/01//Spring reproduced in 2007). Leading change— Why transformation efforts fail. *Harvard Business Review*, 96–103.
Kübler-Ross, E. (1969). *On death and dying: What the dying have to teach doctors, nurses, clergy and their own families*. Taylor & Francis.
Levesque, M. (2020). Leadership as interpreneurship: A disability nonprofit Atlantic Canadian profile. *Politics and Governance*, 8(1), 182–192.
Lewin, K. (1946). Action Research and Minority Problems. *Journal of Social Sciences*, 2.
Lichtenstein, B. B., Uhl-Bien, M., Marion, R., Seers, A., Orton, J. D., & Schreiber, C. (2006). *Complexity leadership theory: An interactive perspective on leading in complex adaptive systems.*
Lilius, J. M., Worline, M. C., Maitlis, S., Kanov, J., Dutton, J. E., & Frost, P. (2008). The contours and consequences of compassion at work. *Journal of Organizational Behavior: the International Journal of Industrial, Occupational and Organizational Psychology and Behavior*, 29(2), 193–218.
Lines, R., Selart, M., Espedal, B., & Johansen, S. T. (2005). The production of trust during organizational change. *Journal of Change Management*, 5(2), 221–245.
Locke, M. G., & Guglielmino, L. (2006). The influence of subcultures on planned change in a community college. *Community College Review*, 34(2), 108–127.
Lucas, C., & Kline, T. (2008). Understanding the influence of organizational culture and group dynamics on organizational change and learning. *The learning organization*.
Mcardle, K. L., & Reason, P. (2008). Action research and organization development. *Handbook of organization development*, 123–136.
Memon, A. R., & Kinder, T. (2017). Co-location as a catalyst for service innovation: A study of Scottish health and social care. *Public Management Review*, 19(4), 381–405.
Nadler, D., & Tushman, M. (1997). *Competing by design: The power of organizational architecture*: Oxford University Press.

NDIS. (2020). *Delivering the NDIS.* https://www.ndis.gov.au/news/4889-delivering-ndis-roll-out-complete-across-australia-christmas-and-cocos-islands-join-world-leading-scheme

Nechully, S., & Pokhriyal, S. K. (2019). Choosing grounded theory and frame work analysis as the appropriate qualitative methods for the research. *Journal of Management, 6*(1), 130–145.

Noble, J., Richardson, H., George, R., Hansford, P., Sheridan, R., & Thirkettle, J. (2017). P-243 Driving change in hospice care-reflecting on the successes and the scars. *BMJ Supportive & Palliative Care, 7,* A97.

Oreg, S., & Berson, Y. (2016). Leaders' impact on organizational change: Bridging theoretical and methodological chasms. Academy of Management Annals, (0138.R5).

Page, L., Boysen, S., & Arya, T. (2019). Creating a culture that thrives. *Organization Development Review, 51*(1), 28–35.

Rosenbaum, D., & More, E. (2021). Complex change in the Australian nonprofit sector. *Change Management: An International Journal, 22*(1), 18–36.

Rosenbaum, D., More, E., & Steane, P. (2017). A longitudinal qualitative case study of change in nonprofits: Suggesting a new approach to the management of change. *Journal of Management & Organization, 23*(1), 74–91.

Rosenbaum, D., More, E., & Steane, P. (2018). Planned organisational change management: Forward to the past? An exploratory literature review. *Journal of Organizational Change Management, 31*(2), 286–303.

Rosenbaum, D., Taksa, L., & More, E. (2019). The role of reflection in planned organizational change. *Change Management, 18*(3–4), 1–22.

Senge, P. M. (1990). *The fifth discipline: The art and practice of the learning organization.* Doubleday.

Shin, J., Taylor, M. S., & Seo, M. G. (2012). Resources for change: The relationships of organizational inducements and psychological resilience to employees' attitudes and behaviors toward organizational change. *Academy of Management Journal, 55*(3), 727–748.

Taffinder, P. (1998). *Big change: A route-map for corporate transformation.* John Wiley.

Tan, V., & Tiong, T. N. (2005). Change management in times of economic uncertainty. *Singapore Management Review, 27*(1), 49–69.

Uhl-Bien, M., Marion, R., & McKelvey, B. (2007). Complexity leadership theory: Shifting leadership from the industrial age to the knowledge era. *The Leadership Quarterly, 18*(4), 298–318.

Van Dierendonck, D. (2011). Servant leadership: A review and synthesis. *Journal of Management, 37*(4), 1228–1261.

Venus, M., Stam, D., & Van Knippenberg, D. (2019). Visions of change as visions of continuity. *Academy of Management Journal, 62*(3), 667–690.

Waddell, D., Creed, A., Cummings, T. G., & Worley, C. G. (2019). *Organisational change: Development and transformation*. Cengage AU.

Wilkinson, K., Boyd, K., Pearson, M., Farrimond, H., Lang, I., Fleischer, D., & Rappert, B. (2019). Making sense of evidence: Using research training to promote organisational change. *Police Practice and Research, 20*(5), 511–529.

Yan, X., Lin, H., & Clarke, A. (2018). Cross-sector social partnerships for social change: The roles of non-governmental organizations. *Sustainability, 10*(2), 558.

Zhai, R. L., Watson, J., Gilchrist, D., & Newby, R. (2017). Non-profit vulnerability: An exploratory study. *Financial Accountability & Management, 33*(4), 373–390.

CHAPTER 19

When Everything Matters: Non-market Strategies, Institutions and Stakeholders' Interests

Angelina Zubac

INTRODUCTION: NON-MARKET STRATEGIES

A non-market strategy addresses the non-market environment as opposed to the market environment. The *non-market environment* "includes those interactions that are intermediated by the public, stakeholders, government, the media, and public institutions. These institutions differ from those of the market environment because of the characteristics such as majority rule, due process, broad enfranchisement, collection action, and publicness". The non-market environment may stimulate both voluntary actions and involuntary actions. The *market environment*, on the other hand, "includes those interactions between the firm and other parties

A. Zubac (✉)
University of Queensland, Brisbane, QLD, Australia
e-mail: a.zubac@business.uq.edu.au; angelina.zubac@aim.com.au;
az@strategylink.com.au

© The Author(s), under exclusive license to Springer Nature Singapore Pte Ltd. 2022
A. Zubac et al. (eds.), *Effective Implementation of Transformation Strategies*, https://doi.org/10.1007/978-981-19-2336-4_19

that are intermediated by markets or private agreements". Such interactions are likely to be voluntary and designed to improve the organisation's financial position (Baron, 1995: 47).

To make sense of both the market and non-market environments, it is necessary to understand the institutional superstructure within which it is contained, including why some institutions have risen to a place of prominence within the superstructure. It is also important to appreciate that organisations and markets are both institutions. This is because "institutions are humanly devised constraints that structure human interaction". Institutions can be informal or formal. Informal institutions are usually observed out of habit or convention. Examples of informal institutions are queuing for the bus, paying gratuities to service providers, speaking to the elderly or the village leadership in respectful terms and throwing one's cap into the air upon formally graduating. Formal institutions usually form because people have organised to ensure that certain standards, rules or regulations are followed. Examples of formal institutions are fiat money, the system of government, the judiciary, the police and building codes. Many organisations will develop their own institutions internally over time too, such as a culture where certain ethical practices or norms are observed. The institutions that matter the most within both the non-market and market environments are those which stimulate or require the observance of very specific behaviours and responses. These will differ depending on the country or institutional system being considered (North, 1994: 360).

If seeking to formulate and implement a strategy of any kind, whether it be market-based or not, the challenge is to find an acceptable way to classify the market and non-market institutions which can impact the organisation. According to Zubac et al. (2007, 2012 & 2021), this can be achieved by classifying an institution that can impact an organisation as belonging to one of the four of these categories: (1) capital markets, (2) product & service markets, (3) resource markets and (4) non-market institutions. In other words, the strategy any organisation pursues will be essentially an amalgam of four sub-strategies, that is, the organisation's (1) financial, (2) customer value creation, (3) resource and (4) non-market strategies, as illustrated in (Fig. 19.1). It shows that the corporate or (overall) strategy is influenced by the organisation's financial, customer value creation, resource and non-market strategies which emerge at the organisation. All of these sub-strategies are primarily impacted by one category of institution, that is, the relevant capital markets, product &

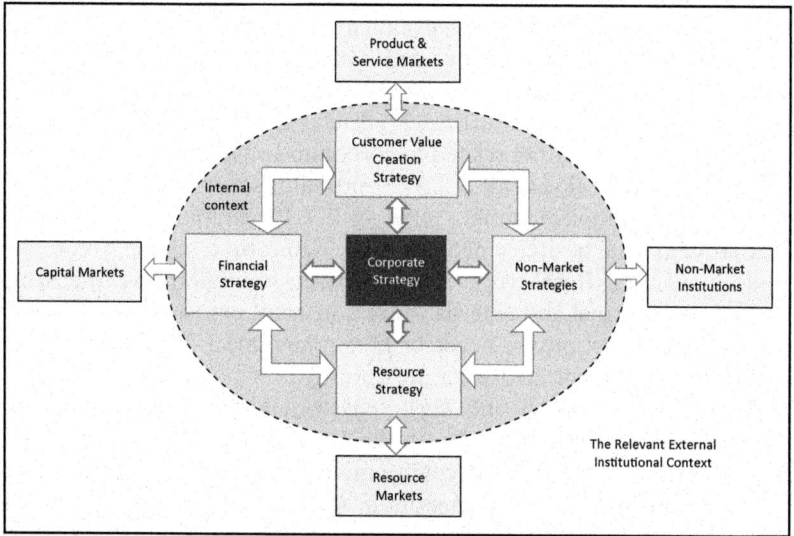

Fig. 19.1 The firm's strategic context (*Source* Adapted from Zubac et al., 2007)

service markets, resource markets and non-market institutional environment, respectively. The double-headed arrows in (Fig. 19.1) indicate that each sub-strategy influences the other. Ideally, the organisation formulates and implements a strategically aligned corporate strategy because the different parts of the organisation coordinate well.

These ideas are consistent with Baron's (1995: 47–48) definition of a market and non-market strategy: A *market strategy* is "a concerted pattern of actions taken in the market environment to create value by improving economic performance" while a *non-market strategy* is "a concerted pattern of actions taken in the nonmarket environment to create value by improving its overall performance". The critical difference between the two definitions is the words "economic performance" and "overall performance". When an organisation is profit-maximising, the non-market environment must be carefully managed. This is because it can directly and indirectly impact economic performance. Indeed, regardless of whether the organisation is profit-maximising or not, a failure to address the non-market environment could lead to the organisation underperforming in other critical areas of performance. Market and non-market strategies should be integrated for this reason.

Taking these ideas even further, Mellahi et al. (2016) argue that non-market strategies are either related to corporate social responsibility (CSR) or corporate political activity (CPA).[1] Although some organisations may concentrate on implementing a CSR or a CPA strategy, a CSR and a CPA strategy can be implemented at the same time and in a complementary manner. Both types of non-market strategies have the same fundamental internal and external drivers in common, such as the desire to satisfy managers' private needs or obtain legitimacy. Both also involve the same fundamental mediating mechanisms, such as *bridging* between parties to gain legitimacy and *buffering* to defend or lobby against an undesirable change in the law. Given the moderating effects of the organisation's external and internal environments, both types of non-market strategies can lead to the organisation achieving good things, such as an improvement in the organisation's reputation or its financial performance. However, a non-market strategy could do the opposite to what was intended. For instance, it could lead to more scrutiny rather than reduce the risk of excessive scrutiny by outsiders. The political ties established by the organisation can sometimes be perceived cynically, especially after entering another country or when the organisation does not have a public affairs function or that function operates inefficiently (Leidong et al., 2017). It can be extremely difficult to build strong social or political ties independently or with other organisations to gain access to useful information or financial incentives and/or build a coalition to influence policymakers (Hillman & Hitt, 1999).

There are potentially many social, political and legal matters or "issues, institutions, interests and information" that can impact an organisation, and many individuals, and organised groups of people or organisations that the organisation must interact with over time to achieve its strategic objectives (Baron, 1995: 48). In a nutshell, non-market strategies are about making both the market and non-market environments easier to navigate (Funk & Hirschman, 2017). In addition, many organisations must operate in environments with weak institutions. When this is the

---

[1] An organisation implements a CSR strategy to positively contribute to society while a CPA strategy is usually undertaken to change the political environment or influence someone politically.

case, it may be necessary to work independently or with others to implement non-market strategies that are: (1) adaptive where the objective is to make the best out of a bad situation, (2) additive through which new rules and regulations are introduced to lower costs, including in consultation with a decentralised body, or (3) transformative where the goal is to change the rules to lower costs or increase them for others (Dorobantu et al., 2017). To be able to navigate the non-market environment, exemplary non-market environment management assets and capabilities must be developed, such as a reputation for ethical dealings or the know-how to deal with governments, the press or activists. Such assets and capabilities may be co-developed or shared with other organisations, including with competitors (Baron, 1995).

However, in the past, non-market strategies have been formulated and implemented as if the management of institutions and stakeholders' interests are entirely separate matters, as if neither have little to do with each other. This has created a conceptual disconnect. With this in mind, the institutions literature is briefly reviewed in the next section. The review demonstrates that institutions determine how people and organisations should interact to develop exchange relationships and other relationships, and build valuable forms of knowledge. In the section that follows, the stakeholder literature is briefly reviewed. The review demonstrates that stakeholders determine how institutions evolve over time. In the final section, a framework is developed that can be used to understand the recursive relationship which exists between institutions and stakeholders, and how non-market strategies can be formulated and implemented to achieve advantaging adaptive outcomes for the organisation. The chapter concludes with a brief discussion of the implications for management and research.

INSTITUTIONS AND ORGANISATIONS

In the last decades, it has become increasingly important to consider institutions when analysing and addressing an organisation's problems. As both the sociological and economics-derived literatures have shown, institutions can explain an organisation's evolution, especially why organisations in the same institutional environment end up resembling each other over time despite competing with each other for customers and resources (Oliver, 1992). Institutional analysis can also be used to understand how organisations and the knowledge they develop over time contributes to endogenous economic growth and positive social change (Glückler et al., 2018).

Indeed, Peng and et al. (2009: 63) argue that the analysis of institutions represents a third leg of the strategy tripod. Although industrial organisation (IO) economics and the resource-based view (RBV) are useful for understanding the benefits of positioning the organisation appropriately in its industry against competitors, and acquiring and developing a unique capability base to differentiate the organisation, respectively, an "institution-based view" can also explain the four fundamental questions of strategy, that is, (1) why organisations differ, (2) how do organisations behave, (3) what determines an organisation's scope and (4) what determines the success or failure of an organisation. By understanding the pressures that different institutions can exert on an organisation to adopt a particular form, one can understand why organisations in the same institutional environment become similar over time. By analysing the informal and formal rules that characterise an institutional environment, one can understand why adaptive rather than optimising strategic decisions are made more often than not. Also, IO economics and the RBV suggest organisations are constrained for geographic or product-related reasons. However, some rules and regulations or even cultural impediments can limit scope outright.

Lastly, rather than explaining performance in terms of the industry position obtained or the uniqueness of the organisation's resource base, the presence of some institutions may be particularly advantaging for some organisations. For instance, the latter can explain choice of entry mode if planning to do business in another country. In countries with weak institutions, joint ventures are usually the preferred mode of entry because valuable local resources can be more readily accessed. Acquisitions can be more constructive when the institutions are strong (Meyer et al., 2009). It is also apparent that when organisations operate with an ecosystem structure, organisations tend to align. Individual organisations are incentivised to emulate other organisations to benefit from being part of the ecosystem and/or gain advantage over another ecosystem (Jacobides et al., 2018).

Two Organisational Literatures

As mentioned, two streams within the management literature examine the subject of institutions. One is more micro in its focus and has its origins in sociology. The other is more macro in its focus and has its origins in institutional economics. According to Peng et al. (2009), Scott and North have been especially influential. Indeed, Scott's (1995) thesis can be considered to be representative of the micro stream while North's (1990) thesis can be considered to be representative of the macro stream. Scott argued institutions are either regulative (coercive), normative or cognitive in how they impact individuals. North argued institutions are either formal or informal in how they impact organisations. That is, the two literatures have in common the idea that laws, regulations, rules are examples of regulative (coercive) and formal institutions while norms, cultures and ethics are examples of normative and cognitive institutions and informal institutions. Although both streams are concerned with people and organisations, the macro stream is much more concerned with how organisations contribute to economic change.

Neo-Institutional Theory (Sociological/psychological)

The term neo-institutional theory is normally used to describe the micro and more sociological/psychological stream of the institutional literature in management. Initially, concerned with examining how bureaucratisation and rational forms of decision-making lead to organisations resembling each other over time, neo-institutional theory began to explore how (disciplinary or professional) fields emerge over time and stimulate isomorphic change. DiMaggio and Powell (1983) found that some fields can exert *coercive* pressure on people and organisations to behave a certain way. However, organisations in the same industry tend to imitate the practices and structures of successful organisations. This form of isomorphism is essentially a *mimetic* response. It is prevalent especially during periods characterised by uncertainty. Fields can also exert *normative* pressure, especially when certain ways of doing or modes of behaviours are associated with professionalisation. This is similar to Scott's (1995) ideas about *regulative*, *cognitive* and *normative* pressures being placed on people and/or organisations by institutions. It also represents a break from the idea that the State dictates and defines the sorts of institutions that can and do emerge over time. Organisations are seen to have a role here despite being institutions themselves (Zucker, 1987).

Similarly, it has been argued that organisations tend to resemble each other over time within the same institutional environment for legitimisation reasons. *Processes of legitimisation* emerge over time because people from within and outside of the organisation identify practices and procedures the organisation should adopt to be perceived as legitimate. Change initiatives are undertaken to introduce the legitimising practice and ensure it is accepted. The opposite occurs when it is perceived that a practice is no longer legitimate. This could be because the organisation is failing or the practice is no longer favourably perceived by a significant group of people. The rate of change depends on a number of factors: "Political, functional and social mechanisms both within and beyond the organization are proposed as determinants of deinstitutionalization. Entropy and inertial pressures are proposed as inherent and competing processes in organizations that moderate the rate of deinstitutionalization; organizational entropy tends to accelerate the process of deinstitutionalization, whereas organizational inertia tends to impede it" (Oliver, 1992: 566). Legitimacy can be further subdivided into "three primary forms.... pragmatic, based on audience self-interest; moral, based on normative approval; and cognitive, based on comprehensibility and taken-for-grantedness". What form of legitimacy ends up being emphasised depends on the system of norms, values, beliefs, and definitions" of relevance (Suchman, 1995: 571).

These ideas complement RBV theory which argues resource heterogeneity, that is, the ability to access, combine and/or use resources that are unique, explains high performance. Since organisations under some circumstances must conform to normative pressures and can become institutionally isolated if they do not, organisations are more likely to achieve their performance objectives if they invest in institutional capital. As opposed to resource capital, defined "as the value-enhancing assets and competencies of the firm", institutional capital is "the context surrounding resources and resource strategies that enhance or inhibit the optimal use of valued resource capital". For instance, by fostering a culture of continuous improvement, the organisation may be able to make better use of its resources, including using them innovatively (Oliver, 1997: 709). An organisation may also become good at strategic political management, including anticipating, reacting to, defending against and proactively addressing political change because it is flexible or has the required capabilities (Oliver & Holzinger, 2008).

In an effort to better understand the cognitive aspect of institutional change, neo-institutional theory researchers have recently focused on understanding the symbolic systems or mental maps which lead to certain behaviours and cultures evolving within an organisational setting. This includes learning about how different actors respond to different institutional pressures and the governance decisions that are ultimately made by decision-makers on the organisation's behalf, as well as the relevance of certain institutional logics. As institutional theory matured, it shifted away from explaining soft institutions because all organisations operate in institutional environments which are market (technical) or non-market based to some extent; it is the degree to which they operate in one or the other that matters. For instance, a bank is more likely to operate in an environment with high technical requirements than a health club (Scott, 2008). The reality is that some institutional settings are far more complex and diverse than others (Vermulen et al., 2016).

The problem with neo-institutional theory is that it essentially evolved to become a theory of everything. It was easier to say what an institution was not rather than commit to a parameterisable definition. For instance, a review of the literature reveals that "institutional logic" has been described as an institution and as a mechanism of institutional change. The challenge now is to "avoid tautologies, avoid narrow theoretical discussion and problematization" (Alvesson & Spicer, 2018: 208).

Neo-Institutional Economics

Neo-institutional economics attempts to expand upon the ideas of the earlier institutionalists from the nineteenth century (Hodgson, 1998). It refutes many of the ideas from neoclassical economics, in particular, the idea that institutions and time do not matter. Neoclassical economics theory is essentially a static theory. It assumes economies can achieve equilibrium when in reality economic change occurs dynamically. Neoclassical economics has power but is limited in what it can explain at the same time.

Institutions "form the incentive structure of society, and the political and economic institutions, in consequence, are the underlying determinants of economic performance". Because institutions are "the humanly devised constraints that structure human interaction", they involve choice and continual processes of learning. If laws, regulations and norms are the rules of the game, then organisations, and the managers and entrepreneurs who operate them are the players. These players need to be incentivised in a variety of ways. These ideas are different to those of neoclassical economics. Neoclassical economics assumes organisations, managers and entrepreneurs are rational, self-interested and make efficient resource allocation decisions. In contrast, neo-institutional economics assumes these "players" stimulate adaptative forms of efficiency when they use society's scarce resources (North, 1994: 59 & 60). Neo-institutional economics deconstructs neoclassical's rational actor model because managers are more likely to make non-optimising decisions than optimising decisions (Hodgson, 1998).

Drawing on Schumpeter's, Penrose's and North's theses about institutions, Moran and Ghoshal (1999: 407) demonstrate the role organisations play in creating adaptively efficient, pluralistic institutional environments. They build on simple exchange principles to develop a process model which shows that, through a process of trial and error, organisations can become good at identifying useful resource combinations, and make exchanges which are both cost-effective and value creating. They demonstrate that institutions are introduced to countervail inertial forces if and when they arise. These institutions allow new resource combinations and complementarities between organisations and their resources to emerge. This shifts the productive frontier forward to a point where all the organisations and markets in the economy (the institutional environment in question) are more value creating than they would have been otherwise. These authors' arguments are important because they demonstrate that neo-institutional explanations for why firms (organisations) exist can be substituted to replace or used to augment the theories generated by classical market theory. Moral and Ghoshal's arguments also suggest that transaction cost economics arguments insufficiently explain why organisations exist. Despite transaction cost economics being an eminent theory within neo-institutional economics, organisations "are seen as a means of containing the damage of market failures". When organisations share productive (new) knowledge and build social capital as a result, knowledge may be repurposed, leading to the building of more social capital over time. This is over and above anything that is possible through the market system alone (Nahapiet & Ghoshal, 1996).

Neo-institutional economics, like neoclassical economics, is still concerned with explaining resource allocation, aggregate income, income distribution and the role of organisational decision-making but by using dynamic explanations. Even though price can indicate value, it is how value is "ensconced in institutions, social structures and behaviour" which is of most interest. Neo-institutionalists acknowledge the role of culture and cultural processes by which people's identities, goals, preferences and lifestyles are ultimately formed (Samuels, 1995: 574). However, a wider range of human-centric and economic problems can be more easily explained by combining economic, political and ideological rationalisations, such as when wanting to understand what might occur if markets remain unfettered or governments intervene in the economy excessively (Rutherford, 2001).

Institutional Change: Institutional Entrepreneurship and Work

The reasons and methods by which institutions change has been considered by authors in both the neo-institutional theory and neo-institutional economics literatures. Two strands in particular have shed light on what change involves: research on *institutional entrepreneurship* and *institutional work*.

According to Greenwood et al. (2002: 59), despite playing a regulatory role—acting as standard and rule setting agents—professional associations are often at the forefront of institutional change, including processes of de-institutionalisation. This is because they are well-placed to start and manage the debate on important professional matters and reframe the way in which the profession should be perceived in future. However, well-networked and influential large organisational professional members may dominate such debates, as was observed when studying the accounting profession. This is only a problem if these elite members resist positive change. Elite organisations' network position "can sharpen [their] awareness of alternatives ..... central organizations are more likely to come into contact with contradictory logics because they bridge organizational fields. Further, they become immune to coercive and normative processes because their market activities expand beyond the jurisdiction of field-level regulations ..... when low embeddedness is combined with a motivation to change, central actors become institutional entrepreneurs" (Greenwood & Suddaby, 2006: 27).

Institutional change is not always the result of an exogenous shock. It can be the result of endogenous forces, including through the efforts of individuals, groups of individuals, organisations or groups of organisations within the field. However, although institutional entrepreneurs are change agents, "not all change agents are institutional entrepreneurs. Actors ..... must fulfill two conditions to be regarded as institutional entrepreneurs; (1) initiate divergent changes; and (2) actively participate in the implementation of these changes" (Battilana et al., 2009: 68). Likewise, they may not always want to take on an institutional entrepreneurial role. The changes they instigate may lead to the creation of a new vision or involve mobilising resources and allies. They are different to social entrepreneurs who focus on achieving some sort of social good because existing institutions cannot make such changes.

Institutional entrepreneurship can be differentiated from the concept of institutional work because of institutional entrepreneurship's "heroic conception of agency". The concept of institutional work is described in deliberately more mundane terms. It is any form of agency directed at creating, maintaining and disrupting an institution. This work can be undertaken by individuals, groups of individuals, an organisation or groups of organisations too. Institutional work is a multi-level phenomenon where the actions of people and organisations are nested within the societal structure (Decker et al., 2018: 615). A recursive relationship must be established between change agent(s) undertaking institutional work and the institution(s) of interest. The process by which change is achieved depends on the agent's level of awareness of what is possible, and their skill and reflexibility. Likewise, it depends on the agent's ability to put boundaries around the institution or institutions of relevance, and the practices for exacting change that are used, which are in themselves the product of institutionalisation. Institutions may be created, maintained or disrupted for a variety of political, practical, cognitive, technological and moral reasons (Lawrence et al., 2009).

Institutional Strategies and Strategic Change: Achieving Legitimacy

Organisations achieve legitimacy by building capabilities of value to society. However, these capabilities are rarely the result of managers making rational, optimising decisions consciously. There are other adaptive forces at work (Langlois, 2003). However, most organisations need to compete while also taking a balanced approach to emulating the actions of other organisations to gain legitimacy (Deephouse, 1999). This is not the same as improving an organisation's reputation. Legitimacy is about gaining social acceptance by following regulations and learning to use resources responsibly. It is a different kind of relative concept to that of reputation (Deephouse, 2005). Institutional strategies clarify how the organisation will cooperate within the institutional environment but also work to create, maintain and/or transform critical institutions (Lawrence, 1999), including how they will create value for customers, owners, managers and employees while shaping but also being shaped by the institutional environment (Kern & Gospel, 2020). This is not to say all organisations develop effective institutional strategies. For instance, not all organisations will improve their environmental practices when put under coercive or normative pressure to use greener methods. Though some may go well beyond what is required to satisfy stakeholders, others will do very little. So much depends on the extent to which the disparate parts of the organisation are expected to act in an aligned manner (Delmas & Toffel, 2004).

Legitimacy has been defined in many ways but all the definitions have in common the idea that it is obtained by socially constructing some sort of reality. Logically, it is also a shared reality involving a particular audience who have achieved consensus (actual or apparent) about what is or is not legitimate. Legitimacy is achieved through a legitimation process with four distinct stages: (1) the need for the social innovation is established at the local stakeholder level, (2) the social innovation is validated at the social level by demonstrating how it aligns with what is already considered to be culturally acceptable, (3) the social innovation is diffused into other domains, and (4) the social innovation is widely embraced because it was accepted across multiple domains within society. The same process can also be used when the objective is to change people's preconceived ideas about what is legitimate. When this is the objective, it is important not only to establish the propriety and validity of the practice, norm, etc., but also to achieve widespread consensus (Johnson et al., 2006).

Of course, the success of the legitimation process will in part depend on whether the institutions in question are stable or undergoing some sort of change (Bitekine & Haack, 2015). Propriety, validity and consensus are distinct concepts. They occur at the micro, meso and macro levels. Together, they represent a multi-level phenomenon (Haack et al., 2021). Not surprisingly, the legitimisation process is possible to bypass altogether by taking on a strategic alliance partner who can "serve an important legitimating function". Such partners help organisations to achieve a range of market, relational, social, investment and/or alliance legitimacy advantages (Dacin et al., 2007: 169).

STAKEHOLDERS AND ORGANISATIONS

According to Hall and Soskice (2003), who are well-known for their work on the varieties of capitalism, some countries have a *comparative institutional advantage* over other countries. This means some countries have developed institutions and complementarities between their institutions that are particularly beneficial. Moreover, the organisations within their particular system of capitalism possess unique relational qualities. Hall and Soskice also argue in the same article that organisations are the means by which value creating relationships can be formed but the extent to which value can be created depends on the institutional superstructure within which the organisation is situated. Agreeing with Williamson (1985) that organisations form to some extent to minimise transaction costs by establishing hierarchies, contracts and a capability base, Hall and Soskice also argue that organisations create value in a variety of ways because of the existence of five unique institutional spheres: (1) industrial relations, (2) vocational training and education, (3) corporate governance for safeguarding investors, (4) inter-firm relations and (5) employees. These spheres enable the establishment of all manner of value creating stakeholder relationships within and across organisations, and within the whole institutional environment. Put yet another way, the extent to which value can be created depends on the quality of the relationships which organisations form through their stakeholders, including suppliers, customers, collaborators, partners, trade unions, business associations and governments. The institutional superstructure and the complementarities between the institutions which emerge in these spheres can be particularly advantaging for some organisations and, consequently, some countries.

These rather grand and highly respected ideas correspond with those of Freeman (2004), who originally introduced the idea that stakeholders are important and should not be ignored by those in management or researching management. Freeman believed large differences in organisational performance and strategic focus can be explained by understanding how stakeholders behave in different organisational and societal settings; different narratives about stakeholders and what they believe to be responsible organisational behaviour differed depending on the organisation. Freeman was also influenced by Williamson's (1985) ideas. Despite Williamson focusing on explaining the implications of ex-post opportunism, including the degree to which contracts can anticipate all possible contingencies,[2] he realised that organisations needed to be structured to

---

[2] Readers wanting to learn more about the implications of being unable to write contracts when transacting that pre-empt all possible contingencies should read Williamson's (1979) "classic" article or Mahoney's (2016) chapter on transaction costs theory in the *Economic Foundations of Strategy* on the topic.

minimise of the cost of getting managers (a key stakeholders group) to act in a way which was consistent with the organisation's strategic objectives. Stakeholder explanations could be used to explain why organisations are different to markets and, thus, their role within capitalism. Freeman makes it clear that he did not deliberately set out to make CSR an important area of study. This was just one of the outcomes of his musings (Freeman, 2004).

Stakeholder theory is also important because it provides insight into the role organisations play within civil society. The study of civil society defines how the existence of the State affects the individual economically, politically or cognitively whereas stakeholder theory "encompasses all the intermediary groups located between two extremes: the firm and the interests of individuals". This has very real implications for how organisations are governed. Boards of directors are required to concern themselves with a great variety of social and cultural matters, and not just those matters which can affect an organisation economically. "Stakeholder theory ratifies the institutionalisation of the firm in that stakeholders prefigure an open or fragmented, society largely dominated by corporations" (Bonnafous-Boucher & Porcher (2010: 206). Organisations depend on stakeholders for their very survival and, hence, must be governed with this in mind (Freeman, 1984; Freeman et al., 2021).

Stakeholder theory is also important because of its potential to extend RBV theory, which is arguably the dominant theory within strategic management. If RBV theory assumes the uniqueness of the resources an organisation possesses explains its performance, it follows that some organisations are high performing because they can build enduring stakeholder relationships. These relationships allow organisations to operate effectively in the marketplace but also within the non-market environment. This means that in addition to explaining sustainable competitive advantage, RBV theory must also explain the benefits of cooperating. RBV theory has traditionally treated people as economic objects, describing them in contractual and cost-minimising terms. However, according to stakeholder theory, stakeholders are "the final end", not the means (Freeman et al., 2021: 5). It explains why some people have a say in an organisation, the implications of a broad stakeholder base, and what is involved when co-creating or collaborating with others (McGahan, 2020). When organisations implement competitive strategies and stakeholder strategies that complement each other, the organisation can develop a performance-enhancing structure but also culture (Zollo et al., 2018).

Three Stakeholder Streams of Literatures—Descriptive, Instrumental and Normative

The stakeholder literature contains three streams: the descriptive, instrumental and normative streams. The descriptive stream explains the corporation in stakeholder terms. The instrumental stream considers whether the way in which stakeholders were managed can explain organisational performance in some meaningful way. The normative stream, on the other hand, considers if stakeholders have legitimate interests and whether these give them a say in the running of the organisation. However, an examination of the three streams demonstrates descriptive and instrumental arguments eventually revert to a consideration of the normative; in other words, normative arguments underlie both the descriptive and instrumental streams. This in part clarifies why organisations must be governed with the interests of stakeholders in mind. Stakeholders are the ultimate arbiters of organisational value. Thus, it is inevitable that the value they associate with the organisation will be defined in normative terms at some point even if it is not initially. Indeed, the stakeholder literature is replete with examples of different stakeholder value systems having a significant impact on an organisation, including cases where managers made self-interested, morally hazardous decisions (Donaldson & Preston, 1995). It is likely that the collective social and normative priorities of stakeholders within an organisation will converge over time (Jones & Wicks, 1999).

Stakeholder Identification and Effectively Governing

It can be a challenge to identify who should be classified as an organisation's stakeholder. According to Mitchell et al. (1997), the task can be rendered less challenging if stakeholders are considered using normative principles. However, some stakeholders can be described as having genuine claims while others as influencers. The problem is that not all claimants are influencers and not all influencers are claimants. Using a Venn diagram in their highly regarded paper to illustrate how stakeholders can be better understood, Mitchel et al. argue stakeholders can be defined in power, legitimacy and/or urgency terms. These researchers argue that stakeholders have low salience if they are of one type—a stakeholder with power, legitimacy or urgency. Their demands are *latent* in that they exist but they are not apparent to others and/or articulable yet. In contrast, *definitive* stakeholders have high salience because they have power, legitimacy and urgency. There can be no doubt that they should have a say in how the organisation is run. When a stakeholder possesses only two of the attributes, they are *expectant* stakeholders. They have moderate salience. They expect the organisation to act in their favour. Stakeholders with power and urgency, can become *dangerous*. They are more likely to use coercion to get what they want, including violence. When stakeholders have power and a legitimate claim, they expect to get attention. They are *dominant* stakeholders because it should be clear to others that they can act on their claims. Lastly, when stakeholders lack power but have an urgent and legitimate claim, they depend on others to have their claims heard. They are *dependent* stakeholders. Others are more likely to act on their behalf or advertise their claim, such as what tends to happen after an oil spill.

Alternatively, stakeholders can be identified by considering if a party is enfranchised and has claimancy rights. *Enfranchisement* "describes who is in and who is out of the organization's internal decision-making process and, hence, is a foundational element of governance structure". *Claimancy rights* "establish which individuals and groups can capture the value created by the organization". The benefit of classifying stakeholders in this way is that one can understand how an organisation's governance system may need to change when the institutional environment changes and stakeholder equity concerns are uncertain too. For instance, when the Tokyo Electric Plant got hit by a tsunami, an architectural change became necessary. Enfranchisement and claimancy rights for some stakeholders needed to be totally renegotiated (Klein et al., 2019: 10). This method for identifying stakeholders becomes challenging when important influencers are ignored. Unless all stakeholders' (potential) claims are categorised, heard, negotiated, prioritised and disputes resolved, all manner of economic and non-economic hindrances could end up plaguing an organisation (Amis et al., 2020).

In recent times, using transaction cost economics and RBV theory arguments, it was also argued that non-shareholder stakeholders are stakeholders if they are also residual claimants, that is, if they can make a claim on the organisation in the same way a shareholder can if the organisation is liquidated. That is, it is possible to calculate what they are owed in potentially or in real terms as a proportion of the resources they made available to organisation. It was also argued that instead of using some sort of moral standard to identify an organisation's stakeholders, "stakeholder resource-based theory makes specific predictions about how profit-maximizing firms will operate"; by pre-empting stakeholders' claims and negotiating in advance, an organisation can minimise potential losses and potentially maximise its gains (Barney, 2017: 3321). However, as Freeman et al. (2021) argued, people are not economic objects or a means to an end. Further, stakeholders can be the source of endogenously created value and shared value. However, it can be difficult to determine how such resources can be understood and governed (Cabral, 2019). In a nutshell, there are very many good reasons why all organisations are now required to be governed with the welfare of stakeholders in mind (Tirole, 2001).

An Integrated Approach: Critical Knowledge Flows and Social Interactions

Reviews by Lee (2011) and Aguilera et al. (2007) discuss two important facts: (1) institutions determine how people and organisations interact to develop exchange and other relationships, and build valuable forms of knowledge, and (2) stakeholders determine how institutions evolve over time. There is a recursive relationship which exists between institutions and stakeholders which must be reconciled.

These are ideas that have not been lost on other researchers. According to Lee (2011: 281) who studied how institutions affect stakeholders, and vice versa, when formulating and implementing a CSR strategy, "while institutions affect firms' social behavior by shaping the macro-level incentive structure and sources of legitimacy (distal mechanisms), firms' stakeholders can amplify or buffer the institutional forces by acting as mediators (proximate mechanisms)". In other words, the collective action of stakeholders stimulates institutional change, leading to certain regulations, norms, cognitions or cultural conditions gaining legitimacy within an organisation. However, stakeholders play a mediating role. They determine whether a particular CSR initiative will be implemented.

Aguilera et al. (2007: 836), take this idea slightly further. These authors integrate multiple micro- and macro-level theories, namely, ideas from organisational justice, corporate governance, and varieties of capitalism to argue "organizations are pressured to engage in CSR by many different actors, each driven by instrumental, relational, and moral motives". They found that both internal and external stakeholders determine the adoption of a certain CSR strategy. These stakeholders, which include employees and actors embedded within government or an NGO, are motivated in different ways and, thus, will use a variety of micro- and macro-mechanisms to put pressure on the organisation to adopt a certain CSR strategy to create social change. The combination of motivations and mechanisms occurring at different levels determine what will be contained and implemented through a CSR strategy.

All of these ideas are consistent with *new stakeholder theory* (McGahan, 2021: 1734). In this theory, it is argued that "because stakeholders bind resources to organizations, neither the resource-based view nor the new stakeholder view is complete without the other". Individuals interact with the organisation either for their own reasons or on behalf of an organisation. They give organisations access to valuable human capital, making it possible for organisations to address a range of market and non-market challenges. By the same token, Oliver and Holzinger (2008: 496 & 514) argued that organisations are likely to benefit if they develop "dynamic political management capabilities". Political strategies are successful because of the "firm's internally and externally oriented dynamic capabilities". People are key because these dynamic capabilities "are grounded in knowledge and influence acquisition and use".

No matter the theoretical lens that is used to understand institutions and stakeholders, the recursive relationship that exists between institutions and stakeholders occurring at multiple levels needs to be understood. There may be many micro-, meso- and macro-level factors that need to be understood too to make sense of how institutions change stakeholders, and vice versa. This is in the context that some institutions and some stakeholders may be organisations. Likewise, a stakeholder may be someone who is internal to an organisation or external to it. A particular stakeholder may play multiple roles. For example, a manager may be required to liaise with a standard setting body to provide feedback about a proposed change in a professional standard. However, in addition to being an employee/agent of the focal organisation, the manager is also a member of the standard setting organisation. Clearly, the manager must reconcile the two roles somehow. Of course, it is also likely that the same stakeholder may need to consult with another institution of which they have no existing stakeholder relationship or role, such as might be the case if the manager needs to consult with the members of an environmental group because the proposed change in the standard has environmental implications.

These ideas are illustrated in (Fig. 19.2), which reflects Zubac, et al. and's (2007, 2012 & 2021) arguments about the need to develop a strategy which addresses, through its sub-strategies, the institutions of most relevance to the organisation. On the left-hand side of the diagram, the idea that it is important to have integrated market and non-market strategies is illustrated (Baron, 1995). These both inform the corporate strategy. As indicated, they also determine how the organisation will be governed since it is now taken as given that organisations will be governed with the welfare of stakeholders in mind (Tirole, 2001). In line with both the institutions and stakeholder literatures, the market strategies are economic strategies and the non-market strategies are non-economic strategies. However, the market and the non-market strategies still influence each other, as the double-headed arrows indicate. The extent to which they influence each other varies. This depends on the organisation, including its history and priorities. Although it has been argued that non-market strategies can only be of two types, that is, either be a CSR or CPA strategy Mellahi, et al. (2016), the diagram assumes that organisations may need to deal strategically with stakeholders who are part of a network, for instance, part of an ecosystem, and/or who are stakeholders within institutions who may not be, strictly speaking, a CSR or a CPA-related institution. It depends on how CSR and CPA are defined by the focal organisation's key decision-makers. However, there is also just too little research to be able to say that all non-market strategies fall into only two categories. Hence the reference to "other institutional strategies".

On the right side of (Fig. 19.2), the stakeholder matrix indicates that some stakeholders may be internal to the organisation while some of the organisation's stakeholders may be external to the organisation. External stakeholders of note are likely to be embedded in an institution and will be recognisable as such. When the institution is informal and not organisation-based, identification is likely to be more difficult. Thus, when an institution is not organisation-based, for instance, it is more informal or normative or cognitive, then the emphasis will be on interpreting how the organisation can "interact" without a human point of contact. As indicated, on the far right of the diagram, some organisational stakeholders may be embedded in several institutions and some internal stakeholders could be too because they have some kind of (vested) interest

19 WHEN EVERYTHING MATTERS: NON-MARKET STRATEGIES ...   471

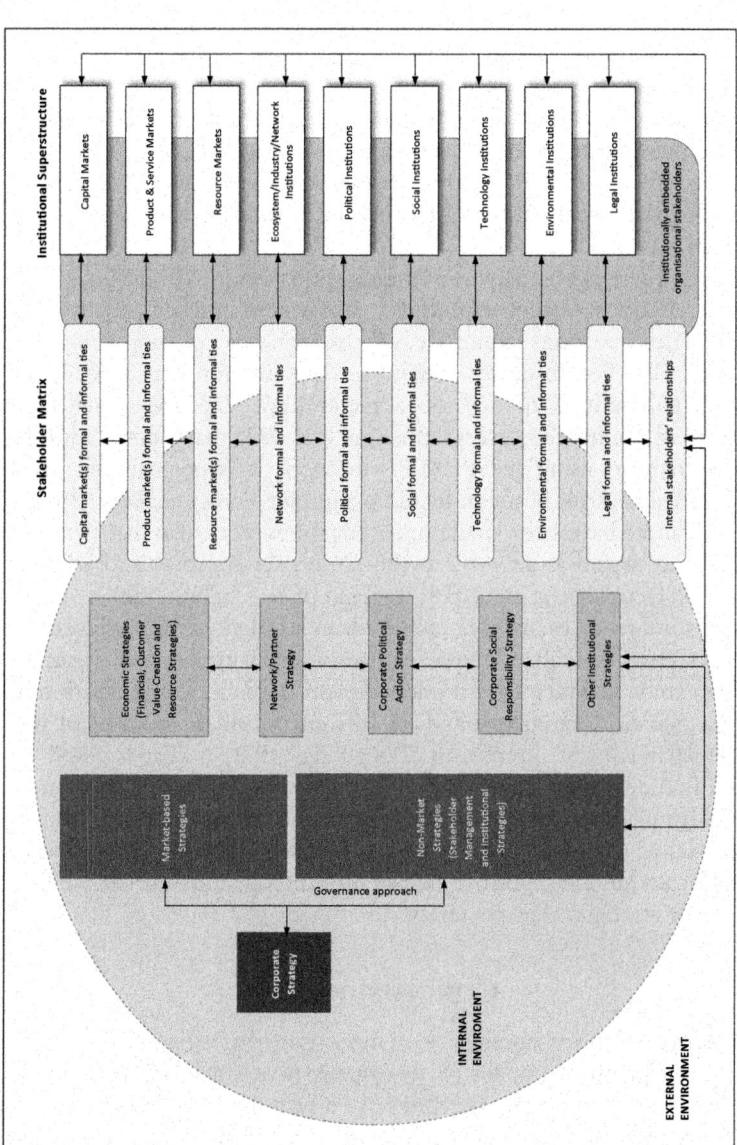

Fig. 19.2 Formulating and implementing integrated market and non-market strategies: The critical internal and external Knowledge flows and social interactions

in an external institution of relevance to the organisation. The institutions itemised within the superstructure, reflect the extant literature. Notably, it also demonstrates PESTEL principles. PESTEL is a widely used method for analysing an organisation's external environment, that is, the political, economic, social, technological, environmental and legal institutions within the external environment. In (Fig. 19.2), the economic institutions are the capital, product & service and resource markets of relevance to the organisation. All other institutions are non-economic institutions.

However, there is one proviso. Organisations often have dealings with other organisations within an industry, ecosystem and/or as part of a network. These dealings could be of an economic or non-economic nature or both. For instance, sometimes organisations need to cooperate with competitors to develop a technology. This too is reflected in (Fig. 19.2). Industries, ecosystems and networks have not traditionally been analysed using the PESTEL method. It is normally assumed that industry analysis is best conducted using Five Forces analysis (Porter, 1980). Advances have been made in recent times to ensure that network position or an organisation's role within an ecosystem can also be better understood (Jacobides, et al., 2018; Rosenkopf & Schilling, 2007). These institutions influence each other, as the double-sided arrows indicate. In short, it is clear that all of these institutions will impact the organisation. The extent to which they do depends on the specific organisation in question, including its history and its current priorities. With all of this in mind, what is most interesting about (Fig. 19.2) is that it could be used as a framework for comprehensively analysing the external environment to formulate (emergent) strategy or analyse how a strategic change was approached at a given organisation, including to identify if there were intended or unintended, positive or negative endogenous effects brought about by the strategic changes enacted.

Conclusion

The objective of this chapter is to demonstrate that all organisations—whether a for-profit or not-for-profit organisation, small or large, simply structured or very complex—need to have a non-market strategy and the ability to implement it. This was achieved by acknowledging that it is no longer feasible for an organisation to formulate and implement strategies that address the market environment only, as Baron (1995) argued, and by reviewing the institutions and stakeholders literatures.

The reviews made it abundantly clear that (1) institutions determine how people and organisations interact to develop exchange and other relationships, and build valuable forms of knowledge, and (2) stakeholders determine how institutions evolve over time. A recursive relationship exists between institutions and stakeholders which must be continuously reconciled; it is not logical to think about the institutions that could impact the organisation without thinking about the stakeholders who have a say in how these institutions form, and vice versa. Critically, the interactions which this recursive relationship stimulates may occur at multiple levels. Some of the organisation's stakeholders, including internal stakeholders may be very interested in advancing the objectives of multiple institutions at any one time too. Managers and researchers need to appreciate all of these things if they are to understand real-life strategic change problems with any degree of accuracy, pertaining to both market and non-market environments. The framework developed in this paper was constructed with this in mind. It is recommended that it can be used as a starting point for such conducting analyses.

REFERENCES

Aguilera, R. V., Rupp, D. E., Williams, C. A., & Ganapathi, J. (2007). Putting the S back in corporate social responsibility: A multilevel theory of social change in organizations. *Academy of Management Review, 32*(3), 836–863.

Alvesson, M., & Spicer, A. (2018). Neo-institutional theory and organization studies: A mid-life crisis? *Organization Studies, 40*(2), 199–218.

Amis, J., Barney, J., Mahoney, J. T., & Wang, H. (2020). Why we need a theory of stakeholder governance—and why this is a hard problem. *Academy of Management Review, 45*(3), 499–503.

Barney, J. B. (2017). Why resource-based theory's model of profit appropriation must incorporate a stakeholder perspective. *Strategic Management Journal, 39*(13), 3305–3325.

Baron, D. P. (1995). Integrated strategy: Market and non-market components. *California Management Review, 37*(2), 47–65.

Battilana, J., Leca, B., & Boxenbaum, E. (2009). How actors change institutions: Towards a theory of institutional entrepreneurship. *Academy of Management Annals, 3*(1), 65–107.

Bitektine, A. and Haack, P. 2015. The "Macro" and the Micro" of legitimacy. Toward a multilevel theory of the legitimacy process. *Academy of Management Review*, 40(1): 49–75.

Bonnafous, M., & Porcher, S. (2010). Towards a stakeholder society: Stakeholder theory vs theory of civil society. *European Management Review*, 7(4), 205–216.

Cabral, S., Mahoney, J. T., McGahan, A. M., & Potoski, M. (2019). Value creation and value appropriation in public and nonprofit organizations. *Strategic Management Journal*, 40(4), 465–475.

Dacin, M. T., Oliver, C., & Roy, J.-P. (2007). The legitimacy of strategic alliances: An institutional perspective. *Strategic Management Journal*, 28(2), 169–187.

Decker, S., Üsdiken, B., Engwall, L., & Rowlinson, M. (2018). Historical research on institutional change. *Business History*, 60(5), 613–627.

Deephouse, D. L., & Carter, S. M. (2005). An examination of differences between organizational legitimacy and organizational reputation. *Journal of Management Studies*, 42(2), 329–360.

Deephouse, D. L. (1999). To be different, or to be the same? It's a question (and theory) of strategic balance. *Strategic Management Journal*, 20(2), 147–166.

Delmas, M., & Toffel, M. W. (2004). Stakeholders and environmental management practices: An institutional framework. *Business Strategy and the Environment*, 13(4), 209–222.

DiMaggio, P. J., & Powell, W. W. (1983). The iron cage revisited: Institutional isomorphism and collective rationality in organizational fields. *American Sociological Review*, 48(2), 147–160.

Donaldson, T., & Preston, L. E. (1995). The stakeholder theory of the corporation: Concepts, evidence, and implications. *Academy of Management Review*, 20(1), 65–91.

Dorobantu, S., Kaul, A., & Zelner, B. (2017). Nonmarket strategy research through the lens of new institutional economics: An integrative review and future directions. *Strategic Management Journal*, 38(1), 114–140.

Freeman, R. E., Dmytriyev, S. D., & Phillips, R. A. (2021). Stakeholder theory and the resource-based view of the firm. *Journal of Management*, 47(7), 1757–1770.

Freeman, R. E. (1984). *Strategic management: A stakeholder approach*. Pitman.

Freeman, R. E. (2004). The stakeholder approach revisited. *fwu Zeitschrift für Wirtschafts–und Unternehmensethik (zfwu)*, 5(3), 228–241.

Funk, R. J., & Hirschman, D. (2017). Beyond nonmarket strategy: Market actions as corporate political activity. *Academy of Management Review*, 42(1), 35–52.

Glückler, J., Suddaby, R. & Lenz, R. 2018. On the spatiality of institutions and knowledge. In J Glückler, R. Suddaby and R. Lenz (Eds.), *Knowledge and*

Institutions (pp. 1–22). Springer Open. https://link.springer.com/book/10.1007%2F978-3-319-75328-7.

Greenwood, R., Suddaby, R., & Hinings, C. R. (2002). Theorizing change: The role of professional associations in the transformation of institutional fields. *Academy of Management Journal, 45*(1), 58–80.

Greenwood, R., & Suddaby, R. (2006). Institutional entrepreneurship in mature fields: The big five accounting firms. *Academy of Management Journal, 49*(1), 27–48.

Haack, P., Schilke, O., & Zucker, L. (2021). Legitimacy revisited: Disentangling propriety, validity, and consensus. *Journal of Management Studies, 58*(3), 749–781.

Hall, P. A. & Soskice, D. 2003. An introduction to varieties of capitalism. In P. A. Hall and D. Soskice (Eds.), *Varieties of Capitalism: The Institutional Foundations of Comparative Advantage.* Oxford Scholarship Online. https://doi.org/10.1093/0199247757.001.0001

Hillman, A. J., & Hitt, M. A. (1999). Corporate political strategy formulation: A model of approach, participation, and strategy decisions. *Academy of Management Review, 24*(4), 825–842.

Hodgson, G. M. (1998). The approach of institutional economics. *Journal of Economic Literature, 36*(1), 166–192.

Jacobides, M., Cenmamo, C., & Gawer, A. (2018). Towards a theory of ecosystems. *Strategic Management Journal, 39*(8), 2255–2276.

Johnson, C., Dowd, T. J., & Ridgeway, C. L. (2006). Legitimacy as a social process. *Annual Review of Sociology, 32*(1), 53–78.

Jones, T. M., & Wicks, A. (1999). Convergent stakeholder theory. *Academy of Management Review, 24*(2), 206–221.

Kern, P., & Gospel, H. (2020). The effects of strategy and institutions on value creation and appropriation in firms: A longitudinal study of three telecom companies. *Strategic Management Journal*, 1–24. https://doi.org/10.1002/smj.3129(Earlyview)

Klein, P. G., Mahoney, J. T., McGahan, A. M., & Pitelis, C. N. (2019). Organizational governance adaptation: Who is in, who is out, and who gets what. *Academy of Management Review, 44*(1), 6–27.

Langlois, R. N. (2003). Strategy as economics versus economics as strategy. *Managerial and Decision Economics, 24*(4), 283–290.

Lawrence, T.B., Suddaby, R. and Leca, B. 2009. Introduction: Theorizing and studying institutional work. In T.B. Lawrence, S. Fraser, R. Suddaby and B. Leca (Eds.), *Institutional Work: Actors and Agency in Institutional Studies of Organization,* Cambridge University Press, https://doi.org/10.1017/CBO9780511596605

Lawrence, T. B. (1999). Institutional strategy. *Journal of Management, 25*(2), 161–188.

Lee, M.-D. P. (2011). Configuration of external influences: The combined effects of institutions and stakeholders on corporate social responsibility strategies. *Journal of Business Ethics, 102*, 281–298.

Liedong, T. A., Rajwani, T., & Mellahi, K. (2017). Reality or illusion? The efficacy of non-market strategy in institutional risk reduction. *British Journal of Management, 28*(4), 609–628.

Mahoney, J. T. (2016). *Economic Foundations of Strategy.* Sage Publications.

McGahan, A. M. (2020). Where does an organization's responsibility end? Identifying the boundaries on stakeholder claims. *Academy of Management Discoveries, 6*(1), 8–11.

McGahan, A. M. (2021). Integrating insights from the resource-based view of the firm into new stakeholder theory. *Journal of Management, 47*(7), 1734–1756.

Mellahi, K., Frynas, J. G., Sun, P., & Siegel, D. (2016). A review of the non-market strategy literature: Toward a multi-theoretical integration. *Journal of Management, 42*(1), 143–173.

Meyer, K. E., Estrin, S., Bhaumik, S. K., & Peng, M. W. (2009). Institutions, resources, and entry strategies in emerging economies. *Strategic Management Journal, 30*(1), 61–80.

Mitchell, R. K., Agle, B. R., & Wood, D. J. (1997). Toward a theory of stakeholder identification and salience: Defining the principle of who and what really counts. *Academy of Management Review, 22*(4), 853–886.

Moran, P., & Ghoshal, S. (1999). Markets, firms, and the process of economic development. *Academy of Management Review, 24*(3), 390–412.

Nahapiet, J., & Ghoshal, S. (1998). Social capital, intellectual capital, and the organizational advantage. *Academy of Management Review, 23*(2), 242–266.

North, D. C. (1990). *Institutions, institutional change, and economic performance.* Harvard University Press.

North, D. C. (1994). Economic performance through time. *The American Economic Review, 84*(3), 359–368.

Oliver, C., & Holzinger, I. (2008). The effectiveness of strategic political management: A dynamic capabilities framework. *Academy of Management Review, 33*(2), 496–520.

Oliver, C. (1992). The antecedents of deinstitutionalization. *Organization Studies, 13*(4), 563–588.

Oliver, C. (1997). Sustainable competitive advantage: Combining institutional and resource-based views. *Strategic Management Journal, 18*(9), 697–713.

Peng, M. W., Sun, S. L., Pinkham, B., & Chen, H. (2009). The institution-based view as a third leg for a strategy tripod. *Academy of Management Perspectives, 23*(3), 63–81.

Porter, M. E. 1980. *Competitive Strategy: Techniques for Analyzing Industries and Competitors.* The Free Press.

Rosenkopf, L., & Schilling, M. A. (2007). Comparing alliance network structure across industries: Observations and explanations. *Strategic Entrepreneurial Journal*, *1*(3–4), 191–209.
Rutherford, M. (2001). Institutional economics: Then and now. *The Journal of Economic Perspectives*, *15*(3), 173–194.
Samuels, W. J. (1995). The present state of institutional economics. *Cambridge Journal of Economics*, *19*(4), 569–590.
Scott, W. R. (1995). *Institutions and organizations*. Sage.
Scott, W. R. (2008). Approaching adulthood: The maturing of institutional theory. *Theory and Society*, *37*(5), 427–442.
Suchman, M. C. (1995). Managing legitimacy: Strategic and institutional approaches. *Academy of Management Review*, *20*(3), 571–610.
Tirole, J. (2001). Corporate governance. *Econometrica*, *69*(1), 1–35.
Vermeulen, P. A. M., Zietsma, C., Greenwooed, R., & Langley, A. (2016). Strategic responses to institutional complexity. *Strategic Organization*, *14*(4), 277–286.
Williamson, O. E. (1979). Transaction cost economics: The governance of contractual relations. *Journal of Law & Economics*, *22*(2), 233–261.
Williamson, O. E. 1985. *The economic institutions of capitalism: Firms, markets, relational contracting*. The Free Press.
Zollo, M., Minoja, M., & Coda, V. (2018). Toward an integrated theory of strategy. *Strategic Management Journal*, *39*(6), 1753–1778.
Zubac, A., Dasborough, M., Hughes, K., Jiang, Z., Kirkpatrick, S., Martinsons, M. G., Tucker, D., & Zwikael, O. (2021). The strategy and change interface: Understanding "enabling" processes and cognitions. *Management Decision*, *59*(3), 481–505.
Zubac, A., Hubbard, G., & Johnson, L. W. (2007). Extending strategic management's reach: Towards a resource investment explanation for firm existence. *Academy of Management Proceedings*. https://doi.org/10.5465/ambpp.2007.26516093
Zubac, A., Hubbard, G., & Johnson, L. W. (2012). Extending resource-based logic: Applying the resource-investment concept to the firm from a payments perspective. *Journal of Management*, *38*(6), 1867–1891.
Zucker, L. (1987). Institutional theories of organization. *Annual Review of Sociology*, *13*, 443–464.

Index

A

Affect, 32, 33, 35, 39, 41–54, 56–58, 71, 73, 79, 84, 145, 227, 327, 328, 345, 423, 431, 465, 468

B

Business models (BMs), 13, 18, 206, 208, 220–226, 230, 236–238, 241, 242, 293, 295, 299, 388, 412, 416, 424, 429, 435, 440

C

Capital management, 156, 193–195, 197

Change, 1–3, 5, 11, 13, 15, 16, 18–20, 27, 32, 40, 44, 56, 66–68, 72, 74, 76–78, 81, 82, 90, 93–101, 105, 109, 113, 115–117, 120–123, 132, 145, 156, 162, 178, 182–185, 189, 191, 196, 198, 206, 208, 209, 214, 215, 219, 223, 228, 230, 231, 233–237, 242, 266, 268, 271, 275, 281, 304, 320, 323, 324, 327–330, 332, 334–337, 340, 342–349, 360, 361, 378, 383, 387, 389–393, 397, 401, 402, 409, 410, 412, 415, 416, 418–420, 422–426, 428–445, 454–459, 461–463, 467, 469, 470

Change management, 3, 324, 331, 357, 358, 360, 361, 364, 366, 369, 374, 375, 377, 383–385, 415, 418, 420, 423, 428, 438

Complex systems, 105, 107, 111, 117, 119

Corporate strategy, 4, 5, 7, 11, 14, 16, 27, 113, 136, 195, 410, 412, 413, 453, 470

Cross-disciplinary knowledge sharing, 11

Customer value creation strategy, 18, 136, 198, 205, 206, 208

Customer value definitions, 206, 263, 278, 282

Customer value learning, 208, 263, 271, 278, 279

D
Dynamic capabilities, 3, 4, 13–15, 20, 27, 121, 164–166, 209, 272, 273, 276, 278, 279, 281–283, 296, 320, 323, 324, 384, 410, 469

E
Ecosystem, 208, 209, 214, 215, 218, 227, 263, 278, 279, 281–283, 293, 294, 297, 312, 456, 470, 472
Emerging economies, 212
Emotion, 16, 26, 32, 33, 37, 38, 41–43, 51, 52, 55–58, 99, 345, 419
External stakeholders, 16, 167, 220, 242, 244, 414, 469, 470

F
Family firms, 387–403
Finance strategy, 18
Financial strategy, 5, 18, 132, 134, 136, 137, 140, 141, 144, 145, 166, 167

H
Human capital, 154–156, 469

I
Industry, 4, 10, 11, 13, 36, 40, 96, 98, 177, 178, 186, 187, 190, 209, 212, 219, 228, 264, 281, 282, 330, 337, 418, 431, 435, 456, 457, 472

Innovation system, 212
Institutional change, 409, 458, 459, 461, 468
Institutions, 4, 5, 7, 8, 11, 13, 14, 20, 140, 142, 144, 145, 149, 153, 157, 158, 166, 209, 215, 282, 410, 412–414, 451, 452, 454–457, 459–464, 468–470, 472, 473
Institutions strategy, 462, 463, 470
Internal stakeholders, 7, 16, 154, 155, 166, 167, 470, 473
Isomorphic change, 282, 457

L
Large-scale change, 330, 347
Leadership, 3, 4, 85, 111, 116, 212, 216, 235–237, 264, 292, 295, 305, 306, 308, 309, 327–329, 332, 336–338, 341, 342, 344, 346, 348, 355, 357, 360, 366, 373, 381–383, 390–392, 398, 400, 412, 419, 422–426, 429, 433, 438, 441–444, 452

M
Models of change, 3, 426, 427

N
Non-market strategies, 4, 5, 7, 11, 19, 20, 27, 136, 198, 206, 319, 320, 324, 409, 410, 451–455, 470, 472
Non-rational decision-making processes, 3

O
Organisational change, 32, 36, 43, 48, 57, 65, 89–95, 97–103, 112,

114, 116, 118–120, 122, 123, 328, 329, 331
Organisational learning, 112

P

Platforms, 3, 11, 29, 152, 163, 209, 281, 283, 293, 320, 343
Project management, 19, 34, 295, 298, 320, 323, 355, 356, 358, 364, 372, 375–378, 382–385
Project management capabilities, 355
Psychological contract, 324, 387, 394–396, 401, 403

R

Recursive practices, 2, 16, 20
Resource-based theory, 11, 148, 164, 272, 276, 282, 290, 301, 465, 467, 468
Resource investment, 209, 269, 271, 323
Resource strategy, 4, 19, 136, 198, 319, 320, 324, 458
Risk capital, 141, 156–159, 161, 162, 167

S

Stakeholders, 5, 7, 8, 18, 20, 94, 117, 119, 134, 136, 137, 139–142, 144, 146, 149–151, 154, 160, 162, 164, 166, 167, 193, 198, 208, 212, 217, 226–228, 231, 232, 235, 239, 241–244, 272, 278, 279, 290–301, 304–306, 308, 309, 312, 323, 328, 329, 332, 337, 339, 340, 342, 344–348, 356, 361, 366, 367, 372, 374–378, 382, 389, 410, 412, 414, 431, 439, 441–443, 445, 451, 455, 463–470, 473

Stakeholder strategy, 465
Strategic alignment, 132, 272, 323, 358, 359, 384, 435
Strategic analysis tools, 198
Strategic change, 1, 4, 11, 19, 20, 27, 43, 51, 53, 68, 101, 119, 123, 320, 323, 328–349, 424, 426, 472, 473
Strategic cognition, 31, 33, 35, 37, 39, 51, 56
Strategic implementation, 357, 358
Strategic learning, 5, 16, 27, 90, 117
Strategic management accounting (SMA), 18, 134, 178, 185, 190, 193, 194, 196, 197
Strategic programmes of change, 431
Strategy formulation, 25, 27, 66, 68, 81–84, 116, 117, 177, 179, 293, 341
Strategy implementation, 3, 25, 27, 65, 66, 68, 71, 73, 74, 76, 82, 83, 85, 89–92, 100–104, 111–120, 122, 123, 166, 178, 180, 194, 198, 356, 357, 384
Strategy process, 2, 3, 7, 15, 16, 26, 27, 55, 57, 101, 102, 122, 123, 163, 414
Sustainability, 132, 192–194, 206, 208, 214–220, 223, 225, 227, 228, 230–234, 237–243, 416, 417, 425, 428, 439, 440, 442, 444

T

Trust, 19, 85, 115, 150, 151, 215, 231, 232, 234, 244, 324, 345, 364, 382, 387–397, 399–403, 412, 424, 429, 433, 442
Trust-transfer, 19, 320, 323, 388, 393, 394, 402, 403

U
Unique institutional contexts, 11

V
Value co-creation, 292, 299, 303

W
Wayfinding, 67

Printed by Printforce, United Kingdom